The Use of English in Institutional and Business Settings

T0316441

Linguistic Insights

Studies in Language and Communication

Edited by Maurizio Gotti,
University of Bergamo

Volume 34

PETER LANG
Bern · Berlin · Bruxelles · Frankfurt am Main · New York · Oxford · Wien

Giuliana Garzone & Cornelia Ilie (eds)

The Use of English in Institutional and Business Settings

● ● ● ● ● ● ● ● ● ● ● ● ● ● ● ● ● ● ●

An Intercultural Perspective

PETER LANG

Bern · Berlin · Bruxelles · Frankfurt am Main · New York · Oxford · Wien

Bibliographic information published by Die Deutsche Bibliothek
Die Deutsche Bibliothek lists this publication in the Deutsche National-
bibliografie; detailed bibliographic data is available on the Internet at
‹http://dnb.ddb.de›.

British Library Cataloguing-in-Publication Data: A catalogue record for this
book is available from *The British Library,* Great Britain

Library of Congress Cataloging-in-Publication Data

The use of English in institutional and business settings : an
intercultural perspective / Giuliana Garzone & Cornelia Ilie (eds).
p. cm. — (Linguistic insights, ISSN 1424-8689 ; v. 34)
Includes bibliographical references and index.
ISBN-13: 978-3-03-910889-3 (alk. paper)
1. English language—Rhetoric. 2. English language—Business
English. 3. English language—Technical English. 4. English
language—Globalization. 5. Communication in business.
I. Garzone, G. (Giuliana) II. Ilie, Cornelia.
PE1479.B87.U83   2007
808'.066—dc22
2007031950

Published with a grant from the Italian Ministry of Education, University
and Research (Project no. 2002104353) 'Intercultural discourse in domain-
specific English' and from Università degli Studi di Milano (Italy),
Dipartimento di Lingue e Culture Contemporanee.

ISSN 1424-8689
ISBN 978-3-03910-889-3

© Peter Lang AG, International Academic Publishers, Bern 2007
Hochfeldstrasse 32, Postfach 746, CH-3000 Bern 9, Switzerland
info@peterlang.com, www.peterlang.com, www.peterlang.net

Printed in Germany

Contents

Cross Cultural Perspectives on Speech Acts

Intercultural Issues in Face-to-Face Communication

GIULIANA GARZONE

Introduction

This book collects a series of essays that deal with the problems related to the widespread use of English in institutional and business settings and look specifically at its impact in an inter- and cross-cultural perspective. Some of them were presented at a seminar convened by Giuliana Garzone and Cornelia Ilie at the ESSE 7 Conference in Zaragoza in 2004, while others are invited papers that complete the overall design of the book.

The theme is all the more interesting today not only in consideration of the sheer magnitude of this phenomenon and its capillary spread, but above all on account of the pervasive penetration of English into professional and workplace contexts as a communication language also for local/internal communication. Therefore, this chapter will start with some preliminary observations on the use of English as a *lingua franca* and its relevance in terms of intercultural and cross-cultural communication. It will then go on to describe the structure of the book.

1. The spread of English as a *lingua franca*

In the contemporary world the status of English as an international language can hardly be questioned (e.g. Crystal 1997: 139). An intriguing aspect of this virtually unchallenged status is that it is the result of an extraordinary success story, unique in its unprecedented rapidity and proportions: as recently as half a century ago English was still in competition with French – the language that had predominated in culture, diplomacy and international trade for over two centuries – as the tongue for international communication, but only a couple of decades later no other language could rival its prevalence. Today the widespread use of English in international communication is not limited to business and politics, but extends to all other sectors of contemporary life, from science and technology to sports, entertainment and pop music, bringing with it a high degree of prestige in all discourse communities the world over (cf. Gotti 2005).

Of course, some of the historical preconditions and the facilitating factors that have led to the rise of English as an international language are obvious. First and foremost among them is Britain's commercial, political and colonial expansion over the centuries, which contributed to an increased number of speakers, as its use extended not only to those countries beyond Britain itself which Phillipson (1992: 17) denominates 'core English-speaking countries' (Britain, North America, South Africa, Australia, New Zealand) and Kachru (1985) sees as making up the 'Inner Circle' of English users, but also to a number of former British colonies that qualify as 'periphery-English countries' (Phillipson 1992: 23) located in Kachru's 'Outer Circle', as well as to some other regions subject to the influence of Britain's commercial power. But the rapid and unchallenged spread of English as a language for international communication in the last century, and in particular in the last five decades or so, cannot be explained without taking into account the rise of the economic and cultural power of the United States after the Second World War. American products, media and cultural models, associated with a prosperous and technologically advanced lifestyle and supported by an unrivalled economic and political power, have literally invaded the world. In more recent times another parallel and determinant factor has been the drive towards globalization, which has relied on English as one of its fundamental instruments and at the same time has contributed to reinforcing its status as a language for international communication – English being the language through which multinational companies do business and communicate, enacting global discursive practices.

It comes as no surprise, then, that the status of English as prime international tongue has often been approached in critical terms; for many authors it is difficult to investigate it "without political bias" (Crystal 1997: xi) and without interpreting its role as devastating in terms of language ecology, posing a serious threat to the status of other languages and to cultural diversity. If in a not too distant past some authors pointed at the evident connection of the spreading use of English as a language for international communication with all-pervading colonial power and imperialism (cf. Phillipson 1992; Pennycook 1994), today it is also seen as inextricably associated with the expansion of corporate capitalism and rampant globalization (e.g. Holland 2002). In a Critical Discourse Analysis perspective, Fairclough (1996) sees "the beginnings [...] of a global order of discourse", based on an essentially hegemonic project. No wonder that in recent years the academic debate over the status and role of English should have often taken on a controversial tone (e.g. Crystal 2000; Harmer 2000; Phillipson 1999, 2001; Holland 2002).

Another important factor, partially connected with those discussed so far, that has contributed to the high status of English to a primary role in international communication is its growing importance as a language for communication in the professional world, not only in commerce, politics and diplomacy – as already discussed above – but in all fields of specialized communication, also "as the co-genitor of the technological age, the age of information" (Halliday 2001: 416). As Henry Widdowson (1997: 142ff) points out, the spread of many of the varieties and registers of English spoken internationally are largely associated with the "secondary expert communities" that use them to communicate transnationally. Thus the success story of English can also be accounted for "through the development of autonomous registers which guarantee specialist communication within global expert communities" (Widdowson 1997: 144). It is also significant that for the maintenance and evolution of their standards these registers of English do not need the intervention of "native-speaker custodians" (Widdowson 1997: 143-144; see also Widdowson 1994) as they are "endonormatively controlled from within by the requirements of communication across the international community of its specialist users".

The latter factor is especially important as in line of principle recourse to one language by speakers belonging to different national communities and with different mother tongues raises a number of crucial questions. First and foremost among them is the issue of power and inequality which may emerge as a consequence of asymmetry in the linguistic skills of the participants in a communicative act, with native speakers of English and proficient users enjoying an advantage over interlocutors who have a less efficient and effective command of the language (Orletti 2000; Garzone 2002: 249-251). This is an unavoidable problem, which is sometimes only partly attenuated by recourse to an interpreter or a bilingual helper, as is illustrated in Valero-Garcés and Downing's chapter in this volume.

1.1. Research on Lingua Franca communication

Traditionally linguistic research, even in its most specifically data-driven sectors like corpus-linguistics, has only reluctantly looked at ELF texts, considering them basically as a poor relation to Standard (British and/or American) English, although in the last few decades the volume of non-native texts in English has been growing dramatically. It is highly meaningful that only recently has the compilation of EFL corpora started (e.g. the ELFA and VOICE corpora,[1] cf. Mauranen 2005: 278-79; Seidlhofer 2004a). More interest has been given to it in English teaching research (e.g. Seidlhofer 2004b).

In contrast with this limited scientific interest, international English is a variety in its own right, probably the most widely spoken language variety in the world, worthy of investigation in itself from all perspectives, theoretical, descriptive and applied, and at different levels – not only lexico-grammatical but also discursive. Pioneering works are House (2003), Jenkins (2000), Lesznyak (2004) and many of the papers in Knapp/Meierkord (2002). A significant body of studies of ELF texts, although not specifically focused on English as *Lingua Franca* usage, also figures in ESP research where, realistically, native texts and native English are not taken as a reference standard. This has yielded a substantial body of research which looks at international communication in English without considering whether the texts investigated are in native or in *lingua franca* English, whether they were written first-hand or the result of a

---

1   For the ELFA (English as a Lingua Franca in Academic Settings) corpus, which comprises spoken academic international English, cf. <http://www.uta. fi/laitokset/kielet/engf/research/elfa/corpus.htm>; for the VOICE (Vienna-Oxford International Corpus of English) corpus, which consists of naturally occurring, non-scripted and mostly face-to-face conversations in English as a lingua franca (ELF); cf. <http://www.univie.ac.at/voice/>.

re-writing or translation process. For instance, this is the approach that characterizes many of the volumes included in Peter Lang's *Linguistic Insights* Series, edited by Maurizio Gotti, to which this book belongs. Another example, which regards specifically business discourse, is the special issue of *English for Specific Purposes* edited by Nickerson in 2005, entirely devoted to English as a *lingua franca* in international business contexts.[2] An account of research in this area is given in Catherine Nickerson's chapter at the end of this volume (see below).

As the overall content of this book suggests, a further research approach may be one that examines cross- and intercultural problems in *lingua franca* communication, looking at it comparatively as one of several kinds of intercultural communication (e.g. intercultural communication across languages, translator- or interpreter-mediated communication, etc.).

1.2. Cross-cultural and intercultural issues in international communication

In a discussion of the intercultural aspects of communication in English as a *lingua franca*, a preliminary observation is in order: in the case under discussion intercultural issues do not originate principally from the interference of the culture of the home country of the language being investigated, because in actual fact English is no more the language of one nation, and ceased to be one long before its rapid spread as an international language; rather, as pointed out above, it was already used in a range of different countries, either as the native language or as a second language in a context of dyglossia. Further, as House (2001) points out, the enormous increase in the number of non-native users (which she reports to have been estimated as being four times as large as that of native speakers) has contributed to 'de-nativizing' the language. This has both linguistic and cultural implications, which are obviously interwoven. While the implications

---

2   The Editorial introducing the issue is of particular interest for the sake of this discussion as it provides an overview of current research on ELF in business communication.

for linguistic research will be discussed later in this chapter, cultural
aspects have been highlighted by Wardaugh:

> English is the least localized of all the languages in the world today. Spoken
> almost everywhere in the world to some degree, and tied to no particular
> social, political, economic or religious system, nor to a specific racial or
> cultural group, English belongs to everyone or to no one, or it at least is quite
> often regarded as having this property (1987: 14-15).

However oversimplified this may seem, it is certainly true that the
way English is used today in the world reflects "a heterogeneous
mixture of cultures and cultural encounters" (Mauranen 2005: 270),
rather than the culture of any of the original English-speaking
countries. Of course, the prestige of the cultural models associated
with Inner Circle countries, and in particular Britain and the US, is
still high, and the sociocultural load carried by globalized language
use and discursive practices is substantial. However, it is not
exaggerated to state that today English is not completely 'owned' by
native speakers any more. It has been appropriated by a huge number
of 'other' speakers, some of whom have even gone so far as to use it
in their resistance to the cultural load originally associated with
English (cf. e.g. Paganoni's chapter in this volume): "[I]t seems that if
you want to resist the exploitative power of English, you have to use
English to do it" (Halliday 2001: 416).

Thus, more than the interference of the original source culture,
intercultural issues arise from the influence of the original native
tongues and cultures as well as the parent discourse communities of
those who use English for international communication. Language is
never a neutral medium simply reflecting discrete referential
meanings, and – as most language philosophers agree – by necessity
carries with it socially, historically and culturally shaped meanings; so
the use of English in international and transnational communication
involves a multiplicity of voices, many of them inevitably characterized by some degree of alterity and cultural markedness: as M.A.K.
Halliday (2003: 408) authoritatively observes, when a language is
taken over as a second tongue by speakers of other languages, they
will certainly "retain some features of their original form of expression". Incidentally, in this type of context also texts generated in
core English-speaking cultures often exhibit some degree of cultural

markedness, as has been shown to be the case – for instance – for arbitration rules (e.g. cf. Garzone 2003). At the same time, the language has to adapt to the task of expressing 'other' meanings, associated with non-native cultures and/or transnational discourse communities, and this requires an expansion of the language's meaning potential and the activation of "new semogenic strategies" (Halliday 2001: 408-409; 412).

Thus discussing intercultural aspects of *lingua franca* communication does not imply subscribing to linguistic determinism and/or cultural relativism, but involves – on the pragmatic side – the recognition of the significance of intercultural issues connected with social contexts, practices and conventions, and – on the semantic side – the awareness of problems associated with the need to convey specific local meanings for which there is an 'empty box' in the *lingua franca* repertoire (Halliday's 'semogenic strategies' mentioned above).

2. Contents of the book

The body of chapters in this volume is structured into four parts. Each section deals with different aspects of communication in English – written and oral – in an international perspective, and explores a variety of issues emerging from the confrontation of cultures across national, institutional and organizational discourse communities, taking an intercultural or cross-cultural approach.

The first section deals with the linguistic and cultural issues associated with different text genres in the English used in the promotion of products in international trade. More specifically, the first two chapters look at how texts in English are used to present and promote Italian-made products for the international/foreign audience at whom they are targeted, focusing on two categories of goods that are typically associated with Italian identity, fashion and traditional food produce.

PAOLA CATENACCIO examines press releases issued in English by four important Italian international fashion designers, together with their Italian versions, and focuses on the way in which fashion houses discursively communicate their image and identity. The analysis identifies a set of common features that are typically identity-related: an emphasis on variety and contrast, an attempt to establish continuity within a tradition while emphasising novelty, and – most interesting of all – a number of discursive practices aimed at 'objectifying' the collections, thus conferring an identity upon them, while focusing only indirectly on the designers' or fashion houses' identity. As concerns references to Italian culture, implicit or overt reliance on them does not have the same prominence in all the texts analysed as some stylists prefer to emphasise either hybridity and cross-fertiliza-tion, or the international appeal. Equally contradictory is the way in which recurrent culture-specific references are handled. In some cases they are integrated into English press releases with a minimum amount of adaptation and with hardly any addition of supplementary information, so that often they are not readily decipherable by foreign audiences. In some other cases, the references to national culture in the Italian texts are replaced in the English versions by 'symmetrical' references to other cultures. This recourse to cultural adaptation indicates that the English press releases are the result of a process of rewriting rather than of translation proper.

DELIA CHIARO, focusing her attention on a category of products which is inherently connected with cultural identity, i.e. food products, discusses the communicative strategies enacted by 33 Italian companies in the agro-food sector in their advertising campaigns in English on the World Wide Web. Here the basic problem is that ideally the same Web text is assumed to have the same desired effect on recipients from any culture, being addressed to a potentially planetary audience. Thus the production of a company's Web site in English entails not only a translation procedure, but requires some degree of cultural adaptation, i.e. more complex forms of semio-translation, also involving the visual component. In her analysis, Chiaro suggests that in the Italian agro-food sector there is a direct link between company size and the translational strategy adopted, smaller companies tending to opt for intrasemiotic *mot-à-mot* renditions. However, today also these firms tend to be more culturally sensitive, shifting towards intersemiotic or syncretic approaches. As concerns promotion strategies, while many companies still project a pretty stereotypical image of Italy and Italians, most of them go in for a mix of tradition and modernity. If until very recently they either chose tradition or modernity to promote their wares, today more and more firms are moving towards an up-to-date image, yet without denying their sense of tradition. Vice versa, companies who still opt for a traditional image are underscoring aspects such as their ultra-modern industrial plants and use of new technology.

The chapter authored by the research group led by MARRINEL GERRITSEN and CATHERINE NICKERSON at the Business Communication Studies department at Nijmegen (including Corine van den Brandt, Rogier Crijns, Nuriá Dominguez, Frank van Meurs and Ulrike Nederstigt) is also focused on advertising, but takes a different perspective from the previous two, as it does not look at the use of English in the promotion of products for a transnational audience, but rather investigates the role of English in locally-published promotional genres in the Netherlands, Germany and Spain, focusing in particular on the reception of the message by the nationals of the countries involved. The research consists in an extensive corpus analysis of print advertisements in women's glossy magazines, followed by an experimental investigation involving more than three hundred young women. The results reveal an increase in the use of English in the genres analysed compared to 1995, and partly contradict previous research as it suggests that the use of English occurs more often in Spain than in Germany. They also indicate that the attitude towards its use is less negative than found by research a decade ago and that it does not have a negative impact on the image of the products advertised, thus suggesting that English may be already viewed by some consumers as a neutral advertising language.

This could be interpreted as an indication that English is now de-coupled from the national cultures that use it as a first language, such as the US and UK. Accepting this view is tantamount to recognizing that it is no longer valid to consider the use of English in international relations as a form of *inter*cultural communication. This supports the point of view of those who argue that it is thanks to its cultural neutrality that English has by now become the language of international communication (e.g. Wardaugh 1987; House 2001; Mauranen 2005; see above).

The second part of the volume deals in particular with issues raising from the inevitable divergences and variations in conceptualization and categorization across countries and cultures, which are all the more problematic when a *lingua franca* is used, and have an obvious impact on language use and discursive practices.

In the first chapter of the section, CORNELIA ILIE discusses the semantic properties as well as the discursive and argumentative function of the lexicalizations in English and in Swedish of the notion of consensus, i.e. *consensus* and *samförstånd/konsensus*, as they are used in parliamentary debates in the two respective countries. In her parallel analysis she examines two sets of transcripts of debates in the U.K. Parliament and in the Swedish Riksdag, with a view to identifying the semantic and pragmatic similarities and differences in how these roughly corresponding notions are used in the two languages, also analysing to what extent they are rooted in the cultural and political tradition of each country. Ilie's findings indicate that in both parliaments the notion of consensus is assigned similar semantic roles, but in the British parliamentary debates it is prevalently seen as the desirable end-result of negotiations, whereas in the Swedish Parliament it is assumed to be the source or starting point, as well as the final result, of parliamentary discussions. Furthermore, in the Swedish context *samförstånd/konsensus* is attributed a positive value by all members of parliament, irrespective of their political allegiance, since it presupposes cross-party cooperation; the notion is used primarily as rule-based and result-oriented procedure in a debate which concerns above all the negative consequences of non-compliance with previously reached consensus. In contrast, British MPs' views on *consensus* are more polarized, as not all of them consider it equally positive, some viewing it as a lesser alternative to a majority decision; this is associated with an institutionally specific use of this notion, primarily as principle-based and process-oriented procedure. According to the author, the analysis confirms that the meaning attributed to basic political notions varies across countries, and indicates that the preference for certain strategies in debate and argumentation is deeply rooted in political traditions.

The following chapter also takes a cross-cultural approach, shifting attention to the corporate world. It compares the annual company reports of U.S. and Japanese companies, focusing on introductions and on Letters to Shareholders. In her research DANIELA WAWRA looks at three areas where intercultural communication studies have identified the most meaningful differences between the U.S. and Japanese organizational cultures: formality of language, individual/collective orientation, competitiveness. The results of the investigation confirm the findings of previous intercultural research. The reports of the U.S. companies are much less formal in language use and syntactically simpler than those of their Japanese counterparts. In general, American reports tend to have a more individual orientation, while Japanese texts reflect a collective attitude. This is shown by the use of first person pronouns and by the way employees are portrayed, as they tend to be represented more as individuals in the U.S. reports, while they are portrayed more as a value-producing collective in the Japanese reports. As concerns competitiveness, a competitive attitude emerges more frequently in linguistic choices in the U.S. reports, with more comparatives and superlatives, and more words belonging to the 'competition' semantic field. This confirms that, despite globalization, companies' origins are clearly reflected in the contents and language of their annual reports – whether intended or not.

The focus on a cross-cultural comparison with Japanese texts provides a link with the next chapter, which discusses a highly-culture specific and politically controversial topic – whaling – and takes a discourse-analytical and cross-cultural approach to look at the way it is dealt with in British and Japanese newspaper editorials. KUMIKO MURATA explores newspaper discourse from a cultural and linguistic perspective discussing its influence on cross-cultural understanding, particularly in the case of readers with different cultural assumptions. Taking as case studies two editorials, one for each country, from a larger corpus of British and Japanese news articles, she shows that anti- and pro-whaling discourses are formulated through the use of seemingly opposing strategies in the British and Japanese press. This confirms that different cultural assumptions and values could lead to differing discourses on the same issue, with the use of loaded words and rhetoric devices in the British article and more attention to 'facts' in the Japanese text; another important element is that both editorials tend to select for coverage the information that favours the stance of the respective nations on the issue of whaling. The results of this research have important implications for the understanding of the influence of the media on readers with different cultural assumptions and values on the same issue, and simultaneously on the cross-cultural understanding and misunderstanding of the people exposed to different discourses.

In the next chapter, the issues associated with variations in conceptualization across languages and cultures are dealt with by MARIA CRISTINA PAGANONI in an analysis of texts – speeches, interviews, articles, essays – produced within the framework of the Indian no global movement, and in particular by four well-known women activists. The use of English in a post-colonial context by necessity involves the appropriation of the language by people who have inherited it as an alien idiom and now use it as their own, often recontextualizing its notions and categories to adapt them to the local culture. But in the texts examined here this process goes much beyond, as the no global activists appropriate and recontextualize English into the praxis of no global activism for subversive purposes, questioning the assumptions of neo-liberal globalization, e.g. by resemanticizing basic words, like 'ownership', 'privatization', 'property', 'resources', 'freedom', 'development' etc. to incorporate them into the discourse of the war on globalization. Similarly, they borrow from the local languages to confer a positive emphasis on the role of Indian culture in the construction of discourse, while signalling the effort to reframe issues according to non-Western values. Thus cross-cultural divergences are exploited in order to construct no global discourse as a form of opposition ideology.

The third section has a specifically pragmatic focus, dealing with differences in the realization of speech acts across languages and cultures, a crucial problem in intercultural business contacts which may give rise to ineffective communication or even misunderstand-ings.

ORA-ONG CHAKORN concentrates on the Thai business context, where correspondence written in English is commonplace, as in the last few decades the use of English has been boosted by growing foreign trade and investment. In particular she takes into consideration letters of invitation in English as instances of cross-cultural business writing between Thais and native English speakers with the aim of shedding light on their rhetoric in a cross-cultural perspective and identifying the relevant moves and their linguistic realizations. Although a six-move pattern is identified in all the letters examined, differences between Thai and native speakers are found in the rhetorical appeals, thus supporting previous research by Campbell (1998) and Zhu (2001): the native letters generally have a stronger rational appeal or *logos*, while those written by Thais tend to use a combination of *logos*, *ethos* and *pathos*. Further, most Thai letters seem to be oriented towards collectivism and relationship-building, while most native letters tend to be more individualistic. The author suggests that these findings can be seen as supporting Wierzbicka's (1991) claim that 'harmony' is interpreted differently in Western culture and Far Eastern culture; however, writing conventions among international business professionals may have a role in determining the differences.

With GRAHAME T. BILBOW's contribution the attention shifts to oral interactions, still focusing on East-West cross-cultural communication. The chapter contrasts the spoken discourse of local Chinese and Western participants in business meetings held at a large airline company in Hong Kong, and presents a study aimed at identifying the differences between the contributions of these two groups. The results of the research highlight differences in the range of speech acts used and in their lexico-grammatical realization in terms of level of directness, lexical choice, and prosodic features. Interestingly, there is also a difference in the quantity of talk, as Western expatriates tend to speak nearly twice as much as the local Chinese, both in terms of speaking time and in terms of number of words uttered. Furthermore, the local Chinese speakers tend to value silence, which is perceived to be preferable to irrelevant talk. However, when interpreting these findings the author points out that there is significant inter-meeting variation, especially among local Chinese speakers, in the variety of speech acts used and in the quantity of talk. This could be accounted for by the different views that the local Chinese and the Western expatriates have of the sociolinguistic appropriacy of contributing verbally in particular types of meetings, in accordance with Flowerdew's model (1997) which sees Westerners as users of Utilitarian discourse who tend to value vocal contributions for their own sake, and have a broader sense of what constitutes 'on-topic' discourse across a range of meeting types, and the Chinese as users of Confucianist discourse, having a strong sense of what is on-topic, which governs how they behave linguistically in particular types of meetings.

In the next chapter the perspective is intra-European as STEPHANIE ZILLES POHLE presents a case study which illustrates the results of a comparative pilot study of the speech act *offer*, one of the main constituents of negotiation discourse in German and Irish negotiations. This is particularly interesting not only because this speech act (also denominated 'proposal' or 'suggestion' in the non-linguistic literature on business negotiations) has so far received limited scholarly attention, but also because cross-cultural investigations into negotiations have mainly dealt with the North American and Asian context and – in Europe – with Northern and Southern European cultures. The analysis indicates that the Irish negotiators were more indirect than their German counterparts, as is made evident in particular by their choice of offer realization strategies and their more frequent use of mitigating devices compared to the German informants. Besides, Irish negotiators used the *inclusive we* form more often than the Germans, which suggests a stronger personal affiliation with the respective company. The results of the research confirm, to a large extent, the findings of the only previous study of German and Irish intracultural sales negotiations (Martin 2001), as well as the findings of previous works on general characteristics of German and Irish culture.

The chapters included in the fourth, and last, part of the volume also deal with spoken intercultural communication and look specifically at intercultural issues in face-to-face communication.

In the first chapter of the section, GINA PONCINI examines spoken interactions mainly in English during a winery visit involving some wine producers and journalists, organized within an international convention on the Nebbiolo grape. The findings highlight a high degree of collaborativeness on the part of the participants, although the analysis of the parts of the visit where only wine producers (an Italian and two Americans) participated reveals a more consistent use of evaluative language, and co-operation aimed at the mutual understanding of specialized terms, resulting in the creation of "shared worlds and viewpoints" (Carter/McCarthy 2004: 69), while in the parts of the visit when the group was joined by a Croatian wine producer, three journalists and an interpreter, the interaction was more task-oriented and focalized on information provision. The analysis suggests that the differences between successive stages of the interaction may relate not only to nationality and cultural background, but also to the professional roles and values, whereas the participants were seen to share repertoires of verbal and nonverbal practices in connection with the wine industry, which Poncini suggests could be interpreted in the light of the notion of community of practice (Lave/Wenger 1991 and Wenger 1998). All in all, as the author points out, this research provides evidence of the rich and complex backgrounds that interactants bring to intercultural professional encounters in which not only national culture and language come into play, but also professional roles, goals and values.

The remaining two chapters in this section also focus on spoken interactions, but deal with interpreter-mediated communication, which represents one of the two alternatives to *Lingua Franca* use in intercultural communication, alongside 'foreign language communication' (Knapp 1991). They look at some of the issues that are specific of this special type of polylogic communicative events. In their chapter CARMEN VALERO-GARCÉS and BRUCE DOWNING present a study of interpreter-mediated medical encounters between native and non-native speakers of English, focusing in particular on cases where an *ad hoc* interpreter is used and comparing them with others where a professional interpreter is recruited. The setting of their case studies is a small community clinic in the United States; the participants involved are – in addition to Spanish speaking patients – two English speaking doctors and a Spanish/English bilingual nurse called upon to act as an *ad hoc* interpreter (as often happens in the US and in the EU), although not trained for it, thus taking on the role of Bilingual Helper. The study, based on recorded interviews, shows that in this type of encounters there are distinct gaps in doctor-patient interaction. The Spanish-speaking patients appear to be getting good care, but in the process excessive responsibility is delegated to the bilingual nurse, who also provides patient advocacy services by simplifying the doctor's explanations. A comparison with interviews assisted by a professional interpreter indicates that in Bilingual-Helper mediated interviews, the amount of 'direct interaction' between doctor and patient decreases dramatically. This suggests that using a professional interpreter in interlingual doctor/patient interactions respects the patient's or parent's right to direct access to the physician and favours effective communication.

In the last chapter of Part 4, CYNTHIA JANE KELLETT deals with intercultural communication mediated by simultaneous interpretation across an unusual language combination – English to Italian Sign Language (*Lingua Italiana dei Segni* or *LIS*) – in a linguistics conference. The study is based on a multimodal corpus of mediation from English to Italian Sign Language, partly simultaneously interpreted and relayed to LIS, and partly interpreted directly from English to LIS. This chapter investigates more specifically the intercultural aspects of one of the speeches interpreted directly. It explores closely the nature of the intercultural communication at play during conference interpretation from English to LIS, identifying any surface adjustments and disparities as well as any form of intrusion from the source language and culture. The analysis reveals only few instances of intrusion from the English original, while textual recasting and distortion of the original source discourse resulted mainly from omissions, additions and substitutions. As concerns the rendition of cultural specificities, there was little evidence of strategies of removal, avoidance or attenuation; in contrast many instances were identified of intentional substitution or addition by the interpreters to conform with the cultural norms of LIS. These findings provide clear evidence of awareness by interpreters of the need for adjustment during the mediation process to the specific linguistic and cultural traits of the target language. In actual fact, concern for intercultural aspects is crucial in interpreting, often posing an ethical dilemma between the need to make clients aware of cultural diversity on the one hand, and the limits of the mediator's role in terms of personal interference in the interpreted interaction, on the other.

The volume is closed by CATHERINE NICKERSON's contribution on English as a *lingua franca* in a business context which has been chosen as the final chapter in that it provides indications for an appropriate research agenda in the future, identifying three main areas of investigation for research into the use of English as a communication language in organizational contexts. The first one concentrates on the effect of using English rather than another language for communication in business, e.g. within multinationals or in advertising. The second area of investigation focuses on the effects of using specific rhetorical and linguistic strategies in various types of business discourse and genres, in particular, in those situations where the local national or organizational culture may not be that of the Anglo-Saxon 'English' world. The third line of investigation discusses what could be done in order to counteract hegemonic situations that have arisen because of the use of English in international business, which also involves a revision of teaching and training materials available. Although Nickerson's considerations focus mainly on business communication, it is obvious that the lines of research she identifies can also be applied to other institutional and organizational contexts.

Taken together, the various parts of this book provide a diversified picture of the issues involved in intercultural communication in organizational and institutional settings. The sheer variety of the topics explored, the range of settings investigated, and the diversity of the actors involved – in terms of geographical areas, nationalities and roles – testify to the extreme complexity of intercultural communication as an object of research.

References

Carter, Ronald / McCarthy, Michael 2004. Talking, Creating: Interactional Language, Creativity, and Context. *Applied Linguistics* 25/1, 62-28.

Cortese, Giuseppina / Duszak, Anna (eds) 2005. *Identity, Community, Discourse: English in Intercultural Settings*. Bern: Peter Lang .

Crystal, David 1997. *English as a Global Language*. Cambridge: Cambridge University Press.

Crystal, David 2000. On Trying to Be Crystal-Clear: A Response to Phillipson. *Applied Linguistics* 21/3, 415-423.

Fairclough, Norman 1996. Border Crossings: Discourse and Social Change in Contemporary Societies. In Coleman, Hywel / Cameron, Lynn (eds). *Change and Language. Papers from the Annual Meeting of BAAL, Leeds, Sept. 1994.* Clevedon: Multilingual Matters, 3-17.

Flowerdew, John 1997. Competing Public Discourses in Transitional Hong Kong. *Journal of Pragmatics* 28 *(Special Edition on Hong Kong in Transition)*, 533-553.

Garzone, Giuliana 2002. Conflict in Linguistically Asymmetric Business Negotiations: The Case of Interpreter-Mediated Discourse. In Gotti, Murizio / Heller, Dorothee / Dossena, Marina (eds) *Conflict and Negotiation in Specialized Texts. Selected Papers of the 2nd CERLIS Conference*. Bern: Peter Lang, 249-271.

Garzone, Giuliana 2003. Arbitration Rules Across Legal Cultures: An Intercultural Approach. In Bhatia, Vijay / Candlin, Christopher / Gotti, Maurizio (eds) *Legal Discourse in Multilingual and Multicultural Contexts. Arbitration Texts in Europe*. Bern: Peter Lang, 177-220.

Gotti, Maurizio 2005. English in Intercultural Settings: Globalising Trends and Local Resistance. In Cortese/Duszak (eds), 139-165.

Halliday, Michael A.K. 2003, Written Language, Standard Language, Global Language. *World Englishes* 22/4, 405-418.

Harmer, Jeremy 2000. Slaying Dragons. Language Fascism and the Art of the Book Review. *IATEFL Issues* 158, 3-4.

Holland, Robert 2002. Globospeak. Questioning Text on the Role of English as a Global Language. *Language and Intercultural Communication* 2/1, 5-24.

House, Juliane 2001. A Stateless Language that Europe Must Embrace, *The Guardian,* 19 April 2001.

House, Juliane 2003. Misunderstanding in Intercultural University Encounters. In House, Juliane / Kasper, Gabriele / Ross, S. (eds) *Misunderstanding in Social Life. Discourse Approaches to Problematic Talk*. London: Longman (Pearson), 22-56.

Jenkins, Jennifer 2000. *The Phonology of English as an International Language*. Oxford: Oxford University Press.

Kachru, Braj B. 1985. Standards, Codification and Socioliguistic Realm: The English Language in the Outer Circle. In Quirk, Randolph / Widdowson, Herny G. (eds) *English in the World*. Cambridge: Cambridge University Press, 11-30.

Knapp, Karlfried / Meierkord, Christiane (eds) 2002. *Lingua Franca Communication*. Frankfurt: Peter Lang.

Lave, Jean / Wenger, Etienne 1991. *Situated Learning: Legitimate Peripheral Participation and Learning*. Cambridge: Cambridge University Press.

Lesznyák, Anne 2004. *Communication in English as an International Lingua Franca. An Exploratory Case Study*. Nordestedt: Books on Demand Gmbh.

Mauranen, Anna 2005. English as *Lingua Franca*: An Unknown Language? In Cortese/Duszak (eds), 269-293.

Pennycook, Alastair 1994. *The Cultural Politics of English as an International Language*. London: Longman.

Phillipson, Robert 1992. *Linguistic Imperialism*. Oxford: Oxford University Press.

Phillipson, Robert 1999. Voice in Global English: Unheard Chords in Crystal Loud and Clear. *Applied Linguistics* 20/2, 265-275.

Phillipson, Robert 2001. Dragons, Language Fascists and Like Myths. *IATEFL Issues* 160, 2.

Seidlhofer, Barbara 2004a. The VOICE of ELF – English as a Lingua Franca. *What's New?* Autumn/Winter 2004, 8-9.

Seidlhofer, Barbara 2004b. Research Perspectives on Teaching English as a *Lingua Franca. Annual Review of Applied Linguistics* 24, 209-239.

Wardaugh, Ronald 1987. *Languages in Competition: Dominance, Diversity and Decline*. Oxford: Blackwell.

Wenger, Etienne 1998. *Communities of Practice: Learning, Meaning, and Identity*. Cambridge: Cambridge University Press.

Widdowson, Henry G. 1994. The Ownership of English. *TESOL Quarterly* 28/2, 377-389.

Widdowson, Henry G. 1997. EIL, ESL, EFL: Global Issues and Local Interests. *World Englishes* 16/1, 135-146.

English in the Promotion and
Marketing of Products across Cultures

PAOLA CATENACCIO

Constructing Identities in the Fashion Industry: Building Brand and Customer Image through Press Releases

1. Introduction

In the last few years fashion has increasingly come to be recognised as an aspect of culture and as a creative tool for the expression of one's individuality and personality; as a result, growing attention has been devoted to the investigation and the assessment of the influence it exercises on individuals and societies. The fashion industry (which includes international fashion houses creating designs for a restricted elite as well as high-street retailers popularising garments at affordable prices for the mass market) plays an important role in determining – frequently in a way which is culturally determined, although globalisation is widespread in this area – what is socially acceptable/desirable, often stretching the limits of the permissible to accommodate deviance from the norm as a form of individual affirmation. As the primary function of dressing is increasingly identified in individual self-expression, fashion becomes more and more often conceptualised as a repository of self-affirming and symbolic significance (cf. Finkelstein 1991; Featherstone 1999; Kellner 1994), and as a way of communicating identities (cf. Barnard 1996). Hence the growing interest for fashion as a social phenomenon actively involved in the shaping and self-representation of society.

The way in which fashion is discursively constructed has also attracted a great deal of interest in recent years, and a lot of effort has been devoted to exploring the manner in which the discourse of fashion shapes concepts of the body and of the self, as well as of one's (especially women's) place and role in society (cf. Negrin 1999 for an overview). This attention has often extended to studies of advertising, but no attention has been given – to the best of my knowledge – to the verbal explicitation of fashion provided by official statements issued by the fashion industry such as, for example, press releases.

This paper looks at the language of press releases in Italian and in English issued by four Italian international fashion designers (Armani, Trussardi, Cavalli and Dolce & Gabbana)[1], and focuses on the way in which fashion houses communicate verbally (in an effort to unfold in words the iconic density of the design) their image and identity, and to construct the ideal customer(s) at whom their collections are targeted. As all four designers operate in foreign markets, where they have a reputation for outstanding – and typically Italian – quality and style, particular attention will be given to the way in which (if at all) this aspect of their public image is conveyed discursively, especially in the English versions of their press releases. In a contrastive and cross-cultural perspective, the manner in which the language of the press releases considered implicitly channels and/or overtly communicates cultural values to foreign or domestic audiences will be given special attention.

This exploratory paper is based on a small corpus of 129 press releases, all of them collated from the fashion houses' corporate websites, 65 of which were in Italian, with the remaining 64 being their English counterparts (in one case there was no English match for the Italian press release). Only press releases relating to the fashion collections (garments as well as accessories such as watches and sunglasses) were selected. The number of press releases collected for each fashion designer (28 each in Italian and English for Armani, 26 in Italian and 25 in English for Dolce & Gabbana, 6 for each language for Cavalli and 5 for Trussardi) depended on the availability of material on the corporate websites. Because of the limited number of documents and the imbalance in the distribution of material, this study is mostly qualitative, and aims at identifying features and characteris-

---

1   The choice of major fashion designers and not, for instance, high-street brands was determined by the consideration that internationally renowned designers, despite their more limited public, appear to exert a greater influence on fashion trends than any high-street name, as they receive greater publicity and media exposure and are imitated by the latter.

tics which will have to be tested against a larger corpus for more definite results.

Because of the absolute lack of previous studies on fashion press releases, this paper will have a double focus. On the one hand, it will aim at identifying salient features of the genre, as a preliminary step to a more detailed examination of the press releases themselves; on the other, it will focus on cultural references in press releases and on their treatment in the different language versions, with particular attention to the role played by the English language in conveying cultural values.

Albeit with the limitations pointed out above, my research questions can therefore be formulated as follows:

- how is identity communicated in fashion press releases? In particular, how is the Italian identity of the fashion houses considered – so relevant in terms of their positioning in the international market – displayed in the press releases in the corpus? And how is the interplay between Italian identity and international appeal juggled?

- what are the main features of fashion press releases? Are there any significant differences between the Italian and the English versions? Do the writers of the press releases appear to be aware of any differences in discursive organisation and/or kind of information required which has to be taken into account when writing press releases in Italian and English?

2. Fashion press releases

Whereas investigation in the nature and scope of brand identity and image have a long tradition in marketing research (Acker 1991, 1995), and while brand and identity management in the fashion business have been the object of recent studies (Saviolo 2002), little attention has been devoted to the discursive features around which such images are built. In particular, their deployment in press releases – an eminently self-centred genre, and one especially suited to the expression and construction of identity – lends itself to specific discourse-analytical and pragmatic analyses, since press releases have been shown to be characterised by a shift in perspective between writer and reader aimed at manipulating modes of representation to serve the writer's purposes of self-portrayal.

According to Jacobs (1999), press releases are 'preformulated', that is they are written in such a way as to make it easy for journalists to copy them verbatim in their articles, both in terms of form and of content. Although they are ostensibly addressed to the journalists, therefore, they are in fact aimed at their readers. Of course, there is no guarantee that they will reach their target in exactly the same form as they were originally formulated in; even so, their operations are particularly interesting because they lay bare the strategies of communication and discursive construction of the self which are at the heart of the industry.

Among the metapragmatic features of the language of press releases, Jacobs identifies *self-reference* through person, time and place deixis, *self-quotation*, and the use of *explicit semi-performatives* (Jacobs 1999: 20-30). All these features have preformulating functions, either in terms of form, content, or both:

- *self-reference* (especially through third-person reference) makes it easier for journalists to copy part or whole of the text in their piece. The frequent repetition of the company name, for example, encourages copying out chunks of text without losing sight of the body issuing the press release. Example: "A., leader in the fashion industry, presents today a collection …";

- *self-quotation* (which is often fictional) also lends itself to integral transfer to the article, and is particularly suitable for audience manipulation because it allows the issuer to put forward their 'version' without the reporter being compelled to subscribe to it; indeed, this communicative strategy 'objectifies' the information (i.e. it distances it from both the writer and the reader of the press release). Example: "Mr A., the founder and creative director of A., declared: 'A. strives to combine technological research with glamorous elegance …'." This strategy communicates self-promotional material as information, thus facilitating its 'percolation' into the final article; and finally,

- *explicit semi-performatives* (3rd person performatives: example: 'A. announces today…', where the means of the announcement is the press release itself) are often used in press releases because they can function as a bridge between performatives (from the issuer's point of view: 'I, A. hereby announce …) and declaratives (as used in the journalist's article, which reports an event, and has therefore no performative force in itself).

All these features concur in carrying out 'point-of-view operations' whereby the issuer's point of view is turned into the projected journalist's point of view, and hence – if everything goes according to plan – transferred to the readership.

The role of the preformulating features identified by Jacobs in the corpus will be examined below, with particular reference to the way in which they shape and communicate identity. Before moving on to the analysis, though, a few words should be said about the context surrounding the issuing of collection-related fashion press releases.

Fashion designers present their collections (Autumn-Winter and Spring-Summer) twice a year, at different times for men and women. Collections are normally presented during a 'fashion week' – a period of generally 7-10 days during which all designers present their new collections. During a fashion week an average of 10-12 runaway shows take place every day at different locations for an international audience of celebrities, reporters, fashion critics and buyers. The shows are eminently visual events, where the setting, the lighting, the music (and, in general, the style of direction) play a determining role in establishing the mood which will encourage the correct 'reading' of the clothes and of the event itself. They are also usually pretty quick affairs, with as many as 60 different outfits being presented in a very short time. Because of these conditions, often it is not easy for the audience to identify with precision materials, patterns and details. It is to be expected, therefore, that the press releases issued on the occasion of the presentation of the collection will focus on this kind of information, beside providing clues for the interpretation of the outfits in line with the fashion house's established style.

3. Preformulation in the corpus

In this part of the paper a preliminary, macroscopic investigation of the corpus will be carried out to identify the common characteristics of the press releases considered, and to verify the occurrence of Jacobs's preformulating features. In this respect, special regard will be given to the consideration of possible differences in the Italian and English versions of the press releases, with a view to investigating whether preformulating features are structured and/or distributed differently in the two languages.

Jacob's features are present in all the press releases in the corpus, both in the Italian and in the English versions, with the exception of self-quotation, which does not appear at all in the Trussardi press releases, and which has a very limited role in the others as well. However, while the distribution of the features does not vary in the English and Italian versions of the press releases (there is a substantial correspondence, although the two versions – as we shall see later – may differ in other respects), not all of them occur with the same frequency and in the same manner in the press releases by the different fashion houses.

As regards self-reference, an analysis of how this feature is realised in the different texts yields extremely interesting results. Of the designers considered, Dolce & Gabbana appears to be the ones who make the most extensive use of it. However, only three times in the 26 press releases which make up the Dolce & Gabbana corpus is the self-reference to the designers as individuals or as a company, while for the most part the designers' name is used as a pre-modifier, either of the term *collection* ("the Dolce & Gabbana Spring/Summer 2004 collection") or – for the greatest part – of the nouns *man* and *woman* ("the Dolce & Gabbana man", "the Dolce & Gabbana woman"), which suggests that it is indeed the customer (and the customer's identity) that the press releases are about.

While the use of third-person reference to emphasise the centrality of the customer is a peculiarity of Dolce & Gabbana, the tendency to avoid references to the fashion houses in favour of the collections or the customers is shared by the other designers as well. By far the most extensive in all groups of press releases, both in English and in Italian, is the use of the designers' names in pre-modifying position, most frequently referred to the word *collection* and often in association with other terms identifying the particular product line referred to (Dolce & Gabbana, D&G, Armani, Armani Collezioni, Armani Jeans, Cavalli, Cavalli Timewear, Just Cavalli, Trussardi, Trussardi Sport...), as in the following examples:

> Trussardi Jeans proposes a new refined casual look ... (T3)[2]
> Trussardi Sport presents a collection with character ... (T4)
> Trussardi Baby-Junior Spring/Summer 2004 collection lights up with colour (T5)
> The new Just Cavalli Time line follows the extraordinary successful steps of ... (C4)
> Just Cavalli Time watches have been designed for co-ordination ... (C4)
> The new Roberto Cavalli Timewear collection dresses and addresses ... (C5)
> Armani Collezioni for women this upcoming Autumn/Winter 2004/2005 offers a more finely tailored ... (A3)
> The Armani Collezioni men's autumn/winter 2004/2005 collection offers items ...(A4)
> The Dolce & Gabbana man loves life ... (DG1)
> ... these iconic images set the mood for the Dolce & Gabbana women's Fall/Winter 2004/05 collection ... (DG2)
> The Dolce & Gabbana woman is looking for great luxury and refinement ... (DG2)
> La charm of little D&G Junior women is fully satisfied ... (DG3)
> The D&G girl's fascination with fashion is clear ... (DG5)

However, in none of the press releases considered is the brand described or defined; rather, these details are treated as a given, as if there were no need for the journalists (or indeed for their public) to be told or reminded of the peculiarities of the different lines. Hence, there is a singular lack of definite descriptions (identified by Jacobs as a salient accessory feature of self-reference: 1999: 91-94) in the corpus. It also appears significant that both Armani and Trussardi avoid self-reference altogether in the body of the press releases relating to the main collections, while resorting to it for their secondary lines – a behaviour which suggests a need to provide points of reference for the lesser known brands while assuming that the main collection is unmistakably identifiable.

---

2   A legenda for the abbreviations is provided in the Appendix.

As for the communication of personal, corporate or brand identity through self-reference, very little appears to be said about the designers themselves, with all identity-constructing being transferred to the collection or – in the case of the Dolce & Gabbana press releases – to the customer. Of the four designers considered, only Cavalli offers a reference to himself ("the Florence-based designer", C5). Armani's personal stance in the fashion world is referred to once[3], while the Sicilian origins of Dolce & Gabbana are mentioned only indirectly and in so far as they are part and parcel of the collection. Finally, all references to the fashion house as such are emphatically absent from the Trussardi press releases, which appear to be the most objectified and anonymous in the selection. This is perhaps not surprising, given that Nicola Trussardi, the founder, died in 1999, and his son Francesco, who had taken over the company, died too in 2003.

It is also significant that, with very few exceptions, there are no references to the 'Italianness' of the designers (which is one of their main selling points internationally) not only in the press releases in Italian, but also in those in English. This may suggest that this kind of information is assumed to be part of the 'shared knowledge' of the world available to journalists and general public alike.

Moving on to self-quotation, this feature does not appear to occur regularly in fashion press releases. In the corpus under consideration there is only one instance of direct pseudo-quotation ("the D&G woman declares 'J'adore le Vintage' ....", DG2), which is used to establish a mood and, significantly, characterises the ideal customer (it is noteworthy, in terms of cultural characterisation, that the quotation is in French in both the Italian and the English versions). Two more examples of self-quotation[4] are the indirect quotes reported below:

---

3   "Ever since Giorgio Armani started his experiments with deconstruction, there has always been something delicately sensual about his collections. But his type of sex appeal relies on nuance and detail to create that frisson, that unexpected thrill, rather than an obvious assault on form and colour. In his womenswear, Giorgio Armani is famed for travelling a path of gender ambiguity, daring to allow the female to appropriate the male style. Now for Autumn/Winter, he claims some femininity for the male sex, through seductive, soft and gentle clothing which dares to toy with notion of narcissism". (A2)

4   These indirect quotations do not fit with Jacobs's definition of self-quotation, but serve a similar purpose.

All this defines what Giorgio Armani calls *"City Glamour"* – an intense and rebellious seduction …(A6)
Domenico Dolce and Stefano Gabbana believe that there cannot be a future without knowing the past … (DG5)

In both instances, self-quotation is designed to give a key to the interpretation of the collection, and emphasises the (otherwise understated) role of the designers as the creative minds behind the 'objectified' collection. This suggests (in line with the observations on self-reference) that the collections are supposed to 'speak for themselves', with the designers withdrawing from the stage.

This impression is confirmed by the use of semi-perfomatives in the corpus.[5] Only in two instances is the subject of the verb the fashion house (emphasis added):

Once again Sector Group [Cavalli] *presents* a collection of watches … (C4)
Domenico Dolce and Stefano Gabbana *present* a collection … (C21)

In all other examples, the collections (or the product lines) themselves, and not their creators, are in subject position (emphasis added):

Trussardi Jeans *proposes* a new refined, casual look … (T3)
Trussardi Sport *presents* a collection with character … (T4)
The new Roberto Cavalli Timewear collection […] *addresses* women … (C5)
Armani collezioni for women […] *offers* a more finely tailored …(A3)
The Armani Collezioni men's […] collection *offers* items that outline and define the body … (A4)
The Armani Jeans women's […] collection *offers* a mix of 90's and 50's inspired pieces … (A5)
Emporio Armani also *launches* its new range of athletic wear … (A6)
The Emporio Armani men's […] shoe collection *offers* cutting edge design … (A8)
Armani Collezioni for men […] *presents* a selection of items …(A13)
Emporio Armani watches […] *offers* a special collection …(A25)
The D&G […] collection *offers* a rugged romantic approach … (DG 14)

This brief analysis based on the preformulating features identified by Jacobs suggests the following:

---

5   Whether these verbs can be considered as semi-performatives when used as in the quotations is debatable; however, I have decided to consider them as such because it seems to me that the attribution of agency to the collections themselves is significant, as I argue more fully below.

1.   with few exceptions, self-reference appears to be a feature of the fashion press releases considered;
2.   normally, third-person reference is used to refer to the collections (or, in the case of Dolce & Gabbana, the 'projected customer'), and not to the designers/fashion houses;
3.   this results in an 'objectification' of the collections, which become the true protagonists of the press releases; in the Dolce & Gabbana press releases the subject of the identity construction is the customer;
4.   the lack of self-quotations and of semi-performatives attributed to the designers (whether as individuals, or as companies) seems to confirm this impression;
5.   there are no differences, as far as these pre-formulating features are concerned, between the Italian and English versions of the press releases.

The most interesting feature emerging from this brief overview is the 'objectifying' of the collections, which also suggests that the press releases focus primarily on communicating the 'identities' of the collections themselves, and only indirectly those of the designers or fashion houses.

4. Other common features

Beside Jacobs' preformulating features, the press releases in the corpus display other common characteristics. Of course, as they centre on collections, an attention to colours, shapes, fabrics and materials is inevitable (although fabrics may feature more or less extensively in press releases by different designers), but there are other features which appear to be typical of the corpus. The most intriguing ones are an emphasis on contrast, and a focus on establishing a link with the past while emphasising the novelty of the collections.

Contrast is expressed both explicitly (by means of expressions containing the lexical item *contrast*, or through the use of verbs such as *mix*, *combine* etc., or of adversative particles such as *but*, *yet*), and implicitly (by juxtaposing items of clothing which are not expected to 'go together'), as the examples below show (emphasis added):

> Polo shirts, jersey shirts in solid tones and prints *as a contrast to* formal, impeccably tailored suits. (T1)
>
> ...softened crocodile *in contrast with* strings, buckles and rings. (T1)
>
> A youthful image, *but* for a woman. (T2)
>
> 1700's reveries *mix* with a Chinese mood. (C1)
>
> New shapes and cuts for cloaks with an unusual *juxtaposition* of Orient-inspired styles ... (C1)
>
> ... A new taste *mixed* and updated in unusual ... (C2)
>
> ... antique charm *mix* with more modern materials ... (C3)
>
> ... play on patterns reinforced by causal *mixing* and matching (A2)
>
> This typically Armani deconstructed look *mixes* traditional sartorial elegance ... (A3)
>
> The ... collection offers a *mix* of 90's and 50s inspired pieces ...(A5)
>
> Emphasising *contrast*, the unsual color combinations ...(A5)
>
> He loves to *combine* day and evening ... (DG4)
>
> ... in a masterly *contrast* of style ... (DG4)
>
> ... elegance [...] harmoniously *contrasted with* the success of street style ... (DG8)
>
> ... *contrast* is key. (DG8)
>
> ... raw *but* super soft cotton ... (DG9)
>
> ... mini-pulls *and* maxi-trenches (T1)
>
> Loose-fitting suits, slim jackets ... (C2)
>
> Mermaid skirts [...] *worn* with flat-heeled boots ... (A7)
>
> A featherweight jacket *goes with* a sarong ... (A14)
>
> Lavish fox fur stoles *layer over* chiffon tops ... (DG2)
>
> ... satin tuxedo jackets and pinstripe suits *[paired] with* brightly colored sneakers ... (DG4)
>
> ... a denim jacket *over* a pink 'flower power' chiffon floor-length dress ...(DG5)
>
> ... vests are *worn over* sweaters ... (DG6)
>
> ... soft sheer shirts [are] *completed with* heavy wool scarves ... (DG7)
>
> ... oversize sweaters *paired with* lean trousers ... (DG8)
>
> ... Victorian romantic style *paired with* a playful flair ... (DG12)
>
> A fuchsia bolero [...] *paired down with* [...] stretch jeans ... (DG13)
>
> ...sparkling beads attached to a tank top [...] *paired down with* a metropolitan denim shirt ... (DG13)
>
> ... a pink fitted leather jacket *paired down with* slim fitting trousers ... (DG17)

This emphasis on contrast could, of course, simply be the result of a current trend in fashion (all the press releases in the corpus were issued within just over two years), and a longitudinal study would be needed to confirm whether this is a likely explanation. However, I would suggest that by building in contrast and variety as key elements of the collections' identity, the press releases imply comprehensiveness (which might be expected to result in wider appeal), but also instability.

The same idea of a dynamic balance between an 'old' and a 'new' identity is also channelled through the frequent references to past and present, tradition and innovation. This is a crucial aspect of the fashion industry in general (cf. Saviolo 2002: 11), and occurs in all the groups of press releases considered (though not always in the same way). The Dolce e & Gabbana press releases make frequent reference to past and future, tradition and innovation:

> Domenico Dolce and Stefano Gabbana believe that there cannot be a future without knowing the past … (DG5)
> The Dolce & Gabbana man always remains faithful to tradition while incorporating a style that allows him to have fun with what he dresses … (DG8)
> … the D&G girl references the past while creating an entirely new aesthetic … (DG11)

Trussardi privileges comparative expressions (emphasis added):

> … a light*er* approach to *customary* items … (T1)
> … a material *normally* used for gloves, *now* part of a new wardrobe, (T1)
> … a sporti*er* look … (T3),

but also makes reference to the past:

> … a style of today, but with those little touches of yesterday … (T2)

Cavalli, the newest of the designers considered, refers to conventional uses (whether his or consolidated by tradition) while pointing out his innovative attitude (emphasis added):

> Ocelot and jaguar skins *reinterpreted* in unusual colors (C3)
> … *reinventing* the stylist's 'animalier' in a highly original fashion (C5)

Armani also refers to the past, especially in the form of his previous collections and the tradition he has successfully established, which he uses as a starting point for innovation (emphasis added):

... a trend that Armani has been *exploring for some years now*, as he searches for the *unexpected* ... (A2);
... striking *reworked* eveningwear ... (A2)
... a collection of exceptional style and *experienced* taste ... (A4)
... elements that go beyond the *expected traditional* unisex influences ... (A5)

Again, this is a feature which hints at the difficult task which fashion designers have to face when balancing tradition and innovation in their collections.

The first part of this paper has focused on similarities, identifying the common features of the press releases and their role in communicating identity. The provisional conclusions that can be drawn at this stage, can be summed up as follows:

- the identities created and communicated in fashion press releases primarily refer to the collections and/or to the customer (and not to the designers);
- these identities are characterised as dynamic, in a sort of ever-changing, evolving continuity with the past;
- all these features occur in both the English and the Italian versions of the press releases considered, and are strictly parallel in the two versions.

In particular, by suppressing all explicit references to the identity of the designers or fashion houses, the press releases encourage customer identification with the style promoted by the collection. The identity represented is, in a way, 'ready to wear', or even 'made to measure' for a pre-existing, ideal customer ("the D&G woman", for example), a strategy that socio-constructivist theories of advertising have already explored, coming to the conclusion that in assuming the existence of a customer, advertisers are in fact creating him/her (cf. Hackley 1998, 1999; Nairm/Berthon 2003), and whose ideological implications have been frequently pointed out (cf. Fairclough 1989).

5. Communicating culture through press releases

The second part of this paper will focus on the representation and communication of culture in the corpus. In this respect, three areas will be considered: references to Italian culture; references to cultures other than Italian; differences in the handling of these references in the Italian and English versions (with particular attention to issues of cultural adaptation).

The first macroscopic observation is that hardly any explicit reference is made to 'Italian style', either in the Italian or in the English versions of the press releases. References to Sicily abound in the Dolce & Gabbana press releases, but only in so far as they represent the stylists' trademark – an element of continuity in their otherwise ever-changing collections, and often only one of several cultural references.

Besides this initial observation, however, the press releases are characterised by a substantial non-homogeneity in the treatment of cultural references. References to different aspects of culture in the press releases by the four designers can be summed up as follows:

	Armani	Cavalli	Dolce & Gabbana	Trussardi
Italian cultural references	√		√	
References to other cultures		√	√	
Adaptation of cultural references to target public			√	
Use of Italian in English press releases			√	
Use of English in Italian press releases	√	√	√	√
Use of other languages	√	√	√	

Of the four fashion houses considered, Trussardi is the most neutral of all, with no explicit reference to cultural elements detectable in the texts considered. No references to Italian culture, tradition or style are present in the press releases, either in English or in Italian; on the other hand, English terms and phrases are used in the Italian press releases. English – which occurs rarely in the body of the text (where it is employed to describe particular techniques, such as stone-washing) – is used mostly to identify the several product lines (or different styles within a collection). Thus, Trussardi Jeans men's Spring/ Summer collection 2004 is divided into 'cold city', 'ocean blue', 'total summer', while Trussardi Sport man's spring summer collection is composed of 'city race', 'recycling' and 'beach boys'. The choice of English names for the several 'sections' of the collection may be due to a need for easy identification, especially on the international market, and does not appear to be deliberately 'obscure'.

Armani's press releases appear to span from cultural neutrality, to explicit internationalism, to references (sometimes quite specific) to Italian culture. English is used very sparsely. One instance is the introduction of the 'metrosexual' trend (a term explicitly borrowed from American culture, A2), which is cited in both the Italian and English press releases. However, the introduction of the American term and concept suggests, rather than an 'Americanisation' of the Armani style, the introduction of a more international, cosmopolitan appeal (the style is described as being typical of New York).

The international appeal of the collections, often implicit in the lack of cultural references, is occasionally mentioned explicitly in the press releases. In one occasion, significantly, the reference is explicit in the Italian press releases, but absent from the English one:

> Una collezione di grande successo internazionale, che risponde ad un'esigenza autentica del gusto maschile.

> Armani collezioni for men this Spring/Summer presents a selection of items that respond to the real needs of men. (A13)

As far as references to Italian culture are concerned, they are only minimally adapted to the international audience of the English press releases:

> Sensazione di un giorno d'estate. Calore, l'eco del mare, voci che si alzano nell'aria fresca. Nel segno delle vacanze, tra Napoli e la costiera amalfitana, nelle isole del sole. Ma all'improvviso anche una certa aria da passeggiata a Posillipo, un certo modo di fare ardito e scanzonato.

> The collection brings to mind the relaxed mood of a summer's day. The heat, the murmur of the sea, voices carried on the gentle breeze. A feeling of carefree abandon, a holiday on those sun-drenched islands between Naples and the Amalfi coast. Then, suddenly, there's a change of pace: now we're sauntering through lively Posillipo, bold, free and easy. (A12)

Here the English version explicitates the atmosphere more succinctly evoked in the Italian version by the simple mention of the term 'Posillipo'. The same kind of reference receives a similar treatment in another press release:

> Variazione popolar-aristocratica, da scugnizzo di Posillipo, sostenitore del club nautico di rione, del sofisticato stile Quartieri Alti che ha inspirato il design di stagione. (A15)

> This season's theme sees an inspired crossover between the two extremes of Neapolitan life: the street kids of humble Posillipo and the sophisticated inhabitants of the fashionable, smart districts, the *Quartieri Alti*.

Despite the simultaneous expansion and reduction of the English version, the cultural reference is not as effective in English as in Italian. Posillipo, for once, is not part of the 'typical' image of Italy readily available to the international public. The difficulty in communicating culture is also detectable elsewhere. In particular, two press releases are significant in this respect, because they suggest a penchant for intellectual citation:

> A taste for refined elegance with a certain suggestive sensuality that evokes the boudoir bringing to mind the films of Luchino Visconti. (A7)

> For a key to the Armani Jeans Collection, consider the phrase "if on a summer's day, a traveller …", an adaptation of the title of the magical work by the great novelist, Italo Calvino. (A17).

In the first quotation, the reference to Luchino Visconti is not glossed, which suggests that it is expected to be self-explanatory. In the second one, the hint to Calvino is not developed in the rest of the press release. Despite the attempt to gloss the reference, the quotation is unlikely to strike a chord in anybody but the better educated foreign readers, and fails entirely to establish a mood based on Calvino's book. Both examples, however, suggest that Armani may be engaging with 'high culture', adding to the firm's consolidated image of Italian sophistication.

Finally, the use of foreign terms other than English appears to be limited and conventional, confined to expressions such as 'joy de vivre', 'par excellence', with no cultural implications (other than, once again, a deliberate – if culturally neutral – internationalism).

On the opposite end of the scale, Cavalli makes no reference to Italian culture. Rather, his press releases suggest a deliberate effort to introduce a variety of exotic cultural references. If the press releases in English display a desire for cross-contamination and hybridisation of cultures, the extensive use of English in the Italian versions emphasises the 'un-Italianness' of the procedure, for which no Italian description appears to be suitable. The Italian press release about the woman's spring/summer 2003 collection is a clear example in this respect:

> Easter mood, sexy moves. La passerella, iridescente plexigrass tortoise, si trasforma in un palcoscenico del teatro dell'opera. On stage: conturbanti Turandot sfilano su vertiginosi stiletto dorati, nuove geishe seducono strizzate in provocanti abiti *bustier*. Vanità contemporanee. Tra sogni settecenteschi e atmosfere China. Pezzo cult: il corsetto. Sotto il vestito come sensuale impalcatura per scolpire il corpo, sopra come dettaglio-*lingerie* per definire provocanti *silhouettes* alla Allen Jones. Richiami "*boudoire*" con fianchi impigliati in abitini di raso cangiante, in gonne ultrashort, in camicine di tulle trasparente, in vestiti-gioiello dalla leggerezza impalpabile 'incrostati' di pizzi e ricami di jais, diamanti, madreperla. Rosso ceralacca, nero cult, nude color. Capi ultrafemminili mixati con pantaloni oversize d'ispirazione sailor, in pelle increspata e denim light blue. Pelle trattata e stropicciata anche per pastrani *d'antan*: marsine, *redingotes*, frock coats. Nuove linee e tagli inediti per tabarri "reinventati" che accostano in maniera insolita fogge East inspired e originali stampe tartaruga, il nuovo *animalier* firmato Cavalli. Turtle prints, quindi, dai riflessi cangianti, ma anche stampe '700 con arazzi, decori e *trompe d'oeil* di ambienti (la stanza, la musica, il foyer dell'Opera), *chinoiseries* folli con fieri, dragoni e ideogrammi, stampe *lingerie* dai colori pastello. E un finale *flamboyant* con sontuosi abiti da *coup de theatre*.
>
> Oriental mood, sexy moves. Live show: the runaway of iridescent tortoise plexiglass is transformed into the stage of an opera house.
> On stage: disturbingly sexy Tourandots walk by on stunning, golden stiletto heels, modern geishas are seductively squeezed into provocative bustier-dresses. 1700's reveries mix with a Chinese mood. The cult piece: a corset. Under the dress like a sensual scaffolding to sculpt the body, over it like a lingerie detail to define provocative silhouettes à la Allen Jones. Budoire style.

> Hips entangled in shimmering little satin dresses, in ultrashort skirts, in skimpy transparent tulle tops, in impalpably light jewel-dresses 'encrusted' with laces and jet embroidery, diamonds and mother of pearl.
> Sealing-wax red, cult black, nude color. All mixed up with oversize 'sailor' pants, in wrinkled leather and light blue denim. Distressed leather for overcoats of yesteryear. Tails, redingotes, frock coats. New shapes & cuts for cloaks with an unusual juxtaposition of Orient-inspired styles and original turtle prints. Cavalli's new animal design. So, iridescent turtle prints, but also 1700's prints with tapestries, decorations and trompe l'oeil settings (the music room, the Opera foyer), wild chinoiseries with flowers, dragons and ideograms, printed lingerie in pastels. And a flamboyant finale with unexpectedly sumptuous dresses. (C1)

In the Italian text above all foreign terms have been highlighted. English expressions in the Italian texts are underscored, French words are in italics. Some of the foreign words appearing in the text are indeed occasionally used in Italian ("bustier", "boudoir", "lingerie"), but they are still perceived as foreign words (differently, for instance, from "manager", or "decoder"). As a comparison of the two texts shows, English features quite substantially in the Italian text, with French playing a minor role (but notice that the closing expression *coup de theatre* occurs in the Italian, but not in the English text). In one case, an Italian expression is immediately followed by the English equivalent. Code-mixing is constant and deliberate, and appears to be the result of a conscious intent to introduce certain terms into Italian, to the extent of substituting a more foreign-sounding expressions for a phrase that occurs in the English version but probably appeared too familiar to Italian ears ("East-inspired" in place of "Orient-inspired" – the Italian for "Orient" is "Oriente"). While the cultural references are only hinted at, their employment has the clear purpose of conveying an exotic, foreign atmosphere, which aims at hybridising style, culture and language. It is clear from the example quoted above that the Italian versions appear to be much more affected, linguistically, by this attempt.

   If Cavalli appears to engage in an operation of cultural and linguistic hybridisation which challenges identity even in its linguistic manifestation, Dolce & Gabbana seems to be more interested in adapting the identities of its collections to the needs of its target audiences, although the use of English in the Italian press releases is quite extensive ('sneakers', 'oversize', 'cargo' etc.), suggesting that some items are perceived as 'un-Italian' and are therefore 'imported', also linguistically, in the collection themselves.

Beside this need for an 'updating' of the Italian language, however, the most intriguing aspect of the Dolce & Gabbana texts is that Italian and English versions of press releases referring to the same collection sometimes evoke an entirely different atmosphere, even while conveying – presumably – the same 'identity'. Thus, while the Italian press release for the D&G 2003 Spring/Summer man's collection describes a typical Italian family holiday on a popular beach (reference is made to "Rimini, Riccione or Mondello"), complete with oven-baked pasta and watermelon, the corresponding English one evokes a much more Californian atmosphere; 'family' is still mentioned, but 'friends' feature much more prominently, and all references to typical Italian entertainment are replaced by American topics – from baseball to body surfing. Below are the two versions of the press releases, with a literal translation of the Italian one into English to facilitate comparison:

> Potrebbe essere Rimini, Riccione o Mondello, la spiaggia ideale per la famiglia D&G.
> Sdraio, secchielli, pic-nic, ombrelloni, asciugamani e ciabatte, pasta al forno e anguria, questo il colorato mondo dei giovani. Giovani padri che indossano jeans talmente sdruciti da metterci sotto un pantalone di jersey, pantaloni cargo, pantaloncini da tennista, pantaloni oversize in tessuto camouflage, pantaloni trasformisti con zip integrali, tute da idraulici, pantaloni Hawaiani, Speedo e shorts da mare, allegramente mescolati a polo da tennis, giacche da baseball, camicie rigate, T-shirts traforate, impeccabili blazer blu dai bottoni d'oro, bomber Madras e felpe con il cappuccio, gilet multitasche, eleganti polo rigate, canottiere e camicie fiorate, camicie in raso da febbre del sabato sera. Le immancabili ciabatte incrociate, infradito, a fascia, sneakers in tutti i materiali e colori, visiere, fasce e polsiere in spugna, borsoni portatutto, chiavi al collo per non perderle mai. Accompagnati sempre dai bambini che imitano il loro stile con jeans, magliette, minicargo, felpe con cappuccio, zoccoletti e ciabatte per uno stile in tutta libertà all'insegna della vacanza.
> Le mamme si adeguano rubando pantaloni oversize, camicie slacciate sul bikini, asciugamani portati come stole e fasce nei capelli. Anche la nonna non sfugge allo stile con bermuda multitasche, polo da baseball, sneakers e visiera fluo.
>
> *(translated from Italian) It could be Rimini, Riccione or Mondello, the ideal beach for the D&G family. Reclining chairs, buckets, picnics, umbrellas,*

towels and flip-flops, oven-baked pasta and watermelon – this is the colourful world of the young.
Young fathers wear jersey pants under distressed jeans, cargo pants, tennis shorts, oversize camouflage pants, multi-functional trousers with zips, plumber's overalls, Hawaiian pants, swim shorts and beach shorts, merrily mixed with tennis polo shirts, baseball jackets, striped shirts, net t-shirts, impeccable blue blazers with gold buttons, bomber jackets and hooded sweaters, waistcoats with dozens of pockets, elegant striped polo shirts ,flowery vests and shirts, Saturday-night-fever satin shirts. Sandals and flip-flops, sneakers in all colors and materials, visors, terry-cloth headbands and wristbands, all-purpose cloth bags, keyholders to wear round the neck. They are always followed by children who imitate their style with jeans, t-shirts, vests, mini cargo pants, hooded sweaters, sandals and flip-flops for a style in the sign of freedom and in the true holiday spirit.
The mothers also take up this style, and steal from the men oversize pants, shirts which they wear unbuttoned over their bikinis, towels which they use as stoles, and headbands.
The style proves irresistible even for grannies, who wear multi-pocket Bermudas, baseball polo shirts, sneakers and visors in fluorescent colors.

The D&G men's Spring/Summer 2003 collection sets the scene for an idyllic and active day at the beach. Regardless of age, the D&G man can't wait to get beneath the sun, taking as many friends and family with him as he can, insuring he will always have a partner for playing sports. He revels in the crowds that gather by the water and lives by the mentality that more really is merrier. In low-slung cargo pants in lightweight fabrics such as linen and cotton he often wears unzipped down the side or front. They are his favourite pants and he owns them in many colors from military green to dusky pink. Athletic mesh sports pants in bright colours are always on hand so he can pick up a game of baseball with his friends. Always individual he customizes his tops by cutting off sleeves and adding extra buttons to create his own kind of polo shirt. Layering is key whether or [*sic*] its athletic pants under distressed jeans or a polo shirt under a striped button down or satin bomber jacket. As the temperature rises he changes into his cotton or distressed denim shorts and always there is a pair of sexy swim shorts for body surfing or tanning. His accessories help complete his look and add to his personal style. His favorite accessory is his frayed denim visor that has faded to pale pastel from too much sun. Colorful sneakers and sandals are his footwear of choice, while he never leaves home without his terry cloth wrist and headband always ready for a game of tennis. (DG16)

Similarly, the father who takes the kids to the park in the Italian version of the D&G Fall/Winter 2002/03 collection becomes, in the English version, "a young father walking in Central Park with his daughter", or "an older brother teach[ing] his little brother how to skateboard". In the same pair of press releases, the reference to the "Canadian woodcutter" in the Italian version is tactfully omitted in the English one (too provincial?). Other omissions are more significant: in the Italian version of the Dolce & Gabbana 2003/04 Fall/Winter man's collection press release, for instance, there is an explicit reference to the 1968 students' riots, entirely omitted in the English version. Mention of "biological attacks" (rather too superficially associated with potential "sentimental attacks", perhaps) in the Italian version of the 2003/04 Fall/Winter man's collection disappears from the English version.

Elsewhere the changes are subtler: the "Tyrolean style" of the Italian press releases becomes consistently an "Austrian style", and references to past icons may differ in the two language versions depending on the target audience's perceived familiarity with them. So, if in the English D&G Spring/Summer 2004/2004 woman's collection reference is made to Jean Harlow, the Mod's look of the 60s, and Janis Joplin, no reference to these appear in the Italian version, which is safely confined to Coco Chanel and the Belle Époque.

This adaptation to the audience sometimes results in the selection of different outfits as representative of the collection, and nearly always in a different presentation of the material, even when the information remains more or less recognisably the same. This leads to the hypothesis that cultural adaptation of contents may also result in a formal restructuring of the discursive strategies at play in the texts.

6. Conclusions

The analysis of fashion press releases conducted in this study suggests some provisional conclusions. With reference to the first focus of the analysis, it appears that fashion press releases share a set of formal common features. Third-person reference and semi-performatives (two of Jacobs' identifying features) both appear in all text in the corpus, although pseudo-quotation does not. However, it appears that (with very few exceptions) third person reference is never to designers, while being consistently referred to the collections (and, in Dolce & Gabbana, to the customer). As a result, the collections themselves appear to be endowed with their own 'identity', making it easier for the customer to adopt it. Other identity-related common features in the corpus are an emphasis on variety and contrast, and an attempt to establish continuity within a tradition (whether personal or cultural) while emphasising novelty. In this respect, there do not seem to be any substantial differences between press releases in Italian and in English. In particular, writers of press releases do not seem to feel the need to provide foreign audiences with any additional information than that provided in the Italian versions.

Probably because of the designers' absence from the press releases, their Italian identity does not appear to feature prominently in them. In fact, references to Italian culture are only present in so far as they represent a source of inspiration for a particular collection, but they are not a necessary element of all of them.

Of the four designers considered, Trussardi appears as the most culturally neutral, while Cavalli displays an interest for hybridity and cross-fertilisation aimed at reflecting back on Italian culture and its language, which, far from being 'exported', is contaminated by the 'otherness' of exotic atmosphere. Armani, while often keeping a neutral attitude which hints at the international appeal of his collections, makes occasional references to Italian life and culture. Although often culture-specific and not necessarily readily decipherable by foreign readers, these references are integrated in English press releases with a minimum amount of adaptation.

Dolce & Gabbana, on the other hand, makes culture the leading theme of its collections. Its press releases overflow with references to lifestyles, places, atmospheres, icons of the past. It also often (but not always) mentions Sicily (but rarely Italy). The most interesting aspect of its deployment of cultural themes, however, is the way in which it is adapted to their target audiences: thus, while references to Italian culture abound in the Italian press releases, they are often replaced by references to other cultures (most notably American, or generally 'European') in the press releases in English. Similarly, when the inspiration of the collections is foreign, cultural references are carefully calibrated to be self-evident for the Italian readers, while more implicit ones are allowed in the English press releases. In conclusion, it appears that a focus on cultural adaptation may also affect discursive organization and shift the balance – in drafting bilingual versions of press releases – from translation to re-writing.

References

Acker, David A. 1991. *Managing Brand Equity: Capitalizing on the Value of a Brand Name.* New York: The Free Press.

Acker, David A. 1995. *Building Strong Brands.* New York: The Free Press.

Barnard, Malcolm 1996. *Fashion as Communication*, London/New York: Routledge.

Fairclough, Norman 1989. *Language and Power*, London: Longman.

Featherstone, Mike 1991. The Body in Consumer Culture. In Featherstone, Mike / Hepworth, Mike / Turner, Bryan S. (eds) *The Body: Social Process and Cultural Theory.* London: Sage Publications, 170-196.

Finkelstein, Joanne 1991. *The Fashioned Self.* Oxford: Polity Press.

Hackley, Christopher E. 1999. An Epistemological Odyssey: toward social construction of advertising process. *Journal of Marketing Communication* 5/3, 157-168.

Hackley, Christopher E. 1988. Social Constructionism and Research in Marketing and Advertising. *Qualitative Market Research: An International Journal* 1/3, 125-131.

Jacobs, Geert 1999. *Preformulating the News. An Analysis of the Metapragmatics of Press Releases.* Amsterdam/Philadelphia: John Benjamins.

Kellner, Douglas 1994. Madonna, Fashion, and Identity. In Benstock, Shari / Ferriss, Suzanne (eds) *On Fashion.* New Brunswick, N.J.: Rutgers University Press, 159-182.

Nairn, Agnes / Berthon, Pierre 2003. Creating the Customer: The Influence of Advertising on Consumer Market Segments – Evidence and Ethics. *Journal of Business Ethics* 42/1, 83-99.

Negrin, Llewellyn. 1999. The Self as Image. A Critical Appraisal of Postmodern Theories of Fashion. *Theory, Culture and Society* 16/3, 99-118.
Saviolo, Stefania 2002. *Brand and Identity Management in Fashion Companies.* SDA Bocconi Working Papers Series n. 66.

Appendix

The press releases in the corpus are identified by the initial of the issuer (example: Armani → A) and a progressive number (re-starting for each designer). The same number was given to English and Italian versions of the press releases: A15, therefore, identifies the press release for Emporio Armani men's collection s/s 2004 both in Italian and English.

A1   Giorgio Armani women's collection a/w 2004/2005
A2   Giorgio Armani men's collection a/w 2004/2005
A3   Armani Collezioni women's a/w 2005/2005
A4   Armani Collezioni men's a/w 2004/2005
A5   Armani Jeans women's collection a/w 2004/2005
A6   Emporio Armani men's collection a/w 2004/2005
A7   Emporio Armani women's collection a/w 2004/2005
A8   Emporio Armani men's accessories a/w 2004/2005
A9   Emporio Armani women's accessories a/w 2004/2005
A10 Giorgio Armani men's accessories a/w 2004/2005
A11 Giorgio Armani women's accesories a/w 2004/2005
A12 Giorgio Armani women's collection s/s 2004
A13 Armani Collezioni men's collection s/s 2004
A14 Emporio Armani women's collection s/s 2004
A15 Emporio Armani men's collection s/s 2004
A16 Armani Junior collection s/s 2004
A17 Armani Jeans men's collection s/s 2004
A18 Armani Jeans women's collection s/s 2004
A19 Giorgio Armani men's accessories s/s 2004
A20 Emporio Armani women's accessories s/s 2004
A21 Giorgio Armani s/s 2004 'Mediterranean' eyewear collection
A22 Emporio Armani s/s 2004 'Urban Fluo' eyewear
A23 Emporio Armani men's accessories s/s 2004
A24 Emporio Armani watches s/s 2004
A25 Giorgio Armani Occhiali s/s 2004
A26 Giorgio Armani women's accessories s/s 2004

A27   Armani Collezioni women's collection s/s 2004
A28   Armani Collezioni men's collection s/s 2004

C1   Roberto Cavalli women's collection s/s 2003
C2   Roberto Cavalli men's collection s/s 2003
C3   Roberto Cavalli Underwear collection s/s 2003
C4   Roberto Cavalli Timewear January 2003
C5   Roberto Cavalli Timewear collection s/s 2003
C6   Roberto Cavalli Eyewear collection s/s 2003

DG1   Dolce & Gabbana mens collection f/w 2004/2005
DG2   Dolce & Gabbana women's collection f/w 2004/2005
DG3   D&G Junior collection f/w 2004/2005
DG4   D&G men's collection f/w 2004/2004
DG5   D&G women's collection f/w 2004/2005
DG6   Dolce & Gabbana men's collection f/w 2002/2003
DG7   Dolce & Gabbana men's collection s/s 2003, *Italian version only*
DG8   Dolce & Gabbana men's collection f/w 2003/2004
DG9   Dolce & Gabbana men's collection s/s 2004
DG10 D&G woman's collection f/w 2002/2003
DG11 D&G woman's collection s/s 2003
DG12 D&G woman's collection f/w 2003/2004
DG13 D&G woman's collection s/s 2004
DG14 D&G men's collection f/w 2002/2003
DG15 D&G men's collection s/s 2003
DG16 D&G men's collection f/w 2003/2004
DG17 D&G men's collection s/s 2004
DG18 D&G men's collection f/w 2002/2003
DG19 Dolce & Gabbana women's collection f/w 2002/2003
DG20 Dolce & Gabbana women's collection s/s 2003
DG21 Dolce & Gabbana women's collection f/w 2003/2004
DG22 Dolce & Gabbana women's collection s/s 2004
DG23 D&G Junior collection s/s 2003
DG24 D&G Junior collection f/w 2003
DG25 & Dolce & Gabbana collection f/w 2002/2003
DG26 & Dolce & Gabbana collection s/s 2003

T1   Trussardi manswear collection s/s 2004
T2   Trussardi womanswear collection s/s 2004
T3   Trussardi Jeans men's collection s/s 2004
T4   Trussardi Sport men's collection s/s 2004
T5   Trussardi baby-junior collection s/s 2004

DELIA CHIARO

A Question of Taste:
Translating the Flavour of Italy

1. Introduction

The New Economy has widened the marketing horizons of businesses throughout the world by facilitating trade relationships both in terms of B2B ('business to business') and B2C ('business to customer'). But over and above the opportunities created by the World Wide Web such as the wealth of on-line shopping facilities which allow customers to buy directly from producers, the Internet provides an endless shop window in which manufacturers are able to exploit an infinite amount of space for the promotion of their wares. Not only, but the so called modern-day Far West of the Net allows companies to promote more copiously and in much greater detail than ever before. Traditional advertising via the media of print, radio and TV not only entails high costs, but is also impaired in terms of actual space made available for promotion. There is a limit to what can be shown and said about a product on a billboard, in the pages of a magazine or the few seconds of a TV commercial. Yet, for the initial outlay of a 'dot.com' and the know-how of a webmaster, the space and promotional possibilities available to businesses on the Web are boundless. On the other hand, sophisticated technology is not sufficient for successful transnational promotion. Companies must not forget the need to employ both an expert in marketing communication and a team of professional translators.

Nevertheless, the apparent freedom of advertising on the World Wide Web raises two questions. The first regards the way in which the medium affects the text, or rather, how Web texts differentiate themselves from print texts. The second issue involves the textual strategies necessary for a campaign aimed at transnational readership. In other words, print and/or TV advertisements are usually aimed at specific language communities. But how can a single Web text, available to anybody, have the same desired effect on any reader from any culture? Of course there are huge multinational campaigns which in the past have hinged on a verbal code that is kept to a minimum of words in English so that the same promotion could be used pretty much globally e.g. *Coca Cola* "Enjoy"*, Nike* "Just do it"; "United Colors of Benetton"; *MacDonald's* "I'm lovin' it", etc.; yet, marketing strategies are changing as companies are beginning to see that an English slogan may not automatically work transnationally simply because English is not necessarily as universally understood as one might imagine (De Mooij 2004: 180). Similarly, campaigns which seem to remain culturally and linguistically neutral like *L'Oreal* ("Because I'm / you're / we're worth it") and easily translatable – at least hypothetically – have also met up with problems transnationally (Munday 2004: 207). For example, while the Shell slogan "I love Shell" worked to the company's advantage in French with the slogan "C'est celle que j'aime" in which the closeness of 'celle' and 'Shell' made it effective, in France Esso's 'Tiger in your tank' was "so bizarre it had to be translated as putting a tiger in your engine" as "…it is not just translation that is necessary but the transposition of a concept into another culture" (Paliwoda 1993: 235).

However, it is fair to say that most print and/or TV promotional texts appear to be especially created for specific language communities and this is evident from the diversity of advertisements for the same product from country to country. For example, large corporations such as Coca Cola make minor modifications in promotional campaigns to the way they present themselves to each culture. Despite standardization, local agencies are allowed to edit commercials to highlight close-ups of local faces (Solomon 2004: 585). Similarly, care needs to be taken when translating brand names.

> There is no good reason to explain why a Fiat Ritmo which sold well in Europe could not sell well in Britain, or why it should sell better as a Fiat Strada in Britain when 'Strada' only means street. [...] Sales of Tide in Denmark were low until it was deduced that it was the Danish word for menstrual flow. (Paliwoda 1993: 235)

Stories of blunders in translating brand names are rife in the field of marketing (Solomon 2004: 484), yet such issues represent only the tip of the iceberg of problems facing the translation of promotional texts. The mere breadth of the Net coupled with a culturally unidentifiable readership may well run the risk of multiplying such problems endlessly.

Websites can be created in as many languages as one desires although it seems to be the case that the tendency is to construct them in the source language plus English and perhaps a few other languages too. While many companies do indeed have different websites for countries which share the same language (e.g. the German multinational *Dr Oetker* has three separate sites for Germany, Austria and Switzerland) thus highlighting a certain sensitivity towards cultural specificity and not taking for granted that same language equals the same culture, what appears to be more common on the Net is a tendency to create an international site in English. This, of course, opens up a can of worms regarding issues as diverse as whether English is indeed the Lingua Franca which is understood by all and sundry (De Mooij 2004) and the fallacy that translation is simply about converting words in one lexico-grammatical system into another and presuming that the same meaning will be conveyed.

So, the question is, just how far is lingua-cultural sensitivity widespread in commercial enterprise? And to what extent is such understanding simply in the possession of the large multi-nationals who have the economic power to afford extensive research into culture-specific perceptions?

Italy is a case in point. The Italian agro-food industry, for example, is certainly one of the most important sources of international trade in the country, yet businesses are mainly small and medium sized. The question we ask ourselves is how are these companies faring with the new competition created by the ever growing free for all of the World Wide Web. More precisely, how are these small to medium sized companies coping with the lingua-cultural requirements of transnational navigators? Are they sensitive both to the linguistic and cultural needs of specific overseas markets or do they consider translation to be simply a case of translating words from one language to another and stringing them together with the right grammar and syntax?

This study will present an outline of the way 33 firms in the Italian agro-food sector present themselves via the World Wide Web.

Particular attention will be paid not only to translational strategies adopted, but also to what I would like to label 'textual sensitivity', by which I refer to the awareness that texts on the Net should differ from print texts simply because of the difference pertaining to the medium itself.

2. Advertising on the Web

2.1. Translational strategies for promotional material

Quentin Tarantino's cult movie *Pulp Fiction* (1994) opens with a scene in which Vincent (John Travolta) is in a car joking with Jules (Samuel L. Jackson) about the intercultural differences which exist between Europe and the USA. Both are surprised not only by the fact that in Holland it is not a criminal offence to buy, sell or consume marijuana, but above all by the names of products in fast food outlets which are not the same in the two continents. What follows is the dialogue in which the two actors discuss these 'little differences':

> VINCENT: Well, in Amsterdam you can buy beer in a movie theatre. And I don't mean in a paper cup either. They give you a glass of beer, like in a bar. In Paris, you can buy beer at Macdonald's. Also, you know what they call a Quarter Pounder with cheese in Paris?
> JULES: They don't call it a Quarter Pounder with cheese?
> VINCENT: No man they've got the metric system, they don't know what the fuck a Quarter Pounder is!
> JULES: So what do they call a Quarter Pounder with cheese?
> VINCENT: They call it a *Royale* with cheese.
> JULES: *Royale* with cheese.
> VINCENT: That's right.
> JULES: What do they call a Big Mac?
> VINCENT: A Big Mac's a Big Mac only they call it *Le* Big Mac.
> JULES: *Le* Big Mac. What do they call a Whopper?
> VINCENT: I don't know, I didn't go in a Burgy King. You know what they put on French fries in Holland instead of ketchup?
> JULES: What?
> VINCENT: Mayonnaise!

If on the one hand this conversation highlights the role which translation plays and will continue to play in the process of internationalization, on the other it underscores the importance of the 'little differences' which are in fact, not in the least bit, 'little' at all. The kind of textual adaptations exemplified in the dialogue are hard to recognize as results of translations yet somewhere in their journey across the Atlantic a translation must have occurred to turn two US labels into two recognizably French ones and as examples of successful transnational commercial communication. Now, our cinematic hero quite rightly notes that the same products in France and in the USA are labelled differently as he reminds us that the planet has been inundated with thousands of written and oral texts which, although not necessarily the product of translation in the strictest sense, represent interlinguistic and intercultural mutations which originated in a different language. Amongst such adaptations or rewritings we find the birth of relatively new English textual genres, destined for a transnational readership which is not necessarily proficient in English. Furthermore, these texts, which may have well been written or produced by a non-native speaker of English, may also be the product of interaction between a human being and a software programme designed to generate translations automatically. And of course, scholars of translation do not need the help of Tarantino to come up with examples of brand names, packaging, menus, brochures and billboards which are different across the globe yet at the same time strikingly similar. And promotional texts on the Web are an example of such a newly born genre.

As is well known, the term 'globalization' refers to the process which allows the image of a company to be recognized outside its country of origin which then leads to the consumption of its products by people who live in different sociocultural and economic environments. Corporations which want to be part of this process need to measure up to another concept too, i.e. localization or the process of customizing a product in the environment in which it is to operate. In the case of hi-tech products such as computers, mobile phones, cars etc., every single product is adapted for each specific locale (the place where it is to be sold). For example the Italian car manufacturer FIAT, makes cars with right hand drive in order to sell them in the UK. This kind of technical accommodation strategy works equally well in the agro-food sector. It would appear that the taste buds of consumers vary from culture to culture, thus the taste of Italian Coca Cola is slightly different from the same product on sale in other countries; well known ice cream products such as 'Cornetto' and 'Vienetta' are sold in different flavours in Italy and the UK, thus the fact that Europeans put mayonnaise on their chips in Europe may seem strange to John Travolta, but for Macdonald's, supplying sachets of it to European customers was a winning marketing move.

Localization, however, is not only a question of adapting products according to culture-specific tastes, but it also involves communication and above all the translation of texts connected with the product from the brand name, packaging and traditional advertising, to the company website. Stecconi (2000) highlights the importance of semio-translation in the process of globalization by demonstrating how successful companies such as the Swedish multinational IKEA have promoted their products via the World Wide Web by diversifying not only linguistically, but also semiotically. In other words, not only is a new verbal text produced for the target culture, but care is taken to produce a visual text which is appropriate for that culture too. Rather like the way in which Coca Cola adjusts its TV ads to include faces which 'belong' to the target locale, IKEA's virtual catalogue contains 36 embedded websites, not only in different languages but also with different culture-specific visuals, each one unmistakably British, Italian, Japanese or whatever. By offering a verbal translation combined with culture-specific non-verbal texts IKEA attempts to satisfy the needs of a transnational readership.

Although promotional texts have been the object of study in the fields of economics and marketing (Solomon 2004), communication studies (Dyer 1988; Wells et al. 1989; Leiss et al.1990), linguistics (Leech 1966; Cook 1992) and, more recently, translation studies (Adab 1998; Fuentes Luque and Kelly 2000; Adab and Valdés 2004), it has only been of late that scholars have been investigating the notion of Web promotion (Stecconi 2000; Chiaro 2004). In particular, Stecconi's empirical analysis of promotional texts on the Web points to the use of one of three different translational strategies, namely 'intrasemiotic translations' in which the source text (verbal) is deconstructed and then reconstructed in the target language; 'intersemiotic' translations in which not only language, but the entire semiotic system is recreated in the target text and 'syncretic' trans-lations in which only parts of the texts (verbal and non) are changed for specific locales.

2.1.1. The Italian agro-food sector and translation

A study carried out by Chiaro (2004) reveals that in a traditional print corpus of Italian food and drink advertisements collected in the UK in 2003, only five out of sixteen brands were genuinely Italian companies and not simply part of larger multi-nationals or companies producing Italian foodstuff who were not Italian yet sported Italian names. The latter firms were labelled "pretend Italian" (2004: 317) because they are getting away with being truly 'made in Italy' to British consumers yet have little to do with Italy in reality. What is especially interesting about corporations who are pretending to be Italian is that the way in which they choose to convey Italianess in their promotional texts which can tell us a great deal about the way the UK sees Italy, or rather the way in which cultural stereotypes are strengthened by the media. It is the so-called pretend brands, for example, who prefer comic stereotypes like the moustachioed muppet Carlo and accompanying *Mama* promoting *Dolmio*'s pasta sauces (Mars corporation) or the sexually active senior citizens of *Bertolli* olive oils (Unilever).

Furthermore, Web promotion of Italian foodstuff reveals a direct link between the size of the company and the translational strategy adopted. Small companies appear to opt for intrasemiotic, *mot à mot* renditions. In other words, the Source Text (ST) is simply deconstructed and re-constructed afresh in the Target Language (TL). On the other hand, the larger multinationals choose either an inter-semiotic or a syncretic translational approach. Never is it just the verbal text which changes, but also at least part of the non-verbal text too. Furthermore, the larger the company the greater was the tendency to adopt an intersemiotic translation. Not only, but the larger the multinational, the more intersemiotic is the approach in terms of higher verbal and visual differentiation between culture-specific sites (Chiaro 2004: 324-325).

3. Advertising Italian food products transnationally

3.1. Advertising Italian food on TV

In 2004 two Italian brands were promoted on British TV, namely *Bertolli* olive oils and spreads and Goodfella's frozen pizzas. Interestingly neither brand is truly Italian as Bertolli is now part of the Unilever group and Goodfella's belongs to Green Isle Foods, a subsidiary of Northern Foods based in Co. Kildare, which bought the *San Marco* brand from the multinational giant Heinz. We can thus safely hypothesize that their advertising campaigns were not made in Italy. However, it is to be said that in the case of such merging (e.g. *San Pellegrino* mineral water with *Nestlé*; *Martini* vermouth with the *Bacardi* group etc) while forcing autochthonous companies to give up their independence, much is to be gained both in terms of financial gains through wider international exposure, but also in terms of marketing experience. The multinational giants have decades of successful promotional know-how behind them from which smaller Italian companies have only to learn. And even totally pretend brands like *Dolmio* and *Goodfella's*, who have little or nothing to do with Italy other than their labels, can teach small and medium sized companies quite a bit.

Now, as expected, both these brands promote their products on TV via comic stereotypes. The two Bertolli commercials feature large, matriarchal Italian families. One ad is a parody of the opening credits of eighties soap Dallas in which the Texan plains and herds of cattle are replaced by a single sheep roaming the Tuscan hills and the Ewing's are replaced by the huge Bertolli family, "The Olive Oil Baron's of Italy". The other spot features a very active grandfather Pietro who like other "people in the Mediterranean" lives longer and is more vigorous because he consumes olive oil. Intertextually linked to each other, to previous TV commercials and parallel print promotions for other Bertolli products (e.g. a senior citizen driving a historic car with the copy "thanks to the right oil she still goes like the clappers" and the 2003 print campaign featuring Italian senior citizens labelled "It-girl – the new name for woman about town" and "Babe magnet"), the *Bertolli* campaign plays on the stereotype of the Latin

Lover who is still sexually active despite his or her age (Chiaro 2004: 323).

Interestingly, in the case of Bertolli, we find an example of a 'glocalized' product. Adab coined the term 'glocalization' for a hybrid translation made up of a "globally relevant ST, based on a message which will have similar impact across different cultural contexts" (1998: 224). Although Italians use olive oil as part of their dietary habits, olive oil spreads are certainly not consumed. In fact they do not even exist on the Italian market as they are not part of the Mediterranean diet. *Bertolli* olive oil spread can thus be considered a sort of 'translated product', a glocalization.

The Goodfella's Pizza campaign also works on comic stereotypes. It consists of two TV ads, one of a grandfather in Italy who, in Italian, publicly disowns his grandson for not having made a success of his *Pizzeria* business in Britain. The ad is translated by an off screen voice-over from which we learn that the reason why the grandson's business has failed is due to the excellence of Goodfella's frozen Pizza. Why go out to a *pizzeria* if there is an 'authentic' pizza in your freezer? The other ad features the grandson explaining in broken English why his *Pizzeria* is empty. Thanks to Goodfella's pizza we learn that "It looks like closing time for Pizzerias". The stereotype speaks for itself. The label and the slogan both recall the typecast of the Italian link with organized crime while the ads evoke decades of Italian immigration and migrants who ventured abroad and typically went into self-employed catering by opening up restaurants, sandwich bars and ice-cream parlours outside Italy.

3.2. Advertising Italian food on the Web

3.2.1. The corpus

A previous study carried out by the present author on the promotion of Italian foodstuff indicated that across 16 brands, both print and web ads could be classified according to two broad categories labelled 'Traditional Italy' and 'Modern Italy' (2004: 319). The traditional strategy tended to promote Italian food products via images of large families seated round a table surrounded by sunny hills and country spires. On the other hand, adverts for beverages (both alcoholic and non) opted for endorsing the image of a more modern Italy inhabited by trendy, good-looking, sun-glassed young people whizzing about busy cities on scooters. Comic stereotypes were only adopted by non-Italian corporations. In order to verify these findings, a larger corpus of thirty-three websites which represented what could be considered representative Italian food products was collected. Included in the corpus were 15 sites promoting pasta (*Agnesi*; *Antonio Amato*; *Barilla*; *Buitoni*; *Carmine Russo*; *Corticella*; *De Cecco*; *Divella*; *Garofalo*; *Giuseppe Cocco*; *Granarolo*; *La Molisana*; *Paone*; *Pasta Russo*; *Setaro*); two producers of tinned tomatoes (*Annalisa* and *Mutti*), five brands of olive oil (*Berio, Bertolli, Carapelli, Monini, Sasso*); three brands of pickles, spreads and antipasti (*Coelsanus, GiA'* and *Saclà*); the *Birra Peroni* beer and *Di Saronno* liqueur websites; three companies producing coffee (*Illy, Kimbo, Lavazza* and *Segafredo*) as well as the sites of the national consortia for Parma ham and Parmesan cheese.

3.2.2. Traditional versus Modern Italy

Out of a total of 33 companies examined, the majority promote their products by projecting a pretty stereotypical image of Italy and Italians. In other words, these companies underscore features such as tradition, long standing family businesses, Italian taste for natural, healthy and flavoursome food. Traditional sites also underscore stereotypically Italian personality traits, such as excitement, passion and fervour.

In contrast, companies which opt for a modern image ignore country images of rolling hills and multi-generational families at table. They prefer featuring chic young people in busy cities and, if they are at a table, it is likely to be at a fashionable café surrounded by the innermost circle of an Italian in-crowd. These companies endorse elegance, sophistication and good taste.

As in the previous study, this larger corpus also reveals that Italian beverages, whether alcoholic or non-alcoholic, tend to be promoted transnationally almost exclusively via images of Italian modernity. However, the modern/traditional strategies are crosscut by intrasemiotic, intersemiotic and syncretic translational choices. In other words, a traditional strategy does not necessarily involve an intrasemiotic translation (i.e. the straightforward deconstruction of the source text and reconstruction in the target language leaving all non-verbal elements the same) although a modern approach, according to the findings in the present corpus, generally tends to exclude this. In fact, half of all traditionally promoted food brands used an intrasemiotic strategy and another half an intersemiotic approach. Interestingly, only one 'modern' promotion in the corpus, *Kimbo* coffee, boasted an intrasemiotic translation, all the others opted for more dynamic intersemiotic or syncretic strategies. Thus, most products promoted via modern Italy will be either intersemiotic (i.e. totally reconstructed both verbally and non-verbally from the source text) or syncretic (i.e. *partially* reconstructed both verbally and non-verbally from the source text).

The other interesting element which emerged from our findings was an emphasis in the 'modern' promotions on the term *tradition,* and vice versa, the occurrence of the term *modern* in 'traditional' promotions. In other words, there appears to be a constant need to reassure the public that despite their up-to-date and trendy images, a company is nevertheless longstanding and based upon solid (read 'family') values and traditions. On the other hand, if the company has decided to promote via a traditional strategy, a need for highlighting modernity in production techniques is underscored. Contradictions in words or marketing strategies? To complicate matters further, six websites were a perfect mixture of tradition and modernity rather than one or the other (i.e. the *Parmigiano Reggiano* consortium, *Berio, Bertolli* and *Sasso* olive oils, and *Buitoni* and *Granarolo* pastas). Again, while in the 2004 study (the corpus of which was collected in 2003) a modern strategy was adopted exclusively for web promotion of Italian beverages, what emerges from the present study is the tendency of much pasta promotion to be moving towards the adoption of a modern strategy too. This is also a clear indication of the speed at which changes occur on the Net, but could also be a pointer of a more general trend for Italian goods to be sold by means of a more contemporary image. And interestingly it is pasta, the traditional Italian food *par excellence* to be amongst the first foods, as opposed to beverages, to be promoted through a modern image of Italy.

3.2.3. Traditional Italy on the Web

So, most companies examined promote their products via a traditional image conveyed through a colourful website. Pasta companies, for example, tend to construct their sites in bright blue and gold colours with straight intrasemiotic translations of the verbal texts into English, while sites promoting olive oils tend to be predictably olive green in colour. Splashes of red also seem to be inevitable so that the red, white and green of the national flag is always present. Photographs of fresh fruit and vegetables fill these websites together with luscious images of steaming plates of pasta all in vivid colours. The image is of good, healthy foods which are transformed into nourishing time-honoured Italian dishes. To complete the image of tradition, on *Barilla*'s American website, Andrea Bocelli can be heard singing in the background, thus homing in on the stereotype of Italian love of opera.

A quick glance at company slogans will show how Italy (and traditional food produce) would like to be seen by the outside world "Taste is only a question of substance" (*De Cecco*); "The original Italian traditions" (*Agnesi*); "Live the passion" (*Barilla*); "The passion comes pouring out" (*Carapelli* oil); "The passion for tomatoes. On line" (*Mutti*); "A squeeze of olives" (*Monini*). Reference to tradition, taste and passion occurs over and over across websites and many sites contain 'authentic' Italian recipes. *Buitoni* (part of the *Nestlé* multinational) offers "Our food affair" with nested pages labelled "intimate", "carnival", "passion", "elegance" and "indulgence". Thus traditional Italy is conveyed through an image of conventional families who consume authentic, healthy food, while tending to be playful and passionate!

However, as observed previously, the word *modern* does occur in these verbal texts especially in descriptions of present day production and business which are present in all the hypertexts examined.

3.2.4. Modern Italy on the Web

The *Illy* and *Lavazza* coffee websites are typical examples of how an Italian product is promoted via images of an extremely modern Italy. The *Illy* site is sprinkled with rigorously black and white photographs of trendy young people and the only clue to the Italianness of the product is in the red company label on the metal silver coloured designer container. Thus the effect of the photography is of elegantly filtered nuances of black and white with small splashes of red. The copy reads "It is not just a coffee, it is an *espresso coffee*: a taste of Italy". Similarly, the models in the *Lavazza* website are photographed in colour but they are equally trendy, and both coffee websites are loaded to the tune of a samba to stress the Brazilian origin of the coffee beans. However, the corresponding international (English language) websites are translated syncretically and thus are different in places from the source Italian sites. In other words, the verbal texts are translated and some of the images change too.

A quick look at the *Illy* print campaign also reveals a modern strategy with images of high powered business people and copies which play on the need to get away from stress with a cup of coffee. Yet, copies contain statements like: "It is a great Italian family"; "Today *Illy* is a company on international scale. Because it is a great Italian family, and anything is strong as your roots." So, although the minimalist ads display no traditional connotation of Italianness, they do convey an image of a cool and trendy Italy which has not forgotten its roots: family and tradition, the two classic Italian values *par excellence*. Returning to the website, to set off the image of an up-to-date, yet, at the same time, traditional company, the site contains a simple photograph of the six present-day members of the Illy family, dressed professionally in cool colours, against background which is stark grey except for the red logo. The underlying message is that *Illy* has carried on its family tradition and it has become a guarantee, a symbol of quality.

If we now turn to the *Kimbo* coffee website, we find that it too is modern in type with a predominance of black and white photography and trendy visual effects, however the translation is intra-semiotic. While it is grammatically impeccable, it is hard to imagine that the message is perfectly clear to a non-Italian visitor to the site:

> Undisputed market leader in Campania thanks to the unfaltering superior quality and the adherence to the typically Neapolitan tradition in coffee…

How many people outside Italy are aware of the fact that Neapolitans supposedly make the best *espresso* in Italy? And that Naples is in the region of Campania? What is surely a positive selling point in Italy, will not necessarily be equally successful, or even logical beyond the country's borders.

Another beverage, *Birra Peroni* is promoted via an inter-semiotic translation of the original Italian website. Gone is the sexy, blonde, scantily dressed model sported on the autochthonous site with the slogan *Peroni, sei la mia bionda* where *bionda*/blonde is a homonym for light beer, literally "Peroni you are my blonde". The UK website eliminates anything which might arouse feminist hostility and replaces it with sleek black and white images labeled 'shade', 'ride', 'time' and 'walk' (Table 1). Each minimalist photograph is coupled with a quietly amusing text based on various contemporary Italian stereotypes. For example, 'shades' contains a short text on the Italian love of trendy sunglasses; 'ride' their obsession for *Vespas* and appearance; 'time' on their unpunctuality and 'walk' on their love of beauty. Endearingly self-mocking, but at the same time cool and essential, the English site is an example of a good quality translation which will be appreciated abroad simply because it embodies the British image of an extremely laid-back Italy. Interestingly, as we shall see, the localization of the text lies its use of humour (3.2.5).

Shade:	Ride:
The Italians are nothing if not practical. In a country of near-permanent sunshine and incandescent smiles, eye shades are essential. A nice pair, of course: hand-crafted *with classic Italian styling.* Tinted, polaroid, slight-wrap, oversize – whatever looks good. Worn outdoors and in, at all times of the day, in all weathers, in all seasons. Sunglasses complete *the Italian look.* They amplify style and confidence. They hint at seductive pleasures, un-guessed depths. They make you famous.	They never meant this to happen. When the first scooters were rolled from a Genovese warehouse in 1946, it was not for style. Nor elegance. Nor even for *sashaying down side streets at sunset.* It was for Italy, the shell-shocked, post-War Italy that urgently needed a form of affordable mass transportation to kick-start its broken economy. That was why they designed "The Wasp". Of course it had to look good too. *That's just the Italian way.*
Time:	Walk:
Italians take time over everything. Cooking, eating, going out. It's the ar-tisan tradition. Do it slowly. Do it well. Italian watchmakers embody this ap-proach, dedicating themselves to the *refinement of style and the quest for absolute quality.* Few watches can trump an Italian classic, especially not an 18 carat hand-made number with diamond set dials and a gold case. Like Italians themselves, these time-pieces are unmistakable, rigorous, *fusing modern and traditional style. Unlike Italians, however, they keep perfect time.*	In a country where every street is a catwalk, *paraded by the stylish and the passionate and the beautiful,* footwear is everything. And the footwear of choice is always made from hand-crafted Italian leather. Exactly how this famous material gains its remarkable light, pleasant perfume and soft caress is a secret, *handed down for centuries.* Italian leather is unique. And, like a cellared Barolo or the finest Parmigia-no, it only improves with age.

Table 1. Verbal text of the UK *Birra Peroni* website.

Again, the tendency for large companies to opt for intersemiotic translations is upheld elsewhere in this corpus too. The Italian liqueur *Disaronno* belongs to the huge Bacardi corporation. The website contains the choice of diverting to one of 50 different nested versions for different countries.

However, this corpus reveals that, slowly, food companies are also starting to choose a more up-to-date image in their promotional material. Interestingly, pasta manufacturers, the most traditional of Italian foods, seem to be the first to have opted for modernity. *Pasta Garofalo* has three websites, the original Italian, an English version and one in Japanese. Strictly black and white with a touch of gold, the site contains low key photographs of off-beat perspectives on pasta. The translational strategy is intersemiotic. Again, Giuseppe Cocco who produces hand made pasta for a niche market sector uses a similar strategy. While focusing on the old tradition of the firm, the website is in black and white, and photos and video-clips all contain the crackly, slow motion effect of an old pre-code silent movie, thus recalling the right blend of tradition and modernity. Yet despite the old movie-style effects, the site is clearly modern, the film itself is obviously contemporary and deliberately, falsely old. And perhaps the traditional versus modern can best be illustrated by the diverse portrayal of women on the *De Cecco* site and on the *Garofalo* site. While the image of *De Cecco*'s woman (Fig.1) is that of a handsome Mediterranean peasant in colorful attire with her hair tied back beneath a headscarf and a sheaf of wheat in her arms, *Garofalo* (Fig.2) offers a three-quarter, black and white image of a sensuous woman, lips semi-open, caressing a pack of spaghetti. The former conveys an image of female strength and tradition, the latter of modern sensuality.

Figure 1

Figure 2.

3.2.5. Comic images of Italy on the Web

It would appear that the feature which is missing from most of these promotional sites for Italian products is comedy. While, generally speaking, successful TV campaigns in Britain and in the USA appeal to the public's sense of humour, the same is not true of Italian advertisements. And, generally speaking once again, Italian companies tend to go for a pretty serious image on line too. Now of course, this may be deliberate, knowing that these texts will be seen transnationally and, as we know, not all cultures prefer humorous advertising styles (De Mooij 2004: 195), yet it seems that multinationals do use humour. *Dolmio* for example, is a pretend Italian brand of tinned tomatoes which is part of the *Mars* corporation. Despite the Italian sounding name (*Sole mio?*) the company actually producing and selling the product is based in Eire. Yet, the website is constructed around a family of Italian muppets, *Papa* is dark and swarthy and dons a moustache, *Mama* is plump and is in the kitchen cooking. The family is set against a bright green background with *Mama* holding up a rigorously red and white checked tablecloth stained with red tomato sauce. The characters speak inserting a schwa at the end of every word. "If only my tablecloth was as clean as **a** their plates!" And, in case visitors do not have access to audio, the extra vowel sound is transcribed in the bubbles coming from the mouth of each muppet. The insertion of this pseudo-schwa (the stereotypical interference of

an Italian speaking English) continues in the copy and in the slogan
"When's **a** your Dolmio day?" Whether we like the ad or not, it is
certainly appealing, and we wonder why comic stereotypes are not
more common in authentically Italian sites. Well, humour does not
travel too well, so possibly companies are playing safe. But small
companies who do dare to joke with surfers may well be in for
trouble. For example, *Divella* pasta adopts a short Italian cartoon chef
called Don Ciccio, a typical Italian name, who produces recipes each
day. The image of Don Ciccio is a comic stereotype which is easily
recognizable by Italians. Somehow, in the English version even the
name of Don Ciccio jars. He does remain a stereotype (short, plump
and with a moustache), but is he funny? Probably not. The humorous
dimension of this particular stereotype is non-existent outside Italy.

On the other hand, if *GiA* purées and pastes have a pretty
traditional intrasemiotic English website, they have two audio files on
The Food Masters website which are extremely funny. According to
The Foodmasters who have been "trading since 1986", they are a self
confessed

> privately owned company serving the major multiple trade, the co-operative
> trade and cash'n'carry outlets throughout the UK. Both proprietary brands and
> private label contracts are currently represented in every major grocery outlet
> nationally, outside of the discount stores. *The Food Masters* expertise,
> contacts and volume sales backed by original, imaginative promotional
> support are a feature of the business.

And "promotional support" is certainly imaginative. In an audio-file
promoting tomato purée, a camp voice reveals his "idea of a dream
Italian". The mind boggles as listeners wonder whether he is referring
to a meal or a man as they discover that his dream Italian is "rich,
beefy and one that goes down well (pause) with a bottle of Chianti"
and that the "ultimate Italian dish starts with *GiA* Tomato Purée. You
can taste it straight from the tube but I prefer to go all the way (pause)
to Pasta Bolognaise and beyond". Again, in another ad we are told by
the same actor that *GiA* garlic purée is "pure Italian… intense, tasty
and fresh, well worth getting your mouth round". The point is, over
and above the political incorrectness of the ads and whether or not we
appreciate the sexual innuendos, they do add up to successful
campaigns. And furthermore, *The Food Masters* have effectively

glocalized with specific products for the British market, such as 'Rocket Pesto' and 'Anchovy Puree'.

Finally, visiting the Peroni UK website between noon and 4pm, navigators find the following notice:

SPIACENTI SIAMO CHIUSI

> It's lunchtime.
> Why not go and find a café, enjoy some lunch, watch the scooters and the beautiful people go by.
> Nothing should be open now, including our site.
>
> It's the Italian way. Why not come back and visit us later?
> Are you sure you want to come in?
> In Italy you'd be going out, finding a café, meeting friends, living the dolce vita.
>
> Go out, enjoy yourself. Why not come back and visit us later?
>
> <http://www.peroniitaly.com/>

The reader is at first nonplussed, then quietly amused by the accurate stereotype of Italian shops which close down for three hours each day for long leisurely lunch breaks. Undeniably, the advertising campaign is extremely clever. And possibly, differently from the *Dolmio* campaign, it is unlikely to cause offence to any Italians.

4. Concluding remarks

It is clear from the corpus examined that medium to small companies in the Italian agro-food sector have tuned into the fact that traditional marketing channels have been radically changed by the New Economy. And if until very recently companies either chose tradition or modernity to promote their wares, today more and more firms are moving towards an up to date image, yet without denying their sense of tradition. Vice versa companies who still opt for a traditional image are underscoring aspects such as their ultra-modern industrial plants and use of new technology. Interestingly this is not so dissimilar of a changing Italy which at the level of public services and infrastructures is trying its best to shed its image of outdated systems.

While going to press I came across the website of a medium sized Italian company, *Babbi*, which produces wafers, ice cream and confectionery in general. The way *Babbi* operates transnationally is a good example of successful use of the Internet for promotional purposes. The company's products are not particularly well known nationally, rather they are a niche product in Emilia - Romagna, the region where they are produced. However, through its website we learn that in Japan, *Babbi* has launched numerous coffee shops across the country where its traditional Italian wafers have been transformed into items with a highly luxurious image. Very different from *Starbuck* style outlets where coffee is drunk from polystyrene cups, at *Babbi Gelaterie e Chocobar caffé* it is served in porcelain cups in the name of total elegance. Furthermore, the wafers are gift-wrapped with the logo of other companies such as *Jaguar* and *Fendi*. In other words, *Babbi* along with its coffee and wafers, is selling class and style. Searching the Internet further, I came across a blog named 'Fugu-diaries', all about eating and drinking out in Japan. Regarding *Babbi* outlets the blogger writes:

> The store is decked out in red and white like its logo. You can choose from about 20 varieties [of ice cream]. The television show, where I first heard of Babbi, said the store once won an award in Italy for it's adzuki red bean and black sesame flavors. My personal favorite is tiramisu, but Patrick and I can also recommend banana, pistachio, mint chocolate chip, straciatella (chocolate chip) and green tea.

We can thus see that *Babbi* is an example of a company which has completely understood the meaning of internationalization and which has gone global, at the same time preserving an Italian image (straciatella and tiramisu) while also translating its products to the taste of others (adzuki red beans and green tea) without selling out via hackneyed stereotypes of Italy, but simply through understated grace and refinement. This could well be the path for others to follow.

References

Adab, Beverly 1998. Towards a More Systematic Approach to the Translation of Advertising Texts. In Beeby, Allison / Esinger, Doris / Presas, Marisa (eds) *Investigating Translation*. Amsterdam/Philadelphia: John Benjamins.

Adab, Beverly / Cristina Valdés (eds.) 2004. *The Translator. Special Issue: Key Debates in the Translation of Advertising Material*. Vol. 10, Nr 2. Manchester: St. Jerome.

Chiaro, Delia 2004. Translational and Marketing Communication: A Comparison of Print and Web Advertising of Italian Agro-food Products. In Adab/Valdés (eds), 313-28.

Cook, Guy 1992. *The Discourse of Advertising*. London: Routledge.

De Mooij, Marieke 2004. Translating Advertising. Painting the Tip of an Iceberg. In Adab/Valdés (eds), 179-198.

Dyer, Gillian 1988. *Advertising as Communication*. London: Routledge.

Fuentes Luque, Adrián / Kelly, Dorothy 2000. The Translator as Mediator in Advertising. Spanish Products in English Speaking Markets. In Beeby, Allison / Esinger, Doris / Presas, Marisa (eds) *Investigating Translation. Selected Papers from the 4th International Congress on Translation, Barcelona, 1988*. Amsterdam/Philadelphia: John Benjamins, 235-242.

Leech, Geoffrey N. 1966. *English in Advertising*. London: Longman.

Leiss, William / Sut, Jhally / Klein, Stephen 1990. *Social Communication in Advertising*. London: Routledge.

Munday, Jeremy 2004. Advertising: Some Challenges to Translation Theory. In Adab/Valdés (eds), 199-220.

Paliwoda, Stanley [2]1993. *International Marketing*. Oxford: Butterworth-Heinemann.

Solomon, Michael R. 2004. *Consumer Behavior: Buying, Having and Being*. Upper Saddle River N. J.: Pearson Prentice Hall.

Wells, William / Burnett, John / Jeanne, Moriarty 1989. *Advertising Principles and Practice*. Englewood Cliffs N.J.: Prentice Hall.

MARINEL GERRITSEN / CATHERINE NICKERSON / CORINE VAN DEN
BRANDT / ROGIER CRIJNS / NURIÁ DOMINGUEZ / FRANK VAN MEURS /
ULRIKE NEDERSTIGT

English in Print Advertising in Germany, Spain and the Netherlands: Frequency of Occurrence, Comprehensibility and the Effect on Corporate Image

1. Introduction and background

The use of English in promotional business genres is a common feature of the Dutch consumer landscape. The most recent research at the Business Communication Studies Department, at the Radboud University in Nijmegen, indicates that the use of English is on the increase in the Netherlands in genres as diverse as annual reports and magazines targeted at teenage girls. In addition, there is also evidence that English is fast becoming a feature of certain promotional genres in Germany (Endmark 2003; Kick 2004) and to a lesser extent in Spain (Berns 1995a; 1995b; Graddol 1999). Against this background, however, studies in the nineteen nineties by Gerritsen (1995) in print advertising and by Gerritsen, Korzilius, van Meurs and Gijsbers (2000) in TV commercials indicate that although English was in widespread use, there were relatively low levels of comprehensibility for the English that was used among the target population, coupled with a somewhat negative attitude towards its use. Research in Germany in 2003 (Endmark 2003) reveals similar findings in that less than two thirds of a target population were actually able to understand the English used in a set of advertising fragments. It is this apparent mismatch between promotional information and consumer interpretation that we will explore further in this paper.

Elsewhere we have detailed the specific situation in the Netherlands for the use of English where English is in widespread use in a variety of different domains, including education, the media, and particularly, business (Gerritsen/Nickerson 2004). Figure 1, for instance, which shows a page from the Dutch *Cosmopolitan* from May 2004, is an example of the type of texts that have now become commonplace in the Netherlands, in which the reader, i.e. consumer, needs to be able to comprehend the many English expressions included in the text in order to understand the overall message. We believe that a similar situation may exist in Germany, and that it may prove possible to identify at least similar trends in Spain.

Figure 1. The use of English in the Netherlands.

In print advertising in particular, there has been an identifiable increase in the use of English in many countries in the European Union in the course of the past decade. Table 1 shows the percentage of advertisements in glossy magazines that contained English in 1994 (Gerritsen 1995) compared to data collected both in the present study and by Van Beurden (2004) in 2003. As indicated by the figures, there has been an increase in the use of English in all four countries in advertisements in glossy magazines, e.g. 33% of the ads surveyed in 1994 in the Netherlands contained English, whereas by 2003, this percentage had risen to 81%.

Country	Glossy magazines 1994	Glossy magazines 2003
Germany	33%	56%
Spain	17%	75%
Netherlands	33%	81%
Italy	1%	25%

Table 1. The percentage of advertisements with English in glossy magazines in 1994 and 2003.

Of the existing theories on the use of English in the European context, the most relevant work for our study is that by Berns (1995a; 1995b) and by Graddol (1999). Berns (1995a) draws on Kachru's 1985-model which classified the status of English around the world, and identifies three groups of countries within the European Union as it was in 1995. She classifies the UK and the Republic of Ireland as users of native varieties of English; Belgium, Denmark, France, Greece, Italy, Portugal and Spain as a group of countries where English is used and will continue to be used as a foreign language (FL); and Germany, Luxembourg and the Netherlands, as countries where English is in the process of developing as a second language (L2). Graddol (1999) also gives an account of English in Europe in the nineteen nineties, including predictions for the future. He views Denmark, Sweden and the Netherlands as countries where English will be most likely to attain the status of an L2; he suggests that it may already be part way through that process in the Netherlands and Denmark, and he predicts that it will be least likely to attain the status of an L2 in Spain. Of particular relevance for our study in which we investigate several aspects of the use of English in the Netherlands, Spain and Germany, is the fact that both Berns (1995) and Graddol (1999) predict that Spain is not likely to achieve L2 status for English; both predict that the Netherlands is likely to achieve L2 status (or may have already done so), and their opinion is divided on Germany; Berns suggests the same future L2 status for English in Germany as in the Netherlands and Graddol suggests that Germany is less likely to achieve this than the Netherlands, but is more likely to do so than Spain. In our study of the use of English in print advertising, together with consumer comprehensibility and attitudes to English, we therefore expected that English would be used, understood, and appreciated least in Spain, coupled with the most negative attitudes towards its use, whereas English would either be used most, appreciated most and understood better in the Netherlands than in Germany and Spain, or that the situation would be equivalent for Germany and the Netherlands.

In this chapter we will address the following research questions for product advertisements in glossy magazines and their target groups in the Netherlands, Germany and Spain:

1.   How often is English used in product advertisements in glossy magazines?
2.   Do the relevant target groups understand English?
3.   Do they have a negative or positive attitude towards the use of English?
4.   Does the use of English have an effect on corporate image?
5.   Are there differences between the Netherlands, Germany and Spain on points 1 to 4 above, and does this suggest a re-evaluation of current theories on the differences between the EU countries in their use of English?
6.   Is English indeed increasingly supplanting the national languages in promotional texts, e.g. the advertisements in glossy magazines?

The investigation consisted of two related projects: a corpus analysis using quantitative analyses based on methods drawn from diachronic sociolinguistics, and an experimental investigation, using analytical methods taken from psycholinguistics, sociolinguistics and marketing. It was therefore multidisciplinary and multi-methodological in approach. The team was made up of seven members of staff, each of whom was a native speaker of one of the languages involved, and around eighty students of Business Communication, all of whom were in their final year of study for a Masters degree. Each of the projects will be dealt with in turn in sections 2 and 3 below.

2. The corpus analysis

Three comparable corpora were compiled for each country under investigation. These were *Elle* for July 2003 for Germany and the Netherlands and *Cosmopolitan* for July 2003 for Spain. For each corpus, the frequency of occurrence of English lexical items was determined for all the advertisements of at least half an A4 in size. Words were considered as English if they met the following two criteria:

1. They did *not* occur in the most recent authoritative dictionary in each country. For Germany, this was the Duden dictionary *Das große Wörterbuch der deutschen Sprache* (1999), for Spain the online (2003) edition of the *Diccionario de la Lengua Española* published by the Real Academia Española and for the Netherlands, the *Van Dale Groot Woordenboek der Nederlandse taal* (1999).

2. They did occur in the same meaning as in the advertisement in an authoritative English dictionary such as the *Oxford Dictionary of English* (2003) or the *Macmillan English Dictionary for Advanced Learners* (2002), or on a UK web-site via Google.

The word *manager*, for instance, does occur in the Dutch Van Dale (1999), but the word *fragrance* does not. In the first instance the lexical item has been assimilated into the 'local' language, i.e. Dutch, and was not counted as English (for the Dutch corpus), whereas in the second instance it has not been assimilated and it was therefore considered as an English item. Words were also counted as English words whenever they occurred as part of a complete English phrase, e.g. the phrase "Your last stop before the top" was therefore considered as six English words. This was particularly relevant for lexical items that can also occur in Dutch, German or Spanish, e.g. *stop* and *top* for the Dutch corpus, since *stop* and *top* are also Dutch words.

2.1. Findings of the corpus analysis

Table 2 shows the number of ads in each edition of the glossy magazines, together with the number of ads that contained English, ranging from as many as 81% for the Dutch magazine to 56% for the German magazine. English occurs in more than half of the total number of ads for all three countries, and the differences between the three countries were not significant according to a Chi-square test ($X2=5.96$, $df=2$, $p=.051$). This is an interesting finding that contradicts our hypotheses based on the views of observers such as Graddol (1999) and Berns (1995a; 1995b) as we have discussed above, that less English would occur in Spain than in Germany and the Netherlands, and that the situation would either be equivalent in Germany and the Netherlands (Berns) or that more English would occur in the Netherlands than in Germany (Graddol). When we looked at the total number of words in those ads that contained English together with the total number of English words, we found that the English lexis accounted for between 6% and 8% per cent of the total text (see Table 3). In this case, interestingly, there was a significant difference between Spain and Germany, with the Spanish ads containing the most English words (7.9%) and the German ads the least (6.0%) ($X2=7.90$, $df=2$, $p=.01$). Again this contradicts the predictions made previously on the future status of English within our three target countries.

	Netherlands	Germany	Spain
Number of ads	21	43	53
Number of ads with English	17 (81%)	24 (56%)	40 (75%)

Table 2. Number of ads and number of ads containing English.

	Netherlands	Germany	Spain
Total number of words in ads with English	1501	1999	3941
Total number of English words	98 (6.5%)	120 (6.0%)	310 (7.9%)

Table 3. Amount of English used.

Finally, we looked at the part of the text in which English occurred in the ads. Table 4 shows the results. The percentages were calculated on the basis of the total number of advertisements in which the specific part of the text was included and the total number of advertisements in which this part of the text was partly or completely in English. For example, there were 21 ads in the Dutch corpus with a header, and 8 of these (38%) had a header partly or completely in English. We found that English occurred frequently in the body, slogan and header of the texts for all three countries and was most infrequent in the sales information. It seemed to be the case that corporations resorted to the local language for each country of the target population concerned, in their presentation of important sales information to the consumer.

	Netherlands	Germany	Spain
Ads with (part of) header in English	8 (of 21) 38%	7 (of 34) 21%	11 (of 35) 31%
Ads with (part of) body in English	16 (of 21) 76%	16 (of 37) 43%	29 (of 64) 63%
Ads with (part of) slogan in English	8 (of 14) 57%	9 (of 20) 45%	6 (of 26) 24%
Ads with sales information (part of) in English	3 (of 14) 21%	2 (of 32) 6%	4 (of 28) 14%

Table 4. Part of text where English occurs.

Again, the fact that more English occurred in the Spanish texts than in the German texts contradicts our predictions based on previous commentators in the European situation. One possible explanation for this, however, may be that there has in fact been more officially standardised assimilation of English in Germany and the Netherlands, as is shown by the inclusion of words of English origin in the standard Dutch and German dictionaries, but not in the standard Spanish dictionary, e.g. the word *weekend* occurs in the Van Dale and the Duden dictionaries, but not in the dictionary published by the Real Academia Española, despite the fact that it is used on Spanish websites. This could, of course, account for the lower word count for English items for Germany and the Netherlands compared to Spain, as a result of the dictionary-based classification system we used in identifying the items of English lexis.

3. The experimental investigation

The corpus analysis allowed us to identify a number of advertising campaigns that were being run simultaneously across the three countries in the two magazines. We selected four campaigns including the Siemens 'be inspired' campaign, the Chupa Chups 'I love me' campaign, the Skechers 'redefining style' campaign and the Elizabeth Arden 'smile with all your senses' (see appendix for examples of the Elizabeth Arden campaign used in Spain and the Siemens campaign used in Germany). All four advertising campaigns were used in all three countries, with varying degrees of English included in the text. These four campaigns formed the basis of the experimental investigation, in which we used the original and manipulated versions of several of the standardised campaigns, to investigate the respondents' comprehensibility of the English used, their attitude towards the use of that English and the effects that these may in fact have on the image projected by the product or organisation promoted through the advertising texts. A total of 316 highly educated (young) women responded to a questionnaire designed to investigate comprehensibility, attitude to English and image of product/service, consisting of 120 respondents for the Netherlands and Spain, and 76 for Germany. Highly educated young women were used as respondents as they could be considered as representative of the target group of glossy magazines like *Elle* and *Cosmopolitan.*

The investigation used a between-group design, such that half of the respondents for each country saw the original (English) version of each advertisement, and half of them saw a manipulated, i.e. Dutch, Spanish, or German, version. The research team worked together to produce equivalent test items in Dutch, Spanish and German for the original English texts. We used translation and back-translation to ensure as close a match as possible, and the student research team members proved to be extremely skilful in their manipulation of the different versions. Figure 2 shows the manipulated Dutch version of the Elizabeth Arden 'Smile with all your senses' Green Tea Fragrance Collection advertisement, which was viewed by half of the Dutch respondents.

Figure 2. The manipulated Dutch version of the 'smile with all your senses' campaign.

In order to investigate the respondents' attitude towards the use of English versus the use of their own language, all six groups were presented with a set of 10 semantic differentials made up of contrasting positive and negative items such as *attractive* versus *irritating* and asked to complete a 7-point Likert scale. Half of the respondents completed the items for the English version of the advertisement, and half for the manipulated version in their own language.

We wanted to know whether the use of English in an ad has an impact on the image of the product that is advertised. Gerritsen *et al.* (2000) report that advertising agencies generally claim that they incorporate English in their advertising because it provides the product with a modern, innovative image. We therefore incorporated this aspect of image into the questionnaire, investigating specifically whether the products advertised using English were indeed considered as more modern and innovative than the products advertised without using English. This part of the questionnaire used the same design as the attitude part, i.e. we presented respondents with a set of 4 semantic differentials such as *modern* versus *old-fashioned,* and asked them to complete a 7-point Likert scale. Furthermore, we investigated whether a product advertised in English would be considered as a more expensive product than one that was advertised in the respondents' own language. If that should be the case, then it could provide some empirical justification for the claims made by advertising agencies.

In the comprehensibility part of the questionnaire, the respondents that saw the original English versions were asked to provide a meaning in context for the specific part of the text, i.e. *Smile with all your senses,* for Elizabeth Arden; *Be inspired,* for Siemens; *I love me,* for Chupa Chups; *Footwear; Redefining style!,* for Skechers. At the end of the experiment, the teachers' group met to decide for each individual test item whether or not the translation given could be considered appropriate or not. For instance, the translations for 'Footwear' were only considered as acceptable if they contained the concept of shoes in general, not just an example of one type of footwear, as in 'boots'.

3.1. Findings of the experimental investigation

3.1.1. Attitude towards the English used in the ads

A Cronbach alpha analysis for the ten items that measured attitude to the use of English versus the use of the local language revealed alphas higher than .70 for all the ads. This meant that we could deal with an aggregated set of data for all ten items. The findings showed that the respondents had a neutral attitude towards all the ads, both the versions with English and those in the local language. On a scale where 1 is positive and 7 is negative, the mean for the four ads with English was 3.46, as was the mean for the four ads without English. There was only one significant difference between the English and the

Dutch version of the Skechers advertisement, in that the Dutch respondents had a more positive attitude towards the language used in the ad not containing English (M=3.47) than towards the ad that did (M=3.95) (F(1,118)= 5.96, p=.016). In addition, the Spanish respondents had a more positive attitude towards the language used in the Skechers ad with English (M=3.36) than the Germans did (M=3.89) (F(2, 159)=5.13, p=.007). Our findings therefore did not indicate that ads with English are always more appreciated than those in the local language. They also indicated, once again unexpectedly, that the Spanish may appreciate ads containing English more than the Germans.

3.1.2. Image

A Cronbach alpha analysis for the 4 items relating to whether the image of the product was viewed as modern or old-fashioned showed alphas higher than .70 for all the ads for only three of the four items: *trendy, innovative, old-fashioned*. Our findings here are therefore based on the aggregated data of these three items. All the responses, both for the ads with English and the ads in the local language, showed that the respondents considered the ads to be more modern than old-fashioned. On the scale from 1 to 7, where 1 equated to *modern* and 7 to *old-fashioned*, the means of all the answers were lower than 4. In those instances where there was a significant difference between the two different versions of the ad, the version with English was considered as more modern than the version in the local language, as we had expected. This was the case in three instances, in Spain for the Siemens (with English M=1.74, without English M=2.19, F(1,118)=11.320, p=.001) and Skechers ads (with English M=2.81, without English M=3.64, F(1,117)=1.74, p=.001) and in the Netherlands also for the Siemens ad (with English M=2.11, without English M=2.75, F(1,118)=11.32, p=.001). There were also two significant differences between the different countries, but only one of these obtained for the version with English, in that the Spanish respondents considered the Elizabeth Arden ad with English (M=3.44) as more modern than the Dutch respondents did (M=4.32) (F(2,65)=3.579, p=.04).

The second characteristic related to product image that we investigated, i.e. whether the respondents viewed the products advertised as more expensive if English was included (on a scale from 1 to 7, where 1 equated to *cheap* and 7 to *expensive*), did not reveal any significant differences for the two different versions of the ads. Respondents did not believe that the products advertised in the ads with English were more expensive than those advertised in ads without English. There were, however, differences between the three countries, since the Spanish respondents considered several products as more expensive than either the Germans or the Dutch. This was the case for Siemens for both the ad with English (Spain M=4.32, Germany M=3.50, Netherlands M=3.70, F(2,135)=18.82, p=.001) and without English (Spain M=4.25, Germany M=3.35, Netherlands M= 3.78, F(2,140)=8.89, p=.001) and for Skechers for the difference between the Netherlands and Spain for the version of the ad without English (Netherlands M=3.26, Spain M=3.63, F(2,124)=3.72, p=.027).

3.1.3. Actual comprehensibility

In terms of actual comprehensibility the differences between the three countries were as expected according to the predictions based on previous studies, e.g. Berns (1995). Table 5 presents these results. For all four ads, the Spanish were less able to give a correct meaning for the target items than the Dutch and the Germans, and the difference between Spaniards on the one hand and the Dutch and the Germans on the other hand, were statistically significant for all the phrases except for "Smile with all your senses". Overall, 81% of the Dutch respondents could comprehend the texts, 90% of the Germans respondents, and only 52% of the Spanish.

	Be inspired (Siemens)		I love me (Chupa Chups)		Footwear (Skechers)	
	Correct	Wrong	Correct	Wrong	Correct	Wrong
Netherlands	59 98%	1	50 89%	6	53 90%	6
Germany	34 94%	2	35 100%	0	33 92%	3
Spain	25 46%	29	30 53%	26	22 63%	13
Significance differences According to X2	X2=52.88 df=2 p=.001		X2=32.43 df=2 p=.001		X2=13.98 df=2 p=.001	
	Redefining Style (Skechers)		Smile with all your senses (Elizabeth Arden)		Total	
	Correct	Wrong	Correct	Wrong	Correct	Wrong
Netherlands	30 60%	20	48 80%	12	240 81%	45
Germany	11 69%	5	30 83%	6	143 90%	16
Spain	9 25%	27	39 68%	18	125 52%	113
Significance differences According to X2	X2=13.22 df=2 p=.001		NS		X2=94.58 df=2 p=.001	

Table 5. Percentage of respondents that were able to give a correct description of the meaning of the English phrases.

4. Summary of findings and discussion

If we return to the research questions we posed at the beginning of the paper, we can now provide some answers on the basis of our findings:

1. How often is English used in product advertisements in glossy magazines?

The findings of our corpus analysis showed that English occurs frequently in the product ads in glossy magazines in the Netherlands, Germany and Spain, and that it occurs more often in Spain than in

Germany. In addition, our data show that English occurs in all three countries less often in sales information, a part of the ad that contains important information for the consumer, than in other parts, such as the slogan.

2.   Do the relevant target groups understand English?
Our findings suggested that the German and Dutch respondents were generally – but not entirely – able to understand the English they were presented with. The Spanish were less able to do so.

3.   Do they have a negative or positive attitude towards the use of English?
The respondents had neither a positive nor a negative attitude to the use of English, suggesting that it may be viewed by consumers as a neutral advertising language (see also Piller 2003 on this point).

4.   Does the use of English have an effect on corporate image?
For some products the use of English seemed to be associated with a more modern image. The use of English did not, however, impact the price that the respondents associated with the product.

5.   Are there differences between the Netherlands, Germany and Spain on points 1 to 4 above, and does this suggest a re-evaluation of current theories on the differences between the EU countries in use of English?
The predictions made on the basis of the literature were that the Netherlands should either be equivalent to Germany, or more advanced than Germany, in terms of the amount of English used, the language skills of respondents and the positive attitudes held on attitude and image. Spain was predicted as being less positive, not as proficient and with less English in use. Our corpus analysis revealed more English used in Spain than in Germany, contrary to our expectations based on both Graddol and Berns. There were no significant differences between the countries in terms of attitude to English (again contrary to our predictions formulated on the basis of both Graddol and Berns), and the use of English led to a more modern image associated with the product only in Spain (in line with the expectations drawn from Graddol and Berns). In comprehending the

texts, the Germans and the Dutch had similar skills, and they were better than the Spanish (as we had expected following Berns). We therefore found both similarities and differences to our predictions made on the work of previous commentators, suggesting that a re-evaluation of the status of English within the EU would be timely.

6.   Is English indeed increasingly supplanting the national languages in (the ads in) glossy magazines?

Our findings suggest that English will play an increasingly important role in the future, at least in the ads intended for glossy magazines. We believe that this is supported by longitudinal studies over the past decade for the three countries we investigated, all of which show a consistent increase in the occurrence of ads with English (cf. Table 1). If we compare our data on the comprehension of English (Table 5, final column) with those collected in 1994 by Gerritsen (Gerritsen 2004) we see a large increase in the comprehensibility of English by the target groups; from 34% to 88% in the Netherlands, from 44% to 84% in Germany and from 33% to 49% in Spain. Although the data collected in 1994 are not fully comparable with those collected in 2004 since the comprehension of different English phrases was tested in the two different studies, it is clear that the use of English is increasing in all three of the countries that we investigated. The use of English in Spain was similar to that in both the Netherlands and Germany, which was contrary to our expectations at the beginning of the project, although the comprehension skills shown by the Spanish target group were not as high as those shown by the German and Dutch respondents (cf Table 5). It therefore seems plausible that although English is used as an intralanguage in Spain, it is possible – or indeed probable – that this will lead to communication problems.

5. Limitations and conclusions

Two obvious limitations underlie the design of the research investigation. First, the corpus analysis was based on only one edition of the magazine(s) with a target readership of highly educated young women. And second, the experiment was carried out with a limited number of respondents all of whom were highly educated. In the Autumn of 2004 we expanded our project to include France and Belgium, and we also analyzed more editions of the glossy magazines we referred to for each target country, investigating those published from April to September 2004. We also hope to extend the target groups within the general populations of each country to include different age groups and different levels of education. A third important methodological point is that the more frequent or similar occurrence of English in Spain compared to the Netherlands and Germany that we identified in our corpus analysis, may be attributable to differences in the way in which dictionaries are compiled. This is something we believe needs further investigation in future projects.

In conclusion we can say that we do not believe that English has attained the status of an L2 in any of the three countries in our project. We do believe, however, that the situation is changing, particularly in terms of comprehensibility, suggesting that English is perhaps becoming more embedded in the local languages. The attitudes to English that our study revealed and the negligible effect that the use of English had on the image of the products advertised in Germany and the Netherlands, would certainly seem to suggest that it is already viewed by some consumers as a neutral advertising language. In this respect, it appears that English has been de-coupled from the national cultures that use it as a first language, such as the US and UK, and, at least for the print advertising we investigated, it therefore no longer seems valid to consider its use as *inter*cultural communication. Furthermore, it seems reasonable to assume that the neutral status accorded to English in advertising language that our study revealed, together with increasing levels of English language use and proficiency, could also prove to be the case in other domains, such as education, the media and politics (cf. Gerritsen/Nickerson 2004). With this in mind, since some of the similarities and differences we found between the countries were not as predicted on the basis of previous studies, we believe that it would be appropriate at this point to re-evaluate current thinking on the differences between the countries of the European Union in their use of, attitudes to and familiarity with English.

References

Berns, Margie 1995a. English in the European Union. *English Today* *43* 11/3, 3-11.

Berns, Margie 1995b. English in Europe: Whose Language, Which Culture? *International Journal of Applied Linguistics* 5/1, 21-33.

Endmark 2003. *Englische Werbeslogans werden kaum verstanden*, <http://www.endmark.in-de.net/img/aktuell/MafoClaims.pdf> (19-12-2004).

Gerritsen, Marinel 1995. 'English' Advertisements in the Netherlands, Germany, France, Italy and Spain. In Machová, Bozena / Kubátová, Sláva (eds) *Sietar Europa. Uniqueness in Unity. The Significance of Cultural Identity in European Cooperation.* Prague: Envirostress, 324-341.

Gerritsen, Marinel 2004. Comprehension of and Attitude towards English Product Advertisements in the Netherlands, Germany, Spain and Italy. *Norwegian School of Management. Proceedings of the 3rd International Conference on Research in Advertising*, 142-147.

Gerritsen, Marinel / Korzilius, Hubert / Meurs, Frank van / Gijsbers, Inge 2000. English in Dutch Commercials: Not Understood and Not Appreciated. *Journal of Advertising Research* 40/4, 17-31.

Gerritsen, Marinel / Nickerson, Catherine 2004. Fact or Fallacy? English as an L2 in the Dutch Business Context. In Candlin, Christopher / Gotti, Maurizio (eds) *Intercultural Aspects of Specialized Communication.* Bern: Peter Lang, 105-125.

Graddol, David 1999. The Decline of the Native Speaker. In Graddol, David / Meinhof, Ulrike H. (eds) *English in a Changing World.* Guildford: Biddles, 57-69.

Kachru, Braj B. 1985. Standards, Codification and Sociolinguistic Realism: The English Language in the Outer Circle. In Quirk, Randolph / Widdowson, Henry G. (eds) *English in the World.* Cambridge: Cambridge University Press, 11-30.

Kick, Isabel 2004. *Die Wirkung von Anglizismen in der Werbung. "Just do it" oder lieber doch nicht?* Paderborn: IBF Verlag im Institut für Betriebslinguistik.

Labrie, Norman / Quell, Carsten 1997. Your Language, My Language or English? The Potential Language Choice in Communication Among Nationals of the European Union. *World Englishes* 16/1, 3-26.

Piller, Ingrid 2003. Advertising as a Site of Language Contact. *Annual Review of Applied Linguistics* 23, 170-183.

Van Beurden, Nynke 2004. *Het gebruik van Engels in Italiaanse advertenties in glossymagazines. Een corpusanalyse en een experiment.* MA thesis Business Communication Studies Katholieke Universiteit Nijmegen.

Appendix

Example 1. The Elizabeth Arden 'Smile with all your senses' campaign used in Spain.

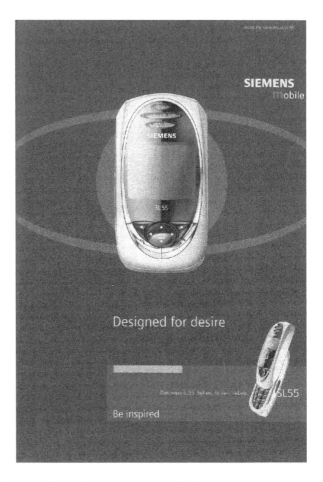

Example 2. The Siemens 'Be inspired' campaign used in Germany.

Concepts and Issues
across Languages and Cultures

CORNELIA ILIE

British 'Consensus' vs. Swedish '*Samförstånd*' in Parliamentary Debates

1. Introduction

The European events over the last decade have provided us with important reminders that parliaments are not only highly institutionalised bodies, but also dynamic institutions susceptible both to undergo and to bring about substantial socio-political changes. The current changing patterns of *consensus* and *dissent* management in the European parliaments raise common issues concerning national and political identities in relation to institutional continuity, rule flexibility, party cohesion and, more importantly, political and cultural debating norms. Achieving consensus requires serious treatment of every group member's considered opinion. Once a decision is made it is important to trust the members' commitment to follow-up action. Consensus usually involves systematic and continued collaboration since it does not mean that one opinion is being adopted by a plurality, but that participants are brought together until a convergent decision is developed.

A number of institutional features shared by the parliamentary discourses in the U.K. and in Sweden, such as procedural rules, patterns of leadership, and decision-making routines, make it possible to undertake meaningful and context-sensitive comparisons of consensus-based strategies. By virtue of lobbying, interest groups in the U.K. have acquired an important role in that they provide the MPs (= members of Parliament) with more information and advice, while challenging and enabling greater effectiveness (Norton 1997). A comparative account of Swedish and British bargaining attitudes and political commitment (Johansson/Melling 1995) shows that the elaboration of a specific political discourse in Sweden redefined power away from direct action and work place control, and towards institutional solutions. According to these authors it was the institutional framework of the two countries rather than the industrial infrastructure which proved critical in the evolution of different bargaining systems. One well-known step in the advance towards the 'historical compromise' between capital and labour in Sweden was the 'Basic Agreement' of Saltsjöbaden in 1938. The period before 1950 saw considerable progress in the creation of a general consensus on the broad goals of economic growth, rationalization and social welfare. The authors argue for an interpretation of bargaining choices and institutional policies as the product of social and political relationships rather than the expression of implicit rationality and organisational logic. This is one of the assumptions on which the present investigation has been based.

2. Aim and method

The present analysis of cross-institutional conceptual features focuses on the roughly comparable discursive uses and argumentative functions of the notions of British *consensus* and Swedish *samförstånd* (= consensus) as they are used in debates that take place in the two respective parliaments. The selection of the analysed key words (and of their collocates) has been conditioned in both cases by the fact they are recurrently used to refer to several institutional events or phenomena: parliamentary debating principles, institutional processes of deliberation and institutional goals. In spite of essential political differences, the British House of Commons and the Swedish Riksdag display significant parallels with respect to issues of procedure continuity and change, as well as a socio-culturally rooted search for stable and effective inter-party solutions. The discussion that follows concerns the shifting semantic properties, as well as the discursive and argumentative functions of the English word *consensus* and the Swedish word *samförstånd* (including its partial synonym, *konsensus*), as well as the connotations that they acquire in connection with their respective collocates in British and Swedish parliamentary debates.

In addition to purely institutional constraints concerning formal procedures, the interaction in parliamentary discourse has to comply with linguistic constraints too. The approach proposed here is located at the interface between a semantico-pragmatic analysis, on the one hand, and an institutional discourse analytical approach, on the other. Starting with a mapping of the semantic fields of the two terms, a microlinguistic analysis is proposed in terms of semantic associations, collocational distributions and semantic roles. The macro-linguistic analysis based on an argumentative discourse analytical frame is intended to identify the ways in which such salient institutional lexicalisations reproduce and reflect ideological positioning and political empowerment in British and Swedish parliamentary interaction.

2.1. Corpus

The corpus that has been investigated consists of two sets of transcripts, namely transcripts of debates in the U.K. Parliament and in the Swedish Riksdag. The British corpus consists of debates in the House of Commons selected from the 1996-1997 Hansard records, the actual title of which is *Hansard (Parliamentary Debates* or *the Official Report)*. These records can be easily accessed from the House of Commons home page on the Internet. The investigation of the British data in this paper focuses on a debate in the House on 23 April 1996 about amendments to a Bill concerning the inauguration of a political forum (Forum for Peace and Reconciliation) meant to ensure the role of Northern Ireland in political negotiations.

The Swedish corpus consists of debates in the Riksdag, i.e. the Swedish Parliament, selected from the 1996-1997 parliamentary records, which can be accessed from the Swedish Parliament home page on the Internet. The investigation of the Swedish data in this paper focuses on a series of debates between Conservative MPs (Deputy Speaker Anders Björck, Lars Tobisson and Håkan Holmberg) and Socio-Democratic MPs (specifically the former Prime Minister Göran Persson) about different positions and arguments about the compliance with consensually taken decisions on foreign policy issues, and particularly in connection with the official level of the Swedish Prime Minister's visit to China in 1996.

3. Institutional key words

In institutional settings, such as parliamentary debates, the connotations associated with major *key words* are often interpretable in terms
of the MPs' political allegiance, ideological convictions and personal
commitments. In order to assess, establish and/or reinforce common
evaluation criteria and debating grounds, one of the MPs major tasks
is to seek agreement among themselves and across party lines as to the
definition and the connotations they associate with central debate
issues that are often lexicalised by means of key words (Ilie 2006).
This is particularly necessary when discussing the formulation of
written legal documents, such as Bill amendments, or the practical
implementation of principle-based policies which are instrumental in
pursuing a consistent and consensual course of action.

In parliamentary debates about particularly important political
and legal issues, which require all-round agreement across party lines
there are a number of frequently used and discussed key words, such
as *consensus, majority decision, confrontation, agreement, unanimity*.
The scope and focus of their semantic connotations and pragmatic
implications is determined to a large extent by their collocates.
According to Hewison (1995: 18), "a country's culture is the means
both of expressing national identity and maintaining – or challenging
– political consensus" (1995: 18). This is another reason why I have
chosen to explore the construal of semantic connotations and
pragmatic functions of the concept of *consensus* when examining the
related key words in British and Swedish parliamentary debates.

3.1. Political consensus

The origin of the word *consensus* is Latin (*consentire*, i.e. to feel
together, to agree). According to several dictionary definitions, consensus has two common meanings. One is a general agreement among
the members of a given group or community, each of which exercises
some discretion in decision making and follow-up action. The other
represents a theory and practice of getting such agreements.
Consensus decision-making is a decision-making process that seeks

not only the agreement of as many participants as possible, but also the settlement or mitigation of objections raised by a minority in order to take the most agreeable decision.

Consensus is usually defined as meaning both: a) general agreement (e.g. "Bishop Colenso is [...] decidedly against what seems to be the *consensus* of the Protestant missionaries", *The Longman Dictionary of the English Language*, 1991) and b) the process of getting to such agreement (e.g. "We are witnessing a decline of *consensus* politics", *The Longman Dictionary of English Language and Culture*, 1992). The concept of *consensus* can thus be envisaged and evaluated as a continuum, both quantitatively and qualitatively. In other words, there can be more or less *consensus* about a specific matter, but there can also be positive and negative connotations and evaluations of *consensus* (Kavanagh 1985). A more politically oriented view on consensus is provided by Chantal Mouffe (1993), who argues that politics is not simply about reaching consensus. It is, rather, about the possibility of manipulating dissent within the framework of an established agreement on how to conduct affairs.

Parliaments are basically confrontational settings that instantiate the polarisation of political power (Ilie 2000). Whereas the confrontation is often expected to be adversarial, this is not always necessarily the case, and it does not apply to all types of verbal interactions that take place during parliamentary proceedings. Instead, the confrontation may take, interchangeably, stronger (overstated) forms of controversy, or milder (understated) forms of controversy (Damgaard 1997). An important element for an analysis of parliamentary discourse is the balance between the consensual and the confrontational orientations of the MPs. The Swedish democratic system of parliamentary government is known to be largely based on consensus, whereas the adversarial politics was a typical description of the British political system in the 1970's. However, Seldon (1994) suggests that consensus and continuity rather than discontinuity and adversarial positioning have been the norm in British politics.

As an illustration of the strategically changing meanings of *consensus*, the present analysis focuses on its various uses and practical implications during a debate in which the political opponents are discussing the advantages and disadvantages of adopting

consensus as a debating procedure, as a mental attitude, as a political
tool and/or as an institutional goal.

4. British parliamentary *consensus*

The British debate that has been analysed regards the amendments to a
Bill concerning the inauguration of a political forum (Forum for Peace
and Reconciliation) meant to ensure the role of Northern Ireland in
political negotiations. The MPs who participate in the debate represent
different political parties, from Labour through Conservative to the
Ulster Unionist and the U.K. Unionist Party. An important issue of the
ongoing discussion consists in the confrontation between two opposite
standpoints, namely *appointment* by *consensus* vs *election* by *voting*.
The question is whether a *consensus* will be reached about the
appointment of the chairman of the Forum, or whether the principle of
majority decision by *voting* will be implemented for the *election* of the
chairman. In example (1) below Eddie McGrady supports a particular
amendment where it is proposed to leave out "*elected* (by the
members)" and insert "*appointed* (by the members)".

(1)   *Eddie McGrady [Social Democratic and Labour Party]*: […] The amendment
       is simple and clear and relates to how the first chairman of the forum *should
       be appointed*. As the *appointment* will be the first exercise by the forum, we
       should like to think that it will be a matter for *consultation* and *consensus* and
       that the *elective process* of a *majority decision*, whether weighted or not,
       would not be a good inaugural activity for the forum. […] We want the forum
       to illustrate some *consensus* in its first activity. The amendment contains
       nothing more significant or hidden than the simple desire and wish that the
       parties attending the forum, by *consensus*, give the chairmanship to the person
       – man or woman – whom they feel will best serve their purposes with equity
       and justice. Consequential to that is amendment No. 57, which refers to
       procedures under paragraph 4, where the word '*election*' appears. Simply to be
       consistent, we ask that the word '*appointment*' be substituted for '*election*'.
       The proposals are straightforward and simple. My party and I hope that they
       will show the *good will* and *consensus* that we sincerely hope will exist in the
       forum during its first activity. (*Debates*, House of Commons, 23 April 1996)

McGrady speaks on behalf of his party when he proposes to appoint rather than to elect the chairman of the new forum. In so doing, he reinforces the distinction between the act of appointing as relatively predictable and unproblematic, and the act of electing as more problematic and unpredictable. As a result, the two lexical items acquire the status of lexical opposites. It is, however, obvious that at the core of the debate concerning the choice of appointment or of election lies the dichotomy between *consensus* and *majority decision* as alternative parliamentary procedures. Their underlying meanings are explicitly outlined by the speaker in that *appointment* is associated with *consultation* and *consensus*, whereas the *elective process* is associated with *majority decision* and it implicitly involves a dissenting minority.

Whereas consensus is a process of synthesising many diverse elements, voting is a means by which one alternative is chosen from among several. Voting is a win or lose model, in which people are more often concerned with the numbers it takes to 'win' than with the issue itself. With consensus people can and should work through differences and reach a mutually satisfactory position. It may be possible for one person's insights or strongly held beliefs to sway the whole group. No ideas are lost, each member's input is valued as part of the solution. Voting does not take into account individual feelings or needs. In essence, it is a quantitative, rather than qualitative, method of decision-making.

In the discourse of Labour MPs, *consensus* collocates frequently with *consultation* and *good will*, which emphasises its positive connotations, as illustrated in example (1) above and example (2) below.

(2)   *Marjorie Mowlam [Labour]*: The official opposition have a great deal of
      sympathy with the spirit of amendments Nos. 60 and 61 in trying to establish a
      set of rules by *consensus*, not *majoritarianism*, and based on *consultation*, as
      the hon. Member for South Down (Mr. McGrady) described. [...] On the
      amendments, it might be helpful if the Committee was assured that the initial
      rules set up and the actual rules of procedure of the forum will be based on the
      principle of *consensus* and *consultation*, rather than on *majoritarianism*.
      (*Debates*, House of Commons, 23 April 1996)

The Labour MP Marjorie Mowlam supports McGrady's proposal when she speaks in favour of establishing the rules by *consensus*

rather than by *majoritarianism*. This reinforces the general assumption
that there is a strong dominance of positive connotations in the use of
the notion of *consensus*. However, on closer inspection, it looks as if
there were several mixed connotations in the use of *consensus* in the
British parliamentary debates, depending to a large extent on the
speakers' party allegiance, strategic goals and inter-party coalition/
opposition, as well as discursive focus. The notion of *consensus* is
used by MPs across the political spectrum from the Social Democratic
and Labour Party to the Ulster Democratic Unionist Party and the
U.K. Unionist Party. Accordingly, as I intend to show in this chapter,
the meaning of *consensus* acquires various, even opposite connotations and serves different, even contrary purposes depending on the
pragma-semantic co-text and context.

Apart from intervening quite frequently in the debate under
consideration, Eddie McGrady, MP and Chief Whip, is also the one
who spells out the task incumbent on the participants in the debate. He
draws a line between *consensus* and *majority decision* by emphasising
the distinction between *appointment*, which is based on *consensus*,
and *election,* which is based on *majority decision.* A polarisation of
two pairs of major key words is thus emerging: on the one hand,
consensus vs *majority decision*, on the other, *appointment* vs *election*.
In so doing, McGrady, like Mowlam, explicitly associates *consensus*
with *consultation* and *good will*, which are two of the most frequently
occurring collocates of *consensus* in this debate, as well as in other
related debates.

As we could see, both McGrady and Mowlam recommend
consensus as the preferred political strategy which ought to be adopted
in the first stage of the Forum for Peace and Reconciliation. In the first
place, consensus is semantically construed in their speeches primarily
as a tool or instrument, e.g. "the parties, *by consensus*, give the
chairmanship", "to establish a set of rules *by consensus*". In the
second place, consensus is semantically construed as concrete
evidence of a favourable debate atmosphere: "We want the forum to
illustrate some *consensus*", "they will show the good will and
consensus". In the third place, consensus is semantically construed
attributively as a principle: "the actual rules of procedure of the forum
will be based on the principle of *consensus*", "on the basis of *consent*
and *consensus*". Table 1 provides in a nutshell the issue that is being

discussed by MPs who are members of the U.K. Social-Democratic and Labour Party: it sums up the comparative evaluation of the two political strategies, *consensus* and *majority decision,*

POLITICAL STRATEGY	*Consensus*	*Majority decision*
POLITICAL PROCESS	Appointment – by consultation	election – by voting
POLITICAL EVALUATION (U.K. Social-Dem and Labour Party)	positive = good will	negative = competition

Table 1.   Positive evaluation of the *consensus* strategy by Social-Democratic and Labour MPs.

According to typological studies of semantic roles (Fillmore 1968; Carlson 1984; Jackendoff 1990), there are primary semantic roles, such as Agent and Patient, and optional roles, such as the Circumstantial roles, e.g. Source, Goal, Instrument and Resultant. Special phrasal and discursive relationships develop in the speakers' utterances depending on the transitive or intransitive type of predication. In their active form, transitive sentences must always contain both an Agent and a Patient, while for intransitive sentences there is a single compulsory role, i.e. the Agent. Given their political commitments, the two speakers above (McGrady and Mowlam) show a preference for the use of the word *consensus* with active transitive predicates and particularly in the Circumstantial role of Instrument ("the parties, *by consensus*, give the chairmanship"), or in the primary role of Affected ("they will show the good will and *consensus*").

Whereas members of the Social Democratic and Labour Party associate *consensus* with a positive attitude towards the political process of consensus-based appointment, an entirely different attitude is conveyed by their political opponents. For example, Ian Paisley conveys an exclusively negative perception and interpretation of *consensus*, as illustrated in (3) below:

(3)   *Ian Paisley [Ulster Democratic Unionist Party]*: […] I suggest to the House – […] – that we are witnessing more and more opposition from those who

initially launched a vicious attack against the very idea of *elections* and a forum. We now have a new parliamentary procedure: it is called *consensus*. We do not take any *votes*; we simply have *consensus*. We would wait a long time to achieve *consensus* in this place – not one Bill or Order in Council would be passed. (*Debates*, House of Commons, 23 April 1996)

Ian Paisley is a member of the Ulster Unionist Party and a notorious opponent to *consensus* policies. The connotations he associates with *consensus* are entirely negative: what he does is to offer the opposite evaluation of McGrady's polarisation between *consensus* as a preferred option and *majority decision* as a dispreferred option. Like McGrady, he uses the notion of consensus transitively, but by denying its Resultant role: *We would wait a long time to achieve consensus in this place – not one Bill or Order in Council would be passed.* A similar attitude is expressed by Robert McCartney, a member of the U.K. Unionist Party, as illustrated in (4):

(4)   *Eddie McGrady*: I am simply attempting to ensure that those who attend the forum, whoever they may be and from whatever party they may come, will deal with one another on the basis of *consent* and *consensus*, not on the basis of *majoritarian rule*. It is most important that the concept of *majoritarian rule* be eliminated as far as possible. No weighted majority of 75 per cent or, indeed, of any other ad hoc fraction or percentage, should be applied to the deliberations of the forum. [...]
        Robert McCartney (U.K. Unionist Party): In responding to the hon. Member for South Down (Mr. McGrady), I must say something about the concepts of majoritarianism and *consensus*. '*Majoritarianism*' seems to be a denigrating reference to the democratic principle that in any body in which there is a difference of opinion, matters are usually decided by a majority of those present. However, it is recognised that in some circumstances the issues to be determined are so grave and significant that it is necessary to have more than a bare majority. I think that the constitution of the United States of America may be changed by a majority of 75 per cent. That figure is reckoned to be a significant loading of a simple majority in such circumstances.
        I am somewhat bemused by the concept of *consensus*. I know the phrase from my experience of the law, where the parties to a contract are said to require a *consensus* ad idem, so that they are thinking about the same thing when they arrive at the subject matter of their contract. However, the way in which the hon. Member for South Down uses the word '*consensus*' suggests that nothing can be agreed on unless the tiniest minority accepts it. People could sit there and as long as they did not participate in the magical process of *consensus*, nothing could be done. If we are to be honoured in the negotiating process by the presence of Sinn Fein, the magical process of *consensus* would render invalid any conclusion reached by those present if it insisted on its

> primary ideas of Brits out and self-determination on an all-Ireland basis. (*Debates*, House of Commons, 23 April 1996)

First of all, McCartney makes a distinction between decisions by simple majority and decisions by a qualified majority of 75 per cent. Just like Paisley, McCartney adopts a rhetorical stance and resorts to irony when he rejects McGrady's proposal concerning consensus. While Paisley concludes sarcastically "We now have a new parliamentary procedure: it is called *consensus*", McCartney shows indirectly his skepticism by ironically referring to "the magical process of consensus". He also construes *consensus* as a process which is only apparently used in the semantic role of External Agent because its agency is strongly denied: "the magical process of *consensus* would render invalid any conclusion reached by those present if it insisted on its primary ideas of Brits out and self-determination on an all-Ireland basis." The message sent by both Paisley and McCartney is that the consensus proposal is not applicable to the current political situation concerning the Forum and therefore it is not to be regarded as a realistic option.

When Paisley refers to consensus as a tool and a procedure, as in example (5) below, he calls into question its efficiency by providing the counter-example of the Anglo-Irish Agreement. He makes it clear that he speaks on behalf of the people of Northern Ireland when he fully rejects the idea of consensus, which he finds useless.

(5)   *Ian Paisley*: [...] Parliament should consider what it has done in Northern Ireland. It says that it is working realistically, but was the Anglo-Irish Agreement brought about by *consensus*? [...] In fact, it launched the greatest divide seen in Northern Ireland for many years. It polarized all parts of the community. In other words, *consensus* means facing down the Unionists. [...] For hon. Members to tell the people of Northern Ireland that they can have no votes but must reach *consensus* on everything is ridiculous and is no way to proceed. [...]. (*Debates*, House of Commons, 23 April 1996)

While the word *consensus* is used in the semantic role of Instrument ('by consensus'), its very function as Instrument is denied. What Paisley particularly reproaches the supporters of the consensus principle is the fact that their procedure is undemocratic because it excludes the people's participation in a democratic process that is of vital importance to them. According to him, the attempt to reach a consensus does not give the people of Northern Ireland the opportunity to have their say. He also considers that the consensus proposal disregards the Unionists' opinions. Paisley's view is shared by his fellow MP John Taylor, who also attacks McGrady's proposal. The brief interaction between Taylor and McGrady in (6) below illustrates in more detail the different ways in which they construe the difference between appointing and electing the chairman of the forum:

(6)   *John Taylor (Ulster Unionist Party)*: [...] I was astounded by what was said by the hon. Member for South Down (Mr. McGrady). We are talking about an *electoral process* in which the people of Northern Ireland, through the *ballot*, will *express their opinion* and *elect* their representatives to a forum, yet the hon. Gentleman *denigrated the electoral process*. He said that he was against *elections* and wanted someone to be *selected* rather than *elected*. How do we select a chairman of a forum? At the end of the day, the chairman must be *elected by the people* who represent the *electorate* of Northern Ireland.
        Eddie McGrady (Labour): Surely this is a gross misinterpretation of what I said. I suggested that the chairman of the forum be *appointed* from among the *elected members* of the forum.
        John Taylor: I challenge the hon. Gentleman to explain the difference between being *appointed* by the elected members of the forum and being *elected* by the members of the forum.
        Eddie McGrady: Consensus. (*Debates*, House of Commons, 23 April 1996)

Taylor goes even further in his rejection of consensus by pointing out that the electoral process is a democratic process, whereas the appointment process is not, since the people are not involved to participate. In his opinion, elections presuppose a popular process, while appointments represent a restrictive process of selection. Consequently the electoral process is regarded by the Unionists as a democratic process, whereas the appointment process is regarded as undemocratic. The Unionists' view on *consensus*, on the one hand, and *majority decision*, on the other, is summed up in Table 2.

POLITICAL STRATEGY	Consensus	Majority decision
POLITICAL PROCESS	appointment = selection	election = people's participation
POLITICAL EVALUATION (Ulster Unionists and U.K. Unionists)	negative = undemocratic	positive = democratic

Table 2. Negative evaluation of the *consensus* strategy by Unionist MPs.

According to the members of the Ulster Unionist Party and of the U.K. Unionist Party, the process of election presupposes the people's possibility to express their opinion and make a choice, while the consensus proposal denies the people's democratic right to express their opinion. By contrast, the appointment process is regarded as undemocratic since it replaces the democratic process of election with a process of selection. Table 3 presents a comparative summary of the different evaluations of the *consensus* strategy made by MPs belonging to opposite political positions.

POLITICAL STRATEGY		Consensus	Majority decision
POLITICAL PROCESS		appointment = selection	election = people's participation
POLITICAL EVALUATION	U.K. Social-Dem and Labour Party	positive = good will	negative = competition
	Ulster Unionists and U.K. Unionists	negative = undemocratic	positive = democratic

Table 3. Opposite evaluations of the *consensus* strategy by the U.K. MPs.

5. Swedish parliamentary *samförstånd/konsensus*

Unlike English, Swedish has two words, i.e. *samförstånd* and *konsensus/consensus*, which cover a wider range of semantic meanings than *consensus*. The very fact that Swedish has two terms where English only has one seems to indicate the existence of more nuanced distinctions that are made in Swedish between the secondary meanings and connotations of this concept. This is particularly significant when we examine the different uses of *consensus* in political discourse, where several circumstantial factors are involved: the magnitude of the issue under consideration and its relevance to different political parties and citizen groups, the legitimacy of particular party-political interests, the implementation of expected outcome(s), the positions and the goals of the MPs and their respective parties, the envisaged or favoured public reactions.

Given the consensus tradition in Swedish political culture, it is generally assumed that in Swedish there is a strong dominance of positive connotations in the use of *samförstånd* and *konsensus/consensus*. However, there are many variations in actual language use, and particularly in special sub-genres of political discourse. As institutional key words, the two variants often convey the under-pinnings of new political trends and policies, the changing balance between the competing and the collaborating forces that shape political or national consensus. The two Swedish equivalents of the English word *consensus* have comparable denotations, but slightly different connotations.

On the one hand, *samförstånd* refers to the relationship between two or several parties who understand each other and may have a mutual agreement between them based on a community of interests. On the other, *samförstånd* refers to the stage of having reached unanimity of opinions or of action between parties with different interests and this particular denotational meaning has both positive and negative derived meanings (*National Encyklopedins Ordbok* 1996). Not surprisingly, the equivalent of the English 'consensus politics' is the Swedish phrase *samförståndspolitik*, while the following are typically Swedish concepts: *samförståndskonferens* (= consensus-building conference), *samförståndslösning* (= compromise solution), *samförståndsarbete* (= consensus work), *samförståndsanda* (= spirit of consensus), *samförståndsman* (= a person who acts in favour of consensus).

As far as the word *konsensus/consensus* is concerned, it is generally defined as the propensity for reaching unanimity between parties with opposite interests (*National Encyklopedins Ordbok* 1996). In very formal circumstances, it is also used with the meaning of consent, concession, approval and/or permission. Quite expectedly, the word *konsensus* is recurrent in the political discourse about Sweden's neutrality politics.

Like most democracies, the Swedish political system works by attempting to strike a balance between consensus and conflict, but, more than other democracies, Sweden has managed to achieve a lower degree of conflict and a higher degree of consensus (Sannerstedt 1992). During the past two decades the Swedish political structures and processes have been undergoing a number of changes, subsumed by Edgerton, Fryklund and Peterson (1994) under the concept of 'political culture':

> Political culture does not primarily deal with what happens in politics, but rather with how people perceive and interpret these events, which is not necessarily the same thing. These perceptions or interpretations can be of three kinds: those based on knowledge, those governed by emotions, and those oriented around values. (1994: 228)

It is particularly the value-related emotions that have been often under-explored in studies of political discourse, although they play a central role in foregrounding politicians' personal profiles, ideological commitments and communicative relationships. One feature of the Swedish 'consensus-style politics' concerns the powers vested in the committees (responsible for scrutinising policy and government departments) and the ease of public access to those committees. There is also supposed to be a much greater degree of cross-party co-operation in the development of new policies in the Swedish Riksdagen.

From the Swedish parliamentary corpus I chose to examine the use of *consensus* in a series of debates in the Riksdagen (from 1996 and 1997) dealing with a foreign policy issue, where the words *konsensus* and *samförstånd* occur relatively often. This choice may be

accounted for by the fact that the foreign policy issue under consideration is comparatively as crucial for Sweden as the British debate
Northern Ireland. The solutions to these issues are decisive for the
respective nations and this is why *consensus* plays a central role. The
examples below illustrate the controversy between Göran Persson, the
former Swedish Social Democrat Prime Minister, and Opposition MPs
about the decision made by the Prime Minister to visit China against
the consensus previously reached in the Foreign Policy Committee
where it was unanimously agreed to plan a visit to China by Swedish
government officials of a lower rank. Particularly significant is the
exchange between Persson and Anders Björck, the First Deputy
Speaker and Conservative MP [a major Opposition party]:

(7)   *Anders Björck (m)*: Alltså blev det inga varningssignaler från Utrikes-
        departementet [...] om att det fanns *konsensus* inom Utrikesdepartementet
        och, om det skulle *brytas* skulle det återupprätthållas i samma form? (*Debates
        in the Swedish Riksdag*, 20 november 1996)
        Anders Björck (First Deputy Speaker and Conservative MP): So there were no
        warnings from [the Swedish] Foreign Office [...] about the fact that there was
        a *consensus* in the Foreign Office and, if it were *violated*, it should have been
        taken up again in the same form? (*Debates in the Swedish Riksdag*, 20
        November, 1996)

(8)   *Göran Persson, statsminister (s)*: Ja, vi redogjorde för min planerade resa till
        Kina. Och diskussionen ägde rum, tror jag, i Utrikesnämnden på Lars
        Tobissons begäran. Efteråt diskuterade vi fördelarna och nackdelarna, men
        märkte att vi inte kunde nå varandra. Vi kunde inte nå *konsensus* [...].
        (*Debates in the Swedish Riksdag*, 20 November 1996)
        Göran Persson, Prime Minister (Social Democrat): Yes, we gave an account
        of my planned trip to China. And the discussion took place, I think, in the
        Foreign Policy Committee on the request of Lars Tobisson [Conservative
        MP]. Afterwards we discussed the pros and cons, but realised that we could
        not agree with each other. We could not reach *consensus* [...]. (*Debates in the
        Swedish Riksdag*, 20 November 1996)

It is relevant to point out that in keeping with the Swedish tradition of
political negotiation, consensus is regarded as a prerequisite, an
instrument and a goal, which explains why interlocutors are normally
striving to both maintain and reach consensus when taking political
decisions. Since consensus pervades cross-party parliamentary interaction, Swedish MPs are hardly prepared to find that previously
reached consensual solutions can be violated. It is against this back-

ground that we are to interpret Björck's challenging and reproachful question with which he confronts former Prime Minister Persson. According to the initial cross-party consensus Persson had accepted the compromise solution that a Swedish official visit to China could take place, but at a lower rank than that of Head of State, Prime Minister or Speaker of the House. This kind of consensual understanding is normally taken seriously and complied with by Swedish politicians. This is precisely the message conveyed by the First Deputy Speaker, Conservative MP Björck, in the following example:

(9)   *Anders Björck, Förste vice talman (m)*: [...] Vi i Sverige har försökt att sträva efter så stor *enighet* som möjligt om utrikespolitiska frågor. Utrikesnämnden diskuterade nivån på besöksutbytet med Kina. Där blev det *konsensus* i Utrikesnämnden om att besöksutbyte på nivå över vice statsminister för närvarande inte skulle äga rum. Det innebär att statschef, talman och statsminister borde avhålla sig från att resa till Kina fram till dess att en förbättring skett vad gäller de demokratiska fri- och rättigheterna i Kina. Därför var det naturligtvis förvånande att statsministern, som ju var väl förtrogen med uppfattningen i Utrikesnämnden, utan att på nytt höra nämnden och utan att rådgöra med den beslutade sig för att åka till Kina. [...] och på så sätt dels informera nämnden, dels försöka se om det fanns någon form av *samförstånd* kring detta. Så skedde alltså inte, utan meddelandet om att statsministern tänkte handla tvärtemot vad som hade sagts i Utrikesnämnden kom via massmedierna ut till de politiska partierna och till de partier som är representerade i nämnden. Det var inte särskilt skickligt handlat. [...] Vi måste naturligtvis från oppositionens sida också uppfatta detta som en onödig konfrontation, och det bidrar naturligtvis inte till att *samförståndet* om utrikespolitiken ökar. (*Debates in the Swedish Riksdag*, 4 June 1997)
    Anders Björck, First Deputy Speaker (Conservative MP): [...] In Sweden we have strived to achieve as much *unanimity* on foreign policy issues as possible. The Foreign Policy Committee discussed the level of the exchange of visits with China and a *consensus* was reached that no visit above the level of Deputy Prime Minister would take place. It means that the Head of State, the Speaker of the House and the Prime Minister ought to abstain from travelling to China until an improvement in the democratic rights and liberties in China has taken place. This is why it came as a surprise when the Prime Minister, who was well aware of the opinion in the Foreign Policy Committee, decided to go to China without even informing or consulting the Committee. [...] and thus first inform the Committee, and second, try to see if there could be some form of *consensus* about it. This did not happen, however. Instead the message that the Prime Minister was planning to act contrary to what was said in the Committee reached the political parties through the media. It was not very cleverly handled. [...] As members of the Opposition we can only interpret this as an unnecessary confrontation which

does not contribute to enhancing the *consensus* about foreign policy. (*Debates in the Swedish Riksdag*, 4 June 1997)

Björck's message is double-layered: on the one hand, he condemns the Prime Minister's unilaterally taken decision and subsequent line of action which practically invalidated the previously reached consensus with the other political parties; on the other hand, he expresses understanding for occasionally changing a political decision due to changing political circumstances, but provided that all political parties are informed and consulted. For Björck it is important that all MPs, including the Prime Minister, live up to the Swedish consensus tradition by ensuring wide cross-party participation in consultations and parliamentary decisions, and particularly on foreign policy issues. According to Björck the Swedish preference for consensus should be taken into account in the Swedish Riksdag when debating issues of national importance. This preference derives from the Swedish propensity for avoiding conflict and confrontation, which is emphasised by Björck: "we can only interpret this as an unnecessary confrontation". Björck's statement is reinforced by several other fellow MPs, including Lars Tobisson (Conservative MP):

(10)   *Lars Tobisson (m)*: Fru talman! När Sveriges statsminister uttalar sig internationellt företräder han hela folket. Vi vill gärna att den som bekläder Sveriges högsta politiska ämbete företräder en linje som är brett förankrad. Därför finns det en strävan till *samförstånd* i utrikespolitiken, vilket leder till speciella regler och traditioner. Göran Persson har med och under sin resa till Kina på flera sätt valt att bryta denna ordning. [...] Sveriges folk måste kunna lita på att dess främsta politiska företrädare internationellt redovisar en politisk linje som det så långt möjligt råder *enighet* om. (*Debates in the Swedish Riksdag*, 4 juni 1997)

   Lars Tobisson (Conservative): Mrs. Speaker! When the Swedish Prime Minister makes declarations on the international arena he represents our whole people. We want the person who holds Sweden's highest official position to stand for a policy that has wide popular support. This is why there is an ambition for *consensus* on foreign policy issues, which implies special rules and traditions. By his visit to China, Göran Persson has chosen to break these regulations in several ways. [...] The Swedish people should be able to rely on the fact that their highest political representatives are promoting a line of policy that is rooted in as much *unanimity* as possible. (*Debates in the Swedish Riksdag*, 4 June 1997)

Both Björck and Tobisson insist on the necessity to follow the Swedish consensus tradition in all political matters and, more importantly, to comply with the provisions of consensual agreements and not break existing regulations. We can detect in their interventions a lot of indirect criticism of the former Prime Minister's violation of parliamentary consensus which is generally regarded as binding. Representatives of other Opposition parties subscribed to this view and supported the necessity to comply with consensually reached agreements. One of them is Håkan Holmberg, a member of the Swedish Liberal Party, and the following is one of his interventions:

(11)   *Håkan Holmberg (fp)*: Alla vet att Folkpartiet har varit och är mycket kritiskt till den svaga känsla för betydelsen av mänskliga rättigheter i Kina som statsministern uppvisade vid besöket i höstas. Det är också väl känt att både vårt parti och flera andra partier i Utrikesnämnden var kritiska till att den här resan gjordes och att den genomfördes på den här nivån. Det hade tidigare funnits *konsensus* om att utbytet skulle hållas på en något lägre nivå. (*Debates in the Swedish Riksdag*, 4 June 1997)

        Håkan Holmberg (Liberal Party): Everybody knows that the Liberal Party has been very critical of the weak emphasis on the importance of human rights in China that the Prime Minister showed during his visit last autumn. It is also well known that our party and other parties were critical in the Foreign Policy Committee about the implementation of this visit and at this level. There had been a *consensu*s according to which the diplomatic exchange would take place at a lower level. (*Debates in the Swedish Riksdag,* 4 June 1997)

In his reply, Persson tactfully acknowledges that it is desirable to reach consensus, but he tries to explain that this is not always possible. Consequently, as illustrated in (12), his view is that more realistic solutions need to be found when consensus cannot be reached.

(12)   *Göran Persson, statsminister (s)*: [...] Vi beklagar ju att vi inte kunde nå enighet och *konsensus* i Utrikesnämnden. Det skulle ha blivit bättre, och det skulle ha varit en styrka. Men, som jag sade förut: om vi tillskriver *konsensus* en överordnad roll, då kan det lätt leda till en veto-situation. Vilket också skulle vara beklagligt. (*Debates in the Swedish Riksdag*, 4 June, 1997)

        Göran Persson, Prime Minister (Social Democrat): [...] We certainly regret that we could not reach *unanimity* and *consensus* in the Foreign Policy Committee. It would have been better, and it would have been a strength. But, as I said before: if we ascribe *consensus* a superordinate role, this can easily turn into a veto situation. Which would also be regrettable. (*Debates in the Swedish Riksdag,* 4 June 1997)

The verbal exchange between Björck and Persson reflects and at the same time reinforces the power relation between the two: as an Opposition MP it is Björck's task to attack and criticise the sitting Prime Minister, as well as to hold him accountable for his policies and actions. However, it is actually Persson as Prime Minister who has the authority and the power to make and change decisions, sometimes (as in this case) without requiring the endorsement of parliamentary committees. The different uses of the key word *consensus/ samförstånd* by the two Swedish parliamentarians indicate the different meanings they deliberately ascribe to them. Their particular evaluations of the notions of *consensus* and *samförstånd*, as well as their respective connotations are summed up in Table 4.

POLITICAL STRATEGY		*Konsensus*	*Samförstånd*
POLITICAL PROCESS		consent, unanimity, approval Tacit agreement & Decision-making	
POLITICAL EVALUATION	Swedish Conservatives	positive = binding - like a contract	
	Swedish Social-democrats	positive = guiding - like a principle	

Table 4.   Different positive evaluations of the *konsensus/samförstånd* strategy by MPs in the Swedish Riksdag.

For Björck, who speaks on behalf of Swedish Conservative MPs, consensus is a binding agreement, i.e. a sort of unanimously finalised contract, whereas for Persson consensus is an agreement, but not a binding one, i.e. a sort of principle or guideline for a course of action. Consequently, the fact that Persson has not complied with the consensus reached in the Foreign Policy Committee is considered by Björck as a serious breech of contract, especially as the Committee was not even informed or warned beforehand. Persson, however, regards his change of policy and non-compliance with the prior consensus simply as a justifiable decision change called for by objective circumstances and motivated by his prerogative as Prime Minister.

On the whole, Björck uses consensus in a wider meaning, which covers the traditional propensity in the Swedish Riksdag to reach tacit understanding and compromise solutions, and to act unanimously in matters of foreign policy. Persson tones down the role of consensus in order to minimise his own violation of a Committee-based parliamentary consensus. The main objection made by Björck does not focus primarily on the fact that Persson violated an officially reached consensus, but on the fact that Persson did not inform the Foreign Policy Committee about his change of plans concerning the visit to China.

It is worth noting that Björck switches between the use of *konsensus* and the use of *samförstånd*. In both (7) and (9) he repeatedly refers to the initially reached consensus in the Foreign Policy Committee by using the word *konsensus*. He resorts to the word *samförstånd* when he envisages it as a tacit agreement and an independently existing understanding: "försöka se om det fanns någon form av *samförstånd* kring detta" (= try to see if there could be some form of *consensus* about it), "*samförståndet* om utrikespolitiken ökar" (= the *consensus* about foreign policy increases). It is precisely in these instances that the word *samförstånd* is used in the Circumstantial semantic role of Locative (the former example) and the central semantic role of Eventive in (7), which highlight the independently occurring consensus. As in the British parliamentary debates, the Circumstantial role of Resultant is instantiated by the notion of consensus through the word *konsensus*, rather than *samförstånd*: "att vi inte kunde nå *enighet* och *konsensus*" (= that we could not reach *unanimity* and *consensus*), in (12), or "Där blev det *konsensus*" (= Consensus was achieved there) in (9). There is, moreover, a particular transitive use of the Swedish *konsensus* which does not occur in the British debate above, namely through the semantic role of Affected which transcends the positive moment of reaching a consensus and concerns the act of breaking a consensus. The ensuing Swedish debate refers to the risks of invalidating a consensus by not complying with it. Whereas the British MPs are discussing the positive and negative aspects of *consensus*, the Swedish MPs agree unanimously on the positive aspects of *consensus*, but their controversy regards the negative consequences of non-compliance with previously reached consensus.

6. Concluding remarks

A comparison between the uses of consensus strategies in British and Swedish parliamentary discourses provides evidence for the fact that the preference for certain strategies is rooted in political traditions, such as higher or lower levels of confrontation and conflict tolerance, higher or lower levels of popular control over political decisions and actions, propensity for consultation and understanding, and higher or lower expectations about the politicians' compliance with unanimously taken decisions. The parallel analysis of the meanings and connotations of the notion of *consensus* in a particular series of British and Swedish parliamentary debates reveals certain institutionally anchored semantic similarities, but several pragmatic differences rooted in particular cultural traditions and historically shaped political principles.

In both parliaments the notion of *consensus* is semantically construed as a Goal, an Instrument and/or a Process, to name a few. Accordingly, it is used in the semantic roles of Resultant, Instrument and Eventive. In the British parliamentary debates *consensus* is ascribed legitimacy especially as Goal, i.e. the desirable end-result of the negotiations, whereas in the Swedish Riksdag *konsensus* och *samförstånd* are assumed to be the Source, i.e. the starting point, as well as the Goal and Resultant of the parliamentary discussions on matters of national importance. In the particular British parliamentary debate under scrutiny the notion of *consensus* is opposed to the notion of *majority decision*, which accounts for the contradictory views supported by the MPs involved in connection with the appointment or election of the first Chairman of Forum for Peace and Reconciliation. In the particular Swedish parliamentary debate under consideration the notion of *samförstånd/konsensus* is discussed and interpreted in terms of the politicians' commitment to and compliance with a previously reached consensual agreement concerning the rank of a Swedish official visit to China. The discussion exhibits severe criticism of the former Swedish Prime Minister's violation of the consensus according to which he was expected to abstain from an official visit to China. It indicates that the political power balance is overarching when negotiating the consequences of non-compliance with consensus-based institutional regulations. To sum up, two main points can be made about the parallel uses of British *consensus* and of Swedish *samförstånd/konsensus* in the parliamentary debates under consideration:

(i) In the British perception and use of *consensus* there is no automatic agreement about the existence of a prior *consensus*-based understanding as the preferred alternative. Moreover, there may even be highly polarised positions, those that claim the legitimacy and those that claim the non-legitimacy of *consensus* (as illustrated by the debate on the inauguration of the Forum for Peace and Reconciliation). The British debate is specifically about consensus as an institutional principle and procedure, while the Swedish debate focuses on consensus as an institutional regulation and commitment.

(ii) The starting point of the discussion about the role, implications, and observance/violation of the notion or principle of *consensus* [*samförstånd/konsensus*] in the Swedish debate is rooted in a shared conviction about its positive value. Swedish debaters tend to ascribe to it a number of positive connotations. The Swedish discussion is not about whether consensus should be used as a basic debate principle, but to what extent it is/has been observed/violated, by whom, and for what reasons. There is a generally shared opinion among Swedish MPs of different political allegiance that *consensus* should be preferred and conflict/confrontation should be avoided.

Two major concerns have been central to this study: (i) to show how divergent connotations are often derived from culture-specific perceptions and competing policy-based evaluations of institutional key words, namely the English *consensus* and the Swedish *samförstånd/konsensus*, as well as their corresponding collocates in parliamentary debates, and (ii) to account for the distinction between the British use of *consensus* primarily as principle-based and process-oriented procedure, and the Swedish cooperation-based use of *samförstånd/konsensus* primarily as rule-based and result-oriented procedure.

References

Carlson, Greg 1984. On the Role of Thematic Roles in Semantic Theory. *Linguistics* 22, 259-79.

Damgaard, Erik 1997. The Strong Parliaments of Scandinavia: Continuity and Change of Scandinavian Parliaments. In: Copeland, Gary W. / Patterson, Samuel C. (eds) *Parliaments in the Modern World: Changing Institutions.* Ann Arbor: The University of Michigan Press, 85-103.

Edgerton, David / Fryklund, Björn / Peterson, Tomas 1994. '*Until the Lamb of God Appears...*' – *The 1991 Parliamentary Election: Sweden Chooses a New Political System.* CESIC Studies in International Conflict 12, Eds Göran Rystad och Sven Tägill. Lund: Lund University Press.

Fillmore, Charles 1968. The Case for Case. In Bach, Emmon / Harms, Robert T. (eds) *Universals in Linguistic Theory.* New York: Holt, Rinehart, Winston, 1-88.

Hewison, Robert 1995. *Culture and Consensus: England, Art and Politics since 1940.* London: Methuen.

Ilie, Cornelia 2000. Cliché-based Metadiscursive Argumentation in the Houses of Parliament. *International Journal of Applied Linguistics* 10/1, 65-84.

Ilie, Cornelia 2006. Micro-level Coherence Patterns in Institutional Discourse. In Chruszczewski, Piotr / Garcarz, Michal / Górski, Tomasz (eds) *At the Crossroads of Linguistic Sciences.* Kraków: Tertium.

Jackendoff, Ray S. 1990. *Semantic Structures.* Cambridge, MA.: MIT Press.

Johansson, Alf O. / Melling, Joseph 1995. The Roots of Consensus: Bargaining Attitudes and Political Commitment among Swedish and British Workers c. 1920-1950. *Economic and Industrial Democracy* 16, 353-97.

Kavanagh, Dennis 1985. Whatever Happened to Consensus Politics? *Political Studies* 33/4, 529–546.

Longman Dictionary of the English Language 1991. London.

Longman Dictionary of English Language and Culture 1992. London.

Mouffe, Chantal 1993. *The Return of the Political.* London: Verso.

National Encyklopedins Ordbok 1996. Höganäs, Bokförlaget Bra Böcker o. Göteborg, Språkdata.

Norstedts Stora engelsk-svenska ordbok 2000. Norstedts förlag.

Norton, Philip 1997. Representation of Interests: The Case of the British House of Commons. In: Copeland, Gary W. / Patterson, Samuel C. (eds) *Parliaments in the Modern World: Changing Institutions.* Ann Arbor: The University of Michigan Press, 13-28

Sannerstedt, Anders 1992. *Förhandlingar i riksdagen.* Lund: Lund University Press.

Seldon, Anthony 1994. Consensus: A Debate Too Long? *Parliamentary Affairs* 47/4.

DANIELA WAWRA

On Course for the Next Stage of Success: The Annual Reports of U.S. and Japanese Companies

1. Globalization and regionalization

'Globalization' has been one of the catch-words of the end of the 20th and the beginning of the 21st century. Theories on globalization can basically be divided into two groups: theories that propagate the homogenization of cultures as a major consequence of globalization and theories that expect the hybridization of cultures (cf. Holton 1998: 163ff, 178ff; Chuang 2000: 19; Crane 2002: 10). An example of the former is the theory of cultural imperialism. Supporters of this approach are of the opinion that a global culture is on its way to replace ethnic, regional and national identities, i.e. to homogenize cultures (cf. Chuang 2000: 22f; Crane 2002: 2). Thus, Beck defines 'globalization' as a 'scare-word' that causes many fears (cf. Beck 2002: 1). Seabrook even states that globalization is a "declaration of war" to all cultures (Seabrook 2004: 1). In contrast, an example for a 'hybridization theory' is the model of cultural networks. Supporters of this theory are of the opinion that globalization rather leads to a strengthening of local identities and thus to cultural hybridization (cf. Chuang 2000: 25f; Crane 2002: 2).

Globalization penetrates all parts of social life in contemporary societies. It is a central topic in sports, fashion, politics, the environment, music, law and business. We speak of a global economy that is characterized by "massive transnational flows of capital and labour" (Holton 1998: 1). This global economy is dominated by 'global players', i.e. companies that operate across national borders. Companies offer global products and services that are consumed in almost every country and region in our 'global village'. Business has been a major driving force of globalization, and in its wake intercultural communication has become more and more important for companies that want to succeed internationally. So far, there is much more literature concerning oral than written intercultural communication. The annual reports of global companies are examples from an important field of intercultural communication. They can provide insights into cultural differences and global trends in this form of communication.

2. Annual reports in intercultural comparison

A company's annual report is an important part of its external communication and can be more specifically categorized among the 'public relations devices'. Through its annual report, a company communicates, above all, to its shareholders, customers and (potential) business partners. It informs them about the current standing of the company in global markets, its financial situation, future prospects and, more in general, about the company's philosophy. The annual report has a significant influence on how a company is perceived by outsiders. It is an important factor in the decision-building process of investors, shareholders and clients: based on the annual report they decide, among other things, if they are going to invest in or buy something from the company. Thus, the annual report influences a company's success or failure in the global marketplace. Consequently, companies consciously use the annual report to build a positive and advantageous identity.

The present study concentrates on the annual reports of companies from the USA and Japan. These two countries have been chosen mainly for two reasons:

1. The United States and Japan represent the world's largest economies. According to the World Bank[1], in 2004 the USA occupied the top rank with a total economic output (GDP) of $ 11,67 trillion. Japan ranked second with a GDP of $ 4,62 trillion.

---

1   Source: *World Indicators database*, World Bank, 15 July 2005.

2. The USA and Japan represent a Western and an Eastern industrial nation, respectively, and their cultures are very different from each other.

The main question that is addressed in this paper is: are the cultural differences between the USA and Japan also reflected in the contents and language of the annual reports of U.S. and Japanese global players, or is the communication and the language used standardized, i.e. truly global?

This study is based on eight annual reports for the financial year 2003 of U.S. and Japanese companies cited in the Forbes 2000 List of "The World's Leading Companies".[2] Seven further reports were analysed to clarify and check some of the points made in the core study. This means that altogether fifteen reports were consulted for the present paper. The Forbes 2000 List is a ranking of the world's business leaders, based on their sales, profits, assets and their market value. The list comprises the best 2000 international companies – 'global players' – of 27 industries (from 'aerospace and defence' to 'utilities') and 51 countries (from Australia to Venezuela). For this study, the best four companies in the banking sector in the USA and Japan were chosen. These are for the USA: Citigroup (C) (rank 1 in the Forbes 2000 list), Bank of America (BofA) (rank 6), JP Morgan Chase (JP) (rank 15) and Wells Fargo (WF) (rank 25). For Japan: Sumitomo Mitsui Financial Group (SMFG) (rank 396), Mitsubishi Tokyo Financial Group (MTFG) (rank 398), Mizuho Financial (MF) (rank 403) and UFJ Holdings (UFJ) (rank 444). All four Japanese banks publish their annual report in Japanese and in English. This demonstrates that it is written for the local Japanese market, as well as for the global market. Another interesting research question – which has not been addressed in this paper – would be if the English translations of the Japanese reports correspond to their Japanese versions or if parts have been left out, added or changed. Here, the English versions of the Japanese reports are compared to the U.S. reports. I decided to concentrate on companies belonging to the same sector, in order to make sure to exclude cross-sectoral differences.

---

2   cf. <www.forbes.com/lists> (20/08/2004).

2.1. Correspondences

At first sight all eight reports have a common structure. They all
contain a letter to shareholders (or stakeholders) and a financial
section. With regard to their content, all reports provide:

•   information on how successful the company was in the past
    financial year;
•   predictions about the future prospects of the company;
•   information on the organizational structure of the company.

In addition, the reports emphasize client orientation and growth. The
basic attitude towards the present and future position of the company
is without exception very optimistic. This is true even in insecure
economic times:

(1)   Our plans are underpinned by the awareness that today's difficult operating
      environment will continue for some time. But we are also well aware of the
      great accomplishments that are possible by drawing on the aggregate strengths
      of the UFJ Group. (UFJ/JAPAN5) The Groupwide management philosophy is
      as follows: - To provide optimum added value to our customers and together
      with them achieve growth - To create sustainable shareholder value through
      business growth (SMFG/JAPAN0) [...] we have to prove that we can
      consistently produce superior results, and that we are disciplined in how we
      use our capital. [...] I have every confidence that we can accomplish these
      goals (JP/USA5).

2.2. Cultural differences

2.2.1. Methodology

From now on the analysis concentrates on the introductions and the
letters to shareholders (or comparable sections) of the reports. This
selection was made as these parts are the most varied and individual
sections of the annual reports, where cultural differences should most
likely be found. The contents and language of these sections will be
examined with regard to culturally marked differences and specifics.

The study is based on qualitative discourse analysis. The
qualitative discourse analysis examines what types of linguistic means
are used in the reports to what effect. This means that the functions of
the linguistic forms in their respective contexts are analysed. In a

qualitative approach the emphasis is not on the rigorous identification and measurement of all instances of a linguistic form, but rather on the interpretation of selected occurrences of forms that are judged as typical and central for the scope of this study (cf. Denzin/Lincoln 1994: 2ff; Wood/Kroger 2000: 100, 105; Wawra 2004: 179f). Thus, the following analysis does not claim to provide a quantatively exhaustive study of the styles of U.S. and Japanese annual reports. It is rather a case study and provides first clues and tendencies that further research can build on. It sketches typical cultural differences between the reports and provides selected examples. The qualitative approach is sometimes complemented by quantitative analysis, when it is regarded as contributing to a better and deeper understanding of an examined feature.

For the analysis, the following categories are used. They have proven to be significant in oral intercultural communication studies:
1.   Formality of language;
2.   Individual – collective orientation;
3.   Competitiveness.

When the topic of cultural specifics is discussed, the reproach of stereotyping often is not far behind. Stereotyping means to assume that all members of a culture share the same characteristics and/or behaviours. Stereotyping is problematic as stereotypes in most cases do not apply to each single member of a group. Stereotyping can lead to self-fulfilling prophecies and is particularly problematic in research contexts: stereotyping makes researchers perceive only selectively what confirms their prejudice (cf. Bennett 1998: 6; for a detailed discussion of stereotypes cf. also Heringer 2004: 181ff and Wawra 2004: 80-85). While there are many problems with stereotyping, 'cultural generalizations' must be made in intercultural studies. Cultural generalizations[3] are different from cultural stereotypes in so far as they assume a 'preponderance of belief':

> Nearly all possible beliefs are represented in all cultures at all times, but each different culture has a preference for some beliefs over others. The description of this preference, derived from large-group research, is a cultural generaliza-

---

tion. Of course, individuals can be found in any culture who hold beliefs similar to people in a different culture. There just aren't so many of them – they don't represent the preponderance of people who hold beliefs closer to the norm or 'central tendency' of the group (Bennett 1998: 6).

In the following section, major differences in the contents and language of the U.S. and Japanese annual reports will be described and selected examples will be provided.

2.2.2. Formality of language

According to a vast variety of intercultural studies dealing with oral communication, Americans tend to have a more informal language use than Japanese people (cf. e.g. Lahiff/Penrose 1997: 55; Weiss/Stripp 1998: 62; McDaniel/Quasha 2000: 315). Is this also true for written communication and more specifically for the language used in the annual reports of the U.S. and Japanese companies?

The answer to this question is positive as the analysis reveals: the language in the reports of the U.S. banks is less formal than the language in the Japanese reports. The following features represent the less formal language use in the U.S. reports:

- simple and active syntactic structures;
- colloquial expressions;
- elisions and contractions;
- citing of employees by Christian names;
- use of questions and exclamations;
- use of direct addresses.

The sentences in the U.S. reports tend to be rather short and *syntactically simple*. The sentences of the Japanese reports in contrast tend to be longer and syntactically more complex. There are more nominal constructions and gerunds in the Japanese reports. The following excerpt from Sumitomo's report demonstrates this:

(2)   Building on the momentum created by the swift and solid progress in reaping the synergies from business consolidation at [...] SMFG was established as a holding company in December 2002. (SMFG/JAPAN2)

In addition, there are by far more *passive constructions* in the Japanese reports than in the U.S. reports.[4] There are altogether only relatively few passive constructions in all of the reports, but there are significantly more of them in the Japanese reports: we find only four passive constructions in all U.S. reports (two in JP's report, two in WF's) but nineteen in the Japanese reports (five in SMFG's, six in MTFG's, three in MF's, five in UFJ's). Here is an example from MTFG's report:

(3)   This significant contribution to income was due mainly to improvement of our loan portfolio through disposals of nonperforming loans, and the more stable credit status of borrowers in Japan as evidenced by the decreased number of bankruptcy filings during the period under review. (MTFG/JAPAN2)

The U.S. reports also frequently contain *colloquial expressions* as well as *elisions and contractions*:

(4)   [...] we spend money like it's our own (C/USA2), If we find something wrong, we'll fix it (BofA/USA3), Guess which business [...] (WF/USA3), At Wells Fargo, we say we don't care how much a person knows until we know how much they care (WF/USA8).

These features are almost absent in the Japanese reports.

The informal language use in the U.S. reports is also shown in the fact that employees are sometimes cited by their *first names* and sometimes even by the abbreviations of their first names:

(5)   Chad Gifford, chairman and CEO of Fleet Boston Financial, [...] Chad will be the chairman of the board in our new company (BofA/USA3), Benjamin F. Montoya, CEO of Smart Systems Technologies [...]. Ben joined our Board in 1996. (WF/USA8), Larry Fuller, who has retired [...] and we wish Larry well. (JP/USA3)

---

4   By choosing to use active or passive constructions the companies portray themselves also as being more in control of their field of business or more reactive to their field. Bolten *et al.* (1996: 418) already state in their examination of the annual reports from the financial year 1991/92 of two U.S. companies (Ford and GM) that the style of the U.S. reports is characterized by more frequent recourse to active verb forms and assumption of responsibility – here in comparison to two German reports (Audi and VW).

The more frequent use of *questions* in the U.S. reports contributes also to a less formal style:

(6)   [...] we are sometimes asked: Can you still grow? Are you too big to grow? Are you dependent on 'big deals' for too much of your growth? (C/USA5)

In the annual report of Fargo Wells, there are a series of questions arranged in the form of parallelisms that start with "Do we care enough":

(7)   Do we care enough to take the time to really listen to customers? Do we care enough to ask them the right questions? Do we care enough not to just push products at them but to recommend the best products and advice for their individual needs? [...] (WF/USA8)

In addition, there are also more *exclamations* in the U.S. reports that contribute to a less formal language: "Our Vision: Unchanged!" (WF/USA2), "Another great year by a truly great team!" (WF/USA8), "It's going to be a great ride!" (WF/USA8).

The less formal style also becomes apparent by the fact that all U.S. reports contain *direct addresses* to the reader:

(8)   Dear Shareholders (C/USA1), Dear fellow shareholders (JP/USA2), you will take this company to even greater heights than any of us ever imagined (C/USA8), your company, those of you who (BofA/USA1), it is for all of you that we strive every day (BofA/USA4), Our report to you [...] (WF/USA1).

Altogether there are only four direct addresses in the Japanese reports: two in SMFG's report and two in MF's report. One of the direct addresses in MF's report is the following: "I would like to take this opportunity to extend my sincere gratitude to our shareholders and customers for your continued support" (MF/JAPAN4). According to conventional language use, 'their' would rather be expected as a pronoun here instead of 'your'. However, none of the letters to share-holders in the Japanese reports starts with a direct address. SMFG's letter to shareholders is titled "Foreword", then the text follows "We are pleased [...]" (1); MTFG titles "Message from management", then follows "Mitsubishi Tokyo Financial Group, Inc. is pleased to report [...]" (2); MF's letter has the title "A Message form the President & CEO of Mizuho Financial Group, Inc.", the letter then starts with the words "On behalf of the Mizuho Financial Group, I would like to take this opportunity [...]" (4); UFJ finally titles "To Our Shareholders" and continues "In the past fiscal year [...]" (2).

The banking sector is predominantly known to be a very conservative one, if not the most conservative there is. This is also reflected in the language of the reports of the U.S. banks, which tends to be more formal than the language of U.S. reports of companies from other sectors examined, as emerges from comparison with the reports of Verizon (Telecommunications Services) (rank 26) and General Motors (Consumer durables) (rank 29). The General Motors report for example already starts with the words: "Here's what's new about GM's strategy this year: nothing." (GM1). Then the letter to shareholders begins with: "You know what it's like when you settle into the driver's seat of a brand new car ... [...] Well, that's the feeling we're aiming for behind the wheel of General Motors [...]" (GM2). Especially the frequent use of expressions like 'you know' and 'well' mark the colloquial language use in both reports as these expressions are rather typical of oral communication. However, the language use of the U.S. banks is still less formal than the language use in the reports of the Japanese banks and even the reports of Japanese companies belonging to other branches.[5] This indicates that the language use in the Japanese reports is more formal than the language of the U.S. reports, independent of the company branch.

2.2.3. Individual – collective orientation

A well founded result of intercultural research in general is that U.S. Americans tend to have a more individual attitude, whereas that of the Japanese tends to reflect more of a collective, i.e. group-oriented attitude (cf. e.g. Hofstede 1991: 53; Bennett 1998: 6; Ramsey 1998: 117, 119, 124, 126; Gibson 2000: 54-59; Scollon/Scollon [2]2001:220). Thus, a Japanese adage says: "Deru kugi wa utareru". The central Japanese concept of *wa* implies the meaning of 'groupism' and 'anti-

---

5   Here, the annual reports of Toyota Motor (Consumer durables, rank 8) and Nippon Tel & Tel (Telecommunications services, rank 30) were consulted for comparison.

individualism' (Wierzbicka 1997: 249).[6] The adage means "The protruding nail is hammered down" (cf. Weiss/Stripp 1998: 84). In order to see if this is also apparent in the language of U.S. and Japanese reports,

- the use of the personal pronouns we/our/us as opposed to I/my/me_is analysed and also,
- how employees are portrayed.

The result of the analysis of the use of we/our/us versus I/my/me is shown in the following table:

Frequency of use	We/our/us	I/my/me
Citigroup	137	31
Bank of America	96	15
JP Morgan Chase	123	6
Wells Fargo	181	12
U.S. banks	**537**	**64**
Sumitomo Mitsui	47	1
Mitsubishi Tokyo	73	0
Mizuho Financial	50	4
UFJ Holdings	39	1
Japanese banks	**209**	6

Table 1. Frequency of use of we/our/us and I/my/me.

Of the six times 'I' is used in the Japanese reports, it is hedged twice, i.e. it is explicitly stated that the speaker speaks on behalf of the company like in the following example: "On behalf of the Mizuho Financial Group, I would like to take this opportunity to extend my sincere gratitude [...]" (MF/JAPAN4). In one case the writer uses 'I' to indicate that he feels personally responsible for the company's success or failure. Thereby his statement is underlined and seems more trustworthy: "I would like to assure you that we aim to make this

---

6   For a detailed discussion of Japanese key words and core cultural values see
     Wierzbicka (1997: 235ff).

year a year of achievement for Mizuho". (MF/JAPAN4) Another time 'I' is used, is when MF's president apologizes for technical problems. He signals that he personally takes the responsibility and protects his employees: "I would also like to take this opportunity to express my deepest apologies for the computer systems problems". (MF/JAPAN4)

Altogether the relation of the frequency of use of *we/our/us* to *I/my/me* for the annual reports of the U.S. banks is 8:1, but for the Japanese reports it is 35:1.[7] Thus, in the U.S. as well as in the Japanese reports 'group' or 'team spirit' is evoked much more often than individuality. But, in comparison, *we/our/us* is used over four times more often than *I/my/me* in the Japanese reports than in the U.S. reports. This reflects a much more collective language use in the Japanese reports than in the U.S. reports.[8]

As regards the *portrayal of their employees*, it is stated in two of the Japanese reports that the employees are still expected to perform better and subordinate to the company's goals. This reflects a collective attitude:

(9)   Moreover, throughout the Group, management will strive to encourage a mindset that prioritizes overall benefit to the consolidated Group. All employees must also adopt the viewpoint of the customer, set high targets for their achievements and be results oriented (MTFG/JAPAN3), Achieving the goals of the Accelerated Business Reform Plan is every UFJ Group member's highest priority. (UFJ/JAPAN3)

In MF's report, employees are mentioned in connection with financial cuts:

(10)   [...] we are implementing drastic management rationalization measures that include a significant decrease in the number of employees and redundant offices ahead of schedule, as well as a reduction in the annual compensation of all senior executives and employees. (MF/JAPAN5)

---

7   537:64≈ 8,39 ≈ 8; 209:6 ≈ 34,83 ≈ 35.

8   It is problematic to compare the results of the quantitative analysis for the U.S. and the Japanese reports directly as the data given in the table are based on a different quantity of text: about 52 columns of text in the U.S. reports are opposed to about 15 in the Japanese reports. This means that about 10 times per column *we/our/us* is used in the U.S. reports but about 14 times per column in the Japanese reports. This confirms that the Japanese reports have a more collective style.

This statement is presented as an achievement on the way to "accelerate cost structure reform" (MF/JAPAN5) and not further commented on. This gives the impression that the company does not see its employees as individual human beings, but rather as a value-producing collective.

By contrast in all of the U.S. reports employees are mentioned as the 'pillars' of the company, and the company says explicitly "thank you" for their contribution to the company's success:

(11)   The photographs in this annual report feature our employees, and for good reason: They are the secret of Citigroup's success. (C/USA7), We are confident of our future, proud of our employees [...] (C/USA7), Most of all, my thanks to our employees, who have worked hard and even sacrificed to ensure the success of our common enterprise. No traveller has ever had better companions. (C/USA8), I am immensely proud of our team's achievement. (BofA/USA1), Finally I would like to thank [...] our associates, who work hard every day to build the company we all envision (BofA/USA4), Our employees have developed a great spirit of giving back, not just in monetary terms, but also through volunteering their time and talents to their communities. (JP/USA5)

Employees are seen as individuals in the U.S. reports, not as a collective:

(12)   [...] people truly feel that, no matter how large we grow, each and every one of us can make a difference (C/USA2)

The achievements of individuals are also partly stressed:

(13)   [...] one individual's contribution stands out. Sandy Weill's genius [...] (C/USA6), "A special thank you this year to Benjamin F. Montoya." (WF/USA8)

Wells Fargo's report explicitly cites the possibilities to promote employee satisfaction:

(14)   At Wells Fargo, we say we don't care how much a person knows until we know how much they care [...]. Do we care enough to create a work environment where it's okay to have fun? If we don't enjoy our work – if we don't look forward to getting up in the morning and coming to work – then what's the point? [...] If our team members are happy and satisfied, our customers will be more loyal to us [...]. We regularly measure the

engagement of our team members – to find out, for example, if they have the opportunity to do what they do best every day, if they've received recognition and praise for doing good work in the last seven days, if they have someone at work who encourages their development, if they have opportunities to learn and grow. (WF/USA4,5)

In addition, there are also very personal passages in the U.S. reports as the following extract demonstrates:

(15)   I've experienced success many times over and endured setbacks. Through it all, I've never looked back or stopped thinking about the possibilities inherent in the financial service industry [...]. I believe Citigroup is the financial company that best embodies these attributes [...]. I'm proud of all these achievements [...]. But what makes me proudest is the family of employees who have been on the journey with me every step of the way [...]. Along with Joan, my wife and best friend of nearly 50 years, I will also devote more of my days to philanthropic activities and my family [...]. (C/USA8)

This also reflects the individual orientation of the U.S. reports: in an annual report an individual gets the space to give an insight into his private life. No comparable passages can be found in the Japanese reports.

Altogether, employees are granted more individuality in the U.S. reports than in the Japanese ones. Their personal satisfaction and happiness matters according to the U.S. reports, whereas the human aspect is never mentioned in the Japanese reports. The Japanese reports give the impression that the prosperity of the company is more important than the prosperity of the individual. If employees are in fact valued more and treated better in U.S. companies than in Japanese ones, it is a different question. This is, however, the impression that is conveyed by the reports.

2.2.4. Competitiveness

A widespread cultural generalization is that U.S. Americans show a more aggressive competitive orientation than the Japanese, who are typically said to be more modest and in search of harmony (cf. e.g. Lahiff/Penrose 1997: 54, 60; Weiss/Stripp 1998: 58; Dore 2000: 51, 55, 143ff). This difference can also be seen in the annual reports of the U.S. and Japanese companies. The language of the U.S. reports is much more competitive than the language of the Japanese reports. The following features add up to the competitive style:

1. The frequent use of *comparatives and superlatives* to make the company's market position clear.
2. The frequent use of words related to the *word field of 'competition'*.

The annual report of Citigroup, for example, contains a longer paragraph in which numerous comparatives and superlatives can be found in a parallelism:

(16)   [...] we have more opportunities to expand our franchise organically – by bringing our best-in-class products and services to these markets and growing our market share – than any other company in our industry. [...] we have more opportunities to grow through cross-marketing than any other company in our industry. [...] we have more opportunity to grow by strategic acquisition than any other company in our industry. (C/USA5)

The letter to shareholders of Citigroup closes with the statement: "Our goal is simple: to be [...] the most profitable, most respected financial services company in the world." (C/USA7). The annual report of the Bank of America even has the title "Higher Standards", which makes the competitive orientation clear from the beginning. "Higher Standards" is a key word of this annual report. It continues to appear throughout the report as a leitmotif. The report ends with the words: "It is for all of you that we strive every day to set – and exceed – a higher standard (BofA/USA4). Right at the beginning of the Bank of America's report, there are a whole series of comparative and superlative wordings:

(17)   2003: Our best year. We served our 28,000,000 customers better than ever before. [...] We served 25,000 midsized companies – more than any other bank. 2,000,000 small businesses made us the nation's number-one small business bank (BofA/USA1).

Wells Fargo's annual report has the title "Measuring the Next Stage of Success" and the following competitive statements follow:

(18)   By virtually any measure, it was another great year. Once again we achieved record revenue and profit. Double-digit increases again in both measures! Our financial performance was among the very best not only in financial services but in any industry. Our bank is the only one in America rated 'Aaa' by

Moody's Investor Services. [...] Only about 20 other U.S. companies have a higher market cap. Our credit quality was among the best in our industry. (WF/USA1)

The report of the Bank of America ends with the words: "And we continue to raise the bar." (BofA/USAI) This wording, "raise the bar", a metaphor taken from sports competitions, more specifically high jump, is typical for the U.S. reports. They frequently contain metaphoric wordings evoking this discipline or belonging more generally to the word-field 'competition' and neighbouring fields:

(19)   [...] our competitors are not standing still (C/USA5), we value people who (...) are intent on winning (C/USA7), We are striving to exceed past accomplishments every day, in all we do. (BofA/USA1), beating our goal in each case (BofA/USA1), we can continue to push our company to even greater heights in the future (BofA/USA1), A commitment to winning is a strong part of our corporate culture. (BofA/USA2)

Although also the Japanese reports do contain statements based on the concept of competition, they are by far less frequent and less exposed than in the U.S. reports.[9] There are neither whole paragraphs centred on the competition metaphor, nor are there any statements based on it right at the beginning of a report or even as a 'motto' of the report. Most often they are used to describe what the company wants to achieve in the time to come (cf. also UFJ/JAPAN5):

---

9   The possibility that the by far less competitive style of the Japanese reports is due to the fact that the Japanese companies (ranks 396, 398, 403 and 444 in the Forbes 2000 list) have been less successful than their U.S. competitors (ranks 1, 6, 15 and 25) can be excluded. First of all, the 'worst' ranked company, the Japanese bank UFJ Holdings, has the most competitive style of the examined Japanese reports. In addition, I examined the reports of the financial year 2003 of three more U.S. banks that are ranked behind the Japanese banks: AmSouth (rank 476), Popular (rank 611) and Sovereign (rank 614). The analysis confirms that the U.S. reports have a very competitive style, independent of the success of the company. Thus Sovereign's report for example starts with the words: "Sovereign's strong and consistent organic growth has been entirely dependent on execution by a top quality team. [...] Sovereign is a driven world class financial services provider, continually outperforming the market in terms of earnings, growth and total shareholder returns." (Sovereign2).

(20)   [...] we moved aggressively from this reinforced position to strengthen the
        foundation for achieving higher sustainable profitability (SMFG/JAPAN2),
        We also made steady headway on all fronts of the Plan to bolster profitability
        by: establishing business models with competitive advantage in several
        strategic businesses (SMFG/JAPAN2), We have also set an aspiration for the
        Group of becoming one of the world's top ten financial institutions by market
        capitalization [...]. (MTFG/JAPAN3)

Even though MTFG/JAPAN has managed to improve its financial
results considerably, this is not particularly emphasized but reported
very factually: "Net income [...] was Y528.9 billion, an increase of
Y425.2 billion, or 409.9% [...]. This major improvement in our
operating results was primarily attributable to [...]" (MTFG/
JAPAN2). A further 'modest' example of competitive expressions in
the Japanese reports is the following:

(21)   [...] we are making every effort in further improving our customer services
        and enhancing competitiveness and profitability. I would like to assure you
        that we aim to make this year a year of achievement [...]. (MF/JAPAN4)

These phrasings are also much more indirect and cautious than the
ones we find in the U.S. reports. Indirectness is also a characteristic
that is typically attributed to the Japanese in intercultural communication studies (cf. e.g. Wierzbicka 1991: 73f; 93ff). The only one of the
four examined Japanese reports which shows more exposed (although
still far less, and compared to the U.S. reports more modest) competitive statements, is the report of UFJ Holdings. This is remarkable,
especially as UFJ/JAPAN is the 'worst' of the four examined Japanese
banks according to the Forbes ranking. The report starts with the
section "Who We Are", and here UFJ's place in Japan and in the
world is explicitly stated: "UFJ Holdings ranks 4th in Japan and 14th in
the world among banks in terms of assets. The UFJ Group is establishing a unique identity among Japan's financial service providers."
(UFJ/JAPAN1) Here again, however, the more modest style of the
Japanese reports shows by its use of "is establishing" as opposed to
"has established". Thus, the Japanese reports are characterized by a
more modest style than the U.S. reports, with less emphasis laid on the
idea of competition.

3. Concluding remarks

The starting point of my study has been to question if internationally operating companies – global players – choose global forms of communication or culturally specific ones. I have then concentrated on whether cultural differences are reflected in the contents and language of the annual reports of global players, based in different countries. The annual reports of U.S. and Japanese banks have been analysed with regard to formality, individual versus collective orientation, the status of employees, the influence of basic values, agency and reactivity as well as competitiveness.

The main findings are:

1. The language of the Japanese reports is more formal than the language of the U.S. reports: the language of the Japanese reports is syntactically more complex and the reports contain more passive constructions. The U.S. reports in contrast contain more colloquial expressions, more elisions and contractions, Christian names, questions, exclamations and direct addresses to the reader.

2. The language of the Japanese reports reflects a rather collective cultural orientation, while the language of the U.S. reports reveals a more individual orientation: the personal pronouns *I/my/me* are used more often in the U.S. reports than in the Japanese reports. The pronouns *we/our/us* are used more than four times more often than *I/my/me* in the Japanese reports than in the U.S. reports. In addition, in the U.S. reports, employees are portrayed more as individuals whereas they are portrayed more as a collective in the Japanese reports.

3. The U.S. reports are characterized by a more competitive language than the Japanese reports: more comparatives and superlatives are used and more words belonging to the world field 'competition' can be found.

The analysis has shown that despite globalization and the international orientation of the examined companies, the cultural origins of the companies are clearly reflected in the contents and language of their annual reports – whether intended or not. Some of the companies explicitly state their role as a global organization with local roots. Thus, Wells Fargo formulates a clear target for the future:

(22)   We want to be the premier provider of financial services in every one of our markets, and be known as one of America's great companies. (WF/USA2)

Other companies, in contrast, do not mention explicitly their local roots. They rather aim to have a purely global image. Nevertheless, language always 'leaks' information on the cultural background of a company and even a global player. While products and objectives (maximization of profits) can be classified as 'global', in the means and roads leading there, cultural specifics can still be found. The emphasis here is on 'still' and the question is, if cultural differences will remain and perhaps even become stronger as a counter-development to advancing globalization in business contexts, as hybridization theories predict. The opposed possibility would be that cultural differences will disappear more and more in the future and give way to a global business culture, as predicted by homogenization theories. A research project for the future would thus be to augment the synchronic study that has been presented in this paper by a diachronic dimension. The data should be gathered over a longer period of time, and the annual reports of different years should be compared with regard to their contents and language. Then we will know if cultural uniformity or cultural diversity will win in the global business context.

References

Beck, Ulrich 2002. *What is Globalization?* Oxford: Blackwell.
Bennett, Milton 1998. Intercultural Communication: A Current Perspective. In Bennett, Milton (ed.) *Basic Concepts of Intercultural Communication*. Yarmouth, Maine: Intercultural Press, 1-34.
Bolten, Jürgen / Dathe, Marion / Kirchmeyer, Susanne / Roennau, Marc / Witchalls, Peter / Ziebell-Drabo, Sabine 1996. Interkulturalität, Interlingualität und Standardisierung bei der Öffent-

lichkeitsarbeit von Unternehmen. Gezeigt an amerikanischen, britischen, deutschen, französischen und russischen Geschäftsberichten. In Kalverkämper, Hartwig / Baumann, Klaus-Dieter (eds) *Fachliche Textsorten: Komponenten – Relationen – Strategien*. Tübingen: Gunter Narr, 389-425.

Chuang, Rueyling 2000. Dialectics of Globalization and Localization. In Chen, Guo-Ming / Starosta, William (eds) *Communication in Global Society*, New York: Peter Lang, 19-33.

Crane, Diana 2002. Culture and Globalization: Theoretical Models and Emerging Trends. In Crane, Diana / Kawashima, Nobuko / Kawasaki, Ken'ichi (eds) *Global Culture – Media, Arts, Policy, and Globalization*. New York: Routledge, 1-25.

Denzin, Norman / Lincoln, Yvonna 1994. Introduction. In Denzin, Norman / Lincoln, Yvonna (eds) *Handbook of Qualitative Research*. Thousand Oaks, California: Sage Publications.

Dore, Ronald 2000. *Stock Market Capitalism: Welfare Capitalism: Japan and Germany versus the Anglo-Saxons*. Oxford: Oxford University Press.

Gibson, Robert 2000. *Intercultural Business Communication*. Berlin: Cornelsen.

Heringer, Hans-Jürgen 2004. *Interkulturelle Kommunikation*. Tübingen: UTB.

Hofstede, Geert 1991. *Cultures and Organizations*. London: McGraw Hill.

Holton, Robert 1998. *Globalization and the Nation-State*. London: MacMillan Press.

Kim, Young Yun 2000. Intercultural Personhood: An Integration of Eastern and Western Perspectives. In Samovar, Larry / Porter, Richard (eds) *Intercultural Communication: A Reader*. Belmont, CA: Wadsworth Publishing Company, 431-443.

Lahiff, James / Penrose, John 1997. *Business Communication: Strategies and Skills*. Upper Saddle River, New Jersey: Prentice Hall.

McDaniel, Edwin R. / Quasha, Steve 2000. The Communicative Aspects of Doing Business in Japan. In Samovar, Larry / Porter, Richard (eds) *Intercultural Communication: A Reader*. Belmont, CA: Wadsworth Publishing Company, 312-323.

Ramsey, Sheila 1998. Interactions between North Americans and Japanese: Considerations of Communication Style. In Bennett,

Milton (ed.) *Basic Concepts of Intercultural Communication.*
Yarmouth, Maine: Intercultural Press, 111-130.
Scollon, Ron / Wong Scollon, Suzanne [2]2001. *Intercultural Commun-
ication.* Malden, Mass.: Blackwell.
Seabrook, Jeremy 2004. Localizing Cultures. *Korea Herald* 13/1, 1-3.
Wawra, Daniela 2004. *Männer und Frauen im Job Interview: Eine
evolutionspsychologische Studie zu ihrem Sprachgebrauch im
Englischen.* Münster: LIT.
Weiss, Stephen / Stripp, William 1998. Negotiating with Foreign
Business Persons. In Niemeier, Susanne / Campbell, Charles /
Dirven, René (eds) *The Cultural Context in Business Com-
munications.* Amsterdam: Benjamins, 54-101.
Wierzbicka, Anna 1991. *Cross-Cultural Pragmatics: The Semantics
of Human Interaction.* New York: Mouton de Gruyter.
Wierzbicka, Anna 1997. *Understanding Cultures through their Key
Words.* Oxford: Oxford University Press.
Wood, Linda / Kroger, Rolf 2000. *Doing Discourse Analysis:
Methods for Studying Action in Talk and Text.* Thousand
Oaks, California: Sage Publications.

KUMIKO MURATA

The Discourses of Pro- and Anti-Whaling in British and Japanese News Editorials: a Comparative Cultural Perspective[1]

1. Introduction

This chapter explores newspaper discourse from cultural as well as linguistic, social, economic and historical perspectives in an exploration into its influence on cross-cultural understanding. In so doing, it investigates the discourse of whaling in both British and Japanese newspapers. Whaling is a particularly relevant topic in this connection since it is highly culture-specific, and the manner in which the issue is discussed could greatly influence readers' understanding, particularly in the case of readers with differing cultural assumptions, resulting in misunderstanding, frustration or incomprehension. The chapter therefore also aims to illustrate how different cultural assumptions and values could lead to differing discourses on the same issue.

Whaling has been one of the most politically controversial issues within the animal rights and environmental protection movements, particularly since the decision by the International Whaling Commission (IWC) to impose a moratorium on commercial whaling in 1982 and its enforcement from 1986 onwards. The issue has been discussed mainly from three different perspectives: 1) the protection of endangered species, 2) the immorality (cruelty) of catching whales or cetaceans in general, and 3) the economic consequences on the

---

1   The following institutions have kindly granted permissions to reproduce materials: The Independent Syndication for 'Harpooned', *The Independent*, 5 May 2000, Nihon Keizai Shimbun-sha for 'Hogei ronsoo wa kagaku to hoo no moto ni', *Nihon Keizai Shimbun (The Nihon Keizai Newspaper)*, 26 April 2002. Thanks are also due to John Bray, Michael Reiss, and Henry Widdowson for their invaluable comments on the earlier version of this paper. Any shortcomings that remain are the author's alone.

whaling communities and industries.[2] The fourth, less frequently discussed, but an equally important issue is the cultural impact of the ban on whaling on existing whaling communities.[3]

All these are intertwined and cannot be discussed separately. The tendency, however, is for the first two viewpoints to be taken up more vigorously by the anti-whaling nations, which include the USA, the UK, Australia, New Zealand, and many of the European nations. By contrast, the importance of the last two viewpoints has been emphasized mainly by the whaling nations, which include Japan and Norway.

In these circumstances, the use of the media has been one of the most effective means for pro- and anti-whaling nations to propagate their opinions, and thus it has extensively been exploited to voice views. This chapter focuses specifically on British and Japanese newspaper discourse on this issue. This is because Britain was one of the major whaling nations in the past and is now one of the leading anti-whaling nations, while Japan has a long history of coastal whaling and is now one of the major pro-whaling nations.[4] The chapter investigates the ways in which newspapers in two countries with opposing views deal with the same issue and how the differing views are represented in each country's press.

In doing so, the chapter also intends to reveal how a certain cultural assumption and value could be exerted and imposed on people with differing cultural backgrounds. The majority of British news reports and editorial pieces carry a strong anti-whaling tone and this in turn seems to be reflected in the opinions of many British people (see

---

2   This applies at least to the British press. The Japanese press takes slightly different stances, taking cultural implications more into consideration.

3   Recently the cultural side of whaling has been recognized in certain cases and some indigenous communities, including Alaskan Eskimos and Native Americans, have been exempt from the moratorium under the 'aboriginal subsistence scheme' (see IWC 2000 Annual Meeting Final Press Release and *The Independent*, 19 May 1999).

4   The coverage of the articles on whaling is far larger in the British press than in the Japanese press. Besides, the articles on whaling tend to appear intensively before international conferences such as the IWC Annual General Meeting and the Convention for the Protection of Endangered Species. New articles on whaling are constantly examined from both British and Japanese newspapers and added to the original data. In this sense, this research is still on-going.

Murata 2004)[5]. Considering that newspapers are a "powerful ideolo-gical and political force" (Gramsci 1985: 386), it is possible that the readers' opinions are subconsciously influenced by the opinion they receive from the newspapers they read regularly. This is particularly true for information on foreign affairs where the media are usually the main source of information.

On the other hand, it also has to be borne in mind that the relationship between the press and its influence on the readers may not be straightforward. It is possible that the press is prioritizing the readers' interests, since, in the case of whaling in the British press, most of its readers are anti-whaling and since "reporters select topics that are a matter of public interest" and "Whaling is one of those topics" (Brown 2001).[6] This may be particularly true in Britain where people's awareness of animal protection is significantly high and where many people belong to various animal welfare organizations.[7] This chapter therefore tries not to draw a hasty conclusion, but examines newspapers in the two nations with opposing views on the same issue of whaling in as fair a manner as possible. This is worthwhile since only a few of the many works on news discourse deal with the same issue across different languages and cultures. We shall first start with a discussion of the frameworks for the study.

---

5   According to a questionnaire administered to 22 British people (mostly academics, teachers and postgraduate students) on this issue by the author in 2000, 18 of them (81.8%) regarded themselves as anti-whaling, while the rest of them (4–18.2%) were neutral. By contrast, the same questionnaire administered to 30 Japanese, mainly postgraduate (and some undergraduate) students studying in Britain in the same year found 17 of them (56.7%) regarded themselves as 'neutral', while 9 of them (30.0%) were pro-whaling and the rest (4–13.3%), anti-whaling.

6   Thanks are due to Paul Brown, the environment correspondent of *The Guardian*, who kindly agreed to be interviewed by e-mail (26 January 2001), on which this quotation is based.

7   Thanks are extended to Michael Reiss, who pointed out this British tendency.

2. The study of news discourse from discourse analytic and cross-cultural perspectives

News discourse has been extensively studied in the past by commentators from media and sociolinguistic perspectives (Bell 1991, 1998), critical linguistics (Fowler *et al.* 1979; Trew 1979; Fowler 1991, 1996; Hodge/Kress 1993; Simpson 1993), critical linguistics and social theory (Fairclough 1989, 1992, 1995a, 1995b, 1998, 2000, 2003), and social cognition backgrounds (van Dijk 1988, 1993, 1996, 1998, 2001). Although their respective backgrounds and approaches to the analysis of news discourse vary, most of these scholars apply their approaches and theories to the examination of news media discourse, apart from Bell, who concentrates more on the analysis of the production and the reception of news.

On the basis of a detailed analysis of discrete structural or lexical features in news articles, they investigate sociopolitical implications and power structures in the text. Or rather, with certain clear prior political stances, they analyze media discourse to interpret it from their political viewpoints (van Dijk 1998, 2001), the mission being the betterment of society (Eagleton 1991; Widdowson 1995a, 1995b, 1996, 1998, 2000a). Together, they are classified as critical discourse analysts.

According to these perspectives, particularly those represented by Fairclough, Critical Discourse Analysis (CDA) bases its micro-level analysis of lexical items and syntactic structures on Hallidayan Systemic Functional Grammar (SFG) (Halliday 1994), utilizing the three functions of ideational, interpersonal and textual in its analysis (Fairclough 1989, 1992, 1995a; Fairclough/Wodak 1997; Titscher *et al.* 2000). These functions are observed in such grammatical features as modality (interpersonal function), and transitivity, including nominalization and passivity (ideational function). The textual function is realized by the overall textual organization, including the coherence and cohesion of the text.

Their approach, however, is not free from limitations, and it has been critically scrutinized mainly for the interpretation of the text on the basis of arbitrary and limited linguistic analysis. In particular, there has been strong criticism of the discrepancy between the analysis of limited lexical items and grammatical features, which are seemingly chosen arbitrarily to meet their specific interpretation, and the lack of objective supports (Stubbs 1994, 1996, 1997; Widdowson 1993, 1995a, 1995b, 1996, 1998, 2000a, 2000b, 2004, among others).[8]

Owing to such constructive criticism, however, CDA is evolving constantly (see Chouliaraki/Fairclough 1999) and the change can partly be observed in some of the works by critical discourse analysts, who, for example, have started incorporating analysis based on corpora in analysing their data to support their claim, albeit not necessarily comprehensively and satisfactorily enough (see for example Toolan 1997; Fairclough 2000).

Apart from the question of how and what to analyse, the inadequacy of attention to the production and the reception stages of news making has also been pointed out (Garrett/Bell 1998; van Dijk 1998; Fairclough 2000). Although Bell discusses the production stage of news making from the journalist's insider point of view and also examines an audience design (Bell 1984, 2000) and van Dijk discusses the importance of considering reception as well (van Dijk 1998), an integrated analysis of news texts has yet to emerge.

The existing works on CDA, albeit taking slightly different approaches respectively to the analysis of texts, share the same ideological stance in that they all seek to find evidence of the inequality of power in society through analysing pieces of texts. In so doing, Fairclough focuses specifically on the 'order of discourse', which is expressed in intertextuality, while van Dijk emphasizes the role of sociocognition as a basis for the formation of 'ideology', and Wodak points out the importance of the historicity of the news context as well in interpreting texts.

This chapter analyses similar news discourse materials to those examined by the above mentioned critical linguists and, specifically, critical discourse analysts, but differs from them in that it looks at the discourses of whaling specifically from a cultural perspective. It examines the wider cultural backgrounds, assumptions and values that influence the formulation of the two opposing discourses – in this case for and against whaling. It does this not only by examining a British

---

8   For the most recent and a persuasive critique of CDA from the perspective of language cognition, see O'Halloran (2003).

newspaper article on whaling but also by comparing and contrasting it with a similar article in a Japanese newspaper. The main objective of this chapter is to illustrate how differing reporting and the interpretation of the same issue are possible depending on different cultural views and values. However, this paper does not intend to promote either pro- or anti-whaling causes, rather, it illustrates how news reports could be partial if they do not pay attention to different cultural values and assumptions, and shows how the same text could be actualized as different discourses among people from differing cultural values and assumptions.

The chapter examines the ways in which anti- and pro-whaling opinions are put forward in the British and the Japanese press respectively, focusing mainly on the following features: 1) the use of specific lexis and syntactic structures, which include the choice and use of certain types of words and grammatical structures rather than others, 2) the use of various rhetorical devices, such as repetitions, rhetorical questions, and parallelism , and 3) text organization and the control of information, including the choice, inclusion and omission of specific information or opinions at the whole text level, since the limited coverage of certain opinions and information leads to a one-sided view (van Dijk 1996).[9] All of these are utilised to enhance either anti- or pro-whaling discourse.

In the following section, I shall briefly discuss the data and the methods for the analysis in the present study.

3. Data and methods

The chapter will analyse British and Japanese newspaper editorials on whaling in a detailed manner within a discourse analytic and cross-cultural perspective. Articles on whaling over the past 14 years (1988-2001) in *The Independent* newspaper were examined mainly in the CD-ROM version. By using the keyword search on *whaling*, 437 articles which contain the word *whaling* in *The Independent* are found

---

9   See van Dijk (1996) on the "patterns of access to discourse" (1996: 84).

during this period.[10] Some of these turned out to be irrelevant for the purpose of the present research, e.g. articles on travel, and were excluded from the present data, thus decreasing the total number of the articles to 173. A similar operation has found a total of 121 articles on whaling in *The Guardian* over the past five years (1997-2001).[11]

As for Japanese newspapers, articles from the past four years (1999-2002) in April, May, June, and July issues of the *Asahi, Yomiuri, Nihon Keizai* newspapers[12] were investigated respectively in their monthly small-printed complete versions (*shukusatu-ban*).[13] In addition, I also investigated the same newspapers in some important years for whaling, such as 1982, when the moratorium on commercial whaling was decided, 1986, the year when the moratorium was enforced, 1987, the year when the actual ban on whaling started, and 1992, the year when the initial five-year moratorium was reviewed. Thus, a total of eight years' articles were examined in the three major Japanese newspapers.

The four months were chosen as the most likely months for the news on whaling to appear in newspapers, since the international conferences related to whaling, such as the Convention on International Trade in Endangered Species (CITES) and the annual general

---

10   *The Independent* is one of the five broadsheet quality newspapers in Britain. Although relatively recently-founded (1986), by contrast with *The Times*, it has now been established as a center-left, liberal newspaper, which is devoted to environmental issues and widely supported by liberals and intellectuals. *The Times* has also a CD-ROM version, but because of its non-availability in the library the author had access to, the search was limited to the articles in *The Independent* and *The Guardian*.

11   The CD-ROM version of *The Guardian* lists articles on an annual basis, and it is therefore possible to limit the amount of information to be dealt with at one time, while *The Independent* lists the relevant information in the past 12 years (1988-1999) simultaneously. However, from 2000 onwards, *The Independent* also lists articles on an annual basis.

12   All these newspapers are members of *The Nihon Shinbun Kyokai (NSK-* The Japan Newspaper Publishers & Editors Association), which is established to "elevate ethical standards in reporting and protect the media's common interest" (<http://www.pressnet.or.jp/info>).

13   The lacking of CD-ROM versions for Japanese newspapers has made it impossible to carry out the automatic keyword search that was utilized in the British newspapers; thus, all searches had to be done manually. This has limited the period of time of the investigation to four years, shorter than the one investigated in the British newspapers.

meeting of the International Whaling Commission (IWC), were held during this period each year. All the articles related to whaling were investigated by checking the indices that contained the Japanese word *hogei* (whale-catching), or *kokusai hogei iinkai* (the International Whaling Commission).

Among these many articles, I have chosen an editorial comment from *The Independent* on the British side and an editorial comment from *Nihon Keizai Shimbun (The Nihon Keizai Newspaper)* on the Japanese side for the present detailed analysis[14]. The editorial comments have been chosen since different opinions are put forward more clearly in the commentary (van Dijk 1998: 21). The selection has been made after reading all the articles on whaling in all the newspapers listed above in both languages and judging that they are fair representatives of the other articles in the newspapers in the respective languages.

As for the procedures for the analysis, first, the British commentary was extensively analyzed, paying special attention to the aforementioned features, i.e., lexical items, grammatical structures and rhetorical devices. Apart from these micro-level detailed analyses, the text was also examined from the perspective of the control and organization of information at the whole text level, considering contextual information. Next, the Japanese commentary was analyzed, examining the same features as the British one in the same manner. After the analyses, both discourses were compared and contrasted for their similarities and differences and for the stances of anti- and pro-whaling. We shall now move on to the exemplification of the analyses.

---

14   *Nihon Keizai Shimbun* is one of the five broadsheet newspapers in Japan and is an equivalent of *The Financial Times*. It enjoys a circulation of more than three million (3,062,860) per day as of November 2001.

4. The discourses of whaling: a detailed analysis of British and Japanese newspaper editorials

4.1. The anti-whaling discourse

On the whole the British editorial examined in this study is strongly characterized by an anti-whaling tone. We shall first examine the ways in which this tone is formulated.

4.1.1. An example from a British news editorial [Text 1]

Text 1 (see Appendix for the full text) is an editorial, and compared to news reports, the specific attitude or opinion of the editor on the topic is therefore put forward more clearly (van Dijk 1998: 21). This is achieved mainly by the use of loaded and provocative words, specific grammatical features, some rhetorical devices, and by the selection of information. We shall now examine these characteristics one by one, starting with the choice of lexis.

4.1.2. Choice of lexis

It is clear by examining the text that the words that convey negative connotations have been explicitly and intentionally used in the text.

To list some of the examples, *kill* and its cognates such as *killing* and *killed*[15] are used frequently where a more neutral word

---

15   The word *killing* is also used in IWC official documents, particularly, when they talk about "whaling killing methods", for example, when they discuss the act itself and where there is no alternative word. Otherwise, when they describe the "Aboriginal Subsistence Whaling", they tend not to use the word *kill* unless necessary. However, the following extract is from the IWC official paper, entitled "The IWC, Scientific Permits and Japan", in which the term *killing* is used ambivalently as can be seen in the following:
"A major area of discussion in recent years has been the issuing of permits by member states for the killing of whales for scientific purposes". (Scientific Permits and Japan, The IWC, 2000)
Here, *killing* seems to have been used, reflecting the content of the discussion. The term must have been actually used in the preceding discussion; thus, the exact term seems to have been used here. Otherwise, this term could have

catch, take, or even *hunt* suffices (see lines 1, 8, 9 of Text 1 in the Appendix)[16]. Or even stronger words such as *slaughter* in "its extended programme of slaughter" (line 6), *corpses* in "50 times as many corpses as another" (lines 11-12) and *exterminating* in "the effect of exterminating the world's population of several species of whale" (lines 17-19) to describe the similar situation, are utilised, where more neutral words can be used. In particular, the use of *exterminating* in this situation is not factually correct if the writer is reporting or knows the exact situation of the current world's whale population (see IWC 2000, Final Press Release). The use of these loaded words reminds us of what van Dijk (1988) states regarding "standard strategies to promote the persuasive process for assertions"; that is, "Facts are better represented and memorized if they involve or arouse strong emotions" (1988: 85).

   Apart from the use of these loaded, provocative words, evaluative or judgmental words, which reflect the author's strong opposition towards the actions of the Japanese as a whaling nation, are used frequently. These examples are *provocative* in a "provocative [decision]" (line 2), *pretend* in "Japan pretends that—" (line 6), *strange* in a "strange kind of science" and a "strange kind of research" (lines 7 & 9). While the first example is a direct evaluation (negative) of the Japanese decision itself, suggesting that Japan's decision will *enrage* people concerned, the second presupposes that Japan is lying since the term *pretend* is classified as "non-factive presupposition", which presupposes "what follows is not true" (Yule 1996: 29) and the actor's intention of deceiving (the *Shorter Oxford English Dictionary*, SOED for short). The third example also indirectly shows the author's

---

        been replaced by the terms such as *catching* or *taking*, which are generally
        used in the official reports of the IWC in describing the same situation.
16   Thanks are due to Barbara Seidlhofer, who has pointed out that the use of
        killing is factually correct in that currently all these catches for scientific
        research are killed, and thus, the use of *catching* or *taking* is an example of
        euphemism. Paul Brown of *The Guardian* also states that the use of "kill is
        short and accurate", whereas the use of "harvest", for example, is "euphe-
        mism" (Paul Brown, Environment Correspondent, *The Guardian*, my
        interview by e-mail, 26 January 2001). However, considering the fact that
        with other animals in a similar situation (cf. for example, foxes, cod, etc.), the
        term *killing* is hardly used (let alone *slaughter*), I still regard this as an
        example of manipulative use of the language.

suspicion of the Japanese action, repeatedly using the word *strange* in describing the nature of Japan's scientific research; and thus, cynically suggesting again that Japan is a liar.[17]

A similar attitude of the author also appears in the use of other words such as *sinister* in "those sinister laboratories" (line 12), *manipulating* in "Manipulating whale DNA" (line 13). The combined use of the terms *sinister* and *laboratories* and the additional use of the term *manipulating* suggest that Japan is engaging in some kind of ominous act, which has an air of *conspiracy* and leads to *disaster* (SOED, LDOCE).

The use of all these expressions strengthens the stereotypes of the Japanese as inscrutable, hypocritical, brutal, and dangerous (in the sense that they can plot anything evil secretly). It strangely echoes the use of the lexis that describes the behaviour of the Japanese during the past war (see Hammond/Stirner 1997; Owens 1997; also BBC 2 documentaries broadcast on the 4th and 5th December 2000). Here, the author intentionally or unintentionally appears to be reinventing the war time image of the Japanese as *brutal, cruel,* and *evil*.[18] These images are also enhanced by the use of certain rhetorical devices, to which I will turn later.[19]

---

17   This is also enhanced by the use of rhetorical devices, which will be discussed in more detail later (see the following section).

18   Kalland/Moeran (1992) points out that:
     "there is a considerable amount of racial prejudice against the Japanese, who also suffer from the cultural imperialism of such countries as the United States and Great Britain. Not only this, but such prejudice is further linked to two other factors – the part played by Japan during the Second World War, and the present imbalance of trade between Japan and most western nations" (1992: 14).
     van Dijk (1996) also points out the use of such terms as 'invasion' and 'army' in describing immigration in the British Press involves the image of 'Immigration is War' (1996: 98, see also van Dijk 1988 and Trew 1979).

19   See also van Dijk (1988), in which he states that "lexical and semantic implications may involve evaluations based on the point of view and the ideology of the reporter" (1988: 71), in discussing the "implications in News Discourse".

4.1.3. Choice of grammatical structures: modality & transitivity

Apart from the explicit use of the specific lexical items mentioned above, some grammatical structures are used to emphasise Japan as an agent of this deplorable action. For example, by the use of transitivity, it is made clear that Japan, whose action the author is accusing of 'hypocrisy', is given a prominent position as an agent of the various brutal actions and hypocrisy. The examples of which can be seen in the following:

> THE JAPANESE decision to start killing sperm whales ... is a provocative one. (lines 1-2)
> Japan pretends that .... (line 6)

In these two sentences, the agents are clearly indicated by being placed in the subject position, although in the first example nominalization is used instead of Japan itself as a subject/agent. It is however clearly entailed that Japan is the agent of this action of "[starting] killing", since the decision was made by Japan; thus, its responsibility for these deplorable actions seems to be emphasized.

The author's determination to promote an anti-whaling cause is also evident in the use of the modal *must* in the final sentence of Text 1, "They must not be allowed to succeed", which shows the high modality of 'obligation' (Halliday 1994).[20]

4.1.3. Rhetorical devices

In addition to the use of specific lexis and grammatical structure mentioned above, various rhetorical devices, including repetitions, rhetorical questions, and parallelism, have also been used to strengthen the argument against whaling.

An example of parallelism can be seen in the second paragraph of the text as follows:

---

20   Van Dijk (1998) also points out that "the recommendation speech act", such as "should not repeat the mistake" is a "standard part of editorials and op-ed articles" and further states as follows:
      "after an analysis of what is wrong (an opinion), it is concluded what should be done, which semantically is also an opinion, and pragmatically an act of advice or recommendation" (1998: 51).

It is a strange kind of science that requires ...
It is a strange kind of research that requires ...

Here, by repeating the same sentence patterns, the author emphasises his/her strong suspicion or doubt about the nature of 'scientific research' that Japan is conducting.

This is further strengthened by the following rhetorical question, "Why does scientific research into one species need five or 50 times as many corpses as another?", which voices direct disagreement with Japan's conduct of 'scientific research'. Of course, here the implied meaning is, 'it doesn't', and accordingly, that 'it is not "scientific research"'.

This is followed by two more questions, showing strong doubt about Japan's action. The first question, "What are they doing in those sinister laboratories in the suburbs of Tokyo?" strengthens the image of Japan as 'inscrutable' and 'plotting', supported also by the use of the term *sinister* as discussed earlier. The second question, "Manipulating whale DNA in order to produce Pokemon?" also strengthens the same line of image, but with more cynicism and mockery.

Moreover, this question, referring to Pokemon, which is an internationally popular children's game invented by a Japanese company, appears to be an attempt to combine Japan's economic image and inscrutability, which describes it as a nation which does anything to achieve an economic objective, even an immoral act. This reference to Pokemon, however, is irrelevant, since it is obvious that one does not need to "*manipulate* whale DNA in order to produce Pokemon". Thus, by using this expression the author implies that Japan is engaging in an unnecessary act, i.e. whaling research, and that it is all the more regrettable because it is killing precious whales for this 'trivial and unnecessary' research. If we follow his/her logic, we can tell that here the author is looking at Japan cynically from an economic perspective.

The rhetorical devices used in the second paragraph are neither logically nor stylistically refined, but just emotionally and sensationally used. Furthermore, they are used together with the heavily loaded and provocative lexis mentioned in the previous section to enhance the effect of persuasion.

In the third paragraph of Text 1, in the form of replying to the rhetorical questions in the second paragraph, the author states clearly his/her opinion that what the Japanese are conducting under the name of "scientific research" is in fact a "simple experiment". That is to say, the purpose of the Japanese experiment is just to see the "effect of exterminating" whales. This is apparently untrue, thus, flouting the *Maxim of Quality* (Grice 1975), and is irrelevant. What the author is implying, then, is that the Japanese authorities are conducting the 'unthinkable', that is, 'lying'. Accordingly, it implicates that what Japan is doing is, in fact, "commercial whaling". This can be illustratively summarized as follows:

```
     The plausible explanation                    Unthinkable possibility

        (Japan is conducting)                              ⇓
          simple experiment
                 ⇓            ⇒ NOT scientific    ⇒      lying
        to see the effect of        research
        exterminating the whales                           ⇓
                 ⇓                                       TRUTH
              unlikely                                     ⇓
    apparently untrue (Grice 1975) ⇒  TRUTH ⇒    commercial whaling
                                                    in disguise
```

Thus, the mounted image of Japan as hypocrite and inscrutable, being projected indirectly in the second paragraph is voiced clearly in the third paragraph, by using more straightforward vocabulary indicating these features. However, here again a slightly indirect and cynical strategy is simultaneously used, activating implicatures as shown above. We shall now examine the overall organization and the control of information of the same text.

4.1.4. Overall organization and control of the information and opinions in the text

It is clear from the text that this is a highly opinionated comment, which is understandable since it is an editorial commentary not just a report. The article, thus, is written for a certain cause, and to persuade readers with the conviction of the actor (van Dijk 1998). According to van Dijk, one of the 'standard strategies to promote persuasive process for assertions' in news discourse is to "provide information that also has an attitudinal and emotional dimensions [sic]" (1988: 85), which exactly seems to be the case with the present text. Furthermore, the text does not include any information about the historical background to the drastic decrease of the world whale population in which Britain as a whaling nation also played a part. In fact, for many years Britain and the USA, together with Norway, Japan and the USSR, had been major whaling nations and contributed a great deal to the present drastic decrease of whale population (Tatou 1985; Morita 1994; Taife 2000). Nor does it include any explanation from the pro-whaling side, that is, in this case, the Japanese side. It does not tell what the Japanese authorities are saying about this 'scientific research'. Nor does it include reports issued by the IWC's Scientific Committee, which describe the present status of the world whale population.

This control of the information by the omission of facts can also be explained by what van Dijk says in one of the subcategories of his "standard strategies to promote the persuasive process for assertions" (1988: 84) as shown in the following:

(C) 2. The truthfulness of events is enhanced when opinions of different backgrounds or ideologies are quoted about such events, but in general those who are ideologically close will be given primary attention as possible sources of opinions (van Dijk 1988: 85).

Thus, this commentary, because of the lack of the fair representation of the both anti- and pro-whaling voices, together with the effect of the use of other devices discussed earlier, has resulted in a very subjective and emotional tone. The same message could have been communicated more effectively, using a more rational tone, which Western discourse prizes. That is, one of the characteristics of Europeans in comparison with non-Europeans listed by Pennycook (1998), quoting Blaut (1993), is "rationality/intellect", while non-Europeans are characterized with "irrationality/emotion/instinct" (1998: 50). Similarly, Said (1978), in discussing "the principal dogmas of Orientalism" states that the West is described as "rational, developed, humane, superior", and the Orient, "aberrant, undeveloped, inferior" (1978: 300). According to these characteristics, here in this text the stereotypical images of Japan as *barbaric, irrational* were described by reversed stereotypical strategies of *irrationality* and *emotion* by the West (see also Scollon/Scollon 1995/2001).

To summarize, I have examined in this section the ways in which anti-whaling messages are formulated and promoted in a British editorial commentary from *The Independent*. It has been observed that varieties of emotive and loaded lexis, various grammatical structures, including modality and transitivity, rhetorical devices, and the control and organization of information are utilized to strengthen an anti-whaling stance. However, it also has to be borne in mind that this discussion illustrates only one type of anti-whaling discourse: news reports as distinct from editorials may use different strategies to influence readers and different newspapers may deal with the same issue in a different manner.[21]

We shall now examine a Japanese editorial on the same issue of whaling to compare and contrast it with the British one.

4.2. The pro-whaling discourse

Compared to the British editorial, the Japanese editorial is characterized by a pro-whaling tone, or rather, most of the articles on whaling in the Japanese press are written on the assumption that whaling is a legitimate activity rather than actively promoting pro-whaling causes. The strategies they usually take when commenting on the criticism made by the anti-whaling nations is to discuss *rationally*, supported by scientific evidence. This is mainly achieved by the provision of *factual* information on the state of whales and whaling and by non-use of emotive language as illustrated in the following text (Text 2).

---

21   As stated earlier, I have mainly examined articles in *The Guardian* and *The Independent*, because of the availability of past articles on whaling on CD-ROM. But more importantly, these two broadsheet newspapers – liberal, left and centre-left - also pay great attention to environmental issues, featuring them weekly.

4.2.1. An example from a Japanese editorial [Text 2]

Text 2 (see Appendix for the full text) is a news editorial appeared in the *Nihon Keizai Shimbun* – a Japanese equivalent to *The Financial Times*. Compared to the English text analyzed above, no emotive or loaded expressions are used in this editorial. Nor is there any direct accusatory tone towards the anti-whaling nations in the whole text. Thus, on the surface it appears neutral. Yet it is clear that the author is taking it for granted that whaling should be allowed. This is achieved by contrasting the rationalistic action taken by the whaling nations represented by Japan with the irrationality shown by the anti-whaling nations. It is also demonstrated by quoting the statements made by Japanese officials that Japan should take a rational strategy in claiming the revival of commercial whaling.

The text starts with factual information on the opening of the Annual General Meeting. The second sentence, by contrast, indirectly asserts the relevance of the whaling nations' claim by inserting the information that the claim by the whaling nations is based on "the discussion at the scientific committee". Thus, in this seemingly neutral first paragraph, the writer tacitly implies that the whaling nations' claim is more rational because it is supported by evidence.

This tone becomes more evident in the next paragraph. After clearly stating in the first sentence that "whaling has been discussed emotionally and irrationally", in the following sentence, the direct relationship between the provision of scientific results and *rationality* is stated. That is, here, disregarding scientific results is equated with irrationality, which, in turn, implies that giving scientific evidence as Japan does is rational. The irrationality of some anti-whaling nations is further emphasized in the following sentence, which describes their unwillingness to accept the scientific evidence.

The next paragraph (Paragraph 3) is important in that it shows more accurate pictures of the present populations of the different species of whales. This shows a stark contrast to the preceding English article, which does not give details of the existing numbers of different whale populations, but uses vague and general expressions such as 'exterminating' (Text 1, line 18) in describing a general status of whale populations. This gives readers an impression that all species of whales are in equal danger of extinction.

There is, however, one similarity with the British text, which is how the decrease of whale population is described. That is, it is described as if the decrease is a natural phenomenon as is the case with the British text. However, this time it is expressed by the use of an intransitive verb *heru* ('decrease') as follows:

> *Kotai-suu*   *ga* ------------------- *heri* -------.   (Tex 2, lines 16-17)
> Species-number TOP   has decreased (and)
> (The number of the species has decreased and ---------.)

In Japanese sentence construction, the use of the intransitive verb *heru* here is a natural means of describing the state of the decreased number of whales. Or rather, it would be very unnatural to use, for example, a passive construction *heras-are-ru* (reduce PSV) to emphasize the victimization of whales by human agents. The same tone can be achieved by just adding an agent to the original intransitive structure, i.e. *heru*, by the use of an agent marker *niyotte*. That is to say, the writer could easily have stated the names of the past major whaling nations, including Britain, USA, and could have emphasized the role the current anti-whaling nations played in the drastic decrease of certain species of whales. However, on the surface the sentence does not show any human involvement in the decrease of whale populations.

Paragraph 4 describes the Revised Management Procedure (RMP), which is recommended by the scientific committee, but which the anti-whaling nations requested to be modified in the form of the Revised Management Scheme (RMS). Here, by showing that the anti-whaling nations are not complying with the recommendation by the scientific committee, the author implies that they are not rational. The author's pro-whaling stance is also shown in the following expression:

> *hogei   saikai   wa   okurete-iru*
> [commercial] whaling revival TOP delayed has been
> (The revival of [commercial] whaling has been delayed.)

Here, it is assumed that the resumption of commercial whaling is matter-of-fact by using the expression *okurete-iru* (has been delayed), with the implication that it has to be resumed. Thus, without using any overt expressions to promote whaling or attack the anti-whaling nations' attitudes towards the whaling nations, the author tacitly indicates his/her pro-whaling stance.

In the next paragraph, the author puts her/himself clearly on the pro-whaling side by introducing a compromise solution which suggests that *we* (= the Japanese – elliptical in the original Japanese version) should give up whaling if *we* were regarded as the villains of the world as follows:

> *--hogei   saikai   wo   akirame-tewa   dooka.*
> [commercial] whaling   revival   TOP   give up   why don't we
> ('Why don't we give up [the idea of] the revival of [commercial] whaling?')

> *Konna   koe   mo   kikoe-te-kuru ga ---*
> such   voice   also   hear   (reach)   but ---
> ([We] also hear such a voice, but ---)

meaning that:

> ([We] also hear such a voice as 'Why don't [we] give up the idea of the revival of commercial whaling', but ---] or [Some even suggest that [we] should give up the idea of the revival of [commercial] whaling ---])

Here, by using the inclusive *we* implicitly, the author makes it clear that s/he is on the readers', i.e., Japanese people's, side and that *we* are for the revival of commercial whaling. By implicitly using *we* to represent the Japanese nation, here, the author is assuming that all Japanese have the same opinion, since even those who are stating different opinions are described as offering a compromise solution. This is illustrated in the use of the conditional "*areru kurai nara* --- (if [we] were regarded ---)" and the expression "*akirameru* (give up)", which implies that giving up the idea of the revival of commercial whaling is against their will. The author then justifies the effort to resume commercial whaling by relating it to the 'sustainable' use of biological and marine resources. It is again made clear that Japan should 'discuss logically and objectively' on the basis of scientific data in persuading the anti-whaling nations. Thus, again Japan's strategy is clearly stated, and the author simultaneously uses the same strategy to persuade readers. Accordingly, this editorial shows a stark contrast to the British editorial shown earlier. The whole article is written on the assumption that "commercial whaling" should be allowed and that this is matter-of-fact.

To summarize, the Japanese news discourse on whaling examined here is characterized by little loaded or provocative lexis and the non-use of direct accusation. In addition, a limited amount of background information on the results of scientific research is given where possible to support its statements or comments. This makes the article sound relatively objective, compared with the British news discourse on whaling, which lacks factual information to support its claim and is loaded with provocative, negatively evaluative lexis and rhetorical devices. Although Japanese discourse patterns in general are often described as *illogical*, *indirect* or *vague* in comparison with English discourse patterns (see, for example, Hinds 1983, 1990),[22] the discourse pattern used in the Japanese editorial in this limited analysis contradicts these stereotypes. By contrast, the English discourse on whaling in this analysis is characterized by irrationality, inconsistency and emotion, from which it usually tries to dissociate itself as can be seen in the following Said's (1978) descriptions of "Westerners" and "Arab-Orientals":

> ---the former [Westerners] are (in no particular order) rational, peaceful, liberal, logical, capable of holding real values, without natural suspicion; the latter [Arab-Orientals] are none of these things (1978: 49).

(see also Pennycook 1998; Scollon/Scollon 1995/2001).

5. Concluding remarks on the news discourse of whaling

This chapter has explored the news discourse of whaling in both the British and the Japanese editorial commentaries. It has investigated how anti- and pro-whaling discourses have been formulated by the use of seemingly opposing strategies in the respective nations' news articles. The British editorial has been shown to utilize anti-whaling

---

22   Kubota (1998) and Maynard (1998) also point out that this is often the case when discussing the characteristics of Japanese written discourse patterns.

campaigners' voices directly in its text, which are emotionally charged and whose arguments are not necessarily coherent or supported by evidence. By contrast, the Japanese editorial appears to be more objective and neutral since its text consists of the description of facts, albeit mostly on the basis of the Japanese government's press releases (see Joseph 1993, Shibayama 1997 and Freeman 2000).[23] The paper has also illustrated how the control of the amount and the content of the information could lead to the manipulation of the understanding of the text. Both commentaries tend to impart the information that favors the stance of the respective nations on the issue of whaling. That is, the stance of the editorials on this issue and that of the respective governments seem to coincide with each other.

Thus, the chapter has clearly illustrated how different ideologies on the same issue are promoted, using different strategies in respective newspapers. Although further investigation is needed, it has great implications for the understanding of the influence of the media on readers with different cultural assumptions and values on the same issue, and simultaneously on the cross-cultural understanding and misunderstanding of the people exposed to different discourses.

Abbreviations used

FTR   future
PST   past
PSV   passive
TOP   topic marking particle

---

23   Joseph (1993), commenting on the Japanese press, states as follows:
      "[The readers] will read a short, factual account: no explanation, no background, no context, no comment. Facts, facts, facts. [...] if the Japanese government's spokesman [sic] says that Japan won everything it wanted at the negotiating table, then that is what will appear in print, even if the rest of the world press is writing editorials on Japan's humiliation at the hands of its fellow summiteers. The press in Japan is not there to agitate, to rock the beat (1993: 118)."
      Although this view is slightly exaggerated, the similar observations are also made by other commentators (see Shibayama 1997, Freeman 2000).

References

Bell, Allan 1984. Language Style As Audience Design. *Language in Society* 13, 145-204.

Bell, Allan 1991. *The Language of News Media.* Oxford: Blackwell.

Bell, Allan 1998. The Discourse Structures of News Stories. In Bell, Allan / Garrett, Peter (eds) *Approaches to Media Discourse.* Oxford: Blackwell, 64-104.

Bell, Allan 2000. Language as Dialogue: Bakhtin and Sociolinguistic Theory. Keynote Speech delivered at the Sociolinguistics Symposium 2000 at the University of the West of England, 29 April 2000.

Blaut, James M. 1993. *The Colonizer's Model of the World.* New York: The Guildford Press.

Brown, Paul 2001. An interview by the author by e-mail. 26 January 2001.

Chouliaraki, Lilie / Fairclough, Norman 1999. *Discourse in Late Modernity: Rethinking Critical Discourse Analysis.* Edinburgh: Edinburgh University Press.

Eagleton, Terry 1991. *Ideology: An Introduction.* London: Verso.

Fairclough, Norman 1989. *Language and Power.* London: Longman

Fairclough, orNman 1992. *Discourse and Social Change.* Cambridge: Polity.

Fairclough, Norman 1995a. *Critical Discourse Analysis.* London: Longman.

Fairclough, Norman 1995b. *Media Discourse.* London: Arnold.

Fairclough, Norman 1998. Political Discourse in the Media: Analytical Framework. In Bell, Allan / Garrett, Peter (eds) *Approaches to Media Discourse.* Oxford: Blackwell, 142-162.

Fairclough, Norman 2000. *New Labour, New Language?* London: Routledge.

Fairclough, Norman 2003. *Analysing Discourse.* London/New York: Routledge.

Fairclough, Norman / Wodak, Ruth 1997. Critical Discourse Analysis. In van Dijk, Teun A. (ed.) *Discourse as Social Interaction.* London: Sage, 258-284.

Fowler, Roger 1991. *Language in the News: Discourse and Ideology in the Press.* London: Routledge.

Fowler, Roger 1996. On Critical Linguistics. In Caldas-Coulthard, Carmen Rosa / Coulthard, Malcolm (eds) *Texts and Practices.* London: Routledge, 3-14.

Fowler, Roger / Hodge, Robert / Kress, Gunther / Trew, Tony (eds) *Language and Control.* London: Routledge & Kegan Paul.

Freeman, Laurie Anne 2000. *Closing the Shop: Information Cartels and Japan's Mass Media.* Princeton, New Jersey: Princeton University Press.

Garrett, Peter / Bell, Allan 1998. Media and Discourse: A Critical Overview. In Bell, Allan / Garrett, Peter (eds) *Approaches to Media Discourse.* Oxford: Blackwell, 1-20.

Gramsci, Antonio 1985. *Selections from Cultural Writings.* Harvard: Harvard University Press.

Grice, Herbert Paul 1975. Logic and Conversation. In Cole, Peter / Morgan, Jerry L. (eds) *Syntax and Semantics, Vol.3: Speech Acts.* New York: Academic Press, 41-58.

Halliday, Michael A. K. [2]1994. *An Introduction to Functional Grammar.* London: Arnold.

Hammond, Phil / Stirner, Paul 1997. Fear and Loathing in the British Press. In Hammond, Phil (ed.) *Cultural Difference, Media Memories: Anglo-American Images of Japan.* London: Cassell, 85-114.

Hinds, John 1983. Contrastive Rhetoric: Japanese and English. *Text* 3/2, 183-195.

Hinds, John 1990. Inductive, Deductive, Quasi-inductive: Expository Writing in Japanese, Korean, Chinese and Thai. In Connor, Ulla / Johns, Ann M. (eds) *Coherence in Writing: Research and Pedagogical Perspectives.* Alexandria, Virginia: TESOL, 87-109.

Hodge, Robert / Kress, Gunther [2]1993. *Language as Ideology.* London: Routledge and Kegan Paul.

IWC 2000. *Final Press Release, 2000 Annual Meeting.* Online at <http://ourworld.compuserve.com/homepages/iwcoffice/conven tion.htm>.

IWC 2000. *The IWC, Scientific Permits and Japan.*

Joseph, Joe 1993. *The Japanese.* London: Viking.

Kalland, Arne / Moeran, Brian 1992. *Japanese Whaling: End of an Era?* London: Curzon Press.

Kubota, Ryoko 1998. Ideologies of English in Japan. *World Englishes* 7/3, 295-306.

Maynard, Senko K. 1998. *Principles of Japanese Discourse: A Handbook.* Cambridge: Cambridge University Press.

Morita, Katsuaki 1994. *kujira to hogei no bunnka-shi.* Nagoya: Nagoya University Press.

Murata, Kumiko 2004. News Discourse and Its Influence on Readers. *The Journal of Asia TEFL* 1/1, 243-266.

The Nihon Simbun Kyokai (The Japan Newspaper Publishers & Editors Association) <http://www.pressnet.or.jp/info>.

O'Halloran, Kieran 2003. *Critical Discourse Analysis and Language Cognition.* Edinburgh: Edinburgh University Press.

Owens, Gina 1997. The Making of the Yellow Peril: Pre-war Western Views of Japan. In Hammond, Phil (ed.) *Cultural Difference, Media Memories: Anglo-American Images of Japan.* London: Cassell, 25-47.

Pennycook, Alastair 1998. *English and the Discourses of Colonialism.* London: Routledge.

Said, Edward W. 1978. *Orientalism: Western Conceptions of the Orient.* London: Penguin.

Scollon, Ron / Scollon, Suzanne Wong [2]2001. *Intercultural Communication.* Oxford: Blackwell.

Shibayama, Tetsuya 1997. *Nihon-gata media shisutem no hookai:21-seiki jyaanarizumu no shinka-ron.* Tokyo: Kashiwa Shoboo.

Simpson, Paul 1993. *Language, Ideology and Point of View.* London: Routledge.

Stubbs, Michael 1994. Grammar, Text, and Ideology: Computer-assisted Methods in the Linguistics of Representation. *Applied Linguistics.* 15/2, 201-23.

Stubbs, Michael 1996. *Texts and Corpus Analysis.* Oxford: Blackwell.

Stubbs, Michael 1997. Whorf's Children: Critical Comments on Critical Discourse Analysis (CDA). In Ryan, A. / Wray, A. (eds), *Evolving Models of Language.* Multilingual Matters, 100-116.

Taife, Dennis 2000. Balance of Nature with Regard to Whales. *Media Releases,* <www.jp-whaling-assn.com/media_releases>.

Tatou, Seitoku 1985. *hogei no rekishi to shiryo.* Tokyo: Suisan-sha.

Titscher, Stefan / Meyer, Michael / Wodak, Ruth / Vetter, Eva 2000. *Methods of Text and Discourse Analysis.* London: Sage.
Toolan, Michael 1997. What is Critical Discourse Analysis and Why are People Saying such Terrible Things about it? *Language and Literature* 6/2, 83-103.
Trew, Tony 1979. Theory and Ideology at Work. In Fowler *et al.*, 94-116.
van Dijk, Teun A. 1988. *News as Discourse.* Hillsdale, New Jersey: Lawrence Erlbaum Associates.
van Dijk, Teun A. 1993. *Elite Discourse and Racism.* London: Sage.
van Dijk, Teun A. 1996. Discourse, Power and Access. In Caldas-Coulthard, Carmen Rosa / Coulthard, Malcolm (eds) *Texts and Practices.* London: Routledge, 84-104.
van Dijk, Teun A. 1998. Opinions and Ideologies in the Press. In Bell, Allan / Garrett, Peter (eds) *Approaches to Media Discourse.* Oxford: Blackwell, 21-63.
van Dijk, Teun A. 2001. Critical Discourse Analysis. In Schiffrin, Deborah / Tannen, Deborah / Hamilton, Heidi E. (eds) *The Handbook of Discourse Analysis.* Oxford: Blackwell, 352-371.
Widdowson, H. G. 1993. Representations in Prose: Setting the Scene. In Sinclair, John M. / Hoey, Michael / Fox, Gwyneth (eds.) *Techniques of Description: Spoken and Written Discourse.* London: Routledge, 143-153.
Widdowson, Henry G. 1995a. Discourse Analysis: a Critical View. *Language and Literature.* 4/3, 157-172.
Widdowson, Henry G. 1995b. Norman Fairclough: Discourse and Social Change. *Applied Linguistics* 16/4, 510-516.
Widdowson, Henry G. 1996. Reply to Fairclough: Discourse and Interpretation: Conjectures and Refutations. *Language and Literature* 5/1, 57- 69.
Widdowson, Henry G. 1998. Review Article: The Theory and Practice of Critical Discourse Analysis. *Applied Linguistics* 19/1, 136-151.
Widdowson, Henry G. 2000a. On the Limitations of Linguistics Applied. *Applied Linguistics* 21/1, 3-25.
Widdowson, Henry G. 2000b. Critical Practices: on Representation and the Interpretation of Text. In Sarangi, Srikant / Coulthard, Malcolm (eds) *Discourse and Social Life.* Harlow: Longman, 155-169.

Widdowson, Henry G. 2004. *Text, Context, Pretext. Critical Issues in Discourse Analysis.* Oxford: Blackwell.
Yule, George 1996. *Pragmatics.* Oxford: Oxford University Press.

Dictionaries quoted

Longman Dictionary of Contemporary English (LDOCE)
Shorter Oxford English Dictionary (SOED)

Newspapers and TV broadcast quoted

BBC 2, *Horror in The East: Turning Against the West.* 4, 5 December 2000.
The Independent, 19 May 1999; 5 May 2000.
Nihon Keizai Shimbun, 26 April 2002.

Appendix

[Text 1]

Harpoone

THE JAPANESE decision to start killing sperm whales and Bryde's whales, which we reported exclusively yesterday, is a provocative one. It comes just weeks after the attempt by Japan and Norway to reopen the trade in whale-meat was rejected by the Convention on International Trade in Endangered Species.

Japan pretends that its extended programme of slaughter is for the purposes of scientific research. It is a strange kind of science that requires so many specimens to be killed. It is a strange kind of research that requires – in addition to the 500 minke already killed each year – 50 Bryde's whales a year and 10 sperm whales. Why does scientific research into one species need five or 50 times as many corpses as another? What are they doing in those sinister laboratories in the suburbs of Tokyo? Manipulating whale DNA in order to produce Pokemon?

Sadly, the only plausible explanation, apart from the unthinkable possibility that the Japanese authorities may be lying, is that they are engaged in a very simple experiment. They want to see what the effect of exterminateing the world's population of several species of whale would be. They must not be allowed to succeed. (*The Independent*, 5 May 2000)

[Text 2]

Hogei ronsoo wa kagaku to hoo no moto ni

1. kokusai hogei iinnkai (IWC) no dai-54-kai nenji-sookai ga katte no hogei-kichi shimonoseki-shi de 25-nichi kara hajimat-ta.

2. kagaku-iin-kai deno giron wo moto ni shoogyoo hogei no saikai wo mezasu nihon nado no shuchoo to eizoku-teki na hogei kinshi kaiiki (sanctuary) no saranaru kakudai wo motomeru han-hogei-koku tono ronsoo wa marude kamiatte orazu setten wa mie-nai.

3. 1982-nen ni IWC de shoogyoo hogei no ichiji-teishi (moratorium) ga kimatte irai hogei mondai dewa goori-sei wo kaku kanjoo-teki na ronsoo ga tuzuite ki-ta. 4. sono gen'in wa seiji-teki na suloogan ga senkoo shite kagaku-teki na ketsuron to kokusai- jooyaku de hoshoo-sare-ta kenri ga keishi sare te kita kara ni hokanaranai. 5. IWC kamei 43-ka-koku no yaku hanbun wo shimeru han-hogei-koku no naka niwa don'nani kujira ga fue-temo ittoo-taritomo hokaku wa yurusa-nai koto wo kokusaku to suru seifu mo aru.

6. IWC no kanri taishoo ni natte-iru 13-shu no oogata-kujira no uchi shironagasu-kujira ya semi-kujira wa 100-nen mae ni kurabete kotai-suu ga juu-bun no ichi toka hyaku-bun no ichi ni heri imadani kaifuku ga okurete-iru ga minku-kujira no yoo ni 100-nen mae no 10-bai ni fue-te-iru shu mo aru.

7. IWC no kagaku- iin-kai wa kono kagaku-teki na ketsu-ron wo moto ni kotai-suu ga fue-te-iru kujira ni kagiri hokaku toosuu wo kiwamete genmitsu ni seigen shite shigen no honntai wo herasazu jizoku-teki ni hogei wo okonau kaitei kanri-hooshiki(RMP) wo kansei-sase sookai ni kankoku shita. 8. han-hogei-koku wa kono ue ni kanshi-seido nado wo fukumu kaitei kanri-seido (RMS) wo mookeru-yoo motomete kooshoo wa nankoo hogei saikai wa okure-te iru.

9. sekai no waru-mono ni sareru kurai nara hogei saikai wo akirame tewa dooka. 10. kon'na koe mo kikoe-te-kuru ga koto wa chikyuu no zaisan de aru kaiyoo wo kashikoi riyoo (wise use) to seibutsu shigen no jizoku-teki na katsuyoo ni kakawaru mondai de aru. 11. nihon wa kagaku-teki na choosa kekka to kokusai-hoo ni rikkyaku shita reisei na ron wo doodoo to tenkai-shi

shinrai-sei no takai shigen-kanri no shikumi wo kakuritsu-shi kakkoku wo settoku suru shika nai.

12. han-hogei wo kakage-te-kita sekai-teki na kankyoo dantai sekai-shizen-hogo-kikin nihon-jimu-sho (WWF Japan) ga 'kibishii shigen-kanri no moto dewa hogei saikai wo hitei-shikire-nai' to hyomei-shita koto wa kataku shikotta hogei han-hogei no fumoo no tairitsu ga ikubun yurumu kikkake ni naru kamo shirenai. (*Nihon Keizai Shimbun*, 26 April 2002)

[Text 2']

Whaling should be discussed on the basis of science and law

1. The 54th Annual General Meeting of the International Whaling Commission (IWC) opened on the 25th (of April) in Shimonoseki, one of the former whaling bases.

2. The argument between the whaling nations, including Japan, which are aiming at the revival of commercial whaling on the basis of the discussion by the scientific committee of the IWC, and the anti-whaling nations, which are aiming at the expansion of the permanent whale sanctuaries, seem to be far from agreement.

3. Whaling has been discussed emotionally and irrationally ever since the moratorium on commercial whaling was agreed by the IWC in 1982. 4. This is because scientific results and the rights guaranteed by the international agreement have been neglected, due to political slogans. 5. Among the anti-whaling nations, which include about half of the 43 IWC member nations, there are even some which claim that their governments' policy would not allow a single whale to be caught even if there is an increase of the whale population.

6. Among the 13 great species of whales which are controlled by the IWC Regulations, there are species such as Blue whales and Right whales, whose numbers have decreased to one-tenths and one-hundredth of the levels of one hundred years ago and are very slow to recover; there are, however, other species such as Minke whales, whose number has increased tenfold compared to 100 years ago.

7. The scientific committee of the IWC has completed the Revised Management Procedure (RMP) on the basis of scientific results, which enables sustainable catching of the whales whose number is on the increase, without reducing the total whale resource by strictly regulating the number of whale catches, and has submitted the suggestion to the general meeting. 8. Following this, the anti-whaling nations have requested that the Revised Management Scheme (RMS), which includes the monitoring system, should

be introduced and thus the negotiation has not been progressing smoothly and the revival of commercial whaling has been delayed. 9. Some even suggest that we should give up the idea of the revival of commercial whaling if we are to be regarded as the villains of the world by insisting on it. 10. This issue, however, is connected to the wise use of marine resources, which is the treasure of the Earth, and the sustainable use of biological resources. 11. Japan should persuade other nations by discussing logically and objectively on the basis of scientific results and international law and establish a highly credible resource management system.

12. The Japanese branch of WWF, which is a global environmental protection group, and which is anti-whaling, has recently stated , 'The revival of commercial whaling cannot be rejected under a strict resource control system'. This might become a trigger to weaken the strong, barren disagreement between the whaling and anti-whaling nations. (*The Nihon Keizai Newspaper*, 26 April 2002, my translation)

MARIA CRISTINA PAGANONI

Recontextualizing Language:
Indian Activists and the Recasting of English

1. Study Design

This paper moves from an interest in no global thinking and aims to investigate the construction of its discourse in contrast with the dominant discourses and practices of economic globalization. It regards the discourse of the Indian no global movement as an emblematic example of this ideological polarization and focuses on the voices of four renowned women activists – Medha Patkar, Sunita Narain, Arundhati Roy and Vandana Shiva. The paper then argues that what these intellectuals perform is an act of recontextualization, by which they invent a subversive 'denaturalizing' discourse that intends to debunk the assumptions of neo-liberal globalization. In order to do so, they appropriate English and articulate their discourse in ways that are functional to their ideology and communicative needs. The research investigates the most salient topics, discursive strategies and linguistic means through which this articulation is realized, under-lining, at the same time, the subversive ideological implications with which no global discourse is encoded.

To this purpose a selection of texts by these Indian activists has been analyzed. The texts, which all appeared over the period from 1997 to 2004, include speeches, interviews, articles, essays and non-fiction books, while the topics all have to do with a number of pressing political, economic and social issues related to globalization: free-market economy and free trade, the internationalization of capital and business, modernizing development paradigms, the protection of the environment and local cultures. At the ideational level, the textual selection is characterised by great topical variety and features different modes of discourse and communicative genres. At the interpersonal level, the emphasis is placed on the translation of specialized abstract knowledge into concise popularized versions of it, which are felt to be more accessible to non-specialized readers. The overall tenor of discourse, therefore, gravitates towards marked empathy and inter-activity with a transnational, non-specialized audience/readership, involved with the no global debate and engaged in cross-cultural communication in hitherto unprecedented ways, for example the annual international gathering of activists at the World Social Forum.

1.1. Methodology

This paper is imbued with the awareness of the relationship between power and discourse that is the central concern of critical discourse analysis. It is structured around the notion of discourse as a form of social struggle and emphasises its ability to bring about change in contemporary 'knowledge-based' and, therefore, 'discourse-driven' societies (Fairclough 2001: 239) by advancing alternative social representations. The insights gained from text analysis are interpreted in the light of social research (Titscher *et al.* 2000; Fairclough 2003), scrutinizing the interplay of the opposite ideologies of globalization that circulate within the order of discourse of new capitalism (Fairclough 1999). Secondly, it relies on the notion that "ideologies typically organize people and society in polarized terms" (van Dijk 2003) and that the oppositional representations of the self (ingroup) and the other (outgroup) are constructed in their discourses through a careful orchestration of topics, rhetorical strategies and linguistic means. Thirdly, it sees no global discourse as a reaction against the discourses and practices of economic globalization, whose "ideology can be seen to 'naturalize' capitalism into a self-protecting, order-maintaining dominant ideology with ambitions of world-wide applications" (Bargiela-Chiappini 2000: 6).

For the detailed interpretation of linguistic data, this paper borrows a number of well-established analytical categories from various key approaches of discourse analysis (Titscher *et al.* 2000) and from theoretical and empirical works dealing with the impact of ideology on representation and discursivity (van Dijk 1998, 2003; Reisigl/Wodak 2001). The argumentative strategies, the rhetorical forms and the linguistic means picked out in the analysis are found to be functional to the construction of new representations and to emphasize the ingroup/outgroup polarization that is typical of ideological discourse. Metaphor is discussed both as a cognitive pattern (Lakoff/Johnson 1989; Judge 1990, 1991) informing the logic of argumentation and as a rhetorical device controlling the global coherence of texts. Metaphor is often linked to irony, and both are interpreted as strategies that intend to reject Western assumptions and to propound alternative paradigms, conveying at the same time some of the sense of displacement typical of the postcolonial experience.

Finally, since recontextualization invests textuality at all levels – generic, semantic, lexical, grammatical and pragmatic – the research draws on other important theoretical contributions. Genre analysis (Bathia 1993, 2000) stresses that generic forms are dynamic constructs that serve changing socio-cognitive needs. Cross-cultural pragmatics (Scollon/Scollon 1995; Wierzbicka 2003) frames this instance of recontextualization as an intercultural phenomenon that taps into the cultural universe of India and involves the confrontation of Indian viewpoints, assumptions and values, as they appear encoded in language, with Anglo-cultural scripts.

2. The appropriation of English

The recontextualization of the Western discourses of globalization could not take place without the appropriation of English, a process originating from colonial times whose endpoint is somehow emblematized by the ways Indian activists use language. Since they have inherited English scripts, they possess the necessary knowledge to borrow the discourses of contemporary history, politics, economics and science from the Western intellectual tradition and to recontextualize them with subversive aims into the praxis of no global activism. Quite significantly, the semantics of such a recontextualization revolves around the postcolonial *topos* of the struggle for reappropriation of material and symbolic goods. In fact, several occurrences of words which are borrowed from the lexicon of possession (i.e. 'monopoly', 'ownership', 'privatization', 'property', 'resources') and that of active resistance (i.e. 'battle', 'boycott', 'fight', 'struggle', 'war') reconfigure metaphorically the act of appropriation as (non-violent) warfare.

Given the emphasis of the *topos* of reappropriation, it is no wonder that the 'struggle over language' (Fairclough 2000: 147) should be a controlling metaphor in the textual selection.

> I think it's vital to de-professionalize the public debate on matters that vitally affect the lives of ordinary people. It's time to snatch our futures back from the 'experts'. Time to ask in ordinary language, the public question and to demand, in ordinary language, the public answer (Roy 2001: 24).

The quotation thematizes "the struggle [...] between legitimizing discourses that validate the dominant Western ideology of free-market economy and subversive discourses that question or reject it" (Bargiela-Chiappini 2000: 2). "To snatch our futures back" seems possible only by reframing the public debate more democratically ("in ordinary language"), along a bottom-up perspective which works against the top-down approach of political and corporate power and generates a rhetoric adverse to the technicalities and euphemisms of technocrats.

3. Questioning globalization

Though they make use of that same standard variety of English usually associated with a "globalized English language culture" (Hasnain 2003: 11), control over global communication and symbolic dominance, Indian activists question the hegemonic narratives which represent economic globalization "as the self-evident contemporary order" (Bargiela-Chiappini 2000: 5). Thus, they rewrite, or recontextualize, the discourses of neo-liberal globalization.

Recontextualization has been defined as "a relationship between different (networks of) social practices – a matter of how elements of one social practice are appropriated by, relocated in the context of, another" (Fairclough 2003: 222). In other words, it amounts to the complex set of processes by which a discourse draws upon, incorporates and dialogues with other discourses.

> Social actors within any practice produce representations of other practices, as well as ('reflexive') representations of their own practice, in the course of their activity within the practice. They 'recontextualize' other practices – that is, they incorporate them into their own practice, and different social actors will represent them differently according to how they are positioned within the practice (Fairclough 2001: 232-233).

The act of recontextualization affects all levels of textuality, as it entails a radical rethinking of the ideational and interpersonal functions of discourse. In what follows, the most recurrent and effective discursive strategies and linguistic means that are deployed in the construction of no global discourse will be discussed analytically.

3.1. The disembedding of genres

Revisiting the repertoire of genres from an oppositional ideological position generates a different perspective on historical, political, scientific and economic discourses, a perspective which postcolonial criticism commonly calls the 'postcolonial gaze'. The espousal of this 'gaze' works through constant and detailed references to Indian culture, politics and history. It decentres privileged viewpoints, imperial and neo-imperial, and reformulates Western discourses according to the cultural frames of the Other, a socio-cognitive effort which takes place in several ways.

First, standard topics in the discourses of global capitalism – free trade, global flows, international politics, development paradigms – are exposed as self-validating and deterministic narratives of progress. In this way, the ideology and practices of the powerful are identified, named and put at a distance as "their ideas, their version of history, their wars, their weapons, their notion of inevitability" (Roy 2004a: 77).

Secondly, an alternative viewpoint is introduced into the polarized arena of ideological confrontation, a viewpoint whose purpose is to displace preconceived assumptions and mystifying narratives. The following quotation, for example, thematizes the exclusion of Indian

people from actual politics, mentioning the disastrous social consequences of dam construction, carried out by India's central government regardless of the uprooting of entire rural communities and of
the damages to the ecosystem.

> Millions of people have been dispossessed by 'development' projects. In the
> past 55 years, Big Dams alone have displaced between 33 million and 55
> million people in India. They have no recourse to justice (Roy 2004b).

This juxtaposition of viewpoints and paradigms heavily affects the
lives of real people.

> The Basmati seed, the aromatic rice from India, which we have grown for
> centuries right in my valley is being claimed as novel invention by RiceTec.
> Neem, which we have used for millennia for pest control, for medicine, which
> is documented in every one of our texts, which my grandmother and mother
> have used for everyday functions in the home, for protecting grain, for
> protecting silks and woollens, for pest control, is treated as invention held by
> Grace, the chemical company (Shiva 1998).

Vandana Shiva is a Western-trained physicist turned into environ-
mentalist activist in close touch with Indian traditions. Consistent with
her ecological and feminist critique of Western science, her narrative
intertwines the affective tones of a matrilinear micro-history ("right in
my valley", "my grandmother and mother") with a grammar of
expropriation which denounces the theft of local resources perpetrated
by multinational corporations through passivization ("the Basmati
seed is being claimed"/ "neem is treated as invention") and the
explicit mention of the agent ("Rice Tec.", "Grace").

Environmental discourse, too, has to be readapted to India's
specificity to avoid the pitfalls of exoticism. For rural people in India
who make a living out of farming and tree cutting, the environment is
"much more than pretty trees and tigers" (Narain 2002). Again, the
Other's viewpoint surfaces in the lecture given by Medha Patkar in the
San Francisco Bay Area in June 2003, in which she asked her
audience

> to visualize a hypothetical scenario wherein the decision to submerge the state
> of California or even the city of San Francisco would be taken by someone
> sitting in Washington DC, without informing the local population or consider-
> ing the impact (Patkar 2003).

Thirdly, the technicalities of historical, political, economic and scientific issues are simplified in favour of higher accessibility to knowledge. As has been seen, a recurrent *topos* in the textual selection is the effort to invent an effective kind of "ordinary language" (Roy 2001: 24) and to deploy it as a demystifying tool. Generic conventions and linguistic resources are therefore manipulated to express new communicative purposes, guided by the need to interact with the greatest possible number of ordinary people. It is no wonder, for example, that the books included in the selection – either collections of speeches and essays, as in Roy's case or, again, concise study cases, as for Shiva's *Biopiracy* and *Water Wars* – should eschew academic lengthiness and verbiage to employ the popularized registers of informative exposition.

> In most indigenous communities, collective water rights and management were the key for water conservation and harvesting. By creating rules and limits on water use, collective water management ensured sustainability and equity. With the advent of globalization, however, community control of water is being eroded and private exploitation of water is taking hold. Water-renewing traditional systems are now decaying. In a study of 152 villages using traditional water-harvesting systems, 79 were dry or polluted (Shiva 2002b: 12).

Just as human activities overlap in real life, so are discourses hybridized and disciplinary boundaries crossed whenever needed. Significantly, another recurrent *topos* is the involvement of economics in all areas of life, again a way of deconstructing the objectiveness of narratives which appear to be uncritically supportive of Western assumptions and vested interests: "Economic policies are not neutral, but ideological – and populist resistance to them is a rational response" (Stiglitz 2003). For example, the interdependence between economics and ecology is constantly stressed, as when Shiva describes the environmental consequences of the use of oil:

> While climate change is creating more flood and cyclones, it is also aggravating drought and heat waves. There is either too much water or too little, and both extremes pose a threat to survival. The most dramatic impact of global warming is the melting of ice caps and glaciers. Although there have always been changes in climate, the scientific community and most governments agree that the present crisis of melting glaciers and polar ice caps

is ecologically connected to the fossil fuel economy and atmospheric pollution (Shiva 2002b: 47).

We can see that the recontextualization, or disembedding, of genres, implies that conventional rhetorical forms are modified to give space to new representations, to convey other meanings and to serve different communicative purposes.

3.2. Argumentation

Since they shape the discursive construction of ideology, cognitive frames have a deep impact on argumentative strategies. No global activists claim that the cognitive pattern which controls the discourses of economic globalization is the so-called 'switch' metaphor, a metaphor which works by implying that there can be only one solution to a problem.

> Many advocated policies are explicitly designed to 'switch' individuals from one condition to the other in each case (e.g. from 'on' to 'off') – from an undesirable condition to a desirable one. And once such a transition has been accomplished, the object is to prevent backsliding into the undesirable condition (Judge 1990).

The 'switch' metaphor betrays "an inability to see the world in terms other than those that the establishment has set out for you" (Roy 2004a: 17). Either you are with 'us' or with 'them', you either manage natural resources or you waste them, your country is either developed or underdeveloped. It follows that the rhetoric of globalization bases its argumentation on "easy dualisms" (Bargiela-Chiappini 2000: 3) and, consequently, that more complex concepts (i.e. sustainable development) do not appear to be seriously taken into account.

On the contrary, the argumentative strategies at work in no global discourse usually adopt "exposition and an explanatory logic" rather than "a logic of appearance" (Fairclough 2003: 95). This is how, for example, after an episode of hunger strike against dam construction, Roy comments upon the redoubtable notion of the "price of progress", an issue clearly informed by the alleged inevitability of binary logic:

That phrase cleverly frames the whole argument as one between those who are pro-development versus those who are anti-development – and suggests the inevitability of the choice you have to make: pro-development, what else? It slyly suggests that movements like the NBA are antiquated and absurdly anti-electricity or anti-irrigation. This of course is nonsense (Roy 2004a: 6).

No global discourse, instead, forges a number of redefinitions that purport to falsify the logic of global capitalism. Redefinitions are statements that establish new relations of equivalence and difference (Fairclough 2003: 88-89). They are often anticipated by questions. Questions make explicit the incessant dynamics of intellectual processes out of which alternative paradigms are seen to be emerging; they are also a strategy to emphasize the interpersonal quality of no-global discourse, constructing it as attentively engaged in dialogue with a local or global community.

Can life be made? Can life be owned? (Shiva 1997: 19).

What is globalization? Who is it for? What is it going to do to a country like India, in which social inequality has been institutionalized in the caste system for centuries? [...] Is globalization about 'eradication of world poverty', or is it a mutant variety of colonialism, remote controlled and digitally operated? (Roy 2001: 13-14).

What then will India's environment look like in the 21st century? [...] The question is: Can we replicate what the West did in one generation? Will India's rivers and cities begin to breathe by the 2020s? (Narain 2002).

Who does water belong to? Is it private property or a commons? What kind of rights do or should people have? What are the rights of the state? What are the rights of corporations and commercial interests? (Shiva 2002b: 19).

Redefinitions are formulated through strings of equivalences and differences in which signifiers collide and meanings expand unexpectedly, reaching out to other cultural universes.

Science is an expression of human creativity, both individual and collective. Since creativity has diverse expressions, I see science as a pluralistic enterprise that refers to different 'ways of knowing'. For me, it is not restricted to modern Western science, but includes the knowledge systems of diverse cultures in different periods of history (Shiva 1997: 8).

> A farmer is not a low-paid tractor driver, that's a modern definition of what a
> farmer is. The real definition of a farmer is a person who relates to the land
> and relates to the seed and keeps it for future generations, keeps renewing it,
> fertility (Shiva 1998).

> The corporate media doesn't just support the neo-liberal project. It is the neo-
> liberal project (Roy 2004b).

We learn, therefore, that science is "a pluralistic enterprise [...] not
restricted to modern Western science", a farmer is "a person who
relates to the land [...] and not a low-paid tractor", and the corporate
media the neo-liberal project itself.

The articulation of the meanings of 'globalization' appears to be
highly divergent from conventional assumptions:

> Globalization has occurred in three waves. The first wave was the
> colonization of America, Africa, Asia and Australia by European powers over
> 1,500 years. The second imposed a Western idea of 'development' during the
> postcolonial era of the past five decades. The third wave of globalization [...]
> is known as the era of 'free trade' (Shiva 1997: 103-104).

> It's not war, it's not genocide, it's not ethnic cleansing, it's not a famine or an
> epidemic. On the face of it, it's just ordinary, day-to-day business. It lacks the
> drama, the large-format, epic magnificence of war or genocide or famine. It's
> dull in comparison. It makes bad TV. It has to do with boring things like jobs,
> money, water supply, electricity, irrigation. But it also has to do with a
> process of barbaric dispossession on a scale that has few parallels in history.
> You may have guessed by now that I'm talking about the modern version of
> globalization (Roy 2001: 13).

As can be seen, the first quotation resorts to a relation of equivalence:
three co-hyponyms ('colonialism', 'development' and 'free trade') are
found and then exploited to represent globalization diachronically as a
multi-faceted and recurrent event. In the second quotation, instead, the
polysemy of the word first generates a rhetoric of difference and
denial that is linguistically realized by a sequence of short paratactic
clauses. Then, corporate globalization, apparently 'ordinary' and 'dull'
in comparison with old colonialism, is in fact redefined as "a process
of barbaric dispossession on a scale that has few parallels in history".

3.3. Semantic redetermination

At the semantic and lexical levels, recontextualization is above all performed by the act of renaming, which signals the effort towards symbolic and material reappropriation. The main linguistic devices through which renaming is realised are the resemanticization of words and phrases and the borrowing of words from Indian languages.

Semantic redetermination works with the help of the rhetorical forms of irony and metaphor. The ironic inversion of meaning and the imaginative quality of metaphoric language manage to denaturalise assumptions and, thus, to reshape an alternative mind framework (Lakoff/Johnson 1989; Judge 1990, 1991).

Irony deconstructs the hypocrisy of language "in this new age of Empire, when nothing is as it appears to be" (Roy 2004b).

> So now we know. Pigs are horses. Girls are boys. War is peace (Roy 2001: 127).

It shows that 'freedom' means in fact 'erosion of freedom', 'development' 'plunder', 'relocation' 'uprooting', 'bioprospecting' 'biopiracy', 'democracy' 'neo-liberal capitalism', and 'structural adjustment program' 'the dismantling of democracy', while 'free market' democracies are exposed as manufactured commodities "just like any other mass market product – soap, switches or sliced bread" (Roy 2004a: 43).

Metaphoric language is applied to disrupt conventional meanings and alludes, besides, to the traumas experienced in periods of old and new colonialism.

> Patents are a replay of colonization (Shiva 1998).

> Large dams are twins of polluting industry and industrial agriculture (Paget-Clarke 2003).

> As for corporate globalization's glittering ambassadors – Enron, Bechtel, WorldCom, Arthur Andersen – where were they last year, and where are they now? (Roy 2004a: 74).
> Debating Imperialism is a bit like debating the pros and cons of rape. What can we say? That we really miss it? (Roy 2004b).

Amenable to the ironic use of metaphor is also the irreverent appropriation of icons and symbols taken from familiar Anglo cultural scripts, especially popular culture (e.g. turkeys and Thanksgiving, Mickey Mouse, soft drinks like Pepsi and Cola). Turkeys, the canonical dish at Thanksgiving – the annual U.S. holiday commemorating the Pilgrim Fathers – are made to stand for the hoards of the world's dispossessed that are too often victims of warfare. George Bush is compared to Mickey Mouse: "The people of the world do not need to choose between a Malevolent Mickey Mouse and the Mad Mullahs". (Roy 2004a: 77) In February 2003 when Sunita Narain disclosed to the public the appalling amount of pesticides retraceable in Indian soft drinks, a journalist, inspired by pop singer Britney Spears' song *The Joy of Cola*, humorously described the findings as "the joy of toxic cola" (Kennedy 2003). The kaleidoscopic list of references to the West's imaginary includes classic fairy tales, Lewis Carroll's *Alice*, French fries, Mc Donald's, Miss World, cowboys, and even notorious criminals such as Jack the Ripper and the Boston Strangler.

Borrowing from local languages is a form of lexical recontextualization, as well as a referential strategy, which should be inscribed and understood within the positive emphasis given to Indian culture in the construction of discourse. Words and quotations from Indian languages appear embedded in the English code as insets that do not detract from the overall textual comprehensibility (a main difference from Anglo-Indian fiction which plays, instead, with pidginisation and creolisation). Rather, borrowing signals the effort to reframe issues according to non-Western values, for example communal values which are typical of Indian collectivistic perspectives (Gudykunst 1998).

> *Navdanya* (nine seeds) or *barnaja* (twelve crops) are examples of highly productive systems of mixed farming or polycultures based on diversity, yielding more than any monoculture can. Unfortunately they are disappearing [...]. In addition, their outputs are diverse – providing all of the nutritional inputs a family needs (Shiva 1997: 124).

Elsewhere, borrowing emphasizes historically-shaped keywords such as *ahimsa* – "India's greatest gift to the world: non-violent resistance" (Roy 2001: 7) – and *satyagraha*[1], which derive from Gandhi's

---

1   *Ahimsa* means non-violence and *satyagraha* struggle for truth. In the quotation that follows *swadeshi* is the spirit of regeneration, and *swaraj* self-

struggle and the years of the nationalist movement. After becoming part of the national heritage, they now circulate with new political meanings.

> By pluralizing our options, we simultaneously create the tools for reconstruction and resistance. In India, a massive movement – the Seed *Satyagraha* – has emerged over the past few years in response to the threats of recolonization [...]. According to Gandhi, no tyranny can enslave a people who consider it immoral to obey laws that are unjust. [...] In the free trade era, the rural communities of India are redefining nonviolence and freedom by reinventing the concepts of *swadeshi, swaraj,* and *satyagraha.* (Shiva 2002b: 124-125)

In spite of the historical, cultural and linguistic references to their country whose values are often represented as superior to Western ones, Indian activists try to avoid idealizing their culture. In fact, they write about India with disenchanted affection and keep asking "some very uncomfortable questions about our values and traditions, our vision for the future, our responsibilities as citizens" (Roy 2001: 12).

3.4. Personalization

A defining trait of no global ideology is to stress responsibility and agency at each societal level, from grassroots communities to government institutions. This approach stands in clear contrast to "some of the linguistic features of the 'naturalising' discourses of economic globalization" which tend to work "as agent-effacing devices instigating consensus when embedded in a style purporting objectivity and factuality" (Bargiela-Chiappini 2000: 5). It follows that the dominant ideology tends to represent global processes as apparently shaped by impersonal factors and to discard human responsibility.

The site of the World Economic Forum (WEF) is quite emblematic in this regard. Annually held in Davos, Switzerland, the WEF gathers chief executives of rich governments, multinational corporations, the World Bank, the International Monetary Fund and the World Trade Organization in order to outline the global economic agenda,

---

rule. Like *navdanja* and *barnaja*, they are all Sanskrit words that are now present in all modern Indian languages.

and is commonly regarded as a defence of power politics and corporate economics. For example, in its mission statement the WEF site mentions the creation of "partnerships to shape global, regional and industry agendas", claims to be "the creative force shaping global, regional and industry strategies", "the catalyst of choice", and stresses that

> In a world characterized by complexity, fragility and ever greater synchronicity, strategic insights cannot be passively acquired (<http://www.weforum.org>).

Very general nominalizations, such as "choice", "complexity", "fragility" and "synchronicity", used to represent the contemporary world, offer an ambiguous description of historical processes, economic practices are vaguely alluded to in the noun phrase "global, regional and industry agenda", while "strategic insights" lack any references to specific social actors. Global capitalism would seem to be constructed as an impersonal agentive entity endowed with irresistible power.

Opting for a demystifying expository logic, no global discourse prefers forms of concrete rather than abstract representation of events (Fairclough 2003: 137-138), thus emphasising responsibility through human agency. To this purpose it resorts to personalization, that is, to the presentation of actors as individuals, communities or institutions that are capable of agency.

> Global corporations are taking full advantage of the demand for clean water, a demand which has resulted from environmental pollution. Even though the corporations tap clean water resources in nonindustrialized, unpolluted regions, they refer to their bottling practice as 'manufacture' of water. (Shiva 2002b: 101)

Though corporate propaganda reportedly attempts to turn 'tapping' into 'manufacturing', Shiva's explanation of water wars describes material processes ("tap clean water", "bottling practice") unambiguously and does not delete agency ("global corporations", "the corporations").

Personalization frames the issues of no global discourse in explicitly political terms, partially disambiguating the assumption that globalization is "'something out there', […] an objective, unstoppable and value-free process" (Bargiela-Chiappini 2000: 1).

India's politicians have not shown any serious interest in controlling pollution. (Narain 2002)

The World Bank only looks at returns on investment. It drags countries into borrowing. (Paget-Clarke 2003)

On the one hand, personalization is deployed to denounce those categories and institutions responsible for the ongoing expropriation of India's resources; on the other, it works as a strategy of ideological re-enforcement, positively emphasizing the resources and the strength of common people.

The adivasis [*i.e. indigenous people*] are asserting their primary rights to water and demanding that the Coca-Cola restore the environment, pay compensation, dose down the factory and quit the country. (Shiva 2002a)

3.5. Use of pronouns

At the grammatical level, the use of pronouns is a referential strategy "by which one constructs and represents social actors: for example, ingroups and outgroups" (Resigl/Wodak 2001: 45).

In no global discourse, 'they' are clearly the outgroup supporting neo-liberal globalization. 'They' are the anonymous bureaucrats of the World Bank, the International Monetary Fund, the World Trade Organization and the multinational corporations.

They are squeezing out loan re-payments by killing water systems and killing people who depend on them. (Paget-Clarke 2003)

With water privatization they demand a full price from the people. (Shiva 2002a)

'They' can also refer to the superpowers with their imperial mythologies and deterministic narrative of progress, as well as to Indian politicians whenever, forgetting their electoral mandate, they enforce unfair policies and thus distance themselves from their own people.

However, the dichotomy between self- and other-representation, characteristically pitching 'us' against 'them', is more subtly articulated in the textual selection, arguably in the attempt to overcome the binary logic of Empire. While in imperial rhetoric 'we' excludes and expunges the Other, in no global discourse 'we' – being interpersonal and dialogic – inclusively embraces "the people of the world", a new transnational civil society that is being shaped by globalizing practices. 'We' sometimes refers to the Indian population – "we, like the rest of the world, have adopted the Western industrial-urban model" (Narain 2002). Finally, 'we' may signify one of the grassroots movements themselves, e g. the Narmada Bachao Andolan (or "Save the Narmada Movement") – "we have proved that we have worked for the people and for the social-environmental impact of these dangerous projects" (Jain 2004).

In all instances the pronoun 'we' refers to a collective agent and describes the engagement of ordinary citizens at a local (i.e. India) or a global level.

> It is for this reason that we need a plan like the Ganga Action Plan, which is now being replicated for other rivers in the country (Narain 2002).

> We all have to challenge these forces, conveying to them that we who resist are not just in nooks and corners of the world. We are together (Jensen 2004).

The pragmatic implications of 'we' aim to underline the effort of no global activists to construct democratic, pluralistic and aggregating practices of participation. Its inclusive meaning, moreover, voices an empathic reaction against the individualism which has informed the Western notion of the self (Scollon/Scollon 1995), a critique which is deeply felt in Indian culture, shaped as it is by a worldview traditionally placing great emphasis on community resources and values.

4. Conclusions

The analysis of the textual selection summarizes the ideological premises of the discourses of neo-liberal globalization, illustrates how no global discourse constructs itself as an oppositional ideology and looks at the several levels of recontextualization performed by Indian activists.

First, in their power struggle over language, they appropriate English while de-hegemonizing it. Secondly, drawing from the domains of history, politics, economics and science, they engender alternative representations to neo-liberal politics and economics and invent a radical counterdiscourse – rooted in Indian history and culture – that, in accepting the Other's perspectives, encodes innovative meanings. In the attempt to democratize knowledge, they recombine well-established genres into more accessible rhetorical constructs. Besides, since "development issues cannot be contained within national boundaries" (Jensen 2004) and local and global practices are affected by mutual interdependence, they address an unprecedented global audience/readership.

Thirdly, they try to overcome the strictures of binary logic, articulating discourse as an incessant interrogation and a sequence of redefinitions and resorting to metaphor and irony in order to expand meaning. They focus especially on the polysemous keyword 'globalization', providing iconoclastic redefinitions of it from their position as postcolonial subjects.

Finally, they creatively exploit linguistic means, such as semantic redetermination, borrowing from local languages, person-alization and use of pronouns, to denaturalize dominant economic assumptions, emphasize the uniqueness of Indian culture, denounce the practices of neo-liberal globalization and encourage the collective action of common people.

So far, arguably, in spite of India's contradictions, their recon-textualization of discourse within a framework of global participation and with respect for diversity has sounded energetic enough to work as an effective form of social action and to look ahead to global democracy. It is upon such vitality that the vision of another possible world – the motto of the World Social Forum – may be constructed.

References

Bargiela-Chiappini, Francesca 2000. *The Discourses of Economic Globalization: A First Analysis.* Unpublished manuscript, at <www.cddc.vt.edu/host/lnc/papers/Bargiela.globalization.doc>.
Bathia, Vijay K. 1993. *Analysing Genre: Language Use in Professional Settings.* London and New York: Longman.
Bathia, Vijay K. 2000. Genres in Conflict. In Trosborg, Anna (ed.) *Analysing Professional Genres.* Amsterdam: John Benjamins, 145-161.
Fairclough, Norman 1999. Global Capitalism and Critical Awareness of Language. *Language Awareness* 8/2, 71-83.
Fairclough, Norman 2000. Language and Neo-liberalism. *Discourse and Society* 11/2, 147-148.
Fairclough, Norman 2001. The Dialectics of Discourse. *Textus* 14/2, 231-242.
Fairclough, Norman 2003. *Analysing Discourse: Text Analysis for Social Research.* London: Routledge.
Gudykunst, William B. 1998. Individualistic and Collectivistic Perspectives on Communication: An Introduction. *International Journal of Intercultural Relations* 22/2, 107-134.
Hasnain, S. Imtiaz 2003. Language Legitimation, Symbolic Domination, and Market Forces in Global Media. *Language in India.* 3/15, at <http://www.languageinindia.com/feb2003/im tiazglobal.html>.
Jain, Shaily 2004. An Interview with Medha Patkar. *Mid Day.* Jan.22, at <http://ww1.midday.com/news/city/2004/january/74611.htm>.
Jensen, Robert 2004. Damn the Dams: An Interview with Medha Patkar. *AlterNet.* February 25, at <http://www. alternet.org/print.html?StoryID=17954>.
Judge, Anthony 1990, 1991. Recontextualizing Social Problems through Metaphor: Transcending the 'Switch' Metaphor. Part I/II, at <http://www.laetusinpraesens.org/docs/metprob.php>.
Kennedy, Miranda 2003. The Joy of Toxic Cola. *AlterNet.* September 5, at <http://www.alternet.org/story.html?StoryID=16717>.
Lakoff, George / Johnson, Mark 1989. *Metaphors We Live By.* Chicago: The University of Chicago Press.

Narain, Sunita 2002. Changing Environmentalism. At <http://www. india-seminar.com/2002/516/516%20sunita%20narain.htm>.

Paget-Clarke, Nic 2003. Interview with Vandana Shiva (2002): Discussing 'Water Wars'. *In Motion Magazine*. March 6, at <http://www.inmotionmagazine.com/global/vshiva3.html>.

Patkar, Medha 2003. Standing Ovation to Medha Patkar. *India Post News Service*. July 11, at <http://www.aidindia.org/medha/ Medha-IndiaPost-071103.pdf>.

Reisigl, Martin / Wodak, Ruth 2001. *Discourse and Discrimination. Rethorics of Racism and Antisemitism*. London and New York: Routledge.

Roy, Arundhati 2001. *Power Politics*. Cambridge, Massachusetts: South End Press.

Roy, Arundhati 2004a. *The Ordinary Person's Guide to Empire*. London: Flamingo.

Roy, Arundhati 2004b. Do Turkeys Enjoy Thanksgiving? January 16, at <http://www.uni-kassel.de/fb10/frieden/themen/Globaliserung/ roy2-orig.html>.

Scollon, Ron / Wong Scollon, Suzanne 1995. *Intercultural Communication: A Discourse Approch*. Oxford: Blackwell.

Shiva, Vandana 1997. *Biopiracy: The Plunder of Nature and Knowledge*. Boston, Massachusetts: South End Press.

Shiva, Vandana 1998. An Interview with Dr. Vandana Shiva. *Rural America/In Motion Magazine*, August 14, at <http://www. inmotionmagazine.com/shiva.html>.

Shiva, Vandana 2002a. 'Ganga' is not for sale. Suez-Degrémont and the Privatization of the Ganga Water. *In Motion Magazine*. Oct. 20, at <http://www.inmotionmagazine.com/global/vshiva2.html>.

Shiva, Vandana 2002b. *Water Wars: Privatization, Pollution, and Profit*. London: Pluto Press.

Stiglitz, Joseph 2003. Don't Trust Technocrats. *The Guardian*, July 16.

Titscher, Stefan / Meyer, Michael / Wodak, Ruth / Vetter, Eva 2000. *Methods of Text and Discourse Analysis*. London: Sage.

van Dijk, Teun A. 1998. *Ideology: A Multidisciplinary Introduction*. London, Sage.

van Dijk, Teun A. 2003. *Ideology and Discourse: A Multidisciplinary Introduction*, at <http://www.discourse-in-society.org/ideo-dis2. htm>.

Wierzbicka, Anna [2]2003. *Cross-Cultural Pragmatics: The Semantics of Human Interaction*. Berlin and New York: Mouton de Gruyter.

Cross Cultural Perspectives
on Speech Acts

STEFANIE ZILLES POHLE

Offers in Irish English and German Business Negotiations: a Cross-Cultural Pragmatic Analysis

1. Introduction

The ever-increasing globalisation of the world economy means that intercultural business encounters are becoming more and more common, among them encounters between Irish and German business people. Misunderstandings, particularly in negotiations, may have severe consequences: if a negotiation goes awry, a company may suffer economic losses, and a potentially long-term business relationship may be jeopardized. The avoidance of intercultural miscommunication on both the business and the personal levels is thus paramount to the success of international business transactions. This, however, presupposes knowledge about the differences which exist between the cultures of the negotiating parties.

This chapter presents a case study which illustrates parts of the results a comparative pilot study of the speech act *offer* in German and Irish negotiations (Zilles 2003). The paper begins with a brief overview of different research approaches to negotiations (Section 2). An outline of the theoretical framework which serves as the basis for the analysis then follows (Section 3). The fourth section of the article deals with the research method and the informants' profiles. In the next section, the results of the study are presented and discussed against the background of a) specific studies of Irish and German negotiations (Martin 2001, 2005) and b) large-scale cultural surveys which aim at a classification of cultures and their value orientations (Hall/Hall 1990; House *et al.* 1999; Szabo *et al.* 2002; Ashkanazy/Trevor-Roberts/Earnshaw 2002; Keating/Martin 2002). The article concludes with a summary of the findings, a description of the limitations of the study, and an outlook for future research.

2. Negotiation research

Intercultural and cross-cultural investigations into negotiation have primarily focused on the North American and Asian context. As far as studies of European countries are concerned, the concentration has mainly been on Northern and Southern European cultures, such as Scandinavia and Spain, although some studies examine the Dutch, German, French and British cultures too. Other countries and language varieties within Europe, among them Ireland/Irish English, also seem worthy of note, given the extensive – and indeed expanding – amount of trade and commerce in the context of the European Union. The only research contribution on negotiations in Ireland so far is Martin's (2001) study of German-Irish sales negotiations.

The importance of offers in negotiations is recognized by several negotiation researchers (e.g. Rubin/Brown 1975; Maynard 1984) and authors of best-selling handbooks on negotiation (e.g. Fisher/Ury/Patton 1999; Baguley 2000).[1] However, research – especially empirical research – focussing on offers remains limited, despite the vast amount of negotiation studies in a wide variety of disciplines (e.g. economic and business studies, social and experimental psychology, sociology, communication studies, linguistics), which approach negotiations from different perspectives. The approaches range from more objective and quantitatively-oriented research strands, including abstract, experimental, and content analytical approaches, to more subjective and qualitatively-oriented research strands, i.e., ethnographic, conversation analytical/ethnomethodological as well as linguistic approaches (cf. Martin 2001: 30-50; also Zilles 2003: 11-18). Despite a general lack of interdisciplinary cooperation, most negotiation researchers apply methods and theories which originate from more than one discipline. Non-linguistic studies addressing the relevance of offers in negotiations have been found in the ethnomethodological/conversation-analytical, experimen-

---

1   It should be noted that the terms *offer*, *proposal*, and *suggestion* are often used interchangeably in works on negotiations, especially in the non-linguistic literature (cf., e.g., Baguley 2000; Fisher/Ury/Patton 1999; Maynard 1984).

tal, and content-analytical research approaches on the one hand, and in the popular literature on negotiation on the other (cf. Zilles 2003).

Linguists who have worked on negotiations have also identified offers and/or proposals as constituents of negotiation discourse. Some of them stress that offers are indeed among the most central elements of negotiations (cf., e.g., Fant 1993: 116; Wagner 1995: 27). According to Fant (1993: 116), for instance, offers belong to the category of 'basic initiatives', which he defines as "acts that are seen as essential to the activity of negotiating...". However, none of these researchers has analysed offers in detail.

The notion of *offer* applied in this paper relies mostly on speech act theoretical conceptions. These will be summarized in the following section.

3. Framework of analysis

3.1. Offers as speech acts

An offer is an expression of one's willingness or intention to carry out a particular future action, and at the same time, it represents a commitment on the part of the speaker to carry out this action. Example (1), a hospitable offer, expresses the speaker's intention and his/her commitment to give the hearer some wine:

(1)   Would you like some wine? (fabricated)

These general characteristics of offers underline the commissive force of offers (cf., e.g., Searle 1975: 80; Hancher 1979: 6; Tsui 1994: 96-97). That which the speaker offers the hearer is in the hearer's interest, e.g., it can be assumed that drinking wine, e.g. at an evening dinner, is – at least potentially – in the hearer's interest (cf., e.g., Searle 1975: 80; Tsui 1994: 96-97; Aijmer 1996: 134).

Offers of, e.g. wine, but also of a product or a service, involve an interactional dimension as the speaker presents the offer to the hearer for acceptance, refusal, or consideration. The speaker expects some kind of reaction or uptake on the hearer's part. In other words, the speaker tries to get the hearer to do something, i.e. in the above example to verbally accept the offer and drink wine or to reject the offer. This aspect relates to the directive force of offers (cf., e.g. Hancher 1979: 6-7; Brown/Levinson 1987: 66; Aijmer 1996: 189).

The speaker's commitment or obligation to do something, however, becomes relevant only if the hearer accepts the offer (i.e., if s/he wants the action to take place), which brings us to Wunderlich's notion of offers as conditional speech acts (cf. Wunderlich 1977: 42-43; also Leech 1983: 217, 219). The condition which underlies all offers can be paraphrased as "*If* you want it, I shall do a" (Wunderlich 1977: 43 [emphasis mine]), or, with respect to example (1), "*If* you like the taste of wine and *if* you would like to drink some now at the evening dinner, then and only then will I give you some wine". The underlying condition is usually implicit in an offer, but it can also be made explicit as in:

(2)   I could give you some wine *if you like*. (fabricated)

It has been shown, therefore, that offering is a complex speech act which combines commissive and directive illocutionary forces. These features apply to all types of offers, both in everyday conversations and in negotiations. It should be noted, however, that this definition of offers has long been and still remains controversial from a linguistic point of view (cf. Barron 2003: 123-126; Zilles 2003: 35-38 for a full discussion).

The nature of the speech event business negotiation, an event which is above all determined by its purpose to close a business deal, influences the specific function of offers employed in this particular context. Rather than being made to show one's concern for the other's well-being, as, for instance, at an evening dinner, negotiators usually make offers because they expect to get something in return, for instance money or the other person's commitment to build up a long-standing business relationship.[2] In other words, it is not only the

---

2   A further major difference between offers in negotiations and in everyday conversations is the topics dealt with (cf. Section 3.3).

hearer who benefits from the predicated action but also the speaker.[3] In addition, if the addressee accepts the offer, the speaker is in a position to demand the other's commitment to do something next time. As Hancher (1979: 7) observes, the directive element of offers can be hidden behind a seemingly generous commissive act: the speaker can formulate an offer in a way that only the speaker's willingness to do something in the hearer's interest becomes obvious. The double nature of offers makes "social and psychological equivocation" and therefore manipulation possible, "for it can be obvious (in a given case) that the act is commissive, but not obvious that it is directive as well" (Hancher 1979: 7). For this reason, an offer made during a negotiation can be regarded as a strategic device. At the same time, the potential manipulation is mutual since both negotiating parties make use of this device.

Negotiations typically imply an exchange between interlocutors who depend upon each other to realize their goals (cf. Wagner 1995: 11). This fact points to a different dimension of the conditional character of offers, a dimension which enhances their directive force: offers can be conditional, but not in the sense of Wunderlich. In an offer such as *ehh we could make that possible, – if it was ((a)) good enough – <P ((package)) P>. [...]* (Ir-Ir, ll. 240-241),[4] expressed by Ir_2 in example (3), the speaker commits herself to a future action (i.e. to make something possible, here referring to the possibility of allo-cating other hotel guests to nearby hotels, cf. Section 4) on condition that Ir_1 accepts not only the offered action, but also the second part of the utterance, an indirect request (i.e., Ir_1 is indirectly asked to do her share to close a satisfying final deal, "a good enough package").

(3)   **Ir_2:**   well, we have a *num*ber of rooms – booked already, I mean, ((you see)), ((but)) ((X)), we *can* actually, – put these eh(.) people in –

---

3   It should be noted, however, that it may also happen in everyday communica-tion that the speaker gets something in return as the hearer may be put under an obligation to return the offer, i.e., he incurs a debt (cf. Brown/Levinson 1987: 66).
4   This example as well as all following ones – unless otherwise stated – are taken from the two transcripts described in Section 4. 'Ir-Ir' stands for the Irish-Irish negotiation simulation, and 'G-G' for the German one (cf. Zilles 2003 Appendix).

> nearby rooms as well. – if,– it comes to it we can block off, you know, fifty, – two rooms and, – just allocate these – to – [nearby hotels].
>
> **Ir₁:**   [but to date] ((it's)) fifty-two rooms – free.
>
> **Ir₂:**   – ehh we could make that possible, – if it was ((a)) good enough – <P ((package)) P>. […]
>
> (Ir-Ir, ll. 235-241)

Following Tsui (1994: 98-99), this second conditional aspect of offers has been termed *contingency* in order to avoid confusion with the notion of conditional speech acts in Wunderlich's sense. Unlike in example (3), this contingency aspect is often only implicit, as, e.g., in price offers:

(4)   **Ir₂:**   that (.)'d be total of say six thousand pounds and for – the night, – which would be a total – for the two nights then of twelve thousand (Ir-Ir, ll. 170-171)

Here, the speaker is willing and intends to rent the room out to the hearer if the hearer wants the room *and* if she is prepared to pay I£ 6,000, or I£ 12,000 respectively, in exchange for it.

Let us now have a brief look at some politeness issues associated with the speech act *offer*. Since the action which the speaker is willing to do when making an offer is of benefit to the hearer, a speaker shows concern for the hearer's wants and needs, thus addressing his/her positive face (cf. Brown/Levinson 1987: 125). An offer potentially leads to the offence of the offerer's own face because the hearer's acceptance will oblige him/her to carry out the predicated action, which is contrary to his/her want of freedom and therefore threatens his/her negative face (although one might argue this imposition is self-made), while the hearer's rejection of the offer threatens the speaker's positive face. At the same time, the directive element of an offer means that the hearer is being imposed on, and an imposition is always threatening to the addressee's negative face wants. The hearer is not only expected to accept or reject the offer, but an offer may even cause him/her to think he is indebted to the speaker (cf. Brown/Levinson 1987: 66) – for instance, s/he might feel s/he is obliged to make an offer in return (cf. also Barron 2005).

Because of the representative roles of H and S as well as their · common objective, i.e., to reach agreement, the degree of face-threat associated with offers can be expected to be valued low by both S and H in business negotiations. It is assumed that the interlocutors' claims to freedom of action and freedom from imposition weigh not as much as their desire to reach a satisfactory outcome at the end of the negotiation, particularly as they expect (and hope for!) a number of offers. It is suggested that counter-offers are not a result of a feeling of indebtedness on the part of the H, but rather related to his/her wish to improve his/her own position with regard to the prospective outcome. Nevertheless, offers remain face-threatening to some extent. In order to counterbalance the potential threat to both the addressee's negative face and to the speaker's positive and negative face, a speaker may use appropriate negative politeness strategies, e.g. hedging or indirectness (cf. Brown/Levinson 1987: 70).

3.2. Offer strategies

The first step towards data analysis was the development of a taxonomy of offer realization strategies in negotiations, since no adequate system was available in the linguistic literature.[5] Seven different realization strategies for offers were identified in the data.[6] These were classified according to their degree of directness and assigned to the three major categories of direct, conventionally indirect, and non-conventionally indirect offers. In this paper, the

---

5   Linguists dealing in detail with the speech act *offer* focus almost exclusively on hospitable offers (e.g. *Have some biscuits*) or offers of assistance (e.g. *Can I give you a hand?*), i.e. on offers typical of everyday conversations (cf., e.g., Hancher 1979; Aijmer 1996; Barron 2003 and 2005). However, the special context of business negotiations makes a particular category system necessary. The data of the present study has shown that offers in negotiations are less formulaic and routinized than offers in everyday speech.

6   The seven substrategies and the three superstrategies are by no means exhaustive. They are derived from a corpus collected for a pilot study (Zilles 2003) which comprises two German and one Irish negotiation simulations. In all likelihood, other data sets require additional and/or different strategies.

focus will be on these major categories (cf. Zilles 2003: 86-94 for further details, especially on the seven realization strategies).

This approach poses a general problem because of the hybrid nature of offers (cf. Section 3.1): it is not possible to determine a strategy's degree of directness concerning both their directive *and* commissive force. It was, therefore, decided to classify offer strategies with regard to their commissive force since it is of special interest in negotiations at what stage of the discourse the negotiators commit themselves to something, i.e., when and how they make concessions on their way to the final agreement. It is important here not to confuse directness with how strong the speaker's commitment is. Rather, the degree of directness of an offer refers to how difficult it is for the hearer to recognize the illocutionary force of the utterance.

In direct offers, the illocutionary force can be derived from linguistic indicators: hedged and unhedged performative verbs and expressions which name the act as an offer. They convey the speaker's intent to commit him/herself directly and unmistakably, as in the following example:

(5)   **Ir₂:**   we could say, – mh, I'm trying to think now, if we could eh, – offer maybe, you know, – an offer of about – a hundred an(.) ten, – – per room, – ehm, – (CLICK) – which would, – bring it up to:, I don't (.) how much that would be, – eh:e:e:e, so *five*, – that'd be five thousand five hundred. [...]
(Ir-Ir, ll. 352-355)

Conventionally indirect offers are, like any conventionally indirect speech acts, characterized by a particular type of pragmatic ambiguity, namely pragmatic duality (cf. Blum-Kulka 1989: 43). Pragmatic duality here refers to the fact that the utterances can be interpreted literally (in example (6) as a statement about one's mood, i.e. being happy), or as the speech act intended, or both simultaneously. The utterances which belong to this category are still quite easily recognizable as offers because they are conventionalized realizations of offers in the context of negotiations. Their interpretation is supported by certain conventionalized phrases (e.g. *be happy/ willing to do A*), as well as conventions combining grammar (e.g. modal auxiliaries: *can/could, will/would*) and semantic contents (i.e., felicity conditions are asserted or questioned).

(6)   **Ir₁:**   [...] you know, we'd be happy to build up a relationship with your company. [...]
(Ir-Ir, l. 68)

In non-conventionally indirect offers, a different kind of pragmatic ambiguity applies: pragmatic vagueness, which means that the utterances have "multiple pragmatic forces" (Blum-Kulka 1989: 43). The offers of this category could also be interpreted as proposals[7] or requests: the speaker tries to get the hearer to do something, i.e., in example (7) to close a deal, and in example (8) to reconsider the offer once more:

(7)   **G₁:**   [[machen wir]] ein abgespecktes ((i.e. Abendessen)), für zehn Euro
'let's do a basic one ((i.e. dinner)), for ten Euros'
(G-G, l. 636)

(8)   **G₂:**   [...] ab   [[[er ich]]]
       G₁: [[[mh]]]
       G₂: ich denke, (H) –, vielleicht sollten wir mh, beide noch mal in uns gehen, [...]
'...but I' 'mh' 'I think, – maybe we should both reconsider it ((i.e. the offer)) once more, ...'
(G-G, ll. 282-285)

However, examples (7) and (8) can also be understood as non-conventional forms of an offer strategy: S commits him/herself to the same action s/he wants H to commit him/herself to. The interpretation of the utterances as offers relies much more on the context because the speaker's willingness to do something (i.e. the commissive force) is not as transparent as in the preceding categories; it only shows indirectly. Since offers of this type can be interpreted as both proposals/requests and offers, the directive force element is stronger than in the other strategies. In fact, there are two different levels of direction: the first level is associated with their nature as requests/ proposals, and the second level of direction has to do with the general,

---

7   The term *proposal* is used in Edmondson's (1981: 142) sense: by proposing something, the speaker predicates a future act A performed jointly by hearer *and* speaker, whereas when making a suggestion, the speaker predicates a future act A done only by the hearer. Thus, offers, proposals, and suggestions differ with regard to their propositional content conditions.

underlying condition of offers in Wunderlich's sense (cf. Section 3.1), which refers to the provocation of H's reaction to the offer itself in terms of acceptance or rejection.

3.3. Offer topics

Offers in negotiations usually refer to issues on an agenda. In the present study four major topic groups were distinguished:[8]

1. Product, service, change in price
2. Price (figure)
3. Communicative, mental, or procedural action
4. Relationship-building

In the first group of topics, a negotiator may talk about the commodities or services s/he is willing to provide (cf. ex. [9]), or the seller may indicate his/her willingness to reduce a price (cf. ex. [10]), or, alternatively, the buyer his/her willingness to increase the price s/he is prepared to pay.

(9)   G$_2$:   wir ham auch standardmäßig, ehm:, – sowieso, immer, ehm, – (.)n
                  Alleinunterhalter noch, […]
                  'it's standard practice, ehm:, that we also have, ehm, a one-man
                  show, too, – anyway, always, …'
                  (G-G, ll. 259-260)

(10)   G$_2$:   […] ja, dann könnte man überlegen eh, – (H) ob man dann mit dem
                  Preis etwas heruntergeht angesichts dieser, langfristigen, –
                  Geschäftsbeziehung, […]

                  '…well, then one could think eh, – about reducing the price a bit,
                  considering this long-term, – business relationship, …'
                  (G-G, ll.179-181)

---

8   Cf. Neumann (1994a: 7, 1994b: 19, 1995: 46) who, in her analysis of requests
      in business negotiations, distinguishes between *business act now*, *business act
      later*, and *procedure*. She does not call these categories *topics*, but subsumes
      them under the notion of *effect wanted*.

The second group concerns explicit price offers made by a negotiator (cf. ex. [4]).[9]
Mental actions (cf. ex. [8]), communicative actions (cf. ex. [11]), and procedural actions (cf. ex. [12]) are included in the third topic group.

(11) **Ir₁:**   [...] we   [6 can 6],
       Ir₂: [6 mh 6]. –   [7 yeah 7],
       Ir₁: [7 dis 7]((cuss)) packages, and insurance
                 packages, [...]
                 (Ir-Ir, ll. 291-293)

(12) **G₁:**   [gut, da]nn:, lassen wir uns ma(.) gleich da zu den, – – *Fak*ten da
                 näher hinkommen, [...]
                 'good, then let's have a closer look at the – – facts, ...'
                 (G-G, l. 104)

Finally, offers made by negotiators to build up a long-standing business relationship with his/her negotiating partner are the topic of the fourth group *relationship-building* (cf. ex. [6]).

3.4. Internal modification

Offers do not only differ with regard to the general realization strategy or with regard to topics. Even within a single strategy type, there may be differences with respect to internally modifying elements (cf., e.g., Faerch/Kasper 1989). There are two general types of internal modifiers: a) lexical, phrasal, prosodic or syntactic elements which weaken the illocutionary force of the utterance, called downgraders (e.g. *possibly*, *only*, *somehow*, *I mean*, *you know*, *let's say*, loud pronunciation or stress of words, subjunctive mood or past tense

---

9   I distinguish price offering from the other offers in negotiations because a price offer represents a very special case of offering: it actually implies 'to offer something for something', not 'to offer to do'. Nevertheless, it could be paraphrased as follows: 'I, the buyer, hereby offer you that I pay you X for good/service Y', and, respectively, 'I, the seller, hereby offer you that I give good/service Y to you for X'. However, a price offer may also be realized by a hearer-oriented utterance such as *You can have the double room for 100*, or by an elliptical utterance in which just the price is mentioned, e.g. *100*.

marker, conditional clauses[10]), and b) upgraders which enhance illocutionary force (e.g. *really*, *very*, *certainly*, *I'm sure, let me stress*, also loud pronunciation or stress of particular words).

The modifiers affect the perceived directness of the respective offer. In the context of negotiations, a speaker may also employ modifiers to promote or play down the attractiveness of the offered good or service.

Choice of perspective contributes to variation in offers (cf. Blum-Kulka/House/Kasper 1989: 19), and it reveals information about the relationship between the interlocutors (cf. Neu 1985: 119-120). It can be regarded as a further aspect of internal modification. The following types of perspective were found in the present data:

- Speaker-oriented formulations: i.e., the speaker either directly (via *I*; German: *ich*, cf. Ex [13]) or indirectly (via *we*; German: *wir*, cf. Ex [6]) refers to him/herself. *We* here is in the sense of *I and my company* i.e., *exclusive/corporate we*.

(13) **G₂:**   das Kombiangebot würde so aussehen, ehm, – daß ich Ihnen, – –
                  (SWALLOW) für beides zusammen, – für die Inklusivleistung,
                  hundert, zwanzich, Euro, pro Nacht bieten kann.
                  'the combined offer would be, ehm, – that I (SWALLOW) can offer
                  you for both together ((i.e. hotel plus bus trip to the city centre)), –
                  for the inclusive service, one hundred and twenty, Euros, per night'
                  (G-G, ll. 207-208).

- Hearer-oriented formulations: i.e., either *you* (German: *Sie, Du*) (cf. Ex. [14]), or *we* (German: *wir*) in the sense of *you and I* (cf. Ex. [11]), i.e., *inclusive we*.

(14) **Ir₂:**   [...]– *and* you will get the, – the – two – free – rooms ((as well)) for
                  your staff.
                  (Ir-Ir, ll. 183-184)

- Impersonal formulations: the impersonal pronouns *you* (German: *man*, cf. Ex. [10]) or *it* (German: *es*), passive constructions, or reference to a third party as in Ex (15).

---

10   Conditional clauses as modifying elements refer to the contingent offers
      mentioned in Section 3.1.

(15)   G₂: [...] das Busunternehmen holt sie ab und bringt sie zurück.
                 '...the bus company will pick them up and bring them back.'
                 (G-G, ll. 189-190)

4. Method and participants

Two German and two Irish businesspeople from three different
companies located in Germany took part in two dyadic intracultural
face-to-face negotiation simulations. They were adapted from Groth's
(2001) "Brit Trips-Midway Hotel Negotiation Simulation". A German
and an English version were devised and adjusted to the German and
Irish cultural context, respectively. The simulations deal with the
booking of hotel accommodation and transport by a tour operator for a
group of soccer fans who are about to travel to a town where an
important soccer game takes place. The tour operator (Ir_1; G_1)
negotiates with the manager of a hotel (Ir_2; G_2). Negotiation concerns
the prices for accommodation and transport to and from the game, but
the participants are free to negotiate other matters as well, e.g. evening
entertainment. Although real-life negotiations would have been a more
desirable basis for analysis, access to such data was not possible (cf.
Martin 2001: 105-106; Fant 1992: 164).

The negotiations discussed in this paper are comparable in
length and outcome (in both, the participants reached an agreement),
and both lasted around 35 minutes each. However, the participant
constellations differed with respect to the informants' sex, education,
profession, and previous negotiating experience.

Dyad		Sex	Age range	Education	Profession	Negotiating experience
Irish-Irish (Ir-Ir)	Ir₁	female	25-30	University degree in German and French	Marketing Assistant in an Irish company in the food and drink sector	limited (no direct sales experience)
	Ir₂	female	25-30	University degree in International Commerce and German	Marketing Assistant in an Irish company in the food and drink sector	yes (negotiation of price reports)
German-German (G-G)	G₁	male	25-30	University degree in Business Studies	Experienced Staff Assistant in an international auditing company	yes (negotiations with clients and investment consultants, negotiation trainings)
	G₂	male	25-30	University degree in Economics	Experienced Staff Assistant in an international auditing company	yes (negotiations with clients, negotiation trainings)

Table 1. Overview of the participants' profiles.

The limited amount of data, the negotiating parties' varying sex as well as the non-authenticity of the negotiations surely represent short-comings of this exploratory study which are not to be neglected in the analysis of the results.

The negotiations were audio- and videotaped and transcribed, and the offer sequences were extracted from the discourse and coded. The coding scheme consists of an Excel database in the form of a matrix in which the head acts of the offers are listed in rows, whereas each column specifies a different aspect of the speech act in question: strategy, topic, upgraders and downgraders, and perspective (plus further aspects which were analysed in the larger project but are not outlined in this paper, cf. Note 1), but also additional information such as speaker identification, reference to lines in the transcript, etc. The total number of offers was 57 in the Irish negotiation, and 85 in the German negotiation. The analysis represents an in-depth case study. Quantitative aspects are limited to a comparison of relative frequencies.

Questionnaires which the participants filled out before and after the negotiations complement the discourse data. They mainly served to provide biographical information about the participants, to elicit their expectations regarding the forthcoming negotiations and also comments on their own as well as their partner's negotiating performance. Moreover, both the Germans and the Irish were asked to write down what they thought were typical differences between German and Irish behaviour in general, and, more specifically, in negotiations.

5. Results and discussion

5.1. Offer strategies

At first sight, the Irish and German negotiations do not seem to differ greatly with regard to the frequency distribution of the major categories for offer realizations (cf. Figure 1).

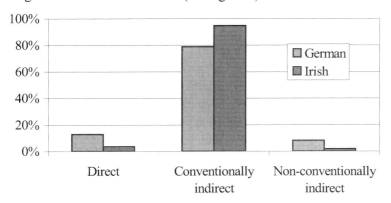

Figure 1. Distribution of major offer categories.

In both cultures, the same tendency can be observed: participants clearly prefer conventionally indirect offers (Germans: 78.8% and Irish: 94.7% of all offers). This pattern is similar to that for German and British English request realizations observed in previous studies such as the Cross-Cultural Speech Act Realization Project (CCSARP) (cf., e.g., Blum-Kulka/House 1989: 125, 134) for requests.

Obviously, both direct and non-conventionally indirect strategies are dispreferred ways of performing offers in the context of negotiations – despite the fact that, pragmalinguistically seen (cf. Leech 1983: 11), both Irish English and German provide the resources for conveying the illocution of offering by direct and non-conventionally indirect means. It is therefore suggested that sociopragmatic factors must be the reason for the linguistic behaviour described above.

It may seem surprising that direct offers are not used more often, given that the predicated future action in offers is to the hearer's benefit (unlike in requests where the action is in the speaker's interest). In other words, one might expect the speaker to want to enhance the hearer's positive face since the threat to the hearer's negative face 'only' refers to the underlying condition which is to be accepted or rejected. This makes offers less imposing than requests.

However, as outlined in Section 3.1, the speaker's negative and positive and the hearer's negative face wants are potentially at risk in other respects as well, which again speaks against a direct offer realization. Other possible explanations for the low frequency of direct offer strategies are, first, that the speaker may be aware that an offer made during a negotiation is far from being to the benefit of the hearer only – instead, the speaker also expects to get something in return, be it money, a service, or the hearer's commitment to a long-standing business relationship, for instance. S/he might therefore choose to avoid direct reference to the speech act in question, thus disguising the aspect of exchange and mutual dependence, which is characteristic of negotiations (cf. Section 3.1). Second, there may simply be no need in negotiations to explicitly name the act performed in negotiations; the conventionally indirect strategies may be sufficient in a business context in both cultures.

Finally, threat to the hearer's negative face would appear to explain the very limited use of non-conventionally indirect offer strategies among the Irish and German informants of the present study. Indeed, by using such indirectness, speakers run the risk of appearing impositive, given the potential interpretation of the utterances as proposals/requests (cf. Section 3.2).[11]

Conventionally indirect offer strategies give the negotiators the opportunity to keep a balance between directly committing themselves to something and directly challenging the opponent's and their own face wants on the one hand, and concealing their own commitment behind the form of a directive speech act (e.g. proposal) on the other.

Despite the similarities between the Irish and German negotiators with regard to the frequency distribution of the major offer categories, the results reveal some interesting differences. Relative to the total number of offers, the German participants (12.9%) make almost four times as many direct offers as the Irish participants (3.5%). By using direct offers, the Germans avoid ambiguity and reduce the risk of being misunderstood more than the Irish. This result is in line with Keating and Martin's observation that "Ireland may have more in common with high-context cultures (Hall 1976) on the basis of the implicit knowledge which the participants in an interaction are assumed to possess. Often what is not said, is more important than what is said and an ability to read between the lines is essential" (Keating/Martin 2002, ch. 2).[12] Martin (2001: 279), referring to the results of her own study, comes to the same conclusion.

This characterization of Irish and German cultures implies that Irish people can be expected to be more indirect, less straightforward, and less explicit than German people. Collaborators of the GLOBE Project (cf. House *et al.* 1999) investigating German and Irish cultures also offer a further explanation which may account for the higher frequency of direct offer realizations used by the German negotiators compared to the Irish negotiators in the present study. It has been found that Ireland displays a moderate level of uncertainty avoidance (cf. Ashkanasy/Trevor-Roberts/Earnshaw 2002: 34; Keating/Martin

---

11   Similar results have been observed in the use of offers in everyday conversation (cf. Barron 2005).

12   The notion of high vs. low-context cultures goes back to Hall (1976), who classifies (West) German culture as a low-context context culture (cf. Hall/Hall 1990: 7; Martin 2005).

2002, ch. 2.2), whereas (former West) Germany shows stronger uncertainty avoidance (Szabo *et al.* 2002: 63; also cf. Martin 2001: 279, 280): where Ireland only scores 4.3, Germany scores 5.22 on a seven-point Likert type scale. Uncertainty avoidance is associated with a preference for risk-avoidance, non-ambiguity and structured-ness.

Interestingly, the Irish negotiators in the present study are also less non-conventionally indirect (1.75%) than the German negotiators (8.2%) in their use of offer realization strategies in the present study. This result corresponds to the GLOBE Project's finding that the Irish culture is lower on the dimension of assertiveness (cf. Ashkanasy/ Trevor-Roberts/Earnshaw 2002: 34; Keating/Martin 2002, ch. 2.2) than the German culture (Szabo *et al.* 2002: 63): 3.92 (Ireland) vs. 4.55 (Germany) on a seven-point Likert type scale.[13] Assertiveness refers to the degree to which individuals are assertive, confrontational, and aggressive in social relationships. It can be argued that non-conventionally indirect offer strategies, which seem to be avoided more by the Irish than by the German informants, imply a higher degree of these characteristics than the other strategies because of their stronger directive and impositive, and therefore face-threatening component.

5.2. Offer topics

In both negotiations, most of the offers concern a service, a commode-ty, or an increase or decrease in price, i.e., the first topic group (Germans: 67.1% and Irish: 40.35% of all offers, cf. Fig. 2), which can be expected to be typical of the speech event negotiation. Interestingly, the German pair is much more creative in their negotia-tion than the Irish pair – they address many different issues in their offers, not only hotel accommodation and transport as prompted by the instructions of the negotiation simulations, but also various possible forms of evening entertainment and dinner, as well as

---

13   Martin (2001: 278), however, does not observe noticeable differences in her study between the German and Irish dyads regarding assertive, confronta-tional behaviour.

additional trips for the group of soccer fans (cf. Section 4). The result is in line with Martin's (2001: 279-280) finding that German negotiators are more oriented towards task and content than their Irish counterparts.[14] Moreover, proportional to the total number of offers, the Irish participants use 4.5 times as many relationally oriented offers (i.e. 15.8%) as the Germans (3.5%) in the present study. Martin (2001: 279) observes a similar behaviour in her study. She writes:

> A further distinguishing feature of the German intracultural dyads is the lesser role attributed to the relational dimension of interaction [...] Certainly, there are examples of interpersonal solidarity initiated by both parties, but there would not appear to be the same efforts made by the interlocutors on the interpersonal level as identified in some of the Irish-Irish negotiations [...]. The fact that there is not, in general, a concerted effort to develop a personal relationship between buyer and seller in the German intracultural dyads ensures that the interaction assumes a more prominent task focus.

The distribution of the offers of the third topic category, i.e. communicative, mental and procedural actions, is also interesting in this regard. These are employed more by the Irish informants (Irish: 15.8% vs. Germans: 9.4% of all offers). Such offers can be used to introduce a new issue to be discussed, or to talk about how or when to implement the decisions made at the end of a negotiation. They can reveal difficulties faced by the interlocutors during the negotiation and also provide an opportunity for the interlocutors to indicate their willingness to think about the negotiating partner's offer or suggestion without committing themselves to a definite answer. Therefore, this type of offer has the potential of preventing the negotiation from reaching deadlock.

---

14   This behaviour might also point to the German participants' greater willingness to take part in the 'game' of simulating a negotiation, or to the difference in their negotiating experience (cf. Section 4).

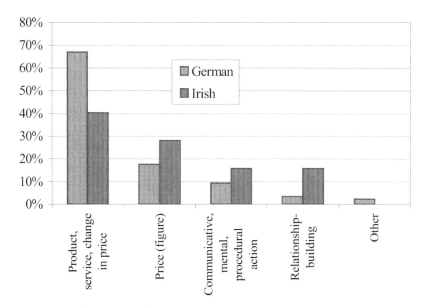

Figure 2. Distribution of major topic types of offers.

Turning finally to the precise price offers, we see that, relatively speaking, more of these are used by Irish participants (28.1% in total) than by German negotiators (17.65% in total). Consequently, it cannot be said that the German participants are more content- or task-oriented per se than the Irish.

5.3. Internal Modification

5.3.1. Upgraders and downgraders

On average, the Irish informants employ approximately twice as many downgraders per offer as the German informants. The German negotiators, on the other hand, employ on average twice as many upgraders per offer as the Irish (cf. Figure 3).

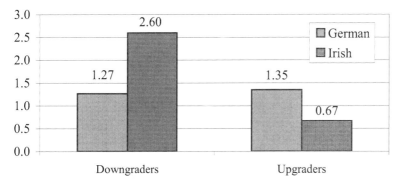

Figure 3. Number of internal modifiers per offer (on average).

Since downgraders have the effect of weakening the speaker's perceived strength of commitment as well as the directive force of the offer, this finding corresponds with the Irish participants' avoidance of direct offer strategies, where the commissive element is strongest, and also with their low use of non-conventionally indirect offer strategies, where the directive element is strongest (cf. Section 5.1). One might argue that by employing more downgrading but fewer upgrading elements, the Irish appear less assertive and confrontational than the Germans – downgraders having often been associated with unassertive, tentative behaviour (cf., e.g., Coates 1996: 171). This would again support again the GLOBE Project's results regarding the dimension of assertiveness. What is more, verbal devices such as *a bit, somehow, eben, vielleicht (maybe)*, or subjunctive mood make a statement less definite and more vague, and this matches the GLOBE Project's finding observation that Germans tend to avoid uncertainty more than the Irish (cf. Section 5.1).

The striking difference between the German and Irish negotiators of the present study concerning the use of upgraders and downgraders, however, may also be explained by the specific participant constellation of the two negotiation simulations. Arguably, the fact that the Irish negotiators are both female may also account for the greater frequency of use of downgraders because studies on female language have shown that "hedges are a valuable resource for speakers, and there is growing evidence that women use them more than men" (Coates 1996: 152). However, Coates (1996: 172) emphasises that this does by no means imply that women are generally unassertive.

5.3.2. Perspective

The hearer-oriented *inclusive we* form, i.e., *we* in the sense of *you and I*, can serve to promote cooperation and solidarity, and to stress common ground between the interlocutors as well as their mutual interests. The Irish use this form more often (14%) than the Germans (3.5%), which supports the assumption that Irish negotiators are more oriented towards relationship-building, a fact also reflected in their choice of offer topics (cf. Section 5.2).

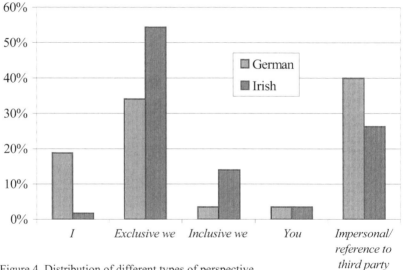

Figure 4. Distribution of different types of perspective.

It is also interesting that the Irish clearly prefer the face-saving *exclusive we* form. It appears in 54.4% of all of their offers. Proportional to the total number of offers in the Irish and the German negotiations, respectively, the Irish employ nearly 1.6 times more offers with this speaker-oriented perspective type than the Germans (34.1%). Saying *we* in the sense of *I and my company* can be interpreted as the Irish negotiators' attempt to avoid direct speaker-reference. They may have wished not to be explicit and straightforward with regard to assuming personal responsibility for the offers and their consequences; they underline the fact that they are acting on behalf of their company. This is why the *exclusive we* can be regarded as a face-saving strategy. The question may of course be raised as to whether the structures in Irish and German companies differ, particularly regarding the power and competence of those conducting negotiations, i.e., if the negotiators themselves are allowed to make a decision or not, and who takes responsibility for such decisions. This is an area of potential future research. On the other hand, the use of the *exclusive we* form may indicate a strong personal affiliation of the speaker with the respective company, which would match the GLOBE Project's results regarding the dimensions of institutional collectivism, which "measures organizational and societal emphasis on collectivism, with low scores reflecting individualistic emphasis and high scores reflecting collectivistic emphasis by means of norms, policies, rules ... or institutional practices" (House *et al.* 1999: 193) and family/ group collectivism, i.e. "the degree to which individuals express pride, loyalty, and cohesiveness in their organizations and families" (House *et al.* 1999: 192): Ireland scores 4.63 and 5.14 on a seven-point Likert type scale (cf. Ashkanasy/Trevor-Roberts/Earnshaw 2002: 34), and Germany only 3.79 and 4.02 so that it has a stronger individualistic orientation than Ireland (cf. Szabo *et al.* 2002: 63). This finding is reminiscent of Ting-Toomey's (1988: 224-230) description of low-context cultures as individualistic and of high-context cultures as collectivistic, and of their ways of negotiating face in conflict communication (also cf. Martin 2005).

This assumption is strengthened when looking at the next perspective type. The two German informants are indeed more self-referenced because about one fifth of their offers are realized by employing the first personal pronoun *I* (direct speaker-orientation), whereas such offers are negligible in the Irish data (Germans: 18.8% vs. Irish: 1.75%). It may also be argued that by directly referring to him/herself, the speaker acts more assertively than by choosing the *exclusive we* form.

One result does not seem to fit in with the other findings which point toward the avoidance of uncertainty and ambiguity by the Germans and the classification of German culture as a low-context culture. Surprisingly, it is the German participants who use more impersonal formulations in the data; it is actually the preferred perspective in the German data (Germans: 40% vs. Irish: 26.32%). Impersonal formulations are a means of weakening the speaker's personal commitment to do something since s/he only indirectly refers to him/herself, and therefore serve to evade explicitness.

Across both cultures, the hearer-oriented perspective *you* is among the least favourite types of perspective (about 3.5% for both groups). This can be accounted for by the fact that when directly addressing the hearer, the directive force element of offers becomes more obvious. This effect may be counterproductive and is therefore avoided by the interlocutors. Apart from that, the very nature of the offer as an expression of the *speaker's* intention to carry out an action in the future – on condition that the hearer accepts – suggests that utterances with reference to the speaker, rather than hearer-oriented formulations, are used more frequently, although the latter are also possible.

6. Conclusion and outlook

In conclusion, one can say that the Irish participants of the present study were more indirect than the German participants so that one may get the impression that they "talk[ed] round the point". This becomes particularly evident in their choice of offer realization strategies and in their more frequent use of mitigating devices compared to the German informants.[15] The two informants from Ireland also made more offers which referred to relationship-building, but it cannot be said that their German counterparts were more content-oriented per se. As far as

---

15   Differences in the interactional structure of offer sequences as well as in the macrostructure of the negotiations also confirm this result (cf. Zilles 2003: 146-155). For instance, the Irish were found to use more externally modifying elements (supportive moves), and they reacted more tentatively to the interlocutor's offers and avoided clear acceptances and rejections. Instead, they preferred to give only feedback, thus signalling that they have heard what the other has said, or that they are considering the offer.

perspective in offers is concerned, the Irish employed the *inclusive we* form more often than the Germans, and the Germans tended to be more self-referenced. The data yields somewhat surprising results in that impersonal formulations are used more by the German than by the Irish participants.

The results of this study correspond, to a large extent, to Martin's (2001) findings regarding German and Irish intracultural sales negotiations, as well as to the findings of previous works on general characteristics of German and Irish culture (Hall/Hall 1990; House *et al.* 1999; Szabo *et al.* 2002; Ashkanazy/Trevor-Roberts/ Earnshaw 2002; Keating/Martin 2002).

The results also match the image which the German and Irish participants of the present study had of their own and the other group's culture and their respective negotiating styles. This becomes apparent from the post-simulation questionnaires (cf. Section 4). Except for one German participant, all participants reported to have had some personal – either professional or private – experience with the other cultural group on which the present study focuses. The German informants believed that Germans were more focused on hard facts, were more formal, but also more efficient. They believed the Irish to be calmer, more relaxed, less direct, more patient and friendlier than the Germans. Similarly, the Irish participants perceived the Germans as being very direct, getting straight to the point ("Germans are more interested in getting to the point quickly"), being more formal, and tending to engage in 'confrontational' behaviour. Small talk and social relationship building were not thought to be valued as highly as among Irish people. By contrast, price and product quality, as well as punctuality and formality, were claimed to be very important to the Germans.

It should be kept in mind that due to the limited amount of data the results of this case study cannot be generalized. Some of the differences can certainly be attributed to the participants' individual style, which is possibly influenced by their age, educational backgrounds, professional experience (especially their previous negotiating experience), and, last but not least, their personalities. One of the major limitations of the study is the fact that, due to the difficulty of finding participants, the Irish negotiators were female, whereas the

Germans were male. There is clearly need of future research which deals with the question as to how far some of the characteristics of the informants' negotiating styles result from gender rather than from cultural differences. Another aspect is that the Irish negotiators' use of the English language may have been influenced by German language use because they had been working in Germany for some period of time when the simulation took place (one of the participants seven months, the other two years).

In order to be able to obtain more generalizable results as far as the Irish and German negotiators' use of German and Irish English is concerned, more quantitatively-oriented research is necessary. Ideally, such future investigations would involve researchers who approach negotiations from different perspectives. Interdisciplinary work would certainly provide more comprehensive insights into the nature of negotiations. Findings could then help to devise new concepts for negotiation handbooks and intercultural trainings.

References

Aijmer, Karin 1996. *Conversational Routines in English*. London/ New York: Longman.

Ashkanasy, Neal M. / Trevor-Roberts, Edwin / Earnshaw, Louise 2002. The Anglo Cluster: Legacy of the British Empire. *Journal of World Business*. 37, 28-39.

Baguley, Phil 2000. *Teach Yourself Negotiating*. Lincolnwood: NTC.

Barron, Anne 2003. *Acquisition in Interlanguage Pragmatics: Learning How to Do Things with Words in a Study Abroad Context* (Pragmatics and Beyond 108), Amsterdam/Philadelphia: John Benjamins.

Barron, Anne 2005. Offering in Ireland and England. In Barron, Anne / Schneider, Klaus Peter (eds) *The Pragmatics of Irish English* (Trends in Linguistics. Studies and Monographs 164), Berlin/ New York: Mouton de Gruyter.

Blum-Kulka, Shoshana 1989. Playing it Safe: the Role of Conventionality in Indirectness. In Blum-Kulka/House/Kasper (eds), 37-70.

Blum-Kulka, Shoshana / House, Juliane 1989. Cross-Cultural and Situational Variation in Requesting Behavior. In Blum-Kulka/House/Kasper (eds), 123-154.

Blum-Kulka, Shoshana / House, Juliane / Kasper, Gabriele (eds) 1989. *Cross-Cultural Pragmatics: Requests and Apologies*. Norwood, MA: Ablex.

Blum-Kulka, Shoshana / House, Juliane / Kasper, Gabriele 1989. Investigating Cross-cultural Pragmatics: an Introductory Overview. In Blum-Kulka/House/Kasper (eds), 1-34.

Brown, Penelope / Levinson, Stephen C. 1987. *Politeness: Some Universals in Language Use* (Studies in Interactional Sociolinguistics 4). Cambridge: Cambridge University Press.

Coates, Jennifer 1996. *Women Talk. Conversation Between Women Friends*. Oxford: Blackwell.

Edmondson, Willis 1981. *Spoken Discourse. A Model for Analysis*. London: Longman.

Faerch, Claus / Kasper, Gabriele 1989. Internal and External Modification in Interlanguage Request Realization. In Blum-Kulka/House/Kasper (eds), 221-247.

Fant, Lars 1992. Analyzing Negotiation Talk – Authentic Data vs. Role Play. In Grindsted, Annette / Wagner, Johannes (eds) *Communication for Specific Purposes* (Kommunikation und Institution 21). Tübingen: Narr, 176-192.

Fant, Lars 1993. 'Push' and 'Pull' Moves in Hispanic and Swedish Negotiation Talk. *Studier I Modern Sprakvetenskap* 10, 112-131.

Fisher, Roger / Ury, William / Patton, Bruce M. 1991, repr. 1999. *Getting to Yes. Negotiating an Agreement Without Giving In*. Boston, Mass.: Houghton Mifflin & Co.

Hall, Edward T. / Hall, Mildred Reed 1990. *Understanding Cultural Differences: Keys to Success in West Germany, France, and the United States*. Yarmouth, ME: Intercultural Press.

Hall, Edward T. 1976. *Beyond Culture*. New York: Doubleday.

Hancher, Michael 1979. The Classification of Cooperative Illocutionary Acts. *Language in Society* 8/1, 1-14.

House, Robert J. *et al.* 1999. Cultural Influences on Leadership and Organizations. Project GLOBE. In Mobley, William H. (ed.)

Advances in Global Leadership, vol. 1. Stamford, Conn.: JAI Press, 171-233.

Keating, Mary A. / Martin, Gillian 2002. Leadership in the Republic of Ireland. In Chhokar, Jagdeep S. / Brodbeck, Felix / House, Robert J. (eds) *The GLOBE Research Project: Country Anthology.* Thousand Oaks, CA: Sage. Preliminary version in <http://www.ucalgary.ca/mg/GLOBE/Public/Links/irishchater. doc> [11 July 2002].

Leech, Geoffrey N. 1983. *Principles of Pragmatics.* London/New York: Longman.

Martin, Gillian 2005. Indirectness in Irish-English Business Negotiation: A Legacy of Colonialism? In Barron, Anne / Schneider, Klaus Peter (ed.) *The Pragmatics of Irish English* (Trends in Linguistics. Studies and Monographs 164). Berlin/New York: Mouton de Gruyter.

Martin, Gillian S. 2001. *German-Irish Sales Negotiation. Theory, Practice and Pedagogical Implications* (Forum Linguisticum 36). Frankfurt a.M. *et al.*: Peter Lang.

Maynard, Douglas W. 1984. *Inside Plea Bargaining. The Language of Negotiation.* New York/London: Plenum.

Neu, Joyce 1985. *A Multivariate Sociolinguistic Analysis of the Speech Event Negotiation.* Unpublished Ph.D. dissertation, University of Southern California, Los Angeles.

Neumann, Ingrid 1994a. Requests in Intercultural Negotiations: on the Method. *Sprak og Marked* 11, 6-8.

Neumann, Ingrid 1994b. Requests in Three Intercultural Negotiations: a Cross-Cultural Study. *Sprak og Marked* 11, 15-20.

Neumann, Ingrid 1995. Realization of Requests in Intercultural Negotiations: on Pragmatic Method. *Hermes* 15, 31-52.

Rubin, Jeffrey / Brown, Bert 1975. *The Social Psychology of Bargaining and Negotiation.* New York: Academic Press.

Searle, John R. 1975. Indirect Speech Acts. In Cole, Peter / Morgan, Jerry L. (ed.) *Syntax and Semantics 3: Speech Acts.* New York: Academic Press, 59-82.

Szabo, Erna *et al.* 2002. The Germanic Europe Cluster: Where Employees Have a Voice. *Journal of World Business* 37, 55-68.

Ting-Toomey, Stella 1988. Intercultural Conflict Styles: A Face-

Negotiation Theory. In Kim, Young Yun / Gudykunst, William B. (ed.) *Theories in Intercultural Communication* (International and Intercultural Communication Annual 12). Beverly Hills, SA: Sage, 213-235.

Tsui, Amy B. M. 1994. *English Conversation.* Oxford/New York: Oxford University Press.

Wagner, Johannes 1995. What Makes a Discourse a Negotiation? In Ehlich, Konrad / Wagner, Johannes (eds) *The Discourse of Business Negotiation* (Studies in Anthropological Linguistics 8), Berlin/New York: Mouton de Gruyter, 9-36.

Wunderlich, Dieter 1977. Assertions, Conditional Speech Acts, and Practical Inferences. *Journal of Pragmatics* 1, 13-46.

Zilles, Stefanie 2003. *Pragmatic Aspects of Irish and German Business Negotiations – An Empirical Contrastive Study.* Unpublished M.A. thesis, Universität Bonn, Philosophische Fakultät, Bonn.

Appendix – Transcription conventions

G₁: / **Ir₁**: **G₂**: / **Ir₂**:	German/Irish tour operator representative German/Irish hotel representative
[ ] *[[ ]]* *[4 4]*	Single, double, and triple square brackets as well as brackets indexed with numbers mark the beginning and the end of simultaneous start-ups and speech overlaps.
[…]	Three dots between square brackets indicate parts of the speaker's turn at talk which are omitted from the quotation.
,	A comma indicates a level pitch movement or a slight rise in pitch, beginning from a low or mid level.
.	A period signals a fall to a low pitch at the end of an intonation unit.
?	A question mark indicates a marked high rise in pitch at the end of an intonation unit.
(.)	A period in parentheses indicates where the speaker omits or appears to swallow one or more syllables or single letters, or the occurrence of a glottal stop.
– – – –	A dash indicates untimed pause or slight hesitation within an utterance. The more dashes in a row, the longer the pause is.
emphasis	Non-italics indicate emphasis.
:::	Colon indicates prosodical lengthening of the preceding sound, proportional to the number of colons.
(H)	audible inhalation
<P P>	Here the text is spoken more quietly than the rest ('piano').
eh, ehm etc.	Hesitation markers or filled pauses.
mh, yeah etc.	Interjection of continuative backchannel responses into a speaker's extended turn, or affirmative responses.
((doubt))	Double parentheses indicate transcriber's doubt.
((X))	Double parentheses with an X in between indicate a syllable that cannot be deciphered by the transcriber.
((i.e. word))	'i.e.' followed by a words in non-italics in between double parentheses indicates an additional piece of information inserted by the transcriber.

GRAHAME T. BILBOW

Speaking and not Speaking across Cultures

1. Introduction

Hong Kong has been a Special Administrative Region (SAR) of the People's Republic of China since its reversion to Chinese sovereignty in 1997. As an SAR, Hong Kong continues to serve an entrepot function for trade between China and the West, and is a base for many international companies interested in trading with China. In such companies, it is common for Western expatriates and local Chinese staff to work closely together using English as a *lingua franca*. This chapter compares the spoken English discourse of Western expatriate and local Chinese participants in a series of business meetings recorded at a large airline in Hong Kong, and makes observations regarding intercultural communication in the context of this type of cross-cultural meeting.

2. The data

This study uses a 140,000-word transcribed corpus of spoken English data audio- and video-recorded in a range of eleven business meetings at a large airline company in Hong Kong. The corpus, which contains meetings that total some eleven hours of spoken data, is called the *Meetings at Work (MAW)* corpus (Bilbow 1997). In terms of their composition, the meetings in the corpus consist of a total of 51 Western expatriate (WE) participants and 36 local Chinese (LC) participants at a range of ranks between junior manager-level and director-level. For the purpose of analysis, certain junior members of staff (e.g. trainee staff) who are sometimes required to attend meetings but not actively partici-pate, have been discounted from calculations. WE and LC speakers are represented at the full range of ranks in the corpus; however, most of the director-level staff are WE, and almost all (92%) of the meeting chairs are middle-aged male WEs. The spoken discourse of these chairs is the subject of discussion in an earlier paper (Bilbow 1998).

The eleven meetings in the MAW corpus serve a range of functions:

- Five of the meetings are *departmental management meetings*, chaired by the same head of department. In these meetings, most of the time is devoted to around-the-table reports by departmental staff, followed by general discussions led by the chair. In the analysis presented below, such meetings are termed *Type A* meetings.

- Five of the meetings are *coordination meetings*, chaired by a range of senior staff across a range of departments. The purpose of these meetings is to bring together staff from a range of departments to consider the progress of major inter-depart-mental projects. These meetings are termed *Type B* meetings.

- The remaining meeting is a *brainstorming meeting*, which is chaired by the head of a large department. The meeting consists of section heads from the department, and its purpose is to brain-storm a matter of general importance to the department (quality service). This type of meeting is termed a *Type C* meeting.

3. Research niche

Since the MAW corpus was compiled in the mid-1990s, the corpus has been used in a variety of ways to illustrate the things people do and say in business meetings and the impact that speakers' words have on other people in such meetings. The range of speech acts used in these meetings has been charted, and this has led to the creation of a putative taxonomy of speech acts used in business meetings. This taxonomy categorises speech acts into *representatives*, *directives*, *commissives* and *evaluatives* (Searle 1976), and identifies speech acts that occur within each of these speech act classes. Two speech act classes have been described in some depth: *directive* speech acts (Bilbow 1997) and *commissive* speech acts (Bilbow 2002).

To date, however, relatively little research has focused on how different groups of participants in meetings behave verbally. While there has been a study of the spoken discourse of chairs ('chair-talk' in Bilbow 1998), there has been no corresponding in-depth study of the spoken discourse of participants, and no comparative study of WE and LC participants' contributions in these meetings. This chapter seeks to fill this gap.

4. Units of analysis: the speech act

The putative taxonomy of speech acts referred to above lists and offers tentative definitions for the following thirty-three individual speech acts, divided into the speech act classes of *representatives*, *directives*, *commissives* and *evaluatives*. Full details of the taxonomy are provided in Bilbow (1998: 180-194). The speech acts identified to date in the MAW corpus are as presented below in Table 1. The abbreviations in brackets after each speech act are used in Tables 3 and 4 later in this chapter.

Representatives		Directives		Commissives	
❖ allow	[all]	❖ direct	[d]	❖ commit	[comm]
❖ conclude	[con]	❖ elicit	[el]	❖ confirm	[conf]
❖ concur	[conc]	❖ engage	[eng]		
❖ confide	[confd]	❖ frame	[fr]		
❖ correct	[corr]	❖ loop	[l]	Evaluatives	
❖ endorse	[end]	❖ mark	[m]		
❖ exemplify	[ex]	❖ nominate	[n]	❖ apologise	[ap]
❖ inform	[i]	❖ request-clarify	[r-cl]	❖ greet/reply-greet	[gr]
❖ metastate	[ms]	❖ return	[ret]		
❖ object	[obj]	❖ start	[s]		
❖ observe	[obs]	❖ suggest	[sug]		
❖ predict	[pred]	❖ terminate	[ter]		
❖ qualify	[qu]				
❖ quote	[quo]				
❖ reformulate	[ref]				
❖ reject	[rej]				
❖ summarise	[sum]				

Table 1. A putative taxonomy of speech acts in business meetings.

The taxonomy in Table 1 is not intended to be exhaustive; indeed, it clearly reflects the limitations of the data from which it was generated. Speech acts are fuzzy categories that defy easy classification; indeed, the process of identifying speech acts is a rather subjective one, since, however explicit and stipulative the definition of a speech act, there is bound to be a measure of discrepancy between how different observers react to utterances and ascribe them to particular speech act categories. In this study, wherever possible, the analyst's observations have been validated against participants' own observations. It is also worth observing that breaking discourse up into short stretches encourages a rather atomistic approach, and there is a danger that the analyst ignores the function of larger discourse chunks. In practice, speech acts in discourse are often grouped strategically so as to produce particular rhetorical effects.

Nevertheless, despite such inherent shortcomings in a taxonomic approach and the notion of the speech act, speech acts are useful units of analysis for representing the things people do in meetings. In the course of this research, the notion of the speech act has been found to be relatively accessible to the non-specialist; this is important if the findings of analysis are presented back to meeting participants themselves, as is the case in this research.

5. Analysis

Bilbow (1998) observes that the verbal behaviours of chairs and participants in meetings differ markedly. One of the most noticeable differences is that chairs in meetings tend, in general, to speak more than participants; 'chair-talk' comprises nearly 40% of all the spoken data in the corpus, despite the fact that participants outnumber chairs by approximately ten to one. Chairs also appear to differ from participants in terms of the speech acts they use in business meetings. Chairs' speech acts are roughly divided between those with a directing function and those with an information-giving function. Perhaps not surprisingly, chairs spend much of their time directing participants to do things through the use of directive speech acts that I have described elsewhere as *command-oriented, elicitation-oriented* and *procedure-oriented* (Bilbow 1998: 164). In contrast, participants in general tend to use a higher proportion of information-related representative speech acts (e.g. *clarifying, correcting, agreeing* and *disagreeing* with information) and commissive speech acts (e.g. *offering* and *promising*) than chairs (Bilbow 2002).

The purpose of this chapter is to investigate whether all meeting participants behave in broadly similar ways, or whether intra-group differences may be discerned in terms of verbal behaviour in meetings; more specifically, whether local Chinese and Western participants use particular speech acts more or less frequently and in different ways.

5.1. Relative quantity of speech

Western expatriates tend to speak more than local Chinese staff in the meetings in the corpus across the board; WEs speak nearly twice as much as LCs in the meetings, both in terms of speaking time and in terms of number of words uttered. This difference cannot be attributed to differences in the number, rank or expertise of participants, since the corpus consists of WE and LC participants of similar rank and expertise, and numbers are factored to account for the slight numerical superiority of WE staff.

5.2. Speech act utilisation patterns of LC and WE participants

A comparison of the range of speech acts used by Chinese and Western participants in MAW corpus meetings also reveals that there are considerable differences in terms of the range of speech acts used by the two groups.

Chinese Participants' Speech Acts		*Western Participants' Speech Acts*	
Speech Act	*% of Speech Acts Identified*	*Speech Act*	*% of Speech Acts Identified*
inform	66	inform	40
suggest	7	return	9
Return	4	suggest	9
engage	4	engage	7
conclude	2	object	6
commit	2	concur	5
concur	2	metastate	3
object	2	request-clarify	2
Mark	2	predict	2
Loop	2	direct	2
exemplify	1	elicit	2
predict	1	observe	2
miscellaneous	5	miscellaneous	13

Table 2. Chinese/ Western Participants' Speech Acts ranked in order of frequency of occurrence.

Table 2 shows that there are several differences in the ranges of speech acts used by Chinese and Western participants across the range of business meetings in the MAW corpus. Although, in general, the most frequent speech acts are shared by both groups (i.e. *informing, suggesting, returning, engaging* and *concurring*), there are nevertheless certain differences between the ranges of speech acts used by Chinese and Western participants, e.g. in terms of *marking, eliciting, exemplifying, metastating, request-clarifying* and so on.

It is useful to group observations regarding similarities and differences between Chinese and Western participants' utilisation of speech acts into the following three categories:

(i)   *Shared speech acts with a broadly similar frequency of occurrence*
      Suggesting and *predicting* speech acts occupy approximately the same proportion of the discourse of both Chinese and Western participants.

(ii) *Shared speech acts with a divergent frequency of occurrence*
In general, Chinese participants make much heavier use of *informing* speech acts than Western participants. This tendency for LC speakers to focus more heavily on *informing* speech acts might partly explain some Western participants' comments in interview that Chinese speakers' discourse appears to be 'mono-functional' while Western discourse gives the appearance of being 'multi-functional'. Relative to Chinese participants, Western participants engage in more *returning* speech acts (clarifying information and intent), *engaging* speech acts (helping conversation flow more smoothly), *concurring* speech acts (expressing agreement with others), *objecting* speech acts (disagreeing with others' utterances) and *predicting* speech acts (forecasting what might happen).

(iii) *Speech acts which are not shared*
It is noticeable that Chinese participants make heavier use of *committing*, *marking*, *exemplifying* and *concluding* speech acts, whereas Westerners make more use of *metastating*, *request-clarifying*, *eliciting*, *directing* and *observing* speech acts.

Such findings, while interesting, may be rather misleading, however. In fact, large differences are discernible in the discourse of each group in the three meeting types represented in the corpus. It is noticeable, for example, that in Type A meetings (management meetings), Type B meetings (coordination meetings) and Type C meetings (brainstorming meetings), local Chinese participants exhibit very different patterns of participation. This is not only reflected in the proportion of talk (Chinese discourse ranged from 23% in Type A meetings, 46% in Type B meetings, to 53% in Type C meetings), but also in the range of speech acts used by local Chinese speakers, the range of speech acts represented in brainstorming meetings being far greater than in management meetings.

Tables 3 (a-c) and 4 (a-c) illustrate the variation that exists between the range of speech acts utilised by Chinese and Western participants respectively in Type A, B and C meetings. In each case, numbers have been factored to account for imbalances in the relative number and rank of participants present in meetings. It can be

observed in these tables that local Chinese speakers behave signify-
cantly differently in the three types of meeting, and that local Chinese
and Western expatriate patterns of speech act utilization are markedly
different.

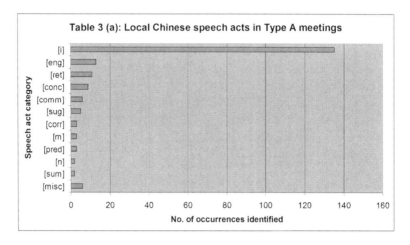

Table 3 (a). (see Table 1 for an explanation of the abbreviations).

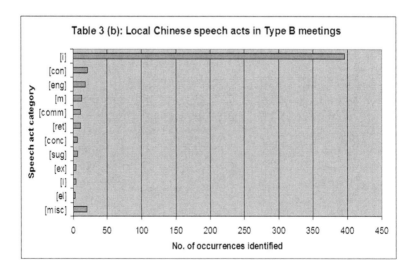

Table 3 (b).

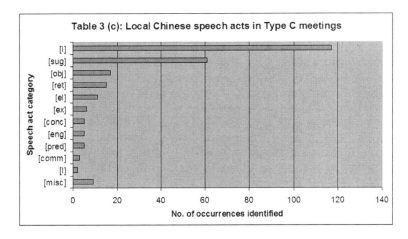

Table 3 (c).

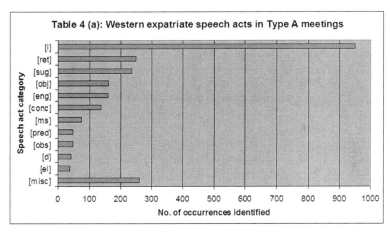

Table 4 (a).

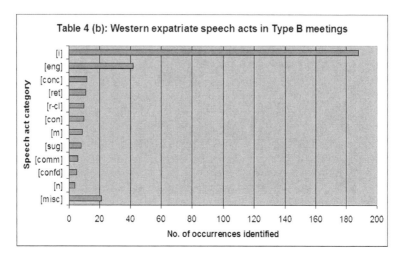

Table 4 (b).

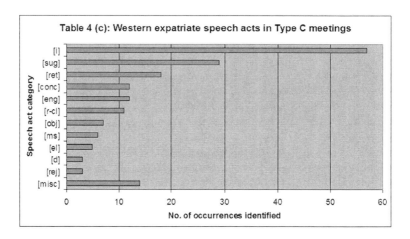

Table 4 (c).

6. Discussion

The above analysis presents a picture of some complexity. Clearly, local Chinese and Western expatriate participants' contributions differ from each other in various ways across the meetings in the MAW corpus. However, each group's participation also varies to some extent across meetings of different types. Local Chinese participants' contributions, for example, vary markedly according to meeting type. Their contributions in management meetings (Type A) are significantly less than in other meetings, and the range of speech acts used by this group tends to be much more varied in the brainstorming meeting (Type C) than in other meeting types. In contrast, the contributions of Western expatriates reveal a considerably lower level of inter-meeting variation; in short, Westerners tend to act broadly the same in all meeting types.

Local Chinese participants appear to make distinctions between different types of business meetings, and these distinctions affect their linguistic behaviour in meetings. In Type A meetings, for example, which consist of around-the-table reports by departmental staff, followed by a 'general discussion phase', local Chinese participants tend to limit their spoken contributions to their reports, and tend not to take part in discussions. When we spoke with participants, we found that local Chinese staff believed it to be inappropriate (and unfruitful) to contribute to the more wide-ranging discussion phase of such meetings, as this was perceived to be 'off-topic'.

In other meeting types, e.g. Type B meetings (coordination meetings) and Type C meetings (brainstorming meetings), however, local Chinese participants viewed discussion as the most vital part of the meeting, and were quite willing to contribute. It therefore emerged from discussion that local Chinese participants have a strong sense of what is on- and off-topic in business meetings that their Western colleagues appear not to possess. For Western expatriate staff, contributions are readily offered, whatever the meeting type, and silence is something that is assiduously avoided. On the other hand, local Chinese participants appear to view silence differently. Silence is quite easily tolerated, and is much preferred to the utterance of irrelevant statements. From our discussions with local Chinese and

Western participants, views regarding silence polarise around the following two 'archetypal' positions.

Chinese archetype	Western archetype
• thoughtful involvement • a strong view of 'appropriate', respectful behaviour • acceptance of change	• unwillingness to become involved • an absence of ideas • resistance to change

Table 5.

This observation is confirmed by research by Flowerdew (1997). In his study of Confucianist discourse (typical of Chinese speakers) and Utilitarian discourse (typical of Anglo-Saxon speakers), Flowerdew observes that Utilitarian discourse emphasises the importance of freedom to express one's views and the need to speak out and sometimes be confrontational (Flowerdew 1997: 536). Conversely, Confucianist discourse attaches importance to collective responsibility, decorum and public order, and leading by example rather than rhetoric (Flowerdew 1997: 543). From our findings, it appears that local Chinese speakers have a somewhat more heightened sense of sociolinguistic appropriacy than their Western colleagues. Quoting the words of the Confucian classics, Flowerdew reports that in Chinese society "Those who know do not speak. Those who speak do not know" (Flowerdew 1997: 538). Western expatriates, on the other hand, appear compelled to speak in every type of meeting, largely irrespective of their level of knowledge.

'Cultural/linguistic critical mass' seems also to affect different groups' volubility in the meetings in the MAW corpus. In meetings in which more local Chinese staff are present, the volubility of local Chinese staff is greater, as it is among Western expatriate staff when they predominate. It is possible therefore that participants feel more comfortable and are more voluble in meetings in which their cultural/ linguistic group is in the majority. This observation certainly merits further research.

7. The realisation of speech acts

As commented above, there are considerable differences in the ranges of speech acts typically used by LC and WE participants in business meetings, and, in the case of LC participants, between meetings of different type. It also appears to be the case that considerable variation exists between Western expatriates and local Chinese meeting participants' spoken discourse in terms of how it is realised lexico-grammatically. While this is no doubt partly due to the fact that local Chinese participants are second language speakers, it also seems likely to be partly attributable to differences in LC and WE speaking style preferences.

While it is not the purpose of this chapter to focus on lexico-grammatical differences between the speech acts of native and non-native speakers, it is worth reiterating some of the most marked lexico-grammatical differences identified between LC and WE spoken discourse in earlier work.

	Local Chinese	*Western Expatriate*
Functional grammatical features	• Mostly direct strategies (mostly direct requesting and suggesting statements, but little use of imperatives or interrogatives in requests or suggestions) • Some use of conventionalised indirectness • Relatively little use of requestive or suggestory hints • Tendency to limit requests to activity inside the meeting room, and suggestions to group-directed activity • Almost all supportive moves were post-posed	• Mostly direct strategies (mostly direct requesting and suggesting statements, but also use of imperatives or interrogatives) • Some use of conventionalised indirectness • Relatively little use of requestive or suggestory hints • Requests tended to relate to a broad range of activities, and suggestions to hearer-, group- and outgroup-directed activity. • Supportive moves were divided between pre-posed and post-posed

	Local Chinese	*Western Expatriate*
	• Principal functions of supportive moves: grounding and elaborating. Absence of imposition-minimising moves.	• Principal functions of supportive moves: grounding, elaborating and imposition- minimising. Presence of imposition-minimising moves assumed the speaker was speaking 'on behalf of the company'.
Prosodic features	• Limited to low-fall and mid-fall, contours which gave speech acts an air of 'finality'	• Broad range of intonation contours, which gave speech an air of emotional expression.
Lexical features	• Formal and impersonal • Little use of indefiniteness • Little use of emphasising and minimising strategies • Little use of bad language • Technically-oriented • Group-oriented	• Informal, idiosyncratic and personal • Some use of indefiniteness • Heavy use of emphasising and minimising strategies • Some use of 'bad' language • Technically-oriented • Company-oriented

Table 6. Functional-grammatical, prosodic and lexical features of local Chinese and Western Expatriate speech in suggesting and requesting speech acts (from Bilbow 1997: 30).

8. Conclusion

This chapter contrasts the spoken discourse of local Chinese and Western participants in a range of business meetings held at a large airline company in Hong Kong. We have noted that there are many differences between the contributions of these two groups. Among the differences we have identified are differences in the quantity of talk, differences in the ranges of speech acts employed, and differences in the lexico-grammatical realisation of these speech acts in terms of level of directness, lexical choice, and prosodic features.

We have noted, however, that significant inter-meeting varia-tion is present, especially among local Chinese speakers in terms of the range of speech acts used. In certain types of meetings (notably management meetings), local Chinese participants tend to speak considerably less and use a more restricted set of speech acts than they do in other types of meeting (notably coordination and brainstorming meetings). Western discourse, on the other hand, tends to be far more uniform across different meeting types.

It has been suggested that one reason for this is that local Chinese and Western expatriate participants differ in their views of the sociolinguistic appropriacy of contributing verbally in particular types of meetings. In Flowerdew's terms, as users of Utilitarian discourse, Western expatriate participants may tend to value vocal contributions for their own sake, and have a broader, more inclusive sense of what constitutes 'on-topic' discourse across a range of meeting types. On the other hand, as users of Confucianist discourse, local Chinese participants may have a strong sense of what is on-topic, which governs how they behave linguistically in particular types of meetings. In contrast with Western speakers, local Chinese speakers tend to value silence, which is perceived to be preferable to irrelevant talk.

References

Bilbow, Grahame T. 2002. Commissive Speech Act Utilisation in Cross-Cultural Business Meetings. *International Review of Applied Linguistics in Language Teaching* 40, 287-303.

Bilbow, Grahame T. 1998. Look Who's Talking: An Analysis of 'Chair-talk' in Business Meetings. *Journal of Business and Technical Communication* 12.2, 157-197.

Bilbow, Grahame T. 1997. Spoken Discourse in the Multicultural Workplace in Hong Kong: Applying a Model of Discourse as 'Impression Management'. In Harris, Sarah / Bargiela-Chiappini, Francesca (eds) *The Languages of Business: An International Perspective*. Edinburgh: Edinburgh University Press, 21-48.

Bond, Michael H. 1991. *Beyond the Chinese Face: Insights from Psychology*. Hong Kong: Oxford University Press.

Crown, Cynthis L. / Feldstein, Stanley 1985. Psychological Correlates of Silence and Sound in Conversational Interaction. In Tannen, Deborah / Saville Troike, Muriel (eds) *Perspectives on Silence*. Norwood, NJ: Ablex, 31-54.

Flowerdew, John 1997. Competing Public Discourses in Transitional Hong Kong. *Journal of Pragmatics* 28 *(Special Edition on Hong Kong in Transition)*, 533-553.

Kress, Gunther 1985. *Linguistic Processes in Sociocultural Practice*. Geelong: Deakin University Press.

Scollon, Ron / Scollon, Suzanne B. K. 1995. *Intercultural Communication: A Discourse Approach*. Oxford: Basil Blackwell.

Searle, John R. 1969. *Speech Acts*. Cambridge: Cambridge University Press.

ORA-ONG CHAKORN

Written Business Invitations:
A Cross-Cultural Rhetorical Analysis

1. Introduction

Invitations to business-related social or professional activities are part of persuasive business communication. With business and social purposes often combined, letters of invitation thus play an important role in both local and international business communications. The use of English in Thailand has been boosted by foreign trade and investment which, during the past few decades, have led to the continuous growth of multinational corporations, foreign companies and joint ventures in this non-English speaking country. Nowadays, the majority of white-collar jobs in Thailand require a good command of English, and business correspondence written in English is commonplace. However, research on cross-cultural business writing between Thais and native English speakers is rare. This study attempts to fill the gap and shed light on the rhetoric of one type of English persuasive correspondence – the letter of invitation – in the Thai business context.

2. Working definitions

An invitation can be regarded as a *performative* speech act. According to Austin's (1962: 6) Speech Act Theory, a *performative* indicates that "the issuing of the utterance is the performing of an action". Although the verb 'to invite' is not mentioned in his seminal study, a link can be created because it reflects the act of 'announcing an intention' (Austin 1962: 98). Following Austin, Searle (1969, 1975, 1976) expands the concept of speech act further by focusing on 'illocutionary acts' or 'indirect speech acts'. He develops a set of those acts, one of which is called 'directives', which range from asking to commanding. Inviting falls into this category according to Searle's (1976: 11) list of directive verbs (i.e. ask, order, command, request, beg, plead, pray, entreat, invite, permit, and advise). Searle (1976: 11) states:

> The illocutionary point of these consists in the fact that they are attempts (of varying degrees, and hence, more precisely, they are determinates of the determinable which includes attempting) by the speaker to get the hearer to do something. They may be very modest 'attempts' as when I invite you to do it or suggest that you do it, or they may be very fierce attempts as when I insist that you do it.

It is interesting that unlike requests in which cross-cultural studies based on speech act have been conducted rather extensively (e.g. Mulholland 1997; Neumann 1997; Blum-Kulka/House/Kasper 1989), invitations seem to be surprisingly understudied in terms of both spoken and written invitations.

To the best of my knowledge, previous studies on letters of invitation are very few and far between. So far I found one published work by Zhu (2001) who compares persuasive strategies in 40 letters of invitation to trade fairs, 20 of which are written in English by native English speakers and the other 20 are written in Chinese by native (mainland) Chinese. My corpus contains more varieties of invitations than trade fair invitations. Therefore, it is essential to formulate a working definition of 'a letter of invitation' for this study.

Before doing so, it is useful to see how a textbook on business letter writing defines 'a letter of invitation'. One interesting description is found in the textbook on modern business correspondence by McComas and Satterwhite (1993). They explain that there are two types of invitations in business correspondence: (1) formal invitations and (2) informal invitations. In their opinion, a formal invitation is in the form of an invitation card following an established pattern which is usually printed with each line centered. (e.g. The Board of Directors of X or Mr. X requests the pleasure of the company of Mr Y at …) Interestingly, they regard a letter of invitation as an informal invitation. They state:

Informal invitations are written in letter format and are more casual than formal invitations. In addition to 'inviting', they should provide the following specifics about the event:
- the day, date, time,
- place
- reason for the function
- who is included in the invitation
- dress requirements (if any)
- a request for a reply. (McComas/Satterwhite 1993: 147)

I agree with them that there are formal and informal invitations. However, formal and informal are not absolute terms. The degree of formality tends to correlate between (a) mode/layout (e.g. spoken vs written / card vs. letter), (b) occasion (e.g. invitation to the opening ceremony of a multinational joint venture vs. an in-house seminar), (c) role/relationship with the audience (e.g. judging from the forms of address such as Dear sir or madam, Dear Mr + surname, or Dear + first name). Written invitations are generally more formal than spoken ones. The invitation to the opening ceremony of a multinational joint venture is more likely to be in the form of an invitation card whereas that to in-house seminar can simply be in the form of a letter or memo. In the business world nowadays, a letter of invitation is more widely used for setting up business meetings, seminars, conferences or visits. It is socially accepted as a formal invitation, which may be attached with a registration form. An invitation card is exclusively used for occasions such as important receptions or grand opening ceremonies. My corpus does not contain any invitation cards, so we will focus only on letters. As outlined by McComas and Satterwhite (1993) above, a letter of invitation tends to include details such as date, time, place, purpose plus a request for a reply. This gives us some general background of letters of invitation. However, there is no definition of what is meant by 'a letter of invitation'. The following set of criteria was then devised to identify the letters of invitation in my corpus.

A letter of invitation contains at least one message which aims to invite the reader to take part in a social-business activity[1] by

---

1   A social-business activity here refers to any activity which is organized for either business purposes alone (e.g. business conferences/meetings/seminars) or both business and social purposes (e.g. corporate receptions for clients/ employees/business guests, club/society events for members). It excludes non-

"pursuing a verbal, physical or cognitive response" (Yli-Jokipii 1996) under the following conditions:

1) The main purpose of the letter is to invite the reader and/or the reader's company to take part in a social-business activity organised by the writer and/or the writer's company on the grounds of corporate and/or personal levels of mutual business relationships.

2) The invitation(s) can pursue a verbal, physical or cognitive response depending on the context. In addition to a verbal or cognitive response, a physical response is involved when the writer asks for the reader's physical appearance in any social-business event such as an organised meeting, seminar, conference, social function or trade-related visit.

3) The invitation(s) can include an invitation to join an organization/club/society (e.g. as a member or honourary member), and an invitation to contribute to a business-related activity (e.g. as chair, member of the board/committee, or special guest). In this case, the invitation pursues a verbal or cognitive response which may or may not involve any immediate physical response.

4) The reader and/or reader's company has an option of refusal. (following Bargiela-Chiappini/Harris 1996).

5) The invitation(s)'s ostensible purpose must not be profit-oriented. The letter asking the reader to buy the writer's product or service is categorised as 'a letter of sales promotion'. When the invitation to a conference or seminar incurs a registration fee, it is categorised as 'a letter of invitation' if its main purpose is to invite (i.e. inviting a particular person whose business is in the same line as the organised event), not to explicitly promote sales to boost profits.

6) The benefits to both sides (the writer and the reader) are primarily in the areas of networking, sharing professional responsibilities, promoting a true image of the company, philanthropy, etc.

---

business-related personal activity such as wedding ceremonies, funerals, individual parties, etc.

The above criteria serve as working definitions for my data collection. Every letter that matches these criteria will be classified as a letter of invitation and will be analysed in this study.

3. Data classification

In my entire corpus of cross-cultural business correspondence there are 40 correspondence texts which can be put in the category of letters of invitation based on the above-mentioned criteria. They consist of 30 letters and 10 faxes. Each fax is in the letter format and shares similar characteristics of a letter (e.g. containing the date, names of the writer and recipient, salutation and complimentary close). Henceforth they will be all referred to as 'letters of invitation'. To ensure confidentiality, some names, phone numbers and addresses in the letter samples shown in the analysis part were changed while their content remained intact. The following table will present the proportion of the letters written by Thais (TH) to that written by native English speakers or non-Thais (NT):

Description	NT	TH	Total number of letters
Letters	18	12	30
Faxes	7	3	10
Total proportion	25	15	40

Table 1. Number of invitation letters.

The NT letters are written by native speakers of English from the United Kingdom or the United States of America whose companies have business contacts with Thai companies or organisations. As we can see from the table, there are 25 NT letters and 15 TH letters. Due to the unequal proportion between both types of letters, I will include an indication of percentage in some comparisons where necessary. The sources of these letters vary from local Thai companies, Thai public enterprises to multinational corporations. There are ten main groups of businesses which I have summarised in alphabetical order as follows:

- Conference Organising Service (e.g. the Economist Conferences)
- Consultancy (e.g. Anderson Consulting, the Boston Consulting Group)
- Consumer Products Industry (e.g. Unilever Thai Holdings)
- Cultural Institute (e.g. the Siam Society)
- Education (e.g. Harrow International School)
- Finance (e.g. Asian Development Bank, Warburg Dillon Read, Bank of England)
- Information Technology (e.g. Microsoft)
- Utility Industry (e.g. the Electric Generating Authority of Thailand)
- Public/Governmental Sector (e.g. embassies, offices in economic/commercial affairs)
- Publishing (e.g. FORTUNE business magazine).

The main purpose of each letter is to invite the reader to take part in a social-business activity as outlined in the above-mentioned criteria. From my corpus of 40 letters of invitation, the types of invitation can be classified into six groups:

1. Invitations to attend conferences (C), including business forums, summits, and panel discussions;
2. Invitations to attend meetings (M), e.g. board meetings, regular/ scheduled business meetings, discussions and briefings;
3. Invitations to join an organisation/club/society as a member, i.e. inviting the reader to take up the membership (MB);
4. Invitations to attend social-business functions or receptions (R), e.g. breakfast, lunch, dinner, cocktail or other types of social-business parties;
5. Invitations to attend seminars (S), including workshops, road-shows and exhibitions;
6. Invitations to join trade-related visits (V), e.g. project/trade visits, visits to exhibitions or to another companies.

The following table shows the proportion of each type of invitation found in the NT and TH letters of invitation:

Types of invitation	Number of letter(s) – N = 40
1. Invitations to attend conferences (C)	14 (NT=12, TH= 2)
2. Invitations to attend meetings (M)	7 (NT= 4, TH= 3)
3. Invitations to take up a membership (MB)	3 (NT=1, TH= 2)
4. Invitations to attend receptions (R)	5 (NT=4, TH=1)
5. Invitations to attend seminars (S)	6 (NT=2, TH=4)
6. Invitations to join trade-related visits (V)	5 (NT=2, TH=3)

Table 2. Types of invitation.

In terms of distribution, there are samples of the TH and NT letters in each type. The most frequently found type here is 'C' (invitations to conferences) whereas the least frequently found type is 'MB' (invitations to take up a membership). There is a disproportionately large number of NT-C letters and attention will be paid to this to ensure that it does not slow the findings. It may be noted that in general the above types of invitation share similar characteristics especially invitations to conferences, meetings, seminars and visits. The classification is for background information. I will first analyse the 40 letters as a whole, and then differentiate the different types of invitations where necessary. Occasionally some examples will be marked with the above abbreviations (e.g. NT09-C, TH33-R) to distinguish the types of invitation.

First of all, I will examine the letters in terms of their length, measured according to the number of paragraph(s) in each letter. In my corpus, paragraphs in both NT and TH letters are of rather equal length and density. The length of the letters ranges from one to eight paragraphs as displayed in Table 3:

Number of paragraph(s)	Number of letter(s) –N = 40 (25 NT, 15 TH)
1 paragraph	1 (1 NT)
2 paragraphs	4 (3 NT, 1 TH)
3 paragraphs	6 (2 NT, 4 TH)
4 paragraphs	10 (6 NT, 4 TH)
5 paragraphs	10 (6 NT 4 TH)
6 paragraphs	5 (5 NT)
7 paragraphs	3 (1 NT, 2 TH)
8 paragraphs	1 (1 NT)

Table 3. Number of paragraph(s).

The letters with 4 and 5 paragraphs are most extensively found. To-gether they account for 50% of the corpus (20 out of 40 letters). Figure 1 presents the number of paragraph(s) in relation to the proportion (in percentage) of the NT and TH letters:

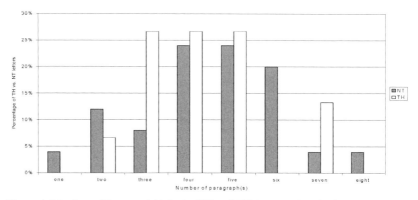

Figure 1. Number of Paragraph(s) in the NT and TH Letters of Invitation.

Figure 1 shows that the majority of the TH letters of invitation contains three to five paragraphs whereas that of the NT letters has four to six paragraphs. As the NT letters outnumber the TH letters (25 NT vs. 15 TH), I chose to examine their number of paragraph(s) in relation to their percentage in order to get a better overall picture. The length of the NT letters seems to be more varied than that of the TH letters. The majority of the NT letters of invitation use four to six paragraphs. Here the average number of paragraphs of the NT letters is 4.44 whereas that of the TH letters is 4.27. This is different from what I found in my cross-cultural analysis of the letters of request in which the NT writers obviously use fewer paragraphs than the TH writers (Chakorn 2006). The NT and TH letters of invitation do not have such difference as most letters range from three to six paragraphs with an average of four paragraphs. Being aware that my corpus is disproportionate, I guarantee that every care will be taken to ensure that this will not interfere with the main findings which focus on the content of the letters

In the next section I will analyse the forty-letter corpus as a whole in terms of rhetorical moves. Each move will be explained and illustrated with examples from my data. Later on similarities and differences between the NT and TH letters of invitation will also be identified.

4. Rhetorical moves in the letters of invitation

From my corpus, it is found that a letter of invitation can be generally characterized by rhetorical moves. Developed along the similar line as Swales' (1990) move analysis and Bhatia's (1993) pattern of moves in sales promotion letters, the rhetorical moves in the letters of invitation here are carefully studied and identified using the data in my corpus. They consist of 6 moves, some of which are deemed obligatory in that they are found in every letter, and some are optional. They are presented as follows:

Move 1	Inviting	*obligatory*
Move 2	Establishing the context (i.e. giving background information, raising the issue, and/or stating purpose)	*optional*
Move 3	Detailing	*obligatory*
Move 4	Soliciting response	*optional* (if missing, then Move 5 appears instead)
Move 5	Anticipating acceptance	*optional* (if missing, then Move 4 appears instead)
Move 6	Expressing thanks	*optional*

In my observation of Move 2, *Establishing the context*, in the invitation letters, I do not take into consideration the inside addresses and salutations although they are part of *establishing the context*. This is because my focus is on the use of Move 2, *Establishing the context*, in the content of the letters. The table below presents the number and percentage of the NT and TH letters that use each of the above-mentioned moves:

Rhetorical Moves	Total NT&TH N = 40	Total %	NT Letters N = 25	NT %	TH Letters N = 15	TH %
1. Inviting	40	100%	25	100%	15	100%
2. Establishing the context	28	70%	19	76%	9	60%
3. Detailing	40	100%	25	100%	15	100%
4. Soliciting response	28	70%	17	68%	11	73%
5. Anticipating acceptance	34	85%	22	88%	12	80%
6. Expressing thanks	2	5%	0	0%	2	13%

Table 4. Rhetorical moves in invitation letters.

Move 1, *Inviting*, and Move 3, *Detailing*, are found in every letter and can be considered as main structural components of a letter of invitation. It should be noted that either Move 4, *Soliciting response*, or Move 5, *Anticipating acceptance*, is obligatory because while many letters have both moves, the others include either Move 4 or Move 5. Move 2, *Establishing the context*, is quite extensively found (70% of the letters, or to be specific, 76% of the NT letters and 60% of the TH letters). Move 6, *Expressing thanks*, is rarely found, which is different from the letters of request and sales promotion. There are only 2 TH letters here that use this move. To illustrate the rhetorical moves as identified above, a detailed analysis of one NT and one TH letter of invitation is presented as follows:

MICROSOFT

December 11, 1996

Mr. Yongyuth Samran
Chairman
Thai Citizen's Bank
924 Bangsamruay Avenue,
GPO Box 1633
Bangkok 10210
Thailand
Dear Mr. Samran:

Please join me as my guest May 7-9, 1997,   *Move 1 Inviting*
when The Microsoft CEO Summit convenes
in Seattle.

Technology is reinventing business practices,   *Move 2 Establishing the context*
transforming corporate structure and realign-   *(raising the issue)*
ing entire industries. The goal of The Micro-   *Move 2 Establishing the context*
soft CEO Summit is to generate and share   *(stating purpose)*
ideas on how we, as company leaders, can
best prepare the corporation for these
challenges and opportunities.

The Summit begins with a welcome reception at the Seattle Four Seasons Olympic
Hotel on Wednesday evening, May 17th. The
sessions will commence the following   *Move 3 Detailing*
morning and will run to the end of the day.
To expand upon the personal relationships
that will have been forged throughout the
day, we will convene at my home for dinner
Thursday evening. The Summit will conclude
at 12:30 p.m. on Friday. Optional activities
will be offered for the remainder of Friday
afternoon. A preliminary agenda is enclosed.

A sampling of Summit participation inclu-
des: Ronald Compton of *Aetna*; Philip Condit   *Move 3 Detailing*
of *Boeing*; Paulo César Ximenes Ferreira of
Banco do Brasil S.A.; Robert Eaton of
Chrysler; Lester Alberthal, Jr. of *EDS*; Fran-
co Bernabé of *Ente Nazionale Idrocarburi
(ENI)*; Andrey Kazmin of Sberbank RF; and
William Esray of Sprint.

Microsoft is pleased to present this Summit in partnership with FORBES Magazine. My staff will follow up with your office to determine your availability. Attendance is limited, so kindly return the enclosed RSVP by Monday, December 30, 1996.

Move 4 Soliciting response

Should you have any questions please call 212-602-1255. I hope I will have the pleasure of welcoming you to Seattle.

Move 5 Anticipating acceptance

Cordially,
(Signature)
William H. Gates Chairman and Chief
Executive Officer

enc.

Move 3 Detailing

Sample 1. Rhetorical Move Analysis of NT01.

Polytechnology Co, Ltd.

Our ref. PLT01/10420/1998
18 December 1998

Khun Wijai Jaruratrungsarit
Manager, Electrical & Process Control
Nestle (Thailand) Co., Ltd.
Tel No. 562-1199 ext. 262
Fax No. 562-1196

Dear Khun Wijai

Subject: Invitation to attend FR Flow Road-show Seminar

Move 1 Inviting

We, Polytechnology Co., Ltd in collaboration with Fisher-Rosemount Singapore Plc.,Ltd would like to invite you to attend 'A One Day Seminar on Fisher-Rosemount Flow Road-show' which will be held on Tuesday 12 January 1999 at 08.30am – 17.00pm (*sic.*) at Radisson Hotel.

Move 1 Inviting

Move 3 Detailing

At this seminar conducted by specialist from Fisher Rosemount Singapore which is not very

Move 3 Detailing

often held, so, we would like you to take this opportunity to attend it for your benefit and knowledge.

We will be very much appreciated if you could be able to spend sometimes with us on this seminar, please kindly reserve your seat in advance by filling in the attached sheet and fax to us at (02) 854-1776, by 4 January 1999 or call Khun Nattawan Nichapa at (02) 690-7050 extension 123.

Move 5 Anticipating acceptance

Move 4 Soliciting response

We very much look forward to hearing from you.

Move 4 Soliciting response

Thank you.

Move 6 Expressing thanks

Sincerely yours
(signature)
Uthai Suwanthip
Senior Vice President

Attchs : Venue
Agenda
Back Ground (*sic.*) Experiences
Map

Move 3 Detailing

Sample 2. Rhetorical Move Analysis of TH38.

We can see that both examples use almost every rhetorical move presented earlier. Both start with Move 1, *Inviting*. This move is followed by Move 2, *Establishing the context* (raising the issue and stating purpose), in NT01. TH38 does not have Move 2. After *Inviting*, it goes straight to Move 3, *Detailing*, which is shorter and not as informative as that in NT01. NT01 states the deadline for reply in Move 4, *Soliciting response*. It does not have Move 6, *Expressing thanks*, and it ends with Move 5, *Anticipating acceptance*. TH38, on the other hand, does not state any deadline, and ends with the formulaic expression '*look forward to* + hearing from you', followed by Move 6, *Expressing thanks*.

The above-mentioned six-move pattern seems to be practical and suitable for my data. It should be noted that the sequencing of six rhetorical moves is flexible. The positions of those moves are not required to appear in the same order as presented although it is obvious that Moves 4, 5 and 6 (*Soliciting response, Anticipating acceptance and Expressing thanks*, consecutively) always appear after Move 2, *Establishing the context*, and, in most cases, after Move 3, *Detailing*. Moves 1, 2 and 3 may alternate to appear at the beginning of the letter whereas Moves 4, 5 and 6 can take turn appearing at the end of the letter. This initial sequencing of the moves is to facilitate the rhetorical analysis as a whole. The following part is aimed at giving detailed description of each rhetorical move in this six-move pattern which includes some linguistic realisations where applicable.

4.1. Move 1 Inviting

Inviting is the essence of the letter. As the main purpose of the letter of invitation is to invite the reader to do something, this move can be considered as the core of the message. The writer usually specifies the person he/she invites in this move, which is normally 'you' (the reader). If the invitation is not directly for the reader, in most cases it is for the representative(s) of the reader's company on whom the reader has an authority to decide. This move consists of at least one invitation message. Unlike a request which can be subtle or indirect, an invitation message is explicit, direct and to the point. This is because the writer normally shows his/her attempt to invite the reader. In my corpus, this move includes two main types of invitation messages: (a) plain invitation, and (b) detailed invitation.

4.1.1. Plain invitation

The writer uses this type of message when he/she extends the invitation without any specific detail on date, time or venue of the event. For example,

(1)   We would like to invite you as our guest for this meeting. (NT27)

(2)   We would be honoured if you could join this function. (NT10)

(3)   It therefore gives us great pleasure to extend formal invitation to you for this exclusive event which will be followed by lunch. (TH35)

When the writer invites the reader to become a member of a society or organisation, the message is considered as plain invitation if the details are not included in the same sentence as the invitation message. For example,

(4)   On behalf of the membership of the Siam Society Under Royal Patronage, it is my pleasure to extend to you an invitation to join our organization. (TH34)

Sometimes the writer may include the reason why he/she invites the reader or the purpose/objective of the invitation in the message. For example,

(5)   Because of your prominence as an executive in THAILAND, we are pleased to invite you to join other international executives and become an International Associate of the Conference Board. (NT07)

(6)   We would like to reconfirm our invitation because your presence, dear Mr. Viravat, would give us the opportunity to discuss topics which might be of mutual interest. (NT18)

It should be noted that most plain invitations are short and precise because the details of the event are presented in preceding or following sentences or paragraphs, or sometimes in attached documents.

4.1.2. Detailed invitation

The type of message involves both Move 1, *Inviting*, and Move 3, *Detailing*, as it contains information on date, time and/or venue of the event in the same sentence as the invitation. For example:

(7)   On behalf of the Economist Conferences, I am pleased to invite you to attend the First Roundtable with the Government of the Lao People's Democratic Republic from April 23 to 25 1997 at the Lane Xang Hotel in Vientiane. (NT02)

(8)   We would be delighted if you would be able to join us at a small luncheon at the Heritage Club –"Governor's Room" on March 10 at 12.00. (NT06)

(9)   We, Polytechnology Co., Ltd in collaboration with Fisher-Rosemount Singapore Plc., Ltd would like to invite you to attend 'A One Day Seminar on Fisher-Rosemount Flow Roadshow' which will be held on Tuesday 12 January 1999 at 08.30am – 17.00pm (*sic.*) at Radisson Hotel. (TH38)

We can see that the main information of the event is presented in the detailed invitation messages above, which represent both Move 1 and Move 3. In addition, the writer sometimes elaborates such information in different sentences or paragraphs, which are regarded as Move 3, *Detailing*.

Plain invitations are considered as Move 1, *Inviting*, while detailed invitations are perceived as Move 1 and Move 3. It is interesting that the TH letters tend to use more detailed invitations (67%) than plain invitations (33%). On the other hand, 60% of the NT letters use plain invitations, and the rest 40% use detailed invitations.

As for the orientations, we can see from the examples above that the writers use both we- and you-orientations in a similar proportion, except for NT07 and NT18 (under 'plain invitations') in which the you-orientation tends to be predominant. The main mood type is declarative. As this move is the core of the invitation letter, the linguistic realisation of the invitation messages written by the TH and NT writers will be discussed in detail in Section 5.

4.2. Move 2 Establishing the Context

In a letter of invitation, the writer frequently makes an introduction which is related to the invitation. I propose to call it 'Establishing the context'. The writer uses this move as an introduction to the business in order to pave the way for the invitation. In my data, this move can be divided into three types: (a) giving background information, (b) raising the issue, and (c) stating purpose.

4.2.1. Giving background information

To establish the context, the writer may begin by giving background of the business which is related to the consecutive invitation. For example,

(10) Harrow has a long and very close relationship with Thai Royal Family for 100 years as you see twenty four Thai Royal Princes including Royal Price Mahidol, father of His Majesty the King, graduated from Harrow. (TH04-MB)

(11)   As you may know, The Conference Board is the premier global network for senior business executives. Companies associated with the Board range from large multinationals to smaller, more entrepreneurial ventures. Executives benefit specifically from exchanging information and experiences with peers from around the world. (NT07-MB)

(12)   Each year The Boston Consulting Group holds a series of Chief Executive conferences focusing on the utility industry sector. (NT17-C)

(13)   As I am sure many of you are aware, this year marks the one hundreth (*sic.*) anniversary of the first visit of His Majesty King Rama V to Europe. This momentous trip, which had such an impact on both Thai foreign relations and domestic policies, is one that we at The Siam Society recognized as an event to not only celebrate, but to look at closely for all its ramifications. (TH20-S)

In *giving background information*, the writer extensively uses the topic-orientation. The purpose is to create a link to the upcoming invitation in following paragraph(s) of the letter. In my data, it is the most widely used type of statement under Move 2, *Establishing the context*.

4.2.2. Raising the issue

This is somewhat different from *giving background information* in that *raising the issue* tends to create an obvious link between the writer or the writer's company and the reader. Here the writer tries to raise the issue involving the reader before moving on to the invitation. In my data, the writer either makes some simple reference or elaborates the frame of reference by stressing the importance of the event. For example:

[Simple Reference]

(14)   We sent a (*sic.*) honorary invitation to you in July and hope that you have received it in time. (NT18-C)

[Elaborate Frame of Reference]

(15)   The introduction of a single Eurocurrency will have wide ranging significance to financial institutions around the globe, as they seek to develop hedging and other strategies in this new market environment. We have asked Robin to provide a brief overview of some of the key issues and developments to a selected group of leading Thai bankers. (NT06-R)

(16)   The previous three conferences were very successful. Almost all those who
        were able to attend (see attached lists from 1996 and 1997) have suggested
        that we hold a similar conference in 1998 and have expressed their intention
        to attend, provided their schedules allow. (NT17-C)

Under 'simple reference', the writer simply raises the issue directly to
the reader without mentioning the background of the business. In
'elaborate frame of reference', the writer tends to capture the reader's
interests by highlighting the expertise and/or achievements of the
company. This characteristic can be compared to Bhatia's (1993)
Move 1, *Establishing credentials*, in sales promotion letters.

Due to the fact that the writer tries to create a link between the
writer or the writer's company and the reader, it is noticeable that
he/she uses both we- and you-orientations. Interestingly NT17-C
makes an elaborate frame of reference to the company's success in
holding conferences in the past. Compared to its previous paragraph
"Each year The Boston Consulting Group holds a series of Chief
Executive conferences focusing on the utility industry sector", which
is categorised as 'giving background information', the paragraph
presented above is different, and thus, is categorised as 'raising the
issue'.

4.2.3. Stating purpose

In establishing the context, the writer may state the purpose of the
event to which the reader is subsequently invited. The examples are as
follows:

(17)   The purpose of the HPC Research Forum is to ensure that we use the best and
        most appropriate science to optimise delivery from the HPC Category
        Research programme. (NT24-C)

(18)   The aim of the Asian Business Breakfast Club is to form a non-political forum
        for successful Asian entrepreneurs in the United Kingdom to enable them to
        get together in congenial surroundings and discuss matters of common interest
        with Government and Shadow Ministers and captains of mainstream business.
        (NT30-M)

(19)   The objectives of organising this reception are to promote and encourage Thai
        fruits to the UK market. (TH33-R)

In *stating purpose*, the only orientation found is the topic-orientation. The keywords for this type of statement are, for example, 'purpose(s)', 'aim(s)', and 'objective(s)'.

In conclusion, the NT letters tend to combine the three aspects of Move 2 together (*giving background information, raising the issue, and stating purpose*) while the TH letters prefer to use one at a time. This move is found in 19 NT letters (76%) and 9 TH letters (60%) as a whole.

4.3. Move 3 Detailing

In this move, the writer informs the reader of the details concerning the invitation. It can be brief or very informative depending on the context. This move typically involves a date/time/venue, which is often included in the invitation messages (Move 2, *Inviting*), as discussed in 4.1. In the invitations to conferences (C), seminars (S) and meetings (M), this move normally includes four main issues:

4.3.1. Structure of the event[2]

This refers to how the general description of the types of conferences/ seminars/meetings including the topic(s) and/or other feature(s) that the writer wants the reader to know.

(20) During this half day seminar we will share with you leading edge technology and applications that businesses implement to enhance their competitive advantage and operation efficiency. (NT40)

4.3.2. Main speaker(s)[3]

This refers to how reference is made to the name(s) of the main or keynote speaker(s) in the conferences/seminars/meetings.

---

2   This refers to the general description of the types of conferences/seminars/ meetings including the topic(s) and/or other feature(s) that the writer wants the reader to know.

3   This regards how reference it made the name(s) of the main or keynote speaker(s) in the conferences/seminars/meetings.

(21)   Speakers include Mrs. Naya Vechinsri, Assistant Governor of the Bank of Thailand and Mr. Gerben Kuyper, Senior Executive Vice President of ABN AMRO Bank. (NT09)

4.3.3. Fee/Funding

This is the description of the condition(s) relating to registration fee and/or funding.

(22)   Pre-registration for the seminar is B1,200, and will take place through December 12, after which registration will be B1,500. (TH20)

(23)   Andersen Consulting offers to fund all your expenses which include round-trip airfare (First Class), hotel accommodation, meals and transportation during the conference period. (TH16)

4.3.1   Evaluation and/or indication of the benefit(s)[4]

Here the writer highlights the benefits that the reader will gain if he/she accepts the invitation, and participates in the conferences/seminars/meetings.

(24)   Interactive workshop sessions will enable you to probe specific operating and investment issues in greater detail. At the end of this two-and-a-half day dialogue, you will come away from the Roundtable with an indepth knowledge of the opportunities and challenges of operating in Laos, a greater sense of the likely future direction of the business environment and have met with the top business and political leadership of the country. (NT02)

(25)   FORTUNE is putting every resource behind this undertaking to ensure that all participants come away with fresh insights and useful information for managing in the global marketplace. The entire event will be executed at the highest level of quality and service, suitable for a group of this importance. (NT11)

(26)   The New Economy is about knowledge and ideas, and we believe your company will benefit from this exchange of knowledge and ideas with our experts. (TH35)

---

4   This is quite similar to, though not as cogent as Bhatia's (1993) Move 2(iii), *Indicating value of the product or service*, in the analysis of sales promotion letters.

As for the invitations to trade visits (V), the writer uses the above-mentioned except *Main speaker(s)*. The emphasis tends to be on the structure of the visit.

Unlike the invitations to conferences/seminars/meetings, the invitations to receptions (R) do not contain explicit evaluation/ indication of the reader's benefits, and rarely incur any charge or fee.

The invitations to take a membership in a society/organisation (MB) involves general details of the membership. This type of invitations also focuses strongly on the evaluation/indication of the benefits to the reader in order to persuade him/her to join in as a member. The following examples will illustrate this point:

(27)   Perhaps, though, the greatest value you will receive from membership in the Conference Board is being part of a global network. You will have the opportunity to develop personal contacts, and through them gain the insights that can help your company excel. (NT07)

To sum up, the presentations of Move 3 in different types of invitation can vary slightly. However, their main aim is the same, that is, to inform the reader of the event to which he or she is invited. This type of information is indispensable for the invitation; therefore, Move 3, *Detailing*, is obligatory in the letters of invitation.

4.4. Move 4 Soliciting Response

This move is similar to Bhatia's (1993) Move 5, *Soliciting response*. While *soliciting response* in sales promotion letters is for boosting sales by initiating new business relations or strengthening the existing ones, this move in letters of invitation is for conducting necessary business routines or procedures concerning the invitation. The writer needs to know whether the reader will accept or decline the invitation so that appropriate preparations will be proceeded. Although replying to an invitation is a social-business etiquette which people should do without being told, many invitation letters tend to include a request for the reader to reply.

In this move, the writer normally asks the reader to respond to the invitation, and gives the name of the contact person and/or a specific telephone or fax number or an email address to encourage response. Sometimes the writer also encloses a registration or reply form with the letter, and asks the reader to return it to the writer's company. For example,

(28) Please complete the attached registration form and fax to ... (NT40)

(29) Enclosed for your review is a complete description of member benefits, as well as your Membership Invitation. Please let us know soon if you are accepting or declining this invitation. (NT07)

When there is a limitation to the invitation such as a limited number of seats in a conference, the writer often informs the reader to encourage prompt reply. For example,

(30) Due to the small number of guests we are inviting, we would be grateful if you could be so kind as to respond at your earliest convenience by fax on ..., or to my attention at the address set forth above. (NT08)

From my data, the most common linguistic realisation of this move is the use of the imperative mood type with the politeness marker 'please'. The declarative mood type is occasionally found. It can be in the form of 'If-clause' as in NT08 above, or in a plain declarative clause with the verbal phrase 'look forward to...', for example, "I look forward to your reply" (NT28) and "In the meantime, my warmest good wishes and I look forward to hearing from you" (NT29). Although this move is regarded as optional, it is found in 70% of the letters (28 out of 40).

4.5. Move 5 Anticipating acceptance

The writer often expresses in the invitation letter that he/she is anticipating acceptance from the reader. The writer expects the reader to accept the invitation, and thus tries to convey this 'anticipation' message to the reader. The statements concerning anticipating acceptance are generally of the declarative mood type. The writer expresses his/her wish that the reader will join the writer or the writer's company in the event the reader is invited to, such as a business meeting, reception or conference. For example, "I hope you will be able to join us in Vientiane in April to ensure that your company – and your views – are part of this important forum for discussion" (NT02).

From my data, the linguistic realisation of this move involves an extensive use of the verb 'hope' and the verbal phrase 'look forward to'. On the surface, the anticipation statements with the verbal phrase 'look forward to' here might look similar to those in Move 4, *Soliciting response*. However, the distinction is that the statements in this move clearly express the positive anticipation of the reader's acceptance, not just their reply. Here the writer often assumes that the reader will accept the invitation, as in "We look forward to meeting you on Saturday, July 29, 2000" (TH35). The writer sometimes makes a strategic statement by adding the adjective of appraisal, for example, "I look forward to your *favourable* reply" (NT32) and "We would be delighted by your *positive* response and hope to see you in Strasbourg" (NT18).

In my corpus, the writer tends to equally use the verb 'hope' and the verbal phrase 'look forward to'. Both we- and you-orientations are extensively found. This move is used in 85% of the letters of invitation. Many letters contain both Move 4, *Soliciting response*, and Move 5, *Anticipating acceptance*. As stated earlier, if Move 4 is missing, then Move 5 appears instead, or vice versa. It is interesting that the writer usually includes positive or optimistic remarks of the reader's acceptance in the letters of invitation.

4.6. Move 6 Expressing thanks

The writer may express his/her thankfulness or gratitude to the reader. This is similar to Bhatia's (1993) Move 7, *Ending politely*, in sales promotion letters. Only 2 Thai letters of invitation in my corpus contain this move. Their expressions of thanks are formulaic, and are preceded by Move 4, *Soliciting Response*. One is a plain expression of thanks: "Thank you" (TH38), and the other is considered as elaborated thanks: "Thank you in advance for your kind assistance" (TH38). It seems that the writer wants to thank the reader for his/her future response to the invitation. This move is very infrequently found in the letters of invitation, and is regarded as optional.

So far I have covered the move analysis of the letters of invitation. The structural description of all six moves is aimed at providing better understanding of the general structure of the invitation letters. Although Zhu (2001: 9) identifies eight moves in her analysis (i.e. *introducing, inviting, advertising, offering incentives, inviting again, registration details, encouraging further contact,* and *polite closing*), I did not follow her move structure because it is designed for the letters of invitation to trade fairs only. Some similarities can be found in her moves concerning *introducing* (similar to *Establishing the context*), *inviting,* and *encouraging further contact* (similar to *Soliciting response* and *Anticipating acceptance*). Zhu (2001) found an extra move called 'Move 5 *inviting again*' (often occurred towards the end) in eight of the 20 Chinese letters in her corpus, which makes them different from her English letters. In my corpus, neither NT nor TH letter has such move. The next section presents the analysis of the invitation messages.

5. Analysis of the invitation messages

In this section, we will examine the invitation messages which are the core of the letters of invitation. The focus is on their positions and linguistic realisation especially in relation to each type of invitation. Most letters contain multi-paragraph texts. There are only four letters with two paragraphs and only one letter with one paragraph. According to Chakorn (2006), the length of the letters of request relatively influences the distribution and positions of requests. However, the length of the invitation letters in this corpus does not have such effect. Many NT and TH invitation letters with four to six paragraphs start the invitation messages early in the first or second paragraphs.

5.1. Positions of the invitation messages

It is interesting that the distribution of invitation message(s) in all 40 letters is within one paragraph. It should be noted that each letter has only one invitation message which is either in the form of a short, simple sentence or a long, complex sentence. So there are 40 invitation messages in total. Their positions are displayed in the following table:

Positions of the invitation message(s)	NT N = 25	TH N = 15	Total N = 40
1st Paragraph	12 (48%)	8 (53%)	20 (50%)
2nd Paragraph	5 (20%)	5 (33%)	10 (25%)
3rd Paragraph	5 (20%)	1 (7%)	6 (15%)
4th Paragraph	3 (12%)	1 (7%)	4 (10%)

Table 5. Positions of the invitation message(s).

It is obvious that both NT and TH writers tend to start the invitation messages in the first paragraph. In fact, among these 20 letters, 16 letters use the invitation messages as an opening sentence which appears right at the beginning of the body of the letters. The other four relegate their invitation messages to the second sentence in the first paragraph, after Move 2, *Establishing the context*. Those sixteen letters whose invitation messages are in the initial position of the first paragraph consist of 9 NT and 7 TH letters. This is worth mentioning here because it is noticeable that the TH writers do not adopt what Hinds (1990) calls a '*delayed introduction of purpose*' or '*quasi-inductive*' style of writing in this type of persuasive letter as they do in the letters of request (Chakorn 2006).

5.2. Linguistic realisation of the invitation messages

In 4.1, I discussed the content of Move 1, *Inviting*. The forty invitation messages belong to this move. It is interesting to see how the invitation messages are realised in terms of their textual and linguistic features. Regardless of their positions, I will examine the linguistic realisation of all invitation messages. First of all, it is useful to divide them into 4 groups. The first group consists of the invitations to conferences (C), seminars (S), and meetings (M). These three types of invitation can be grouped together for this analysis because they share similar characteristics. The second group is the invitations to receptions (R). The third group is the invitations to trade-related visits (V). And the last group is the invitations to take a membership in a society/organisation (MB).

5.2.1. Invitations to conferences (C), seminars (S), and meeting (M)

There are 27 invitation messages of this type (18 NT, 9TH). The most common linguistic feature used is the verb 'to invite', which is mainly found in the form of 'I/We + would like + to invite + you + to attend…', for example,

(31)   We, Polytechnology Co., Ltd in collaboration with Fisher-Rosemount
       Singapore Plc., Ltd *would like to invite you to attend* 'A One Day Seminar on
       Fisher-Rosemount Flow Roadshow' which will be held on … (TH38)

(32)   On behalf of the HPC Research Management Team and the other members of
       the Research Forum, *I would like to invite you to attend* the next Research
       Forum which will be reviewing the Laundry Research programme. (NT24)

The term 'on behalf of' is occasionally used in the invitation messages, and always appears at the beginning of the sentence. Sometimes the writer may use the term 'I am pleased/delighted + to invite…':

(33)   On behalf of the Economist Conferences, *I am pleased to invite you to attend*
       the First Roundtable with the Government … (NT02)

(34)   Following the success of AsiaConnects in Kualar Lumpur and EuroConnects,
       our established annual event in Europe, *I am delighted to invite* a representa-
       tive of Airports Authority of Thailand to AsiaConnects 2000. (NT23)

Another term is 'to extend this/our invitation' which is found in different styles as follows:

(35)   On behalf of Deputy Prime Minister Kang Kyong Shik of the Republic of
       Korea and Mr. Richard McClean, Publisher and Chief Executive of the
       International Herald Tribune, *I take great pleasure in extending this compli-
       mentary invitation for you to attend* the 1997 Korea Summit. (NT08)

(36)   *It therefore gives us great pleasure to extend formal invitation to you* for this
       exclusive event which will be followed by lunch. (TH35)

(37)   On behalf of the TVA, *I would like to extend our invitation to you or your
       representative to attend* the above which will be held on … (TH37)

We can see that the verb 'to attend' is also used extensively. There is one NT example which uses a 'self-obligation' statement in the form of 'If-clause': "We would appreciate it if you are able to attend the ASEAN-UK Business Forum's meeting scheduled for tomorrow – Friday 12th at 9.30a, at the Philippines Embassy" (NT26). The terms 'pleasure' and 'opportunity' are occasionally found, as in the following examples:

(38) It is my *pleasure* to invite you to the next meeting of the Board of Advisors and Governors ... (TH13)

(39) We would like to take this *opportunity* to invite and propose to your goodself our sponsorship scheme. (TH14)

As discussed earlier in 4.1, the invitation messages can be of two types: plain invitations and detailed invitations (in which date, time and/or venue of the event are included). There are 11 detailed invitations here (6NT, 5TH), which accounts for 41%. All letters use the declarative mood type except one NT letter which uses the imperative mood type:

(40) Please join me as my guest May 7-9, 1997, when The Microsoft CEO Summit convenes in Seattle. (NT01)

There does not appear to be a clear-cut distinction in the use the we- and you-orientations between the NT and TH invitations. However, there are a few exceptional cases in which the writer attempts to put an emphasis on 'you' the reader. It is realised through a passive voice where 'you' is the subject. For example,

(41) You are cordially invited to attend this conference on Thursday 29th May 1997 at the Ballroom of the Regent Hotel, 155 Rajdamri Road, Bangkok 10330. (NT09)

(42) You are cordially invited to join us for what promises to be an extraordinary event. (NT11)

(43) You are invited to attend:
Converged Networks – Unifying Your Enterprise Business Strategy, Tuesday, April 11, 2000
The Ballroom, The Regent Bangkok Hotel
8:30-12:00am (NT40)

In the above examples, 'you' is clearly emphasized in the form of 'you are (cordially) invited to…'. It is noticeable that only NT letters use this type of passive voice in the invitation message. The TH writer only uses active voice. To sum up, apart from the passive voice and imperative mood type, there is no other particular difference between the NT and TH invitations in this category.

5.2.2. Invitations to receptions (R)

There are 5 invitations to receptions in my corpus (4 NT, 1 TH). Apart from the verb 'to invite', another common linguistic feature is the verb 'to join' and the indication of the type of reception. For example,

(44) *We would be delighted if you would be able to join* us at a small luncheon at the Heritage Club … (NT06)

(45) *We would be honoured if you could join* this function (official invitation is enclosed). (NT10)

Both NT examples above use the 'self-obligation' statements (i.e. we would be delighted/honoured if…). The only TH example in this category is as follows:

(46) The Office of Commercial Affairs, Royal Thai Embassy *have the great pleasure to invite you to* the Reception of "Exotic Thai Fruits" on Friday 23rd June 2000 from 5.30-8.00pm at Royal Lancaster Hotel, Lancaster Terrace, London W2 2TY. (TH33)

The term 'opportunity' is also used in one NT example: "I would like to have the opportunity to invite you for lunch and also to update you on the products/sales/research capabilities of DMG across Global Markets products and identify business opportunities" (NT32). As there are only a few examples, it is impossible to point out any difference between the NT and TH invitations to receptions.

5.2.3. Invitations to trade-related visits (V)

The common linguistic features of this type of invitations are the verbs 'to invite' and 'to visit'. There are 5 examples: 2 NT, 3 TH. Most invitations in this category use the term 'to invite + you + to visit', for example,

(47)   During that trip, *I would like to invite you to visit* me at EGAT to renew our relationship and to discuss matters of our mutual interest. (TH15)

(48)   Further to our telephone conversation earlier today, *I am writing to formally invite you to visit* Australia as a guest of the Australian Government ... (NT19)

Another way of inviting includes the terms 'pleasure' and 'to extend our invitation' as in the following example:

(49)   *We take pleasure in extending our invitation* to you for a trade visit and discussion to Thailand ... (TH22)

Again, due to a limited number of examples, it cannot be assumed that there is any difference between the NT and TH invitations to trade-related visits.

5.2.4. Invitations to take a membership in a society/organisation (MB)

There are only 3 invitations of this type in my corpus (1 NT, 2 TH). Like some other types, the verbs 'to invite' and 'to join' are prominent. For example,

(50)   Mom Rajawonge Chaftu Mongol Sonakul asked me to see and *invite* you as a founder and shareholder of the best British Public School, i.e. Harrow School implanted in Thailand. (TH04)

(51)   Because of your prominence as an executive in THAILAND, *we are pleased to invite you to join* other international executives and become an International Associate of the Conference Board. (NT07)

(52)   *On behalf of* the membership of the Siam Society Under Royal Patronage, *it is my pleasure to extend to you an invitation to join* our organization. (TH34)

The first two examples have a strong focus on 'you', the reader. The last example is a TH invitation with the terms 'on behalf of' and 'to extend an invitation' which is similar to some examples in Type C-invitation. As there are very few examples, we cannot compare between the TH and NT invitations of this type.

In conclusion, the invitation messages are mainly realised by the common use of the verbs 'to invite', 'to attend', 'to join' which can be presented in different forms of sentence. The NT invitations have a more variety of presentations. It includes the imperative mood and passive voice in the first type (Conference and Seminar), and also the self-obligation statements in the first and second types (Meeting and Reception respectively). Interestingly, no TH invitations use the self-obligation statement at all. The TH writers only use the active voice in the declarative mood type, and tend to use more detailed invitations than plain invitations. However, the lexical choices are somewhat similar between the NT and TH invitation messages.

7. Rhetorical appeals as persuasive strategies in letters of invitation

Persuasive discourse can be studied using the Greek framework of western rhetoric originated by Aristotle. Campbell (1998) examines rhetorical conventions in two business letters written in English by a native English speaker and by a Chinese speaker. Aristotle, as cited in Campbell (1998: 38), noted that there are two kinds of persuasion, one stemming from sources external to the persuader (inartistic or atechnic proofs – witnesses, contracts, tortures, oaths) and those the speaker has to invent – entechnic proofs. "One must use the former and invent the latter" (Aristotle. Translated by Kennedy 1991: 37).

Campbell (1998) focuses on the entechnic proofs (or artistic proofs) which, according to Aristotle, have three parts: *logos, ethos* and *pathos*, all of which are seen as inseparable although they may not have the same level of priority in persuasive discourse. Campbell (1998: 38) states, "the logos represents arguments and evidence in the matter under discussion, pathos (emotion) the reader's stake in that matter, and ethos (character) the claims of the author". His findings show that the English letter has a strong logical appeal (*logos*) and lacks any appeal to either *ethos* or *pathos* whereas the Chinese letter has an inseparable combination of *logos, ethos* and *pathos*. Campbell (1998: 40) concludes that "the concept of reason couched in emotion marks a difference between Chinese and Western rhetorics". He also presents a reconstruction of each letter by improving its rhetorical conventions in order to enhance its effectiveness upon the reader.

Hyland's (1998) study focuses on metadiscourse in 137 CEO's persuasive letters in English that appeared in different annual reports of international and Hong Kong companies. He examines how CEOs use metadiscourse, which is considered as non-propositional material, to realise rational (*logos*), credible (*ethos*) and affective (*pathos*) appeals. According to Hyland (1998), rational appeals are realised through how writers logically define problems, support claims and state conclusions. Credibility appeals involve creating an *ethos* or the writers' integrity and authority essential for credible communication. Pathos or affective appeals mean that the writers attend to the desired effects of his/her text on the readers by "looking at the text from the readers' perspective, addressing their situation, empathizing with their values, and directly inviting them to respond" (Hyland 1998: 238) He concludes that metadiscourse is central to the creation of rational, credible, and affective appeals in CEOs' letters.

Zhu's (2001) comparative study of English and Chinese persuasive strategies in trade fair invitations supports Campbell's (1998) findings. By examining the corpus of 20 authentic English letters written by native speakers and 20 authentic Chinese letters written by mainland Chinese businessmen, Zhu (2001) points out that the English letters have a strong *logos* while the Chinese letters tend to use *logos*, *ethos*, and *pathos* simultaneously as they emphasize an appeal both to logic and to emotions. She cites Aristotle's (1991) concept of persuasive rhetoric and relates it to the Chinese rhetorical tradition in which "there seem to be a clear stress on combining pathos, ethos and logos" (Zhu 2001: 5).

Identifying *logos*, *ethos* and *pathos* in letters of invitation may create a better understanding of some cross-cultural persuasive strategies between Thai and English business professionals. In this study, the three types of appeals are found in the 40 letters of invitation. Logos is usually found in Move 1, *Establishing the context*, in which the writer gives background information, raises the issue, and/or states the purpose of invitation. For example,

[Invitation to a seminar]

(53)   As I am sure many of you are aware, this year marks the one hundreth (*sic*.) anniversary of the first visit of His Majesty King Rama V to Europe. This momentous trip, which had such an impact on both Thai foreign relations and

domestic policies, is one that we at The Siam Society recognized as an event to not only celebrate, but to look at closely for all its ramifications. (TH20)

Sometimes the writer expresses the rational appeals in the main invitation message (Move 2, *Inviting*), for instance, "In order to explore the issues, challenges, and consequences concerning the new currency, ABN AMRO Bank will present a conference titled: [...]". (NT09) Logos is also found in Move 3, *Detailing* (under the evaluation and/or indication of the benefits). For example,

[Invitation to an e-business workshop/seminar]

(54)   The New Economy is about knowledge and ideas, and we believe your company will benefit from this exchange of knowledge and ideas with our experts. (TH35)

Ethos or the credibility appeals are often mixed with *logos* as in the following example,

[Invitation to a conference]

(55)   The previous three conferences were very successful. Almost all those who were able to attend (see attached lists from 1996 and 1997) have suggested that we hold a similar conference in 1998 and have expressed their intention to attend, provided their schedules allow. (NT17)

Ethos can be realized through the description of the socio-business activity to which the reader is invited. For instance, the *ethos* of an invitation to a seminar involves the structure or agenda, main speaker(s), and evaluation/indication of the benefit(s); all of which help establish the credibility of the writer's company and are crucial to the reader's decision whether to accept or decline the invitation.

Unlike the letters of request, *pathos* is less used in the letters of invitation. It is expressed in a rather different way. No letter shows an acknowledgement of the success of the reader's company. Only a few TH letters emphasize the reader's importance by implying that his/her support can make the event successful, for example, "Looking forward to receiving your fullest support to make this forthcoming conference a success in Chiangmai" (TH14I). Most letters with the emotional appeals tend to focus on the writer's strong hope or anticipation for the reader's acceptance of the invitation. For example,

(56)   So, Khun Viravat, I hope you will accept this invitation and join us in Barcelona. (TH16)

(57)   We look forward to your warm participation. (NT40)

(58)   We will be very much appreciated if you could be able to spend sometimes with us on this seminar. (TH38)

The NT writers use little *pathos* which is realized through some formulaic expressions such as 'I/We hope...' and 'I/We look forward to'. On the other hand, the TH writers tend to make more effort in showing their determined expectations for the reader's participation as we can see in the above examples. Another interesting feature of the TH letters with emotional appeals is that the writer sometimes demonstrates common ground with the reader by addressing his/her need or interest before encouraging him/her to accept the invitation. For example,

(59)   I feel that these planned events will be of particular interest to Siam Society members and I very much hope you will have to opportunity to attend. (TH20)

As in the letters of request, collectivism is often expressed in the TH letters of invitation through the explanation of the benefits that the reader can receive at a company level, not just at an individual level. Many TH letters reveal this characteristic, and some explicitly express the mutual relationship-building, for example,

(60)   We hope to provide you with a better understanding of our operations and seek to further strengthen our business relationship and cooperation. (TH22)

In conclusion, my findings extend Zhu's (2001) to a wider corpus of general letters of invitation: the NT letters use stronger logical appeals whereas the TH letters use both logical and emotional appeals at the same time (similar to Chinese letters in Zhu's study). The TH letters also demonstrate a more collaborative image than the NT ones do, which suggests collectivism. This resembles Zhu's (2001: 15) findings about her Chinese corpus as she states, "the host-guest relationship is accentuated throughout the [Chinese] letter".

7. Conclusion

This chapter has studied the rhetorical patterns of the letters of invitation and identified the relevant moves and their linguistic realisations as well as the cross-cultural persuasive strategies. A six-move pattern has been identified and applied to every letter. Both NT and TH letters appear to have similar moves except that Move 6, *Expressing thanks*, is found in only 2 TH letters. Unlike the letters of request in which the NT writers use fewer paragraphs than the TH writers, the majority of the NT letters of invitation have four to six paragraphs whereas that of the TH letters have three to five paragraphs. There is no obvious difference in terms of length as the average is four paragraphs. Interestingly, the TH writers do not adopt what Hinds (1990) calls the 'delayed introduction of purpose' style of writing in their invitation letters as they do in the letters of request. Most invitation messages (both NT and TH) are found in the first paragraph, mainly in the first sentence. Only 2 TH letters have the invitation messages in the third and fourth paragraphs respectively. The concept of 'delayed introduction of purpose' is, therefore, not applicable in this type of persuasive correspondence.

The common linguistic feature used in invitation messages is the verb 'to invite', especially in the form of 'I/We + would like + to invite + you + to attend/join/visit…'. The mood type is mostly declarative. Self-obligation statements are not found in TH invitation messages. The NT invitations sometimes use imperative mood and passive voice whereas the TH ones use only declarative mood and active voice, and tend to include more details of the invitations. The we- and you-orientations tend to be equally found in both NT and TH letters, and the topic-orientation is usually found in Move 3, *Detailing*. In conclusion, local socio-cultural constraints do not seem to be striking in this study. Compared to the analysis of NT and TH letters of request (Chakorn 2006), the letters of invitation in this corpus reveal fewer cross-cultural differences.

My findings on the rhetorical appeals support Campbell's (1998) and Zhu's (2001) in that the NT letters generally have a strong rational appeal or *logos*. The TH letters tend to use a combination of *logos*, *ethos* and *pathos*, although they may not have the same priority.

Most TH letters seem to be oriented towards collectivism and relationship-building while most NT letters tend to be more individualistic. Perhaps this can support Wierzbicka's (1991) claim that 'harmony' is interpreted differently in the western culture and the Far Eastern culture. Still there is a need for more business discourse study which can pin down further cross-cultural differences especially in writing conventions among international business professionals both linguistically and culturally.

References

Aristotle 1991. *Aristotle on Rhetoric: A Theory of Civic Discourse* (Translated by Kennedy, George A.). New York: Oxford.

Austin, John L. 1962. *How to Do Things with Words*. Oxford: Clarendon.

Bargiela-Chiappini, Francesca / Harris, Sandra J. 1996. Requests and Status in Business Correspondence. *Journal of Pragmatics* 28/4, 635-662.

Bargiela-Chiappini, Francesca / Nickerson, Catherine (eds) 1999. *Written Business: Genres, Media and Discourse*. London: Longman.

Bhatia, Vijay K. 1993. *Analysing Genre: Language Use in Professional Settings*. Harlow: Longman.

Blum-Kulka, Shoshana / House, Juliane / Kasper, Gabriele (eds) 1989. *Cross-Cultural Pragmatics: Requests and Apologies*. Norwood, MA: Ablex.

Brown, Penelope / Levinson, Stephen C. 1987. *Politeness: Some Universals in Language Usage*. Studies in International Sociolinguistics 4. Cambridge: Cambridge University Press.

Campbell, Charles P. 1998. Rhetorical Ethos: A Bridge between High-Context and Low-Context Cultures? In Niemeier, Susan *et al.* (eds) *The Cultural Context in Business Communication*. Amsterdam: Benjamins, 31-47.

Chakorn, Ora-Ong 2006. Persuasive and Politeness Strategies in Cross-Cultural Letters of Request in the Thai Business Context. *Journal of Asian Pacific Communication* 16/1, 103-146.

Hinds, John 1990. Inductive, Deductive, Quasi-Inductive: Expository Writing in Japanese, Korean, Chinese and Thai. In Connor, Ulla / Johns, Ann M. (eds) *Coherence in Writing: Research and Pedagogical Perspectives.* Virginia, VA: TESOL, 87-109.

Hyland, Ken 1998. Exploring Corporate Rhetoric: Metadiscourse in the CEO's Letter. *Journal of Business Communication* 35/2, 224-245.

McComas, Donna C. / Satterwhite, Marilyn L. 1993. *Modern Business Correspondence.* Singapore: Macmillan/McGraw-Hill.

Mulholland, Joan 1997. The Asian Connection: Business Requests and Acknowledgements. In Bargiela-Chiappini, Francesca / Harris, Sandra (eds) *The Language of Business: An International Perspective.* Edinburgh: Edinburgh University Press, 94-114.

Neumann, Ingrid 1997. Requests in German-Norwegian Business Discourse: Differences in Directness. In Bargiela-Chiappini, Francesca / Harris, Sandra (eds) *The Language of Business: An International Perspective.* Edinburgh: Edinburgh University Press, 72-93.

Searle, John R. 1969. *Speech Acts: An Essay in the Philosophy of Language.* Cambridge: Cambridge University Press.

Searle, John R. 1975. Indirect Speech Acts. In Cole, Peter / Morgan, James L. (eds) *Syntax and Semantics Vol.3 Speech Acts.* New York: Academic Press.

Searle, John R. 1976. A Classification of Illocutionary Acts. *Language in Society* 5, 1-23.

Swales, John. 1990. *Genre Analysis: English in Academic and Research Settings.* Cambridge: Cambridge University Press.

Wierzbicka, Anna 1991. *Cross-Cultural Pragmatics: The Semantics of Human Interaction.* Berlin: Mouton de Gruyter.

Yli-Jokipii, Hilkka 1996. An Approach to Contrasting Languages and Cultures in the Corporate Context: Finnish, British and American Business Letters and Telefax Messages. *Multilingua* 15/3, 305-328.

Zhu, Yunxia 2001. Comparing English and Chinese Persuasive Strategies in Trade Fair Invitations. *Document Design* 2/1, 2-17.

Intercultural Issues
in Face-to-Face Communication

GINA PONCINI

Communicating within and across Professional Worlds in an Intercultural Setting

1. Introduction

Intercultural encounters are increasingly frequent in business and other professional settings, whether within or between organizations. The growth of multinational and multilingual corporations, according to Harris and Bargiela-Chiappini (2003), has strengthened the perception of English as a *lingua franca* of international business. In today's global marketplace, even small firms have contact with people from other cultural and linguistic backgrounds who are not necessarily native speakers (NSs) of English.

This changing situation is accompanied by an increasing number of studies on intercultural communication involving non-native speakers (NNSs) of English who use this language in business, from Firth's work on negotiations in the early 1990s (e.g. Firth 1990, 1996) up to more recent studies involving the use of English as a lingua franca[1] in spoken discourse (e.g. Louhiala-Salminen 2004; Poncini 2002, 2004) and written discourse (e.g. Nickerson 2000, Gimenez 2002). Research has also focused on case companies, with Louhiala-Salminen, Charles, and Kankaanranta (2005) reporting on spoken and written internal communication in English in Scandinavian companies involved in mergers. A more general interest in English as a global language and its role in international settings continues to grow (e.g. Swales 1997) alongside work on domain-specific English (see e.g. selections in Cortese/Riley 2002). This makes it all the more important to examine how English is used by

---

1   See Vandermeeren (1999: 274-277) for a discussion of *lingua franca* use in business, and Nickerson (2005) for an overview of current research on the use of English as a lingua franca in international business contexts.

native speakers of languages other than English, especially when multicultural settings and technical aspects of business activities and products are involved.

The issue of language choice has also received attention in research into language and communication in business organizations. For example, Nickerson (2000) investigates the use of written English by native speakers (NSs) of English and NSs of Dutch in a Dutch multinational, discussing the interplay between Dutch and English in chains of emails. Charles and Marschen-Piekkari (2002) also give attention to language choice in their examination of horizontal communication in a multinational in Finland. Moreover, in studying multicultural business meetings conducted mainly in English, Poncini (2003) has investigated the role of languages other than English, highlighting the purposes they serve and showing how they help build common ground. As Nickerson (2005: 370-371) has recently stated, "the communicative event is often considerably more complex than the label of English as a *lingua franca* would suggest".

The above studies confirm the importance of taking into consideration the wider professional context as well as the immediate circumstances when investigating discourse in multilingual settings. They also suggest that the use of different languages may serve practical needs or represent a cooperative element and thus such language use deserves attention when examining discourse in multi-lingual professional settings.

1.1. Scope of the present chapter

This chapter investigates spoken interactions mainly in English during a specific event involving participants from different linguistic, cultural and professional backgrounds. The event, a winery visit, was organized within a wider three-day international convention on the Nebbiolo grape, which took place in northern Italy in early 2004 and brought together wine producers from Italy, the U.S., Australia, South Africa and Switzerland.[2] Other participants included vineyard owners,

---

2   I would like to thank the organizing association, the *Consorzio per la Tutela dei Vini di Valtellina* (the Consortium for the Protection of Valtellina Wines)

journalists, researchers, experts on viticulture and wine from around the world, and members of the local community. Participants at the wider convention thus represent not only different cultures but also different professions, but with a common interest in the wine industry.

Data for the present chapter consist of audio recordings of one of the winery visits organized as part of the convention. During the visit, interactants from Italy, the U.S. and Croatia used English and some Italian. The interactants from Italy and the U.S. were wine producers, while those from Croatia consisted of three journalists and a wine producer with an interpreter. The analysis focuses on the use of evaluation (Thompson/Hunston 2000) and specialised lexis concerning grape growing, wine making and wines, with attention given to knowledge already shared by interactants and the linguistic means with which they build shared knowledge and common ground. Attention is also given to switches between English and Italian and the use of Italian terms during discussions in English.

The rest of this chapter is organized as follows: Section 2 discusses data and methods and provides background on the context, while Section 3 presents the analytical approach. In Section 4, examples from the data are analyzed and discussed, followed by concluding comments in Section 5.

2. Data, methods and context

In January 2004, a three-day convention on the Nebbiolo grape was held in Valtellina in the Lombardy region of Italy. This grape is grown mainly in northern Italian regions and is relatively little known in 'New World' wine producing nations. The event, the first of its kind, brought together wine producers from Italy (mainly Valtellina and Piedmont), the U.S. (California, Oregon, Pennsylvania, Texas, and Washington State), Mexico, Australia, South Africa and Switzerland.

for giving me permission to collect data at the event. I would also like to express my appreciation to event participants for their willingness to be recorded and/or interviewed and for taking the time to discuss their professional activities with me.

Other participants included vineyard owners, journalists, researchers, and experts on viticulture and wine from around the world; members of the local community; others involved with the organization; (for some events) the general public interested in wines.

Participants thus represented a hybrid discourse community. By bringing together these participants, the event aimed to compare the Italian experience[3] with that of countries on other continents, and to present and discuss scientific, historical, and cultural research. It also provided occasions to taste Nebbiolo wines from around the world and visit vineyards and wineries in the Valtellina area.

The winery visit recorded for the present study can be divided into three main parts, as shown in Table 1.

Part of the visit	Description
First part: 11.37-13.00. Initial tour of the winery	Participants included a young Italian wine-producer (the 4th generation of the family owning the winery) and two young people who had established a winery in California and spoke some Italian. I was present as a participant-observer. Other Italian participants occasionally joined the group for a short time. Both English and Italian were used during the tour.
Second part: 13.00-13.52. In the wine-tasting room	The second part involved the same participants as the first part. The three wine producers engaged in discussions, mainly about wine-making, and then tasted and discussed the wines tasted.
Third part: 13.52-15.18. In the wine-tasting room	In the final part of the visit, the three wine producers were joined by five Croatians attending the convention: three journalists, one of whom spoke Italian, and a wine producer with an interpreter. An older member of the family who owns the winery was also sometimes present. Both English and Italian, but mainly English, were used during discussions of the winery and its products.

Table 1. The three parts of the recorded winery visit.

More information about the people present during the first two parts of the winery visit is provided below:

---

3   Producers from Italy listed on the invitation are from Piedmont (producers of Barolo, Barbaresco, Boca, Carema, Gattinara, Ghemme, Lessona) and Valtellina, with a few producers from Sardegna and Valle D'Aosta.

- Stefano (a pseudonym[4]; referred to as 'S' in this paper), who is a 4th-generation northern Italian Nebbiolo wine producer (NS of Italian, NNS of English);
- Denise ('D') and Tom ('T'), who produce wines, including Nebbiolo, in their California winery (NSs of English, D speaks Italian, and T understands some Italian and can speak using certain words and expressions);
- Researcher (NS of English, NNS of Italian, has lived in the area of the winery for 26 years).

S, D and T are in their late 20s or early 30s and are somewhat younger than many of the other producers at the convention. In the third part of the visit, the group in the wine tasting facility is joined by five Croatians, as follows:

- Three journalists, one of whom spoke Italian, and all of whom spoke English;
- A wine producer, who did not use English during the visit, with an interpreter who used English with the Italian wine producer.

Although for technical reasons the transcriptions of the third part of the visit are not as complete as those for the first two parts, it is felt that an examination of this data together with field notes is sufficient for providing insights into discourse in the present setting, where participants represent not only different cultural backgrounds but also different professions.

Supplementary data[5] provide an understanding of the wider event and context, and consist of field notes, semi-structured interviews with different participants during the three-day event, and emails, letters, press releases and newsletters sent or prepared during the seven months preceding the event. Audio recordings were also

---

4   All names used are pseudonyms. Other identifying information has been deleted in the extracts used in this chapter.
5   Written and spoken data were collected as part of a wider study, with data originating in the food and wine industry in different countries. The wider study is in turn part of the project, 'Intercultural communication in business settings: linguistic aspects', being carried out by a local research unit, headed by Giuliana Garzone, at the University of Milan, within the framework of the national project (COFIN 2002) *Intercultural Discourse in Domain-specific English*, co-ordinated by Maurizio Gotti.

made during technical presentations during the first two days and at the wine-tasting session on the last afternoon.

3. Analytical approach

In examining spoken discourse involving interactants whose pro-fessional activities concern wine, this chapter examines the use of evaluation (Thompson/Hunston 2000) and specialised lexis relating to grape growing and wine making. It also draws on Goffman's (1979/ 1981: 124-159) participation framework, which distinguishes between the different roles that can be taken on by participants in a situation as opposed to a single category of speaker and a single category of 'hearer'. These approaches are discussed in Sections 3.1 and 3.2.

3.1. Evaluation

3.1.1. The significance of evaluation

Thompson and Hunston discuss evaluation, used as a cover term "for the expression of the speaker's or writer's attitude or stance towards, viewpoint on, or feelings about the entities or propositions that he or she is talking about" (2000: 6-7). Examining evaluation can be a fruitful way to shed light on values underlying a text (see e.g. Hunston 1994, Thompson/Hunston 2000). In addition, evaluation is related to social interaction. As Mauranen (2002: 118) points out, "[e]valuation is a slippery notion for linguistic research because it cannot very readily be allocated to any particular, easily definable set of ex-pressions". Indeed, in presenting a taxonomy of stance features for his investigation of stance in research articles, Hyland (1999: 105) states that he does not claim that the taxonomy includes all stance features in his corpus. Investigating how evaluative language is used during the multiparty discussions can illustrate how it reflects and constructs shared values, whether these shared values concern aspects of wine making, the wine business or the event at hand.

3.1.2. Specialised lexis and evaluative force

The chapter considers implicit and explicit evaluation along the positive-negative parameter (Thompson/Hunston 2000: 22-25), which depends on value systems. This allows considerations as to whether specialised lexis acquires evaluative force (i.e. lexical items that are not inherently evaluative may take on a positive or negative connotation for the group) and whether it seems to help build common ground as a kind of in-group terminology (Brown/Levinson 1978/ 1987). This is important in view of the different linguistic and cultural backgrounds of participants, who do share, however, a (professional) interest in wine and wine making.

3.1.3. Indications of expectedness: presupposing and building shared knowledge

The chapter also considers evaluation along the expectedness parameter (Thompson/Hunston: 22-25), taking into consideration selected manifestations of expectedness (e.g. *of course, as you know*). This allows considerations of whether interactants presuppose shared knowledge and in doing so whether they contribute to building shared knowledge.

3.2. Participant roles

The analysis also draws on Goffman's (1981: 124-159) participation framework. He distinguishes between the different roles which participants in a situation can take on, as opposed to a single category of speaker and a single category of hearer, intended in the acoustical sense. An unratified participant may be a 'bystander' or an 'overhearer' (inadvertent, non-official listener) or an "eavesdropper" (engineered, non-official follower of talk). Goffman's *production formats* relate to the role of the speaker, who can be animator, author and principal. Levinson (1988) refers to these as *production roles.*[6]

---

6   Levinson (1988: 169) points out that in addition to recognizing some ambiguity in the categories, Goffman (1981) uses the term *participation*

The 'animator' physically utters the word(s), the 'author' represents the origin of the beliefs and sentiment (and perhaps also composes the words), and the 'principal' is the person whose viewpoint or position is expressed. The speaker's role may involve all three.

Although some scholars, including Levinson (1988), have further systematicized Goffman's (1981: 124-159) categories (see also Kerbrat-Orecchioni 2004 for a discussion of participation frameworks and multi-participant conversation), the present study does not focus on all possible participant roles, but rather on shifts in participant roles of interest.

3.3. Language choice

Some studies report on the potential of language alternation in facilitating communication in business settings. While the focus of some of these studies was not specifically code-switching, the resulting observations concerning switches between languages in naturally occurring spoken interactions provide a richer understanding of intercultural encounters in business settings.

Charles (2002: 103), for example, discusses an investigation into how Finns and Swedes negotiate meaning and how they achieve cooperation and comprehension, with the investigation suggesting that the choice of language is highly situationalised and pragmatic. She (2002: 103) points out that the meetings analysed "seem to be a mixture of Swedish and English", with the immediate circumstances determining frequent code-switching. In addition, Louhiala-Salminen (2002: 226) suggests that the use of different languages in business situations today may facilitate communication when she describes the language of communication in the interactions she studied as alternating between English and the national language, "with occasional help from other languages as well". Finally, Poncini (2003) focuses on the use of different languages during multicultural meetings conducted mainly in English, showing how this use can serve

---

framework so that sometimes it seems to refer to reception roles only and at other times seems to include both reception and production roles.

practical purposes and more generally helps build common ground and relations.

The present chapter gives attention to switches between English and Italian in discussions of wine-making and products. It does not aim to provide a complete analysis but rather explore selected switches to provide a richer picture of the communicative event.

4. Examples from the data

4.1. Professional discourse and interpersonal involvement: focusing on shared values (Extracts 1-5)

In the data for the first part of the winery visit, the tour, it is especially noticeable that in exchanging information about professional experiences, the three speakers – two wine producers from the U.S. and one from Italy – make linguistic choices contributing to heightened interpersonal involvement. This is done mainly by means of frequent back-channelling (some of it overlapping), repetition, explicit agreement and occasional laughter. The cumulative effect of using these features is that the speakers "create shared worlds and viewpoints" which reinforce relationships, as discussed by Carter and McCarthy (2004: 69). In analyzing their data, they point out that as a result of using repetition, an "affective convergence and a commonality of viewpoint" is created, and they note that this was also observed by Goffman (1981) and Tannen (1989) in their data.

In the data for the present study, it is at first S who especially provides information about making wine with Nebbiolo grapes, since this is the specialty of his family's winery in Valtellina, while it is still new to the California participants. Gradually the two participants from California also relate their experiences and opinions, with the three interactants building common ground and using implicit and explicit evaluation to build on values they share (e.g. experimenting and trying new things in wine-making is 'good').

4.1.1. Extract 1: Early discussions leading to shared values

Extract 1, divided into two parts as shown in Tables 2 and 3, presents an interchange which occurs about 20 minutes after the start of the tour, when the wine producers from Italy and the U.S. know relatively little about each other. Both parts illustrate the frequent back-channelling (underlined and in boldface) during discussions about wine-making processes. This can signal attentive listening and/or comprehension (of content, of language).

1	Denise	so (.) how (did) <u>just so I know</u> how (+) when (.) do you usually pick the Nebbiolo (.) at what date
2	Stefano	usually we begin to pick up the grapes in the middle of October
3	Denise	**ok**
4	Stefano	usually
5	Denise	**ok** 11.51.38
6	Stefano	uh 2001 and 2002 (+) and from the middle of October to the beginning of November ((Denise: **right**)) in three weeks uh (+) we pick up our grapes
7	Denise	and then do you put them in th- a stainless steel fermenter? 11.51.52
8	Stefano	yes (+) we receive the grapes in the winery (less the) and we have to ( ) the grapes ( )
9	Denise	**uh huh**
10	Stefano	we remove the the raspo
11	Denise	**uh huh**
12	Stefano	uhm
13	Denise	sì uh (.) de-stem
14	Stefano	**yes ok** 11.52.06
15		and uh (in steel) (where) it's possible to (.) to control the temperature
16	Denise	what is the (.) temperature you usually ((Stefano: **yeah**)) keep at
17	Stefano	what we are doing + what we did with the wine that you uh (+) you appreciate was (+) that at the beginning (.) we had to increase the temperature but not very quickly
18	Denise	**ok**
19	Stefano	we decide to arrive at (.) thirty degrees ((Denise: **ok**)) centigrade in (.) two days
20	Denise	**ok**
21	Stefano	( ) it's possible to do to increase the ( ) but it (...)

Table 2 Extract 1, Part 1.

Some of the back channels overlap with the speaker (e.g. units 6, 16, 19, 27), and some occur between units or during pauses (e.g. units 3 and 5).

In initiating the discussion about picking Nebbiolo grapes, D uses negative politeness strategies (underlined) in unit 1, giving a reason for her question and minimizing the reason *(just)*. She also rephrases part of the question *(at what date* for *when,* used earlier in the unit), a feature of her discourse observed elsewhere in the data. It can be noted that more questions are used here than later or elsewhere in the data for the visit (in 1, 7 and 16, which starts as a question). D uses self reference (*I* in unit 1) so that the interchange appears to start off as a dyadic interaction, but S's use of *we* to refer to his winery's activities is followed by D's use of *we* in unit 22 (Part 2 of Extract 1), shortly after which T speaks, using *we* in unit 30. Thus once the discussion is underway, speakers evoke the collective nature of their respective wineries rather than their individual identities. Pronouns are in a frame and will be further discussed later in this section.

Part 1 of Extract 1 also provides an example of what can be called 'a collaborative effort' to produce the English term for a specialised term first used in Italian (units 10-14). Though D in unit 11 appears to have understood S's use of the Italian 'raspo' (*grape stalk* or *stem*), when S hesitates in unit 12, D takes on a cooperative role and supplies the English 'de-stem' (which S confirms in unit 14), showing she shares knowledge of this aspect of wine-making and is aware of language concerning the process, both in English and Italian. Similarly, S seems to understand D's question before she completes it in unit 16, showing he can anticipate what is of interest to D and T on this occasion.

Table 3 shows how the positive value in experimenting and trying different things (mentioned earlier by S during the tour of the winery facilities) grows in Part 2. Both D (in unit 27) and T (in units 28 and 30) implicitly evaluate this as positive (underlined), connecting it to the group of three. D in unit 27 shifts speaker roles and by means of "like you said" (boldface, underlined and in italics) explicitly refers to S's earlier mention of experimenting, presented positively. T signals his agreement by back-channelling (*exactly* in unit 27, and in units 28 and 30 he uses repetition to indicate they have tried different things). In addition, S explicitly signals an opinion in unit 33, despite some inaudible speech, and D and T appear to share the same opinion (34 and 36 respectively). Other choices signalling interpersonal involvement include lexical repetition in units 34-35 (D and S).

22	Denise	no but but we're interested 'cause we're still learning
23	Stefano	**yeah**
24	Denise	we've only produced for five years now
25		and it's every year
26	Stefano	**yeah yeah**
27	Denise	and every year you have to experiment ((Tom: **exactly**)) *like you said* and try something different to know the correct temperature (.) the correct length
28	Tom	**we've done very cold fermentation**
29	Stefano	**yes**
30	Tom	**we've done very warm**
31	Stefano	it's uh Nebbiolo needs a temperature (.) at the beginning of the maturation to extract the (the) ((Denise: colours)) ( )
32	Tom	**yeah**
33	Stefano	the colours (+) but I think it's dangerous to (..)
34	Denise	just **too fast**
35	Stefano	**yes too fast** at the temperature
36	Tom	**yeah**

Table 3. Extract 1, Part 2.

In Extract 1, some occurrences of *we* seem to refer to the respective wine producers, for example S speaks for his winery when he uses *we* in units 8, 17 and 19 (though his use of *we* when he speaks of picking grapes in unit 2 could also be interpreted to include other Nebbiolo producers in the area). Similarly, D in unit 24 and T in units 28 and 30 use *we* to speak for their winery. Other occurrences, in contrast, refer to participants in the interaction; for example, D's use of *we* in unit 22 refers to her and T. As will be seen in other data extracts, later in the visit some occurrences of *we* seem to refer to Nebbiolo producers and people interested in Nebbiolo and its promotion.

What begins to emerge in this early part of the visit, however, is an indication of one thing that is of value to people interested in Nebbiolo, whether as wine producers or as experts: colour. The colour of wines made with this grape is an important issue, and recognition of this represents a kind of common ground (e.g. unit 33, despite some inaudible speech). This is more evident in the next example. The colour Nebbiolo of wine is not as dark as that of many other wines, so it is important not to 'lose' colour during wine-making.

4.1.2. Extract 2: Repetition and explicit agreement about shared values

1	Tom	with sugar (left) ((Stefano: **yes**)) for fermentation
2	Stefano	uh because what we want to do (.) the barrique (draws) a net (that keeps the) colour
3	Denise	that's what we learned ((Stefano: **the teacher**)) yesterday=
4	Stefano	=the teacher told yesterday morning=
5	Denise	=two days ago maybe=
6	Stefano	=yesterday=
7	Denise	=**ok**=
8	Stefano	=yesterday morning (.) Professor [LN deleted] ((Denise: **yeah**)) he told sure that the small barrel=
9	Denise	=you get **better colour**
10	Tom	(**yeah**) 11.55.26
11	Stefano	you keep **more colour**
12	Tom	always in the barrels you get **more colours**
13	Stefano	the problem is that to you don't want to cover ((Denise: **no**)) the (aroma) with the grape with the oak ((Denise: **no**))
14	Denise	**mm hmm**
15	Stefano	and in fact it's because we don't use any uh uhm (3) American oak?
16	Denise	**right** neither do we ((Stefano: **no sorry but**)) no no we don't like it ((Tom laughs))
17	Stefano	no I think it's **good** for other kinds of ((Denise and Tom: **unintelligible overlap**)) ((Denise: **for [Grape Variety1]**))
18	Tom	but not for Nebbiolo
19	Denise	but not for Nebbiolo
20	Stefano	maybe [Grape Variety2] can also be interesting with great result
21		with Nebbiolo it's my opinion
22	Denise	no no
23	Tom	I agree=
24	Denise	=we agree ((everyone laughs))
25	Tom	We tried it all
26	Denise	French and Slovenian

Table 4. Extract 2.

Extract 2 illustrates part of an interchange that begins with a shift in production roles, when in units 3-8 D and S draw on a technical presentation made the day before in discussing colour as it relates to barriques / small barrels. Both speakers refer to a previous speaker and, in units 4-8, S and D establish a common point in the past. Co-presence at the event contributes to common ground, so speakers can now draw on what they have experienced in common. It can be noted that the referents for *we* are ambiguous, but include all three speakers, who were at the presentation on the previous day. Back-channelling and overlapping speech emphasize the collaborative effort. In general, many of the features signalling interpersonal involvement noted earlier are also present in Extract 2. For instance, back-channelling is frequent (e.g. units 1, 7, 8, 13, 14) and some of it is overlapping (e.g. 1, 8, 13). Repetition on the part of all three speakers (e.g. D in 9, S in 11, and T in 12) is also common, and T and D echo each other in units 18 and 19 (sets of relative units are outlined in a frame). Overlapping speech and back-channelling are in boldface and underlined.

D and T use a variety of means to show agreement with S's negative evaluation of American oak in units 13 and 15 (in 17 he specifies that the evaluation depends on the grape variety involved). For example, D in unit 16 first agrees, then refers to the behaviour they have in common (not using American oak) and states they don't like it, using *we* to refer to their respective winery. Another example is T's rephrasing in unit 18 of S's evaluation as to the relevance of American oak for certain grape varieties, echoed by D in unit 19. Explicit agreement is evident towards the end of Extract 2, when T and D explicitly agree with S in their latched speech (boldface in 23-24), T using *I* to evoke his individual identity, and D again using *we* to speak for their winery / both of them. Speakers thus highlight their shared viewpoints in a range of ways. Moreover, S shows face concerns when he says he's sorry (overlap in 16) about his negative evaluation of American oak, recognizing that T and D share the same country of origin as the oak.

4.1.3. Extract 3: Discovering common ground: the same ingredient

Similarly, in the interchange in Extract 3, the interactants make linguistic choices that serve to highlight their shared viewpoints and common ground in terms of their professional activities, in this case when they discover that they use the same yeast. They build on this aspect of what they have in common – precise technical names deleted in units 5-7 – by using implicit and explicit positive evaluation. S uses explicit positive evaluation in both English and Italian (*best, buono, fantastico* in units 10, 12 and 14), with T back-channelling his agreement (12 and 15). Using the same yeast is implicitly positive, as it represents another shared viewpoint (D and T in units 8 and 9 partly overlap in supplying this information, which also builds common ground). The group laughs, adding to the interpersonal element.

1	Stefano	uh for example I use a specific yeast selected from the University of
		[Italian city] ((Denise: mm hmm)) for Nebbiolo ((Denise: mm hmm))
2		and this is to respect really **respect** the aroma (of) the colour and uh
		save part of the colour
3	Denise	mm hmm
4	Tom	what yeast did you use (.) do you know the name of the
5	Stefano	([**technical name deleted**])
6	Tom	([**same technical name deleted**]) yeah
7	Stefano	[**three letters plus one number deleted**]
8	Denise	oh so we use ((Tom: it's the)) the **same**
9	Tom	it's the **same yeast** ((laughter))
10	Stefano	it's one of the **_best_**
11	crystal	no we tried one year with our [letter + numbers deleted] (+) because
		((Tom: unintelligible)) we used
12	Stefano	**_buono_**
13	Tom	yeah and
14	Stefano	**_fantastico_**
15	Tom	yeah a lot of a **lot of colour**

Table 5. Extract 3.

4.1.4. Extract 4: Shifts in production roles to introduce a topic

Extract 4 is an example of how a shift in production roles is used to introduce a topic, with D drawing on a technical presentation made the day before. Though in unit 1 she seems to start by immediately asking a question beginning with *how*, she restarts and in Goffman's terms acts as 'animator' for a professor ('author' and 'principal') who spoke at the convention the day before. She thus evokes the small group's shared interest in Nebbiolo and the convention before turning to the question of how often S racks wine. After S uses *travasi* in Italian (boldface in 6), D and T provide alternative terms until D in unit 10 provides the term *rack*, which is then incorporated into the rest of the interchange. These occasional collaborative efforts to supply technical terms in English occur as part of the interaction, as observed elsewhere in the data, and are sometimes accompanied by laughter by all present.

In unit 12, T summarizes his understanding of the information provided by S in terms of whether the racking occurs before or after a certain point of the wine-making process (*malolactic*), with S's back-channelling (*yeah* is used twice) seeming to confirm T's comments are correct. This may help ensure understanding of the technical process. However, in unit 15, S's use of *ok* seems to signal that he understands he must provide T with a specific example, which he provides in the units that follow (not shown).

1	Denise	and (+) how- because the other **interesting** thing (.) one of the professors was mentioning that (.) Nebbiolo needs air (+)
2		and (.) that was one thing we were talking about (+)
3		how often do you (+) ((Tom: rack the wine)) rack
4	Stefano	uh (2) I'd say that Nebbiolo (rack) most the wine ( ) at the beginning (.) mostly when young
5	Tom	exactly ((Denise: hmmmm)) 12.06.41
6	Stefano	yeah and so we call (+) **travasi** I don't know when
7	Denise	(coupled) over
8	Tom	(to rack) ((Aldo: yeah (.) no)) oh (pump) over
9	Stefano	no no no
10	Denise	to rack
11	Stefano	rock ((Tom: rack)) rock is the correct word
12		we do ((overlapping laughter)) we try to do three racks the first year ((Denise: ok)) ((Tom: mmmm)) and then two racks the second year ((Denise: ok)) the big barrel ((Tom: so the first one))
13		in this kind of barrel two (++) you can do two uh (++) two the first year and one again in ( )
14	Tom	so your first one after malolactic is finished ((Stefano: yeah)) you wait till malolactic ((Stefano: yeah)) the first time
15	Stefano	=ok (+) uh 12.07.30 for example the harvest in October (.) the end of the fermentation the fermentation in November [15 units deleted]

Table 6. Extract 4.

4.1.5. Extract 5: The fruttaio: incorporating local elements

		12:09
1	Stefano	and ok (2) a ***good*** thing that we are do with the barrique (+) because you know it's not possible to do with the big barrel the cask uh when we uhm we
2	Denise	when you rack?
3	Stefano	no when we press the grapes up it ((Tom: unintelligible overlap)) ( ) the Sfursat in January (.)
4		the fruttaio (.) is a very cold room (+)
5		it's free
6		so we we bring the barrique and we bring the barrique in the fruttaio
7		it's about 3 4 degrees centigrade
8		so we solve the problem of the (acido tartarico)
9	Tom	the uhm ((Denise: tartaric acid)) tartaric acid tartrates
10	Stefano	yes yeah
11	Tom	so the cold stabilizes (obviously)
12	Stefano	without move the wine with the with the ( ) ((unclear, same word overlaps, Tom or Denise: ( )))
13	Denise	yeah we learned
14	Stefano	because you 12.09.52 the and the wine can ((Denise: yeah)) can keep more oxygen it's=
15	Denise	=exactly=
16	Stefano	=very difficult, it's very difficult
17	Tom	**we do the same**
18		we for one month we keep it we keep the wine at about two degrees for one month (.) for one month
19	Stefano	different countries ((laughter))
20	Tom	we have a room that we built
21	Denise	we also in the beginning part do that
22		we **experimented** with uhm putting just the grapes after we harvest them to keep them cold
23	Tom	we de-stem into a fermenter but uh
24	Denise	it's just a box ((Stefano: yes)) that holds one point five tons (.) so one and a half tons ((Stefano: yeah))
25		and we put it in that room keep cold for two days
26	Stefano	yeah (++) it's a ***good*** thing (.)
27		I like
28	Tom	at zero degrees after five days in the sunshine (.) we inoculate the next day

Table 7. Extract 5. The *Fruttaio*.

The example in Extract 5 shows how T and D are able to contribute to
S's discussion of a typically local aspect of producing a particular
kind of wine, by relating a similar aspect of their own experience, thus
further highlighting a shared world. They do this even though what S
describes is a technical aspect of producing a certain kind of Valtellina
wine, made from grapes that are left to dry in a special room called a
fruttaio (units 1-16, which include some units concerning comments
or questions by T and D). Starting in unit 17, T relates their experience in California, and then both he and D build on it. S uses back-
channels that overlap with D and also uses explicit positive evaluation
(unit 26) and states his appreciation (unit 27).

Other items of interest concern the use of technical lexis and its
relation to knowledge shared by the interactants. For example, S
hesitates over a technical term in English in unit 1 but supplies it
himself in unit 3 (*press*) after D suggests a different one – again *rack*.
When S uses an Italian term in unit 8, both T and D understand,
though T hesitates in supplying the technical term, and then repeats D:
"tartaric acid ... tartrates" (unit 9). The interactants share this knowledge about wine-making, but not about each other's experiences using
the colder rooms. Indeed, when S explicitly explains what a *fruttaio* is
in unit 4 he does not presuppose their understanding of this Italian
term even though D speaks Italian and both have been present in the
area for several days, focusing on wine-making.

4.2.   *Extracts 6 and 7: 'We' as producers of Nebbiolo
and people interested in Nebbiolo*

This section discusses extracts relating to the second part of the
winery visit: interactions involving S, D and T in the wine-tasting
room while tasting wines. Of interest is the greater use of *we* with
ambiguous referents. This contrasts with uses of *we* that refer to the
speakers' respective wineries, more frequent during the beginning of
the first part of the visit consisting of the tour through the facilities.
Also worthy of note are the more frequent switches to Italian in this
part of the visit (e.g. D in unit 13 of Extract 7).

Several examples of *we*-ambiguous are evident in Extracts 6
and 7. For example, S's use of *we* in unit 11 in Extract 6 is ambiguous.

S can be speaking for Nebbiolo producers and people interested in Nebbiolo – a wider group that includes the three of them. Interestingly, the topic concerning "the value of the grape variety" is introduced through a shift in production roles, when S (unit 6) acts as 'animator' of the viewpoint expressed by a convention speaker the day before and then disagrees with it, justifying the presence of producers from other countries at the event (Extracts 2 and 4 provide other examples of an interactant taking on the role of animator for an event speaker).

1	Tom	this is *beautiful*
2	Denise	uh huh it's
3	Stefano	((unintelligible - he asks them something))
4	Denise	like canella *cinnamon*
5	Stefano	è anche *bello* confrontarsi 13.19.55 *it's also good to compare experiences*
6		yesterday (.) Professor [LN] (.) the last one told that we ( ) need (.) we don't need Nebbiolo from other countries
7		but it's *good* for us to have from other country because it show the *value* of the grape variety
8	Denise	it shows *value* of grape value (.) absolutely [two units deleted]
9	Stefano	many people say "I like Nebbiolo"
10		but very few drink Nebbiolo
11		so we must do our best to make sure people drink Nebbiolo
12	Denise	and the quality and the education 13.22.06
13		the cosa più importante è che la persona non solo le persone che comprano e bevono ma anche chi produce deve sapere come si può fare un Nebbiolo più buono [...] *the most important thing is that the person not only the people who buy and drink Nebbiolo but also whoever produces it must know how a better Nebbiolo can be made*

Table 8. Extract 6. *We*-ambiguous – *we* as Nebbiolo producers: S.

Moreover, the alternation between silence and speech during the actual wine-tasting suggests it has own special status within the more general interactions. At times this kind of activity during the winery visit (and as part of the overall industry event) has the nature of a kind of ritual, with moments of silence characterizing the tasting. During the discussions between these moments of silence, the three inter-actants display and build on many of the features mentioned earlier in this chapter (e.g. back-channelling, indications of agreement). An examination of the data suggests that S, who is directly involved in this activity as a member of the family owning the winery whose wines are being tasted, withholds evaluation during and after the actual tasting, though at a certain point he provides information about the wine (name, year, features). He may await or prompt evaluative comments from the participants.

Extract 7 shows a cluster of T's use of *we* with ambiguous referents: the occurrences can refer to the two wine producers from California, the three interactants, or a wider set of individuals interested in Nebbiolo and its promotion. He connects the greater awareness (and consumption) of Nebbiolo not necessarily from Italy to greater awareness and consumption of Sassella (unit 6), a Nebbiolo wine made in Valtellina, implying benefits at a local level resulting from wider exposure of Nebbiolo wines in general.

1	Stefano	bisogna anche spiegare (.) non e' facile da bere (.)
		it's necessary to explain too (.) it's not easy to drink (.)
2		ma puoi anche bere *but you can drink it*
3		anche in Italy (.) great wine (.) but one glass ((Tom: too rich))
		even
4	Tom	I understand ((Denise: una bomba))
		[six units deleted]
5	Tom	so that's where we're starting (+) where we have to start
6		we think if we can get people to drink Nebbiolo like you're saying
		then we can get people to drink Sassella (.) and (.) and on and on
		and on

Table 9. Extract 7. *We*-ambiguous – *we* as Nebbiolo producers.

4.3. Another professional community, another culture

In the third part of the visit, the three wine producers are joined by five Croatians: three journalists, at least one of whom spoke Italian, and a wine producer with an interpreter. As mentioned earlier, this part of the visit is of interest because the participants joining the group have different cultural and professional backgrounds with respect to the original three interactants. Although for technical reasons the transcriptions of the third part of the visit are not as complete as those for the first two parts, the use of in-depth field notes while listening to the audio-recording and reviewing transcriptions allow this part of the visit to be described. Selected transcriptions are also examined.

This part of the visit is characterized by longer speaking turns, little back-channelling, and longer periods of silence during the wine tasting. These features are in turn related to a nonverbal characteristic of this part of the visit: most of the Croatians take notes during the discussion or at least during S's replies (while S and/or D may have taken occasional notes during the visit, this was not as evident during observations). As a result, S's speech at times takes the form of a short monologue (or at least a longer speaking turn).[7]

Moreover, this part of the visit is characterized by additional configurations of interaction, such as simultaneous discussions in lower voices. For example, one of the Croatians, the wine producer, is accompanied by a Croatian interpreter who speaks to him in a low voice (not picked up by the recording equipment) during parts of discussions in English. Sometimes Italian is used, since the journalist taking the most active role also spoke Italian. However, following a specific request by another Croatian participant to speak English, the main language used was English.

Two extracts will be examined in this section, both concerning items discussed by the three wine producers prior to the arrival of the group of Croatians. One (Extract 8) concerns the kind of yeast the winery uses (also the subject of Extract 3 presented earlier), and the other (Extract 9) concerns the *fruttaio* (also the subject of Extract 5 presented earlier).

Extract 8 shows how, in response to a question about yeast by one of the Croatians, S provides information in a longer turn. He appears to presuppose shared knowledge about the role of yeast and the issue of Nebbiolo colours (*you know, you heard* in units 3 and 4) so that he does not risk patronizing any participants who already have this knowledge, and at the same time he provides this information to any participants unaware of this issue. This contrasts with the way yeast was discussed earlier by the small group, shown in Extract 4,

---

7   Contextual information included in the transcripts indicates when there may have been a question or comment from one of the Croatian participants that was only partially picked up by the recording equipment.

where shared knowledge and values were highlighted through repetition, back-channelling, agreement and evaluation, both implicit and explicit. Compared to earlier interactions, this part of the visit involving a larger group takes on a more task-oriented nature.

1	Stefano	yeah that the yeast we use it is the same (.) are studied were selected form the University of [Italian city]
2		and they are specific for Nebbiolo grapes (.) Nebbiolo grape vines. uh what I was looking for was a yeast who will respect the aroma of the grape variety and uh save the colour
3		you know there are yeast that (.) that (.)
4		you heard that Nebbiolo does not have colour, just ( ) present Nebbiolo and the (one) you use
5		14.01.18 ((No voices can be heard. The group is tasting wine. Someone seems to say "bueno"))

Table 10. Extract 8.

The interchange in Extract 9 below occurs about 40 minutes after the one in Extract 8. One of the Croatians asks what happens with acids between October and January. S responds, explaining the *fruttaio*, already discussed by S, T and D (shown in Extract 5) and referring to the regulations ("disciplinary") for making this particular wine. While S continues to appear to presuppose shared knowledge, in the case of regulations concerning this wine (*you know* in 5), he does not presuppose knowledge of the *fruttaio*, explaining the special room in unit 1 and then using the term and explaining it in unit 6.

1	Stefano	ok well you can in the wine not in the ( ) grapes also because we pay attention to let the grapes in **a special room very cold and in dry uh dry houses** ((low voices, one of the Croatians may be translating))
2		you can move the air if you have, if you .... you can move the air, we don't need the control the temperature of ((one of the Croatians speaks in Italian and explains to S that the person asking the question did not know about lack of humidity and would like to try this process. There is some overlap with Stefano.)) 14.42.07
3		from November to the nights most is below zero. of course the cold air, ha sentito il ( ) *you heard the* ( ) ((the Croation speaker says (he) is also trying))

4	Stefano	but you know you have the disciplinary to accept for example the **Sfursat disciplinary says** the drying has to be in ( ) places it's ( ) in the vineyards [3 units, partly unintelligible and deleted] ((Low voices. One of the Croatians asks if the grapes are dried then left in natural conditions or if something is in this room (unspecified, vague)))
6	Stefano	we have two **fruttai** (+) **fruttaio is the is the fruttaio fruttaio is the house where we dry the grapes**
7		one is very close to the vineyards (beautiful position) dry
8		and uh ((overlap)) this is the map [units not included] ((14.45 no one seems to be speaking; only the sound of glasses can be heard))

Table 11. Extract 9.

To summarize this section, the typical features observed when the group expands to include the five Croatians (journalists and a wine producer with an interpreter) include more task-oriented talk and information provision, with examples provided in Extracts 8 and 9, and less interpersonal involvement if compared to interactions during the first two parts of the visit, when the three wine producers discussed their professional experiences.

5. Concluding comments

This chapter has examined spoken discourse in an intercultural setting involving members of different professional communities connected to the international wine industry. During the winery visit under investigation, initial participants – wine producers from Italy and the U.S. – were joined by a group from Croatia consisting of three journalists and a wine producer with an interpreter. Although other factors besides the changing group composition during the visit must be kept in mind (e.g. individual style vs. cultural style), and despite limits characterizing research on spoken interactions in groups (see

Kerbrat-Orecchioni 2004 for a discussion), some considerations can be made about the intercultural interactions characterizing the event.

In the first two parts of the visit, the three wine producers exchange information about professional experiences, with their linguistic choices contributing to heightened interpersonal involvement. This is done mainly by means of frequent back-channelling (some of it overlapping), repetition, explicit agreement, evaluative language, switches to Italian and occasional laughter. The three speakers also collaborate to come up with specialized terms in English when these terms were first introduced in Italian during discussions in English, and they were noted to use more Italian as the visit progressed. In addition, the speakers build on common ground created at the event (e.g. taking on the role of 'animator' to bring up comments or viewpoints expressed earlier by a convention speaker) or emerging during the interaction, for example wine-making processes. As a result, the speakers converge to build 'shared worlds and viewpoints', even when local elements are involved (e.g. using the same yeast; using a 'cold (dry) room' / *fruttaio*).

The highly evaluative language used by the three participants in the first two parts of the visit concerns not only specific wines, but also their own activities and their identity as wine producers. For example, positive values emerging from the discourse include wanting to experiment, to learn, to exchange experiences, and to contribute to the positive status of Nebbiolo wines in the world. This evaluative status of Nebbiolo as representing a special grape variety and wine is supported by other data such as emails sent prior to the event and the technical and historical presentations made during the first two days of event, and is being explored as part of the wider study.[8]

The third part of the visit, which includes the Croatian journalists, wine producer and interpreter, appears to be more task-oriented and focused on information provision. Compared to the parts of the visit involving the three wine producers, during this part of the visit there is very little back-channelling, overlap and repetition on the part of the interactants. As a result, the main speaker (S) takes longer turns that take the form of short presentations or monologues. In general,

---

8   Poncini (2005) investigates email communication and letters in English and Italian connected to the organization of the event.

less evaluative language is used, and when it is used it concerns the wines tasted. While linguistic choices provide information and help build shared knowledge, they seem less aimed at building 'shared worlds and viewpoints' and more task-oriented.

Some of these differences may relate to the professional roles and values of the participants, though national culture and individual style may also influence communication. For example, concerning professional activities in this particular setting, the 'younger' wine producers, whether from the U.S. or Italy, seem to share an interest in learning and exchanging experiences and viewpoints about making wine, both technical aspects and well as commercial and promotional aspects. This interest is closely intertwined with their professional and personal interest in producing wines.[9] The journalists, on the other hand, must naturally report on the event, the wines, and the wineries producing them, and they need to obtain information (and taste wines) to help them meet this goal. The Croatian wine producer, in contrast, seems to seek specific information with his own activity in mind since he does not share information about his own winery and methods with others present. It is conceivable that all participants also aim to build relationships throughout the three-day event to help them further their professional activities and interests (see e.g. Ford 1990 and Håkansson /Snehota 1995 on business relationships and networks, and Poncini 2004: 15-19 for a discussion of business relationships and networks in connection to studies on business discourse).

Whatever the professional role of the participants – wine producers or journalists – they were seen to share repertoires of ways of doing things, for example verbal and nonverbal practices during the wine tasting. The notion of community of practice[10] (Lave/Wenger 1991 and Wenger 1998) holds promise for research in such settings because of its emphasis on practices and values (see Bhatia 2004: 148-149). In the present study, interactants come from different linguistic,

---

9   A kind of longer-term collaboration may have developed during the visit, since later that year during a trip to the U.S., S visited S and D and their winery in California.

10   A community of practice (Lave/Wenger 1991: 98, paraphrased in Bhatia 2004: 149) can be viewed "as a set of relations among persons, activities and the world over time and in relation with other tangential and overlapping communities of practice".

cultural and professional backgrounds yet share certain values and practices in connection with the wine industry. While the data is too limited to make generalisations, the present investigation provides evidence of the rich and complex backgrounds that interactants bring to intercultural encounters. Indeed, not only (national) culture and linguistic backgrounds come into play, but also professional roles, goals and values.

References

Bhatia, Vijay 2004. *Worlds of Written Discourse: A Genre-based View*. London: Continuum.
Brown, Penelope / Levinson, Stephen C. 1978/1987. *Politeness: Some Universals in Language Usage*. Cambridge: Cambridge University Press.
Carter, Ronald / McCarthy, Michael 2004. Talking, Creating: Interactional Language, Creativity, and Context. *Applied Linguistics* 25/1, 62-28.
Charles, Mirjaliisa 2002. Corporate policy and local realities in communication. The case of Nordea. In Lambertsson Björk, E. (Ed.) *Encode 2001 Proceedings, Annual Conference in Halden, Norway*, 91-108.
Charles, Mirjaliisa / Marschen-Piekkari, Rebecca 2002. Language Training for Enhanced Horizontal Communication: A Challenge for MNCs. *Business Communication Quarterly* 65/2, 9-29.
Cortese, Giuseppina / Riley, Philip (eds) 2002. *Domain-specific English: Textual Practices across Communities and Classrooms*. Bern: Peter Lang.
Firth, Alan 1990. 'Lingua Franca' Negotiations: Towards an Interactional Approach. *World Englishes*. 9/3, 269-280.
Firth, Alan 1996. The discursive accomplishment of normality: On 'lingua franca' English and conversation analysis. *Journal of Pragmatics* 26, 237-259.

Ford, David (ed.) [2]1997. *Understanding Business Markets: Interaction, Relationships and Networks*. London: The Dryden Press, New York: Harcourt, Brace and Company.

Gimenez, Julio 2002. New Media and Conflicting Realities in Multinational Corporate Communication: A Case Study. *International Review of Applied Linguistics in Language Teaching* 40, 323-343.

Goffman, Erving 1981. Footing. In *Forms of Talk*. Philadelphia: University of Philadelphia Press, 125-157 ([1]1979).

Håkansson Håkan / Snehota Ivan (eds) 1995. *Developing Relationships in Business Networks*. London: Routledge.

Halliday, Michael A.K. [2]1994. *An Introduction to Functional Grammar*, London: Arnold.

Harris, Sandra / Bargiela-Chiappini, Francesca 2003. Business as a Site of Language Contact. *Annual Review of Applied Linguistics* 23, 155-169.

Hunston, Susan 1994. Evaluation and Organization in a Sample of Written Academic Discourse. In Coulthard, Malcolm (ed.) 1994. *Advances in Written Text Analysis*. London: Routledge, 191-218.

Hyland, Ken 1999. Disciplinary Discourse: Writer Stance in Research Articles. In Candlin, Christopher N. / Hyland, Ken (eds) 1999. *Writing: Texts, Processes and Practices*. Essex: Longman, 99-121.

Kerbrat-Orecchioni, Catherine 2004. Introducing Polylogue, *Journal of Pragmatics* 36, 1-24.

Lave, Jean / Wenger, Etienne 1991. *Situated Learning: Legitimate Peripheral Participation and Learning*. Cambridge: Cambridge University Press.

Levinson, Stephen 1988. Putting Linguistics on a Proper Footing: Explorations in Goffman's Concepts of Participation. In Drew, Paul / Wootton, Anthony *Erving Goffman: Exploring the Interaction Order*. Cambridge: Polity Press, 161-227.

Louhiala-Salminen, Leena 2002. The fly's perspective: discourse in the daily routine of a business manager. *English for Specific Purposes* 21, 211-231.

Louhiala-Salminen, Leena 2004. *Does Business Speak BELF? Examples of Scandinavian Interaction in "Business English*

Lingua Franca". Paper presented at the 6th ABC European Convention, 20-22 May 2004, Milan, Italy.

Louhiala-Salminen, Leena, Charles, Mirjaliisa / Kankaanranta, Anne 2005. English as a *lingua franca* in Nordic corporate mergers: Two case companies. *English for Specific Purposes* 24, 401-421.

Mauranen, Anna 2002. "A Good Question." Expressing Evaluation in Academic Speech. In Cortese, Giuseppina / Riley, Philip (eds) *Domain-specific English: Textual Practices across Communities and Classrooms.* Bern: Peter Lang, 115-140.

Nickerson, Catherine 1999. The use of English in electronic mail in a multinational corporation, in Bargiela-Chiappini, Francesca / Nickerson, C. (eds) *Writing Business: Genre, Media and Discourses.* Essex: Longman, 273-291.

Nickerson, Catherine 2000. *The Corporate Language Game.* Amsterdam: Editions Rodopi.

Nickerson, Catherine 2005. English as a lingua franca in international business contexts. *English for Specific Purposes* 24, 367-380.

Poncini, Gina 2002. Investigating Discourse at Business Meetings with Multicultural Participation. *International Review of Applied Linguistics* 40, 345-373.

Poncini, Gina 2003. Multicultural Business Meetings and the Role of Languages other than English. *Journal of Intercultural Studies* 24/1, 17-32.

Poncini, Gina 2004. *Discursive Strategies in Multicultural Business Meetings.* Bern: Peter Lang.

Poncini, Gina 2005. Constructing an International Event in the Wine Industry: An Investigation of Emails in English and Italian, in Gillaerts, Paul / Gotti, Maurizio (eds) *Genre Variation in Business Letters.* Bern: Peter Lang, 205-231.

Swales, John M. 1997. English as *Tyrannosaurus rex. World Englishes* 16/3, 373-382.

Tannen, Deborah 1989. *Talking Voices: Repetition, Dialogue, and Imagery in Conversational Discourse.* Cambridge: Cambridge University Press.

Thompson, Geoff / Hunston, Susan 2000. Evaluation: An Introduction. In Hunston, Susan / Thompson, Geoff (eds) *Evaluation in Text: Authorial Stance and the Construction of Discourse.* Oxford: Oxford University Press, 1-27.

Vandermeeren, Sonja 1999. English as Lingua Franca in Written Corporate Communication: Findings from a European Survey. In Bargiela-Chiappini, Francesca / Nickerson, Catherine (eds), *Writing Business: Genre, Media and Discourses*. Essex: Longman, 273-291.

Wenger, Etienne 1998. *Communities of Practice: Learning, Meaning, and Identity*. Cambridge: Cambridge University Press.

Appendix – Transcription conventions

Pauses: (.) short pause under 0.3 seconds
(+) about 0.4 – 0.7 seconds
(++) about 0.8 – 1.7 seconds
(no.) no. of seconds in parenthesis, rounded to the second (if 2 or more)
Translations into English are in *italics*
?: indicates upward intonation
= adjacent to a word: word= =word indicates "latched speech" between two speakers
Contextual information is in double parenthesis (( ))
Back-channels that overlap with a speaker are inserted into his or her utterance
Stefano: we decide to arrive at (.) thirty degrees ((Denise: ok)) centigrade in (.)
Square brackets [ ] are used for changed or deleted names e.g. [wine name].
Inaudible or unclear speech is indicated by parenthesis ( )
Transcription with a degree of uncertainty is in parenthesis (some)
Alternative transcriptions are placed one above the other in parenthesis (sun)
Capitals indicate speaker emphasis: OUR products
Names and identifying features have been changed or deleted: [LN] means a last name has been deleted. [FN] = first name.
Time from DAT recording is in hours, minutes, and seconds: 9.12.05 = 5 seconds after 9:12 a.m.
Units are roughly the equivalent of Halliday's (1994: 215) clause complex, a head clause together with related clauses..

CARMEN VALERO-GARCÉS / BRUCE DOWNING

Modes of Communication between Suppliers of Services and Non-native English-speaking Users: Doctor-Patient Interaction[1]

1. Purpose and design of the study

Interviews involving physicians and patients or parents of minor patients[2] in a community clinic serving a largely Hispanic clientele in Saint Paul, Minnesota, U.S.A., were recorded, transcribed and analyzed to investigate features of the interaction in three communicative modes. In two recorded interviews, both the doctor and the patient speak English. In another two interviews a bilingual nurse, the clinic's usual interpreter, mediates between a Spanish-speaking patient and the English-speaking doctor. In the third pair of interviews a professional interpreter interprets the English/Spanish doctor/patient communication consecutively and using the first-person in reference to the speaker. We refer to these three conditions as the Monolingual Mode, the Bilingual Helper Mode, and the Interpreted Mode.

The purpose of this research was to:

1. describe the differences between an interaction that does not require an interpreter and a professionally interpreted doctor/

---

1   Catherine Athorp, an undergraduate student at the University of Minnesota, was a significant contributor to this research, collecting and carrying out a preliminary analysis of a portion of the data. Her contribution is hereby gratefully acknowledged. We also wish to acknowledge the expert assistance of Patricia Aedo, who transcribed or edited the transcriptions and translated the Spanish portions of the texts.
2   The data analyzed here are drawn principally from pediatric interviews in which a mother and one or more children are present. Thus when we speak of a 'doctor-patient' interaction, the person addressed by the doctor is most often the mother rather than the patient.

patient interaction;
2.   compare the role taken by an ad hoc interpreter (a bilingual nurse) during a doctor/patient interview with that of a professional interpreter;
3.   investigate the nature and effectiveness of communication in the Bilingual Helper and Interpreted modes in comparison with an unmediated same-language interview.

2. Method

2.1. Setting and participants

A small community clinic that serves a multi-lingual immigrant population was selected as the site for this study. The primary participants in the study were two English-speaking doctors, one Spanish/English bilingual nurse, who does ad hoc interpreting in the clinic, and six adults who were either patients or the parent of minor patients. Each of these participants signed a consent form that briefly explained the project and their role. Consent forms were available in both Spanish and English. A copy of the consent form was provided to each participant.

2.2. Data

During the course of one day, four interviews were recorded on audio cassette. Two of the interviews were conducted entirely in English (Monolingual Mode) and two required the intervention of a bilingual, a nurse doing double duty as an interpreter (Bilingual Helper Mode). On a later date, two additional bilingual interviews were recorded, this time involving the services of a professional interpreter who was not a health care provider (Interpreted Mode). No researcher was present in the room during the first two sets of interviews, but a researcher observed from a corner of the room during the final two interviews.

2.2.1. Organization of the data

The data, recorded on cassette tape, were first transcribed, and the Spanish portions of the texts were translated into English. The typed transcripts of the bilingual interviews were then arranged in a special script format. This format suggests the flow of speech from participant to participant. Translations of the Spanish-language utterances, presented between parentheses and in italic script, were inserted directly following each Spanish counterpart.

To simplify visualization and analysis, the successive turns were presented in four columns, representing the contributions of the monolingual provider in column A and the patient (or a parent of a juvenile patient) in column C. The utterances of the bilingual who provided interpretation were divided between two columns, B and D. We placed in column B the Spanish-language utterances of the bilingual addressed to the patient, usually relaying what the doctor had said, but in some cases representing utterances initiated by the bilingual. We placed in column D what the bilingual said in English, speaking generally to the provider and usually, but not always, relaying the utterances of the patient (or patient's parent). An example of this script format is shown in Table 1.

The advantage of this format is that it makes it simple to determine who is speaking and to compare the utterances of the doctor and the patient to those of the bilingual. It also facilitates comparison of the monolingual and interpreted interactions. The columns and rows are labeled for easy reference to a specific cell.

This format is used in order to

a)   easily compare interpretations to the utterance that is interpreted;

b)   determine which portions of the doctor's and the patient's speech are interpreted, and which are not;

c)   more easily identify speech produced by the bilingual which is not an interpretation of another's speech and identify to whom it is directed.

	A	B	C	D
	Doctor	Bilingual to patient	Patient (or parent)	Bilingual to doctor
1.	Okay. Is this the first time she's been here for our well child check? Is that right?			
2.		¿Es la primera vez que nos trae para el control de niños o no? *(Is this the first time that you've come in for her well child check, or not?)*		
3.			Sí. *(Yes.)*	
4.				Yes.
5.	Que bueno. *(Fine.)* All right, and she is now ... nine months old.			
6.		Ahora tiene nueve meses. *(She's nine months old now.)*		
7.			Sí. *(Yes.)*	
8.				Yes, nueve. *(..., nine)*
9.	Ah, okay.			

Table 1. Example of a formatted transcription.

We found it possible, and useful, to analyze the interviews into a series of *exchanges*, each consisting of a sequence of *turns at talk* by the different parties. Exchanges most often contained, at minimum, a question and answer or a statement and response. The example in Table 1 contains two exchanges, the first ending with the doctor's rejoinder, "All right", in 5. In the same turn, the doctor begins a new interrogative exchange, which ends at turn 9. The two interchanges in

Table 1 were typical, containing three basic elements: a question, a response, and an acknowledgement or rejoinder, along with the bilingual's interpretations (Prince 1985). Interestingly, rejoinders are often not interpreted, even by professional interpreters (Downing/ Swabey 1998).

2.3. Pattern of interaction

In a 'textbook example' of an interpreted interview, in which the interpreter role is limited to relaying messages between the other parties, each of the utterances of the doctor and the patient would be interpreted, and the interpreter would only rarely be an active participant in the interview. In other words, the *pattern* of verbal interaction would be identical to that of a monolingual interview involving only two parties, but for the 'repetitions' produced by the bilingual party. The patient would hear, after a brief delay, what the doctor had said, and vice versa, through the mediation of the bilingual.

We were interested in discovering whether each utterance of the bilingual party (columns B and D) served as an interpretation of what one monolingual party had said, for the benefit of the other, or whether it had some other function, and what those functions might be. Obviously, in monolingual interviews there are just two speakers, corresponding to columns A and C in the bilingual interviews. The monolingual interviews provided a basis for comparison with the interviews that included either a professional interpreter (Interpreter Mode) or a bilingual nurse brought in to assist in the communication (Bilingual Helper Mode).

2.4. Function analysis

In this paper we have not attempted a complete functional analysis, but we will refer to some utterances as representing any of six functional categories. (Analysis of the informational content of the exchange or of the accuracy with which meanings are transferred from English to Spanish and Spanish to English lies outside the scope of this paper.) The six functional categories are as follows:

1)   *Questions*: Utterances that ask a question.
2)   *Tag questions*: A special category of questions with a variety of functions. Usually one or two words, e.g. "Okay?" "Isn't it?" "Right?"
3)   *Answers*: Utterance that directly respond to a question.
4)   *Initiating Statements*: Utterances that initiate a topic or elaborate on the same speaker's topic.
5)   *Response Statements*: Utterances that are made in direct response to another's statement or an elaboration. Elaborations of questions by another party are also classified as 'response statements'.
6)   *Acknowledgements*: Short phrases, most often a single word, which follow an answer or response offered by another. Also called *rejoinders*.

3. Analysis of the data

3.1. Patterns of interaction

No attempt was made to control the length or content of the medical interviews that we studied. We recorded, transcribed, and analyzed six complete naturally occurring interviews. By chance, these interviews were somewhat diverse in content. One monolingual interview involved an adult patient, whereas the others were pediatric appointments in which one or more infants or children were present in addition to their mother. One pediatric appointment was a routine well-child interview, while in the other the mother had brought two sick children, and this appointment was frequently interrupted while the doctor went to the lab for test results. Nevertheless, all were basically one-on-one interview situations and appeared generally comparable in content and scope.

The number of turns taken by the participants in each interview provides a basis for comparison of their length. As the following table shows, the number of turns per interview was reasonably uniform, the longest being Interpreted Mode #1, in which the doctor saw two patients, the two boys with cold or flu symptoms.

	MONOLINGUAL MODE		BILINGUAL HELPER MODE		INTERPRETED MODE	
	#1	#2	#1	#2	#1	#2
TOTAL TURNS	302	310	265	316	446	376
Doctor	151	155	111	118	147	118
Patient/ Mother	151	155	45	74	104	86
Helper (nurse)			109	124		
Interpreter					189	165
Child (patient)					4	0
Other (nurse)					2	
Social Worker						7

Table 2. Total turns and turns taken by each participant.

As shown in Table 2, the Monolingual interviews and the Bilingual Helper interviews appear to be very close in length – averaging 306 turns for the monolingual ones and only slightly fewer, 290 turns, for those in the Bilingual Helper mode – an average difference of only 16 turns. The Interpreted Mode interviews (the longest of which included physical examination of two patients, the mother's two sons) were both longer, averaging 411 turns. It is not surprising that the number of turns was greater in these interviews, given that each utterance by the principal interlocutors was interpreted by the interpreter. As we will see, in the Bilingual Helper Mode only a fraction of the utterances were repeated for the benefit of the third party.

More significant, however, is *the amount of speech produced by the principal participants*, the doctor and patient (or parent of the patient) *that could be understood by the other party*. In the Monolingual Mode, doctor and patient alternate in speaking to each other and the number of turns taken by each is identical. Every utterance is direct and comprehensible. In the Interpreted Mode, fewer turns are taken by the mother of the patients than by the doctor, 104 compared to 147 (29% less) in one case and 86 compared to 118 (27% less) in the other. But every utterance by either party was either interpreted or could be understood without interpretation (*okay*, *no*, etc.). In the two interviews mediated by a bilingual nurse (Bilingual Helper Mode), the mother speaks even less: 45 turns compared to the doctor's 111 turns (59% less) in the first interview and 74 compared to 118 turns (37% less than the doctor) in the other.

The number of turns taken by each participant cannot tell the whole story, however. A better way to compare the three modes of interaction is to examine the extent of 'direct interaction' between the health care provider (the doctor) and the patient (or parent of a patient). In the monolingual interviews, the doctor and the patient speak the same language and therefore have the potential to understand everything the other says. There is 'direct interaction' between them for the entire interview. In the Interpreted Mode, there is direct interaction in the sense that the principal participants address each other when they speak and the interpreter relays each utterance to the other party in language each party understands. This is the usual mode of interaction in these Interpreted interviews. For example, in Interpreted Mode #1, 99% of the interpreter's turns are interpretations of what another party has just said, and 98% of what the doctor or patient says is interpreted (or in the case of some responses, is easily understood without interpretation).

This is not the case in the interviews mediated by the bilingual nurse. The doctor and the patient can interact 'directly' in the Bilingual Helper interviews only when the bilingual acts as an interpreter. Very often, however, the bilingual nurse instead speaks directly to one party or the other, entering into the conversation rather than interpreting for others. In these cases, no interpretation is provided for the party who is not being addressed, so that party cannot be expected to understand what is being said. In sum, doctor/patient interaction is being replaced by nurse/doctor or nurse/patient interactions.

Here is what further analysis reveals. In the first Bilingual Helper interview:

•   Of the 111 utterances spoken by the doctor, only 51 (46%) were interpreted in some fashion to the patient.

- Of the 45 utterances spoken by the patient, only 16 (36%) were interpreted to the doctor.

Similarly, in the second Bilingual Helper interview:

- Of the 118 utterances spoken by the doctor, 67 (57%) were relayed to the patient.
- Of the 74 utterances spoken by the patient, 36 (49%) were relayed to the doctor.

Thus, the 'direct interaction' in these two interviews was only 67 utterances, accounting for only 43% of the combined doctor and patient utterances for the first interview; and 103 utterances, or 54%, for the second.

The bilingual, who was also a nurse on staff at the clinic, contributed to the interviews in ways that were not, strictly speaking, interpretation.

- In the first Bilingual Helper interview, there were 109 utterances spoken by the bilingual. Of these, 42 (39%) were not interpretations of another's speech. Of these bilingual-originated utterances, 11 (26%) were directed to the doctor and 31 (74%) to the patient.
- In the second Bilingual Helper interview there were 124 utterances spoken by the bilingual. Of these, 70 utterances (41%) were not interpretations; 28 (40%) were directed to the doctor and 42 (60%) to the patient.

4. Findings

4.1. The Monolingual Mode

When both patient and provider speak English there is direct one-to-one communication between the health care provider and the patient. In both of our monolingual interviews, the doctor and the patient alternated turns, without exception, throughout the entire interview, so that the patient took exactly as many turns at speech as the doctor.

4.2. The Interpreted Mode

The professional interpreter, who is not a health care provider and was present solely to interpret, maintains a narrowly defined interpreter role. This is facilitated by the fact that the doctor addresses the interviewee, the patient's mother (or in some cases, the minor patient), rather than the interpreter, and the mother responds directly to the doctor. The interpreter introduces herself and her role briefly to both parties at the beginning of the session. After each turn at speech by either the doctor or the mother of the patient, she interprets what was said, generally quite accurately, into the other language. The exceptions – the instances in which she does not interpret – fall into these categories:

1) Brief responses, most often by the mother, which are readily understood without translation: *Sí, okay, uh-hum, no*. Sometimes she *does* offer an interpretation for such responses. The doctor in the interpreted interviews knows some Spanish, and occasionally speaks in Spanish, so it is not surprising or inappropriate that sometimes even longer utterances in Spanish are not interpreted for her.

2) Responses and especially rejoinders by the doctor which end one exchange and which are immediately followed by the initiation of another exchange by the same speaker. The interpreter regularly interprets only the latter portion of the utterance which begins a new exchange. In some cases the response or rejoinder by the doctor could be understood by the mother without translation, but in cases where the doctor is offering praise, encouragement, etc., the failure to interpret these comments could have a negative effect on the rapport between the doctor and the mother of the patient. In both Interpreted Mode sessions there are a few interesting instances where the interpreter speaks directly to one of the parties rather than merely relaying what has been said.

4.2.1. Comparison: monolingual interviews and interpreted interviews

Apart from the professional interpreter's exceptional interventions outlined above, the interaction between the health care provider and the patient/parent proceeds in essentially the same way in the Interpreted Mode as in the Monolingual Mode. The two parties address each other directly, and they respond to each exchange initiated by the other. The non-essential difference is that, in the Interpreted Mode, the interpreter makes it possible for each party to hear everything said by the other party even though the other is speaking a different language. This, of course, is the aim of professional interpreting.

4.3. The Bilingual Helper Mode: nurse or interpreter?

In the Bilingual Helper Mode the bilingual seems to move freely between the roles of interpreter and nurse. As interpreter, she is frequently involved in relaying the doctor's questions and counsel to the mother, and reporting the mother's responses to the doctor. In the role of nurse, she frequently takes over the doctor's role of questioning and counseling the patient, leaving the doctor in position of merely observing or supervising the exchange. Whenever the bilingual speaks directly to either the doctor or the patient, no interpretation of her utterance is available to the third party. In addition, replies and acknowledgments are often not reported. Judged by the standards of professional interpreting, the nurse as interpreter does a very poor job of facilitating communication between doctor and client.

Looking specifically at Bilingual Helper Mode interview #2, however, it becomes apparent that the nurse is not acting in the role of interpreter at all. Rather, in a fashion described by Briskina (1996), she is merely providing bilingual assistance to the doctor. The nurse participates in two intertwined conversations: one in English, with the doctor, and one in Spanish with the mother and children. The key fact that forces this analysis is that after the initial introductions, the doctor almost never specifically addresses the mother, but instead communicates with the nurse *about* the mother and her child. The nurse communicates with the doctor and then, responding to questions and directives from the doctor, turns to the mother to obtain the requested information or to give the suggested advice. The doctor is focused on the information she wants to obtain from or give to the patient through the bilingual nurse, but acts in a supervisory role, guiding and supervising the work of the nurse, who is actually the person interviewing the patient.

To see how this works, let us look at a passage from the transcript of Bilingual Helper Mode #2, shown in Table 3.[3]

turn	DOCTOR	BILINGUAL HELPER (NURSE)	MOTHER/PATIENT (CHILD)
1.	Muy bien, mamá. (*Very good, mom.*) Who lives in their household now?		
2.		¿Quién vive en su casa ahora? (*Who lives in your house now?*)	
3.			Em, mi esposo, los dos niños y mi hermana. (*Um, my husband, the two children and my sister.*)
4.		¿Y su hermana? (*And your sister?*)	
5.			Unha.
6.		Okay, her husband, two, the two children …	
7.	Two children and the maternal aunt.		
8.		Yes.	
9.	Okay. Que bien. (Okay, fine.) All right. Now…this baby's growing well, baby passed her Denver Developmental. Um, does mom know how to make the Similac up correctly?		

---

3   Here for clarity we have used just three columns for the three speakers instead of separating the bilingual's English and Spanish utterances into separate columns as in Table 1.

turn	DOCTOR	BILINGUAL HELPER (NURSE)	MOTHER/PATIENT (CHILD)
10.		¿Usted sabe como hacer el Similac? (*Do you know how to make the Similac?*)	
11.			No.
12.		No. [to the doctor]	
13.		La leche con la ... (*The milk with the ...*)	
14.			Esta con agua y – y – hecho dos, dos copas?¿ de leche para cuatro onzas de agua. (*This with water, and ..., and I make 2, 2 cups? of milk to have 4 ounces of water.*)
15.		Okay. Perfect. She says 4 ounces of water and two ...	
16.	Scoops.		
17.		...scoops.	
18.	Perfect, okay. She knows to run the water for 3 minutes 'cause of the lead?		
19.		Yes. I told her about that when I was ...	
20.	Okay. Good.		

Table 3. Bilingual Helper Mode #2 excerpt.

In turn 1, the doctor speaks directly to the mother, in Spanish, congratulating her on her answer to a preceding question posed by the nurse. Then, in the same turn, she addresses a question to the nurse rather than to the mother (referring to "their household" rather than "your household"). To obtain the requested information, the nurse then addresses the mother directly: "Who lives in your house now?" (ignoring the semantic difference between 'household' and 'house'). In turn 4, the nurse requests confirmation of the answer, which she receives. The nurse then turns to the doctor in turn 6 to respond to the doctor's question with her newly obtained information. The doctor, having overheard the Spanish exchange, completes the answer for her in turn 7. The nurse's next utterance, in turn 8, is not a translation to the mother but an acknowledgment that the doctor understood correctly. The doctor's evaluative comment in turn 9 is in Spanish and therefore presumably addressed to the mother.

But again the doctor continues by addressing a statement and a question to the nurse, referring to the mother in the 3rd person ("Does mom …"). The doctor in turn 9 also uses technical language that the mother would not understand ("her Denver Developmental"). In turn 10, the nurse ignores both the non-technical and technical comments of the doctor, and merely turns the question *about* the mother posed to her by the doctor ("Does mom know how to make the Similac up correctly?") into a question *for* the mother. Receiving a negative answer, the nurse follows up by beginning an explanation (which in a monolingual or interpreted interview would come from the doctor). In turn 14 the mother demonstrates that she does in fact know the answer to the question, at which point (turn 15) the nurse says "Okay," indicating that she now has the answer to the doctor's question, and she demonstrates the mother's knowledge by partially repeating what the mother has said, in English, with help from the doctor in turn 16. This time the doctor's evaluative comment (turn 18) is in English and is not translated for the mother's benefit – suggesting that the nurse assumes the remark to have been addressed to her.

As before, the doctor then continues by addressing another question to the nurse: "She knows to run the water for three minutes 'cause of the lead?". This seems to be a prompt not for the nurse to echo the question but for the nurse to instruct the mother about running water from the tap before using it for drinking and also to explain the reason for this – the danger of lead poisoning. This time, the nurse already knows the answer to the doctor's question, and therefore in turn 19 she neither interprets the question to the mother nor carries out the implied directive; she simply explains how she knows that the mother has the desired knowledge ("Yes, I told her about that when I was…"). Thus there is no interpretation of the doctor's question, the nurse's response, or the doctor's evaluative rejoinder. The mother is excluded from this portion of the dialogue.

We see in this example, and throughout this interview, how two conversations, one in English and the other in Spanish, are interlocked. At the same time, we see that there is minimal direct communication between the two principal parties, that the nurse's questions are often not direct interpretations of the doctor's questions or directives, that utterances by the nurse that are not interpretations of another party's speech are not interpreted for the other party (a violation of the interpreting standard of 'transparency'), and in fact that even statements or questions by the principal parties are frequently not interpreted in this mode.

4.4. Comparison: Interpreted Mode and Bilingual Helper Mode

Comparison among the three modes reveals that in the case of the Bilingual Helper Mode, there is an underlying agreement between the doctor and the bilingual nurse that the latter will act as nurse rather than as interpreter for the major portion of the interview. While this saves time, avoiding the repetition of utterances from one language to the other, and the doctor evidently feels that the nurse has the skills and knowledge to obtain information from the client and to give out accurate information, details and instructions, it does greatly lower the amount of direct doctor/patient interaction.

One of the ways the bilingual nurse contributes to the communication is to explain technical terminology when it is needed. At this point we must say that the language of the medical profession is specialized and there are terms which even same-language-speaking patients may not clearly understand; obviously it is even more difficult for non-native speakers to understand (Valero 2004a, 2004b). In this case, a similar situation to that reported by Valero is handled differently according to our data. Thus, while in the Monolingual Mode the doctor assumes that the patient knows the term or concept, or it is not important that the patient understand what it is, in the Bilingual Helper Mode the bilingual, feeling no obligation to interpret precisely what was said, provides advocacy by using simplified language or elaborating on the message when the doctor uses technical jargon.

On one occasion the Bilingual Helper leaves out part of the original message. Then, she asks for clarification, but she tends to ask more specifically for the information she had forgotten rather than trying to repeat what the doctor says again. There is no counterpart for any of these functions in the Monolingual Mode or the Interpreted Mode, except that in the latter case an interpreter might suggest that a doctor clarify terms or explanations, rather than undertaking to do so herself.

In situations where the doctor speaks to a juvenile patient, using very short utterances, the Bilingual Helper comes closer to providing a direct interpretation. In this context, the bilingual is not an independent participant in the interaction, and the role of care-giver is retained by the doctor. However, in those cases where the bilingual acts in the role of nurse or advocate, the doctor is removed to a supervisory position and has less direct interaction with the patient than in either of the other modes of interaction.

5. Conclusion

Because of the increasing number of non-English speakers in the United States – and in EU countries too – there is a greater need for interpreter services in order to provide adequate medical care for patients who do not speak English. The ideal situation for health care would be to have health care providers who speak the language of the patient. The second best choice is to have trained interpreters who specifically interpret in health care situations. However, the most common method of providing bilingual health care services in hospitals and health care centers is to maintain a list of bilingual employees who can be called upon to assist or to let the patient bring to the appointment a bilingual relative or friend. This is what we have called the Bilingual Helper Mode of interaction.

The data for this study come from recorded conversations in a clinic in the USA. The interviews are analyzed in terms of the pattern of interaction among the principal participants. In this study the focus has been on the role played by a Spanish-English bilingual nurse called upon to provide language assistance in a role that is ambiguous between that of a nurse and that of interpreter. The bilingual nurse has no training as an interpreter. The doctors in our recorded interviews relied heavily on her to provide health care for the patients and she did so with what appeared to be a high level of skill and capability. She also occasionally provided interpretation of what the doctor and patient, or the patient's mother, said to each other. In using simplified language while addressing the patient, rather than repeating the technical explanations offered by the doctor, the bilingual could be seen as providing patient advocacy services. These multiple tasks would seem to be a large burden to place on one individual (Downing 1992). Had she been a bilingual who was not a nurse or other health care provider, she might not have been asked to fulfill the other roles so extensively.

However, since the nurse had experience but not formal training in interpreting and the doctors had no training in how to best use an interpreter, there were distinct gaps in doctor-patient interaction in the Bilingual Helper interviews. The Spanish-speaking patients appeared to be getting good care, but the process depended heavily on the bilingual nurse's knowledge and care-giving expertise. A great deal of responsibility was delegated to her that was the doctor's responsibility in the monolingual or professionally interpreted interviews.

Comparing the Bilingual Helper Mode with the Interpreted Mode, we see that the amount of 'direct interaction' between doctor and patient changes dramatically, being higher in the Interpreted Mode. This suggests that using a trained interpreter in interlingual doctor/patient interactions respects the patient's or parent's right to direct access to the physician and favors effective communication.

References

Briskina, Galina 1996. Interlingual Doctor-Patient Communications: Understanding the Role of a Professional Interpreter. Presented at the American Association for Applied Linguistics Conference, Chicago.

Downing, Bruce T. 1992. The Use of Bilingual/Bicultural Workers as Providers and Interpreters. *International Migration* (Special issue: *Migration and Health in the 1990s*, edited by H. Siem and P. Bollini) 30, 121-129.

Downing, Bruce / Swabey, Laurie. 1998. "Okay, Good for You. Does It Still Itch?": An Analysis of Non-interpreted Rejoinders in Medical Discourse. Paper presented at the Second Critical Link Conference, Vancouver, British Columbia, Canada.

Prince, C. D. 1985. *Hablando con el doctor: Communication Problems between Doctors and their Spanish-Speaking Patients.* Ph.D. dissertation, Stanford University, USA.

Valero-Garcés, Carmen 2004a. Terminología Médica Especializada en la Interpretación en los Servicios Públicos. Retos y Estrategias. Paper presented at the IX International Conference on English for Specific Purposes, March 2004. Alcalá de Henares, Madrid, Spain (forthcoming).

Valero-Garcés, Carmen 2004b. Los lenguajes especializados y la terminología en la entrevista médico-paciente inmigrante. Realidad y necesidades. Paper presented at the Third International Conference of the European Association of Languages for Specific Purposes (AELFE), September 2004, Granada, Spain.

CYNTHIA KELLETT BIDOLI

The Linguistics Conference Setting: A Comparative Analysis of Intercultural Disparities during English to Italian Sign Language Interpretation[1]

1. Introduction

Over recent years, attention has been increasingly focussed on the study of English/es used in international communication from an intercultural perspective, to investigate disparities in language use in English texts from different countries of origin, from a variety of specialized domains and to analyse if and how during international intercultural communication English intrudes upon the discourse patterns of foreign languages (Crystal 1997, Cortese/Riley ·2002, Cardinaletti/Garzone 2004, Candlin/Gotti 2004). This chapter introduces one such intercultural investigation in Italy: intercultural communication mediated by simultaneous interpretation across an unusual language combination in a particular institutional setting. A multimodal corpus was compiled of mediation from English to Italian Sign Language (*Lingua Italiana dei Segni* – LIS) during four academic conference presentations delivered by American native speakers of English.

The Italian Deaf community or more specifically, the approximately 877,000 Italians with some form of hearing impairment from partial to total, of which 92,000[2] are pre-lingual deaf individuals, are

---

1 This investigation is part of research on *Intercultural Practices and Strategies of Textual Recasting* conducted by the University of Turin unit within the Italian national research project (MIUR COFIN), *Intercultural Discourse in Domain-specific English* coordinated by M. Gotti: <http:/www.unibg.it/cerlis/ progetti.htm>.

2 Information is based on data provided by the Italian National Statistics Institute (ISTAT), see <http://www.handicapincifre.it>.

an integral part of Italian society, and like their hearing fellow countrymen, come into contact with English in its written or spoken forms. The majority of profoundly deaf people communicate amongst each other in sign language, which for some of them, those born of deaf parents, is their first language. The Italian Deaf attend the state school system and therefore are expected to learn and communicate in Italian and learn English as a compulsory second language like mainstream hearing children, but their ability to learn spoken language varies greatly from person to person.[3] Since 1992, all Italian deaf children have had the legal right to assistance in their studies from nursery school to university through the services of hearing assistants, specialized in classroom communication, and deaf educators as well as interpreters when necessary to mediate between Italian and LIS. Also deaf adults can rely on an interpreter service for help during every day 'community' related communication of institutional nature such as in courtrooms, in hospital, during parent teacher meetings, in municipality and other local authority offices or at conferences organized by official associations or universities. Some deaf individuals do not learn to sign at all but depend solely on lip reading or on any residual hearing they may have retained with varying degrees of success; yet others speak in class or at work and sign at home. But if coping with spoken and written Italian is difficult enough for them, contact with a foreign language like English adds to the challenge of daily life even more for severely deaf individuals (Kellett Bidoli 2004: 128-129).

2. The institutional setting

As part of this intercultural investigation into English-LIS contact in Italy, a survey was conducted in 2003 on interpreter-mediated communication, principally to identify the workplace settings of professional interpreters and the extent of English to LIS mediation (Kellett Bidoli forthcoming a). A questionnaire which surveyed a very small

---

3   For research into the teaching of English to deaf adults see Ochse 2001, 2004.

sample of Italian LIS interpreters (approximately 12%) revealed that a larger proportion of them than expected know English well, though when working for the Deaf they tend not to work directly from English to LIS but interpret from English relayed through a spoken Italian interpreter from spoken Italian to LIS in a trilingual combination. Therefore a double filter is often at play; the English source text is filtered through spoken Italian before being perceived visually by the Deaf. Investigation into the working environment of interpreters showed that although interpretation from English is infrequently encountered, several domains in institutional settings do emerge:

- interpreting from English at conferences related to Deaf issues (60% of sample responses);
- educational experience with English at university level in English language classes and in the fields of information technology, linguistics, neurolinguistics, political science and psychology (33%);
- interpreting from English in the medical context (20%);
- interpreting from English in social contexts such as at cultural and sports events (13.3%);
- interpreting from English on television (13.3%).

Conferencing emerged clearly as being the most frequent context in which English is used. Responses to an open-ended question on 'other interpreting events' netted in several more socially related fields, which included interpretation during religious events, tourist excursions, public examinations, unspecified training courses and unspecified 'informal situations'. Taking the total of multiple responses to all interpreted events of social nature it was found that 73.3% of the interpreters worked in this social 'institutional' field; an even higher response frequency than the 60% obtained for conferencing and composed of a wide range of genres well worth further investigation.

A closer look at conference typologies encountered on the job revealed several domains which in order of frequency are: linguistics (77.8% of the sample), psychology (33.3%), science and technology (33.3%), deaf culture and history (22.2%), deaf education and learning (11.1%), law (11.1%), medicine (11.1%), and social assistance (11.1%).

The next stage of investigation was to focus more closely on the nature of the intercultural communication at play during conference interpretation from English to LIS and assess any surface adjustments in the form of disparities such as culture-bound textual shift and different linguistic usage. More specifically the aim of this present study is to observe whether there is awareness of and respect for cultural specificity during the mediation process or whether there is some form of intrusion from the source language and culture producing linguistic and cultural distortion. Detailed analysis was conducted to pinpoint any strategies of removal, avoidance or attenuation of cultural specificities or vice versa to identify those occurrences respectful of cultural differences: 'good practice'.

3. The corpus

Four representative texts were accordingly selected and converted into a small digital corpus of multimodal nature for electronic comparative/contrastive analysis containing 12,616 tokens (Kellett Bidoli forthcoming b). More precisely, the corpus consists of the video recordings of four academic speeches within the domain of linguistics, presented at two major Italian conference events by American-English native speakers, scholars of sign language and/or interpretation. One was presented at the First National Symposium on Italian Sign Language (*1° Convegno Nazionale sulla Lingua dei Segni*) organized by ENS the Italian National Deaf Association in 1995 (Caselli/ Corazza 1997).[4] The remaining three were presented at the conference *The Meeting of Sign and Voice* organized by the SSLMIT (*Scuola Superiore di Lingue Moderne per Interpreti e Traduttori*) of the University of Trieste in 1997, on theoretical and practical aspects of signed language interpretation and training (Gran/Kellett Bidoli 2000).[5] The videos included insets of the speakers' presentations with the LIS interpreters communicating gesturally on full screen. Three of the speeches were simultaneously interpreted into Italian and then

---

4   A paper by W.C. Stokoe on the evolution of sign language.
5   W.P. Isham, *Research on Interpreting with Signed Languages*, C.J. Patrie, *Sequencing Instructional Materials in Interpreter Education* and B. Moser-Mercer, *Acquisition of Interpreting Skills*.

relayed to LIS for a mixed hearing and deaf audience, whereas one speech was interpreted directly from English to LIS.

Software[6] capable of handling the multimodal source data contained in the corpus (images and sound) was used to transcribe the spoken English into written text and the signed interpretation into glosses. The original VHS video taped English versions underwent a complex transference to convert them into a format for digital viewing on a computer where the images, sound and written transcriptions were combined and synchronized to run simultaneously on the screen: as the media file played, the text scrolled and manual transcription of the English or signed discourse was undertaken by extracting sound or visual information from the video file. The parallel transcription process took four months to complete owing to the trilingual nature of the study and the three-dimensional form of signs as well as gestures that often produce meaning not easy to gloss. The glosses were checked by a profoundly deaf adult, a teacher of Italian Sign Language. Despite numerous technical problems that arose (Kellett Bidoli forthcoming b) the following multimodal parallel corpora were obtained:

- audio/video recordings of the original spoken English conference discourse;
- video recordings of the signed interpreted discourse in LIS;
- a written transcription of the source discourse (**in bold**);
- glossed transcriptions of the interpreted LIS in Italian (following the conventional rules for the transcription of signs in *ITALICS* upper case);
- a written 'interpreted' version of the LIS in standard English to enable an international readership to compare the interpreted message with the original (*in italics*);
- a written 'interpreted' version of the LIS in standard Italian to enable both a professional interpreter and the profoundly deaf teacher to check the accuracy of the meaning conveyed by the glosses/signs.

LIS glosses in this chapter have all been translated into English for the convenience of readers. Signed languages are composed of a simulta-

---

6   Code-A-Text Integrated System for the Analysis of Interviews and Dialogues (C-I-SAID: Scolari, Sage Publications).

neous combination of signs, gesture, body movement and facial expression to convey meaning which is extremely difficult to represent graphically in 'written' form (Kellett Bidoli 2004: 137-138). The non-manual signals that are part of the signed discourse are inserted in lower case letters above the glosses on a line. Conventional symbols for non-manuals have been omitted in order to simplify understanding of the examples below for a readership unacquainted with the conventions of sign language transcription. Two glosses joined by a hyphen indicates that two words are needed to gloss one sign, single letters joined by a hyphen indicate use of the manual alphabet (fingerspelling) and words between double quotation marks in italics represent lexical items that were mouthed to provide the lip pattern of the spoken equivalent of the signs. This is useful if a sign is not clear or a concept is difficult to interpret; the mouthed equivalent can often clarify doubts.

On completion of transcription of the LIS glosses a resulting continuous string of unpunctuated text was broken down into meaningful segments according to the natural 'intonation' markers, pauses, particular gestures and facial expressions of the interpreters. This enabled segmentation of the transcribed LIS text into small manageable units using the customary 'musical score' format for the transcription of bilingual mediation, in order to detect any micro-textual elements during the subsequent detailed comparative analysis once the English and LIS texts had been aligned. Punctuation was also necessary in order to respect the requirements of the software used, which is programmed to parse segments of dialogue chronologically and horizontally in the form of sentences or paragraphs.

Analysis of the first half of the corpus (Kellett Bidoli forth-coming b) uncovered extensive textual recasting in LIS predominantly in the form of omissions, additions and substitutions as well as several intercultural features of interest. In the two speeches analysed it was extremely difficult to identify direct interference from the English language as the double filter mechanism was at play and no recordings of the Italian interpretation were available. This chapter focuses more specifically on intercultural aspects uncovered from the one speech interpreted directly from English to LIS. Subsequent personal contact made with the interpreter revealed that although *chuchotage* (whisper-ing) from English to Italian was provided at the conference, it was not availed of until two-thirds through the speech when the interpreter's concentration was tiring. However, after attempting to follow the Italian for a minute or two, the interpreter found that listening to two languages simultaneously was more of a disturbance than an aid and reverted back again to listening to the original source language.

4. Lexico-grammatical disparities

Through color-coding the omissions, additions and substitutions became immediately visibly ubiquitous but in order to identify linguistic and cultural intrusions leading to semantic misrepresentation or distortion in greater depth, a more detailed comparison of segments at microtextual level was necessary.

Firstly, word order asymmetries were checked. Whereas English is essentially a 'fixed-word-order' SVO language (subject [S] followed by verb [V] and then object [O]), LIS has predominantly an SOV order, but sometimes an OSV order with a slight pause after the object can be found. For example:

(1)   **The interpreter** [S] **translates** [V] **the discourse** [O],

in English, is rendered in LIS as:

(2)   *INTERPRETER* [S] *DISCOURSE* [O] *TRANSLATE* [V]

or:

(3)   *DISCOURSE* [O] minimal pause *INTERPRETER* [S] *TRANSLATE* [V]

S and O inversion can occur when the subject is evident (the discourse cannot translate the interpreter) or when using directional verbs, which entail movement (left or right) from the spatial location of the subject or the object, which have been previously fixed.

English word order transpired in a few instances as in:

(4)   *I [S] UNDERSTAND NOT [V] ITALIAN [O]* – *I don't understand spoken Italian*

This should have been interpreted *I [S] ITALIAN [O] UNDERSTAND NOT [V]*.

(5)   [...] *MUST CARE-FOR CHILD* [...] – *[...] they had to care for [their] children [...]*

instead of the correct *MUST CHILD CARE-FOR.*

Non-manual movements such as shoulder or head rotation and arm movements are essential grammatical markers in signed languages and by simply reading the transcribed glosses it is often difficult to establish cohesive links; who does what to whom. Furthermore, LIS like Mandarin Chinese relies on a topic-comment structure whereby the subject of the topic being talked about is indicated through a sign (maybe appearing only once). This is followed by one or several subsequent comments that share the initial topic but which are not linked by evident clause structures, but simply each link in the chain has some connection with the initial topic (subject). If one does not follow the non-manual signals very carefully to identify ellipted reference and cohesive clues in the topic chain structure, this leads to serious problems of disambiguation of meaning for a hearer (like myself) during the mental translation process from LIS and recourse to inference mechanisms. Zero anaphora will result from the glosses unless the non-manual referential signals of body movement and gaze are transcribed too. Because of topicalization and resulting sparse referential tracking, translation of the corpus glosses was made impossible at times without recourse to the non-manual clues on the video or the acute visual perception of the deaf expert.

Occasionally it was the LIS interpreter who caused perplexity by omitting the initial subject altogether, though in most cases it could be inferred from the context:

(6)   **The first [development] in two recently published papers [...]** – *FIRST THERE-ARE CLEAR THERE-ARE 2 RECENT PUBLISH [...]*

Here the subject 'papers' is missing.

As mentioned above, when referring to people, places or things in contrast (for example, novice interpreters versus experts) instead of using familiar agreement features which exist in English or Italian, the interpreter places them in a specific spatial location so that anaphoric reference can be achieved by turning the body in that direction or pointing to that specific point in space. Multiple referents in space can be set up too:

(7) *STUDENT ABILITIES 3 SECTOR, SECTOR, SECTOR BEGINNERS, INTERMEDIATE, ADVANCED SO, SO, SO, COMPETENCES 3 ITS-COMPETENCE, ITS-COMPETENCE, ITS-COMPETENCE CAN, BUT ORDER THUS NO, CAN EXCHANGE FOLLOW THUS NO, MUST CHANGE SO, SO, SO, TAKE, TAKE, THEN TAKE WHICH*
[We can divide] student skills into three categories: beginners intermediate and advanced, as follows. You don't have to keep to the order of these three levels of ability, beginners, intermediate and advanced, but you can change. You don't have to keep this order but you can change it. You can change tasks according to need

In this example three referents have been established. As the interpreter signs 'sector' she appoints three specific locations with parallel hands in the neutral space in front of her. She then signs 'beginners, intermediate and advanced' in the same locations respectively and from then on in the discourse she need not use those three signs again, but refers to the three categories by signing additional information in those locations. 'Its-competence' repeated in each of the three locations means the competences, abilities or skills in each of the three previously mentioned categories. The same applies in the following example:

(8) *DIFFICULT, CATEGORY MATERIAL, CATEGORY MATERIAL, CATEGORY MATERIAL DIFFICULT*
It's difficult to find material for beginners, intermediate and advanced students

Reference may be made by pointing to the referent (person or thing) without recourse to signing or fingerspelling a name:

(9) <u>   Points to Moser   </u>
ALREADY BEFORE HEAR SPEAK, HEAR SPEAK
You heard [Barbara Moser] speak [about this] earlier

or:

(10) <u>   Points to slide   </u>
THERE OUTLINE SEE [...]
There [on the overhead] you can see [...]

Reference may also be indicated through the use of verbal directionality (Corazza 2000) by changing the direction of the verb from the spatial location of the subject to the object. In LIS there are three verb classes. The first comprises those non-directional verbs, which are articulated on a location of the body such as *EAT* (MANGIARE) or

THINK (PENSARE) requiring a preceding referent: pronoun or noun. The second class articulates the verbs in space without subject reference, which is obtained through directionality of the sign, which leads one to understand, who is acting or who receives the action. Examples of directional verbs frequently used in the corpus are *LOOK-AT* (GUARDARE), *GIVE* (DARE), *SPEAK* (PARLARE), *SIGN* (SEGNARE), *TELL-TO* (DIRE). According to the directional movement (linear, arched, circular) or repetition of directionality, one can express 'give you' (singular or plural), 'give each', 'give to all', and 'always give'. The third class is subdivided into verbs which are signed either in the location of the subject or the object such as *GROW* (CRESCERE).

Sign language glosses of verbs are given in the infinitive,[7] which gives the false impression that there is no tense perception in LIS. In English, verbs are marked according to tense and aspect whereas in LIS there is the use of time signs together with specific markers or indicators at the beginning of the sentence in relation to the linear concept of time that runs along a 'time line' from the far front of the body (future), through to the immediate front of the signer in neutral space (present), to the back of the signer's body (past). Once the tense of a verb has been established, all successive verbs will be in that tense until a new marker is supplied. Time is associated with signs such as *WEEK* (SETTIMANA), *MONTH* (MESE) *YEAR* (ANNO), numbers, names of months and days. 'Last year' will entail the *YEAR* sign moving back towards the shoulder, 'in three hours' will entail **3** incorporated in the *HOUR* (ORA) sign moved forwards and 'long time ago' will require a repeated past tense marker (the double motion of the hand back across the shoulder). Temporal aspect, such as the signalling of duration ('for a long time') and frequency ('often') of an action are accomplished by inflectional signs. These are similar to directional verb movements (linear, arched and circular), which indicate the desired aspect.

Another marked difference between LIS and English is the frequent conversion of spoken affirmative statements into signed

---

7   An exception is the sign for the verb **DO** (FARE) and the separate sign for **DONE** (FATTO). **DONE** can act as a tense marker e.g. **I EAT DONE** (IO MANGIARE FATTO) – *I have eaten.*

interrogative forms. The interrogative can be expressed by: *yes-no* questions (during casual conversation); *wh*-word questions that use an interrogative sign like, *WHAT?* (COSA?), or *WHERE?* (DOVE?) that are normally placed at the end of the sentence with accompanying non-manual signals and are normally accompanied by an answer; and *rhetorical* questions. In the corpus there was extensive cultural adjustment to the use of *question-answer* forms that provide the signer with a means of introducing new information that can be supplied in an answer. These interrogative forms have been kept where possible in the interpreted transcription to convey their illocutionary effect, (however where this infringed the semantic rules of English or Italian they were transformed into near equivalent affirmative statements):

(11) **Some of the most important facts about sign language are being discover-ed by Deaf researchers** – *What was one of the most important things that emerged? It was that the Deaf were doing research*

(12) **Equally positive is the collaboration between deaf and hearing research-ers** – *Who was doing real research? Both Deaf and hearing people together*

There are several signed negative forms in LIS in diverse locations glossed as **NO** or **NOT** (NON), most frequently signed by the right hand index finger after the verb, and often accompanied by head negation. Additional negations at the end of sentences are *IT-ISN'T* (NON-C'È) *NEVER* (MAI), *NOT-YET* (NON-ANCORA), *NOTHING* (NIENTE) or *NO ONE* (NESSUNO). Signed negation may be omitted altogether and indicated by head negation alone. Here is an example of the 'no' negative and double 'O' negative for *NOTHING*, which can cause problems in interpretation as they come right at the end of sentences:

(13) *THERE-IS GROUP CHILDREN THERE-IS TEST KNOW* _____
"vocabulary"
WORD WORD KNOW PRESENT AFTER RESULT NOT-LIKE RESULT FOLLOW THAT COLOR SKIN OR GENES NO, NOTHING
[They have been working with] a group of children and have tested their knowledge of vocabulary. They found that it wasn't the color of their skin or genes [that was the determining factor for their knowledge]; not at all

A negative can be conveyed by 'blowing' into the air:

(14) **Interpreters have to describe a map without seeing it**
blowing into the air

INTERPRETER MUST REPEAT MAP SEE

Direct speech forms were substituted by indirect forms as in:

(15)   **Thus an older more skillful toolmaker could show a younger one, "Not that way, not that way, do it like this"** – *The toolmaker working with the hammer stone could show [another person] how [to work]. He could explain the process. The young toolmaker could watch and copy how to work by hitting too*

Overall, as found in Cokely's investigation (1992) little syntactical intrusion from English was found in the corpus.

An English lexical intrusion in the Stokoe speech was identified in the use of the single term *LINGUA* for 'language' whereas, both Italian and LIS have two distinct terms and signs: *LINGUA* meaning a set of conventions necessary to communicate orally or gesturally between individuals in a particular community of practice, and *LINGUAGGIO* meaning man's faculty to express himself through articulated sounds in the form of words or movement and gesture in the form of signs.

Another example of English lexical intrusion was found in the choice of a verb:

(16)   **I know Virginia**
        IO SAPERE CONOSCERE VIRGINIA
        I know Virginia

In English there is only one verb for both 'to know something' and 'to know someone' whereas in Italian and LIS there are two separate verbs *sapere* and *conoscere* respectively. Here the interpreter chose the wrong one before immediately making the correction.

A metaphor was substituted by:

(17)   **This broadening [...] of language knowledge to include sign languages [...] will bring another flower like that, that happened back home at times** – *This could also mean the beginning of a new approach in Italy, the opening of new horizons*

which omitted the intended meaning of success and comparison with what has happened in the USA, but ended the speech on a positive note all the same.

5. Cultural disparities

Fingerspelling (the use of the manual Roman alphabet) is kept to a minimum in LIS and can be considered a cultural intrusion of the spoken/written language forms used by the hearing population. Fingerspelling is used only to spell out proper names of unfamiliar people and places or technical terms. The Italian Deaf avoid it in normal 'conversation' preferring gesture, mime or description in signs where possible. It was found in the corpus with accompanying mouthed lip patterns:

- only two Italian fingerspelt words: *S-E-M-I-O-T-I-C-I* (Italian plural form of 'semiotic') and *T-R-A-S-L-I-T-T-E-R-A-Z-I-O-N-E* (transliteration) which are linguistic terms uncommon in everyday signed speech. Two clear instances of English intrusion of the letter 'N' were found in *T-R-A-N-S-L-I-T-T-R-A-Z-I-O-N-E*;

- acronyms: *O-N-U* (U.N.), *C-N-R* (C.N.R.);

- one foreign loan: *C-L-O-Z-E*;

- unfamiliar proper names which in some cases when of foreign origin were spelt incorrectly: (*C-H-I-O-M-S-K-Y* /Chomsky, *C-O-K-L-E-Y* /Cokely, *H-U-R-T* /Hart, *L-A-M-B-R-T* /Lambert, *L-I-V-S-T-O-N* /Livingstone, *M-E-R-T-S* /Mertz, *R-E-S-L-E-Y*/ Risley, *S-I-P-L-E* /Sipple, *V-A-L-I* /Valli). Two Italian names were misspelt too (*F-A-B-R-O* /Fabbro, *U-M-B-E-T-R-O*/ Umberto). Sign names[8] were used when referring to people known to the deaf audience together with mouthing;

- unfamiliar place names, e.g. *K-I-O-T-O* /Kyoto which was fingerspelt and immediately identified by a 'roof or pagoda-like' sign which was used hence forth. Sign names were used for 'Gallaudet' and also 'Washington DC' known to Italian deaf

---

8 Sign names are signs which rapidly identify a person being referred to, usually according to some physical feature, character trait, or initials, which immediately distinguishes him/her during normal conversation between the Deaf. For example two consecutive, downward-moving 'V' signs refer to Virginia Volterra, well known among the Deaf in Italy for her research on Italian Sign Language and interest in Deaf issues.

people as both the US capital and the location of Gallaudet
University for the Deaf; *Geneva* mentioned in the source
discourse was omitted;

- and unfamiliar foreign technical terms *D-É-C-A-L-A-G-E* (lag
time) and *S-H-A-D-O-W-I-N-G*. In the case of 'décalage' a sign
was invented by the interpreter immediately after the fingerspelling which after two occurrences of the term was used
alone. 'Shadowing' is a technique used in interpreter training
when students are asked to listen to discourse and repeat it
simultaneously to exercise their speed of delivery, lag time and
eventually correct mistakes added purposefully. Deaf people
would probably not have understood this term, which was not
explained.

Fingerspelling slows down the communication process despite its
incredible rapidity by expert hands. This may explain an omission of
the second name in a list of four authors: Olga Capirci, Jana Iverson,
Elena Pizzuto and Virginia Volterra. The first name was fingerspelt
which probably increased lag time and either the interpreter missed
the second or, in order not to miss too much new incoming discourse,
instead of fingerspelling the second unfamiliar American name,
avoided it altogether and continued by using only the rapid sign names
of the last two Italian authors familiar to the deaf audience.

Another specific cultural trait in signed languages is the use of
mime or body language to convey additional semantic meaning to
signs often more forcibly than in the original which cannot be glossed.
Stokoe's interpreter respected this cultural specificity in particular.
For example when Stokoe describes early hominids shaping stones:

(18)   **An early maker of stone tools […]**

The interpreter conveyed more semantic meaning than in the original
by signing *MAN* together with a bent over ape-like posture and
primitive animal-like facial expression. Anaphoric reference was thus
later conveyed through body posture without the sign for *MAN*;

(19)   **[…] he hits the hammer stone down across the other one**

This was inferred through the miming of the striking action several
times as if holding the stones;

(20)   **A hunting dog goes to ground, sniffs signs that tell it another animal has passed [...]**

The interpreter signed *DOG SNIFFS* but intensified the meaning through body posture and movement to convey that it was intent on sniffing and was moving here and there;

(21)   **The cat rubbing against its owner's leg is making a kitteny sign and that sign means "Feed me Momma"**

The interpreter signed *CAT* and then mimed a cat rubbing against something followed by *OWNER* in such a way as to convey the act of the cat looking upwards and begging to be fed;

(22)   **Before gestural communication begins from birth onwards, the infant needs to be talked to, or signed to [...]**

No signs were needed for 'from birth...infant' as the interpreter cradled an imaginary baby signing at it with the free hand making one infer the mother as the agent of the action. But when the interpreter's gaze switched to an upward direction with the sign *SEE*, one automatically inferred it was the baby perceiving the outside world.

In the following example it is interesting to note that the distant transatlantic American perspective implied by 'your' is adjusted to the Italian perspective by 'here in'. In addition, 'Umberto' was incorrectly fingerspelt:

(23)   **Your countryman Umberto Eco [...]** – *Here in Italy [...] Umbetro Eco [...]*

An evident adaptation by the interpreters to Deaf culture was found in the whole corpus in the numerous references to sight and gesture. 278 items associated with sight and gesture were found compared to 232 associated with speech and hearing. It is evident that conferences lying in the domain of linguistics and specifically on sign language contain a greater than average number of lexical items in the source discourse referring to sight and gesture, but many instances were found of intentional substitution or addition (underlined) by the interpreters to conform with the cultural norms of LIS:

(24)   **There are signs that stand for objects and for beings [...]** – *Like signs for objects or something you can see [...]*

(25)   **[...] when we work we are going between two languages that are very different in structure [...]** – *Many people see the two languages, sign language and spoken language, as having a different structure*

(26) [...] **a brief introduction on the, development of expertise with particular reference to interpreting** – *[...] an introduction on the development of expertise looking in particular at interpretation*

(27) **We found out and not just in interpretation and translation that there are differences between experts and novices when it comes to the kind of factual knowledge that students have** – *I only looked into the fields of interpretation and translation and I saw there are differences between experts and novices in the knowledge students have*

(28) [...] **novices will always focus on what they don't know [...]** – *Novices only look at words they don't know [...]*

In this case the verb 'look' was signed twice for emphasis to mean 'focus on';

(29) **This is all about understanding points of view [...]** – *This is all about having to see how to understand different points of view [...]*

Another culture-specific adaptation is found in the following:

(30) **Above all, to be [an infant] that others directly communicate with** – *Whoever speaks or signs to the infant must do so directly and not turn their shoulders*

Here the interpreter through shoulder and head movement explicitly emphasizes '**directly**' in that whoever is signing or speaking to the child must not do so while turning away because to the Deaf seeing the meaning of language is essential.

6. Conclusion

Little attention has hitherto been directed on the conference genre in the field of English for Academic Purposes (Ventola *et al.* 2002: 9). Conference genres are dynamic entities, which may unfold unexpectedly according to unpredictable situations and events (*ibidem*: 31). They are composed of spoken discourse, which may be read from a written text or be presented in the form of spontaneous speech with or without the aid of notes. Data from conferences is less immediately available to the researcher than written discourse found in text corpora like the British National Corpus and Brown Corpus or on the World

Wide Web (research papers, legal texts, newspaper articles, websites etc.). The lack of readily available written data for the conference researcher to work on necessitates the audio recording of events and adoption of conversation analysis techniques. If one adds an interpreted multilingual dimension to the conference event then analysis becomes even more complex to handle. Add a multimodal dimension across diverse semiotic channels by including a signed language and one ends up with a daunting task. A mixture of curiosity and determination has led to this attempt to unravel intercultural aspects subtly hidden from immediate scrutiny.

In the present study on a small representative corpus of conference interpretation from voice-to-sign (and in this paper in particular on direct English to LIS interpretation), clear evidence has been found of awareness by interpreters of the need for adjustment during the mediation process to the specific linguistic and cultural traits of the target language. Few instances of intrusion from the English were found. Textual recasting in the form of distortion of the original source discourse resulted principally from omissions, additions and substitutions (reported in Kellett Bidoli forthcoming b). Further detailed analysis is yet to be conducted on the fourth speech in the corpus.

Word counts revealed a total of 3,075 different English types out of the 12,616 tokens from which approximately 500 terms were selected according to their specialized usage in the conceptual field of linguistics. Concordances were generated for each to detect particular collocations or patterns. Corresponding sign glosses were identified in the LIS corpus and likewise concordances were analysed. From these it has been possible to begin the compilation of a glossary on CD-ROM of terms and expressions representative of the specialized language of linguistics that a LIS interpreter would most likely encounter when interpreting at a conference from English. The purpose of this English-LIS glossary is to provide Italian trainee interpreters with a useful tool to prepare them for one of the most demanding of tasks: complex intercultural and interlinguistic mediation across audio, visual and gestural channels of communication.

References

Candlin, Christopher / Gotti, Maurizio (eds) 2004. *Intercultural Aspects of Specialized Communication*. Bern: Peter Lang.

Cardinaletti, Anna / Garzone, Giuliana (eds) 2004. *Lingua, mediazione e interferenza*. Milan: FrancoAngeli.

Caselli, Maria Cristina / Corazza, Serena (eds) 1997. *LIS. Studi, esperienze e ricerche sulla Lingua dei Segni in Italia. Atti del 1° Convegno Nazionale sulla Lingua dei Segni*. Tirrenia (Pisa): Edizioni del Cerro.

Cokely, Denis 1992. *Interpretation: A Sociolinguistic Model*. Burtonsville, MD: Linstok Press.

Corazza, Serena 2000. Aspetti morfofonologici dei verbi in LIS. In Gran, Laura / Kellett Bidoli, Cynthia (eds) *Signed Language Interpretation and Training: Theoretical and Practical Aspects*. Trieste: Edizioni Università di Trieste, 19-28.

Cortese, Giuseppina / Riley, Philip (eds) 2002. *Domain-specific English: Textual Practices Across Communities and Classrooms*. Bern: Peter Lang.

Crystal, David 1997. *English as a Global Language*. Cambridge: Cambridge University Press.

Gran, Laura / Kellett Bidoli, Cynthia (eds) 2000. *Signed Language Interpretation and Training: Theoretical and Practical Aspects*. Trieste: Edizioni Università di Trieste.

Kellett Bidoli, Cynthia 2004. Intercultural Features of English-to-Italian Sign Language Conference Interpretation: A Preliminary Study for Multimodal Corpus Analysis. In Candlin, Christopher / Gotti, Maurizio (eds) *Intercultural Discourse in Domain-specific English*. In *TEXTUS. English Studies in Italy* 17/1, Genoa: Tilgher, 127-142.

Kellett Bidoli, Cynthia Forthcoming a. Investigation into Linguistic and Cultural Mediation between the English-speaking World and the Italian Deaf Signing Community, in Bondi, Marina / Maxwell, Nick (eds) *Cross-cultural Encounters: Linguistic Perspectives*. Rome: Officina Edizioni, 159-173.

Kellett Bidoli, Cynthia Forthcoming b. A Multimodal Approach in a Multilingual Context: Interpretation from English to Italian to

Italian Sign Language. Paper presented at the 25th ICAME Conference, *Corpus Linguistics: the State of the Art Twenty-five Years on*, University of Verona, Italy 19-23 May 2004.

Ochse, Elana 2001. EFL with Adult Deaf Students: Two Cultures, Two Approaches. In Cortese, Giuseppina / Hymes, Dell (eds) *'Languaging' in and across Human Groups Perspectives on Difference and Asymmetry*. In *TEXTUS. English Studies in Italy* 14/2, Genoa: Tilgher, 447-471.

Ochse, Elana 2004. Language – English – Difficult//Question – You – Think – What? In Candlin, Christopher / Gotti, Maurizio (eds) *Intercultural Discourse in Domain-specific English*. In *TEXTUS. English Studies in Italy* 17/1, Genoa: Tilgher, 143-158.

Ventola, Eija / Shalom, Celia / Thompson, Susan (eds) 2002. *The Language of Conferencing*. Frankfurt: Peter Lang.

.

CATHERINE NICKERSON

English as a *Lingua Franca* in Business Contexts: Strategy or Hegemony?

1. Introduction

The use of English as an international language, often as a *lingua franca*, both in business contexts and beyond is hardly headline news. Research over the course of the past decade has confirmed over and over again, that English is a dominant, and dominating, language in many different social domains – from education, through the media to business – and that this dominance, particularly for the international business arena, seems unlikely to change at least for the next fifty years (cf. Graddol 2004). But is this all there is to it? Are we simply to accept the dominance of English and shape our research agenda accordingly? Or are there other issues that should be of interest to us, such as the interface between English and other languages and/or the effect that the use of English may have on those that are obliged to use it in order to get their work done? These are the issues that I would like to explore in this chapter, looking first at what we have learnt through our research about the use and nature of English in international business contexts, continuing on with what we do not yet know, and concluding with a discussion on what this could, or perhaps should, tell us as a research community.

2. English in business contexts

In general, we know that the use of English is on the increase in many different social domains. And incidentally, this is one of the criteria proposed by Braj Kachru in the nineteen eighties for when English can be considered as an L2 rather than as a foreign language (Kachru 1985). In our research at the Radboud University in Nijmegen, for instance, we have documented an increasing use of English every-where, most especially in promotional genres, and we believe that this process is quite advanced in some parts of the European Union in particular, notably in the Netherlands and in Scandinavia (e.g. Gerritsen/Nickerson 2004, Nickerson/de Groot 2005). This is amply illustrated in Gerritsen *et al.* (this volume), which in particular reports on the use of English in advertising in the Netherlands, in Spain and in Germany.

If we focus on international business contexts and communica-tion in multinationals in particular, then we can see that the dominance of English has been reported by researchers working in a variety of different national contexts, and we can certainly assume that it is an immutable fact of life for many business people working across the globe. If we take only a few examples dating from the beginning of this century, then we see Akar reporting on the use of English in the Turkish business context, Chew confirming the continued need for English in the banking sector in Hong Kong, Louhiala-Salminen, Charles and Kankaanranta detailing the decision to use English for internal communication at two Swedish-Finnish multinational cor-porations, and Gimenez who investigates the role played by English in the communication between a European Head office and its Argentinean subsidiary (Akar 2002; Chew 2005; Louhiala-Salminen/ Charles/Kankaanranta 2005; Gimenez 2002). David Graddol has suggested recently that English may ultimately be replaced by languages such as Chinese, Hindi/Urdu or Arabic as the *lingua franca* of the international business arena (Graddol 2002). This seems unlikely to occur, however, within the next fifty years, suggesting that an understanding of the role played by English will remain for the time being at least of key interest.

So what then are the hallmarks of recent research into the use and nature of English in international business contexts? The studies I have briefly profiled above, and the many others that have revealed similar findings, show that there has been a shift from the analysis of the language used in isolated written texts or speech events, towards the analysis of contextualised communicative genres. As a result, researchers have become increasingly concerned with the way in which organisational and/or (national) cultural factors contribute to the realisation of the individual text/event under investigation. This discursive turn is apparent in the work of many researchers investigating English in business contexts, whatever their geographical location or the genre(s) they have chosen to study (see Nickerson 2005, for an overview). In addition to this, many researchers looking at the use of English in international business contexts have also identified and deconstructed the strategies used in various genres and contexts (e.g. Nickerson 2000; Poncini 2004; Planken 2005). As a result, we know quite a bit about what Anne Freadman has eloquently referred to as "the tricks of the trade" for the (English) genres used by the business people we have investigated, i.e. the strategic ways in which business people get their work done (Freadman 1994, my paraphrase).[1] Business discourse and those that construct it, have been revealed in turn as being strategic, persuasive and promotional, and interestingly, there also seems to be a consensus that experienced business people are strategically competent despite the fact that they may not have high levels of proficiency in English.

Alongside research that has focussed specifically on the use of English, often as a *lingua franca,* there has also been a certain amount of work done on the use of other languages in international business contexts together with the way in which those languages interface with English. The landmark study by Vandermeeren, for instance, shows that both French and German were used in communication between French and German companies – and, crucially, that English did not dominate (Vandermeeren 1999). Vandermeeren's work contains an interesting discussion on the consequences of language choice for export performance, looking specifically at the relationship between 'standardisation', i.e. the selection of English as a lingua franca for all transactions, versus 'adaptation', i.e. the conscious

---

1   I believe that for written discourse at least Bhatia's concept of discriminative and non-discriminative elements may be a particularly useful way of thinking about business discourse. Bhatia (1993) has discussed the relationship between moves and strategies in a genre in terms of discriminative elements (moves) and non-discriminative elements (strategies) – within which we can also distinguish between rhetorical strategies and their linguistic realizations (see also Nickerson/de Groot 2005 for further discussion).

choice of using your business partner's language. At least for the French corporations who responded to her survey, the choice of German in correspondence with German business partners seemed to be associated with a better export performance than where companies had 'standardised' their correspondence and chosen English. Vander-meeren's final comments in her 1999 account of the project are succinct in explaining the importance of understanding the impact of foreign language use and business performance. She states:

> Managers who dismiss the negative consequences of insufficient language skills as a marginal issue may not realise that a company's linguistic adaptation to its clients can make the difference between failure and success in establishing and maintaining a business relationship. (1999: 289)

Elsewhere in Europe, Hagen's work within the framework of the European Union in projects such as the REFLECT project and ELUCIDATE project, shows that languages such as French, German, Italian and Spanish are used, in addition to English (Hagen 1999, 2002), and Lavric and her colleagues at the Wirtschaftsuniversität (WU) in Vienna have completed a series of fascinating studies within Austrian business (and other professional contexts) and have found that French, Italian and Spanish are in use (e.g. Lavric 1991; Kubista-Nugent 1996; Daublebsky 2000). The recent study by Bäck within the Viennese research group in particular, involving a detailed case-study of three export-oriented middle-sized Austrian companies, has revealed that German, French, Spanish, Portuguese and Italian are used by Austrian corporations – English being reserved for communication with Asia only (Bäck 2004). Finally, Poncini's work on multinational and multilingual business meetings in Italy, details at least one context where the participants opt for other *linguae francae* in their interactions, involving a total of eight languages other than English (Poncini 2004). The work of these researchers, and others like them, suggests that the realities of the business context are often considerably more complex than the simple label of English as a *lingua franca* would imply.

To summarise what we know about the use of English in international contexts, we know that English is widely used around the globe in a variety of different genres, sometimes on its own and sometimes in co-existence with other languages. We know that some non-native speakers of English at least, can communicate both strategically and effectively. We know that other languages are also used, when it is strategic to do so – to cement a relationship with a business partner, to establish common ground with a business partner or for reasons of shared proficiency. Our research has revealed something about the relationship between the national or organizational context and the use of language as discourse, together with the various factors that may play a role in an organization's communication practices. Finally, we know that organizational discourse is highly strategic and we also know something about the rhetorical and linguistic strategies that are used by business writers to get their work done.

The research I have selectively reviewed above would seem to suggest that the decision to use English is largely a strategic choice, viewed both in terms of the other language choices available and in terms of the ability of the majority of business people to communicate in English effectively. In the next section I will go on to discuss some of the practical difficulties that may also be associated with the widespread use of English in international business, together with the possibility that opting for English may lead to a certain amount of disempowerment amongst employees, or indeed to the creation of hegemony.

3. Strategy or hegemony?

In general terms, attitudes towards the widespread use of English may not always be positive. In a recent protest in Belgium, for instance, a sign containing the partly English phrase "Kiss en ride" was forcibly removed from outside a railway station, and in the Netherlands in 2004, protesters demonstrated at Schiphol Airport in Amsterdam, where Schiphol is given the title "Amsterdam Airport" only without a Dutch equivalent. It seems then, from examples such as these, that the dominance of English is not universally appreciated, even – or perhaps especially – in (national) contexts where the use of English is prevalent. In business contexts in general, and multinational corporations in particular, previous research has suggested that not only can the (indiscriminate) use of English lead to practical difficulties, it may also create situations in which some employees are more equal than others. It is these two related issues that I will go on to discuss in the remainder of this section.

During the mid nineteen nineties, I was lucky enough to have been given access to a large email corpus collected at one of the Dutch divisions of the Shell multinational corporation (see Nickerson 2000). The following extract was taken from an email sent by a supervisor to a middle manager, at a time when English was being adopted throughout the Dutch divisions as the corporate language and the message from senior management was "become competent in English or accept the consequences for your career". The supervisor writes "Wel zijn er onder ons nog collega's die geen Engels spreken/lezen en toch met procedures/werkvoorschriften moeten werken" (*But there are certainly employees within the group who neither speak or read English, who still have to be able to work with manuals and procedures [in English]*; my translation). Essentially behind the smokescreen of an official language policy, there is the potential for disempowerment due to a lack of proficiency in English, as the supervisor acknowledges, and not only that, there is also the potential for a catastrophic failure of communication. This, it seems, is not an isolated incidence of the consequences of using English, since other researchers have systematically collected information and reported on similar situations in various contexts around the world. I will illustrate this by referring to examples taken from the banking sector in Hong Kong (Chew 2005), and from multinational corporations in Argentina (Gimenez 2002), and in Finland (Charles/Marschan-Piekkari 2002).

Chew's recent study of the banking sector in Hong Kong is based on detailed interviews with sixteen new bank employees. It reveals a communication setting in which "almost all written communicative tasks are carried out in English while most oral communicative tasks are carried out in Cantonese, the language of the majority of people in Hong Kong" (2005: 430). The only exceptions to this were those occasions where there was a non-Chinese speaker present, a rare event for most of the informants. As a result of the language choice most usually associated with the medium of the task, i.e. written tasks in English and oral tasks in Cantonese, there was also a considerable amount of Chinese-to-English translation that took place in order to produce a written English version of information collected from (mostly) Chinese sources. Ten out of the 16 informants reported that they had difficulties with the language demands posed by the communicative tasks required of them, and this was most especially the case for those employees working in environments alongside colleagues who spoke English as a first language.

Language difficulties are also reported by Gimenez (2002), in his study of the communication between the European Head Office of a multinational corporation and its Argentinean subsidiary. His analysis shows that the local corporate reality, which included the low level of English of some managers and the need to translate key documents and hold electronic discussions of policies in Spanish, contravened the globally-adopted conventions preferred and indeed imposed by the European Head Office, which in fact stipulated that there should be no translation and that electronic discussions should take place only in English. Gimenez observes what must be a common feature of this type of situation in multinational corporations, i.e. the emergence of a group of employees with sufficient English language skills who are called upon to 'help' their less proficient – and often more senior – colleagues.

These are also issues that are dealt with in detail by Charles and Marschan-Piekkari (2002), who write eloquently about the consequences of using English within the multinational corporation Kone Elevators. English had been adopted by Kone Elevators as the company language in the early 1970s, so the study took place more than thirty years after the implementation of that decision. 110 staff at Kone were interviewed, representing 25 corporate units in 10 different countries in Europe, Mexico and the Far East. The interviews were held in English, Finnish, Spanish and Swedish, and a further six interviews were also held with key people within the organization for additional information on language training and the specific role that language is perceived to play in horizontal communication (2002: 14). Charles and Marschan-Piekkari report that almost 60% of the Kone employees they interviewed viewed language as a communication barrier in the course of their work, succinctly encapsulated in the following quotation taken from a top Finnish manager:

> There is actually no other practical barrier than language when we have co-operation and meetings with each other. These Scandinavian units [in Sweden, Norway and Denmark] get along rather well, but for us [in Finland] it is a constant challenge to find staff who could participate because of language issues. The same persons tend to get overloaded by these duties. (2002: 19)

As in the study by Gimenez, the Finnish manager identifies a group within the corporation who find themselves in a key position as a result of their language proficiency.

Charles and Marschan-Piekkari analyze the communication problems at Kone in detail, and identify five main areas of concern including both practical difficulties and issues of power (2002:19). The first was the difficulty of finding a common language for the interactants to use, *despite* the assumption that English would be widely spoken (my emphasis), the second – again as in the Gimenez study – was the comprehension problems that the interviewees reported as a result of insufficient translation of corporate documenta-tion into the various languages spoken at the subsidiary companies, and the third was the difficulty that employees experienced in understanding the various accents in which English was spoken internationally – particularly at lower levels in the hierarchy. Specifically in terms of power relations, the fourth area of concern was the "centralization of power into the hands of those who were able to obtain and disseminate information through knowing the official corporate language or the parent company language", and finally, the fifth concern was the "feeling of isolation in those with lacking or inadequate skills in the corporate language, resulting in communication flows determined through language rather than job requirements" (Charles/Marschan-Piekkari 2002: 19). It seems that where one group of employees may benefit from their language skills – whilst at the same time perhaps being overloaded as a result in the words of at least one of the managers interviewed – a second group is clearly disadvantaged and will not have access to the same quantity of information. In an earlier study at Kone, Marschan-Piekkari, Welch and Welch summarise this as "a shadow structure, based on language clusters and individuals who were language nodes and mediators" going on to say that "because of the power of language they had the capacity to influence the formal communication lines and even threaten the intended functioning of the formal organizational structure" (1999: 436-437).

The studies from around the world I have summarized here briefly, suggest that although a decision to adopt English may be a strategic one which facilitates some communication to some extent, it may also give rise to issues of power, including inequalities and powerlessness due to a lack of language skills, as well as creating certain practical difficulties associated with a lack of comprehension and the sometimes false assumption that everyone speaks English. In the next section I will go on to discuss how these issues might contribute to three main areas of investigation in an appropriate research agenda in the future.

4. Towards a new research agenda

The studies I have reviewed above suggest that there are three areas of investigation that could be usefully combined in research into the use of English as a *lingua franca* in business contexts. The first of these stems from the fact that we know very little about the effect of using English rather than another language in a given business context. We know, for example, from our research at the Radboud University in Nijmegen into the use of English in print advertising around the European Union, that not all consumers are equally able to comprehend the texts – Spanish consumers being less able to comprehend English texts than their German and Dutch counterparts – but we do not yet know enough about other genres, contexts and (national) cultures. I believe that we need to collect a body of knowledge on the specific communicative situations relevant to business in which English is used. For instance, we could begin by investigating the comprehensibility of different varieties of English in different business contexts, the attitudes held towards the use of English, and the other problems signalled in previous studies like Charles and Marschan-Piekkari (2002) where native speakers of English, in particular, both experienced problems and caused problems in communication within multinationals.

As well as the effect of opting for English in general in business contexts, we also know very little about the effect of using specific strategies, both rhetorical and linguistic strategies, in various types of business discourse, in particular, in those situations where the local national or organizational culture may not be that of the Anglo-Saxon 'English' world. In this respect we have tended to be largely descriptive in our research thus far – and although this has undeniably provided us with a wealth of important information on the strategies used in various business genres, I would suggest that we could now take a more prescriptive stance, or at least a self-reflexive one in developing a future research agenda. In the Netherlands and Belgium in particular, at least for written discourse in business and technical contexts, the multidisciplinary field of Document Design has made some promising advances in establishing the effects of using a particular strategy in a particular communicative genre. This type of research complements our existing knowledge of how language as discourse realizes effective communication in business contexts, and it could usefully provide the next necessary step towards a more prescriptive relationship with the business world.

The third and final area of investigation that we could focus on is to look at how to counteract hegemonic situations that have arisen because of the use of English in international business, such as those I discussed in the previous section. Applying what we know about the use of English as a *lingua franca* in business contexts to the development of appropriate teaching or training materials, could be one very important – and indeed ethical – step forward in our own ideology as a research community, not just in terms of political correctness or a critical stance, but in the form of concrete usable recommendations. In Nickerson (2005) I discuss the lack of published teaching materials focused on English in business contexts that are apparently based on empirical research findings, despite the fact that many of us are involved both with teaching and with research. Projects such as the Language in the Workplace Project (LWP) based at the Victoria University Wellington in New Zealand (see Holmes 2000), the Teaching English to Meet the Needs of Business Education project in Hong Kong (see Bhatia/Candlin 2001), and individual studies such as the investigation by Charles and Marschan-Piekkari (2002), all provide excellent examples of how empirical research can be used as a resource to inform teaching and training materials for people in business. Similar work would help in the future to identify and then address those situations in the international business arena in which a 'shadow structure' may exist.

References

Akar, Didar 2002. The Macro Contextual Factors Shaping Business Discourse: The Turkish Case. *International Review of Applied Linguistics in Language Teaching* 40/4, 305-322.

Bäck, Bernhard 2004. *Code Choice im Österreichischen Export in die Romania. Ein Modell und drei Fallstudien.* Unpublished PhD Dissertation, Wirtschaftsuniversität Wien: Vienna.

Bhatia, Vijay K. 1993. *Analysing Genre: Language Use in Professional Settings.* London: Longman.

Bhatia, Vijay K. / Candlin, Christopher N. (eds) 2001. *Teaching English to Meet the Needs of Business Education in Hong Kong.* Hong Kong: City University of Hong Kong.

Charles, Mirjaliisa / Marschan-Piekkari, Rebbeca 2002. Language Training for Enhanced Horizontal Communication: A Challenge for MNCs. *Business Communication Quarterly* 65/2, 9-29.

Chew, Kheng-Suan 2005. An Investigation of the English Language Skills Used by New Entrants in Banks in Hong Kong. *English for Specific Purposes* 24, 423-435.

Daublesky, Stefan 2000. *La Langue Française dans le Monde du Travail: Étude sur les Diplômés des Années Quatre-Vingt de l'Université de Sciences Économiques de Vienne.* Diplomarbeit Wirtschaftsuniversität Wien.

Freadman, Anne 1994. Anyone for Tennis? In Freedman, Ann / Medway, Peter (eds) *Genre and the New Rhetoric.* London: Taylor and Francis, 43-66.

Gerritsen, Marinel / Nickerson, Catherine 2004. Fact or Fallacy? English as an L2 in the Dutch Business Context. In Candlin,

Christopher N. / Gotti, Maurizio (eds) *Intercultural Aspects of Specialized Communication*. Bern: Peter Lang, 105-125.

Gimenez, Julio C. 2002. New Media and Conflicting Realities in Multinational Corporate Communication: A Case Study. *International Review of Applied Linguistics in Language Teaching* 40/4, 323-343.

Graddol, David 2002. The English Language and Globalization. Paper presented at the Language and Global Communication Seminar. Cardiff: Centre for Language and Communication.

Graddol, David 2004. The Future of Language. *Science* 303, 1329-1331.

Hagen, Stephen (ed.) 1999. *Communication Across Borders. The ELUCIDATE study*. London: CILT.

Hagen, Stephen 2002. *The REFLECT Project*. <www.Reflectproject. com>.

Holmes, Janet 2000. Victoria University's Language in the Workplace Project: An Overview. *Language in the Workplace Occasional Papers 1*.

Kachru, Braj. B. 1985. Standards, Codification and Sociolinguistic Realism: The English Language in the Outer Circle. In Quirk, Randolph / Widdowson, Henry G. (eds) *English in the World*. Cambridge: Cambridge University Press.

Kubista-Nugent, Agnes 1996. *La lingua italiana nelle imprese austriache – un'indagine sul fabbisogno della lingua italiana condotta nella zona di Vienna*. Diplomarbeit Wirtschaftsuniversität Wien.

Lavric, Eva 1991. Welche Sprachen für Europa? Fremdsprachliche Lernerbedürfnisse in Österreich im Kontext der EG-Annäherung. In Griller, Stefan / Lavric, Eva / Neck, Reinhard (eds) *Europäische Integration aus Österreichischer Sicht: Wirtschafts-, Sozial – und Rechtswissenschaftliche Aspekte (Schriftenreihe des Forschungsinstituts für Europafragen 3)*. Wien: Orac, 357-388.

Louhiala-Salminen, Leena / Charles, Mirjaliisa / Kankaanranta, Anne 2005. English as a Lingua franca in Nordic Corporate Mergers: Two Case Companies. *English for Specific Purposes* 24, 401-412.

Marschan-Piekkari, Rebecca / Welch, Denice / Welch, Lawrence 1999. In the Shadow: The Impact of Language on Structure, Power and Communication in the Multinational. *International Business Review* 8, 421-440.

Nickerson, Catherine 2000. *Playing the Corporate Language Game: An Investigation of the Genres and Discourse Strategies in English Used by Dutch Writers Working in Multinational Corporations.* Amsterdam: Rodopi.

Nickerson, Catherine 2005. English as a Lingua Franca in International Business Contexts. *English for Specific Purposes* 24, 367-380.

Nickerson, Catherine / de Groot, Elizabeth 2005. Dear Shareholder, Dear Stockholder, Dear Stakeholder: The Business Letter Genre in the Annual General Report. In Gillaerts, Paul / Gotti, Maurizio (eds) *Genre Variation in Business Letters.* Bern: Peter Lang, 325-346.

Planken, Brigitte 2005. Managing Rapport in Lingua Franca Sales Negotiations: A Comparison of Professional and Aspiring Negotiators. *English for Specific Purposes* 24, 381-400.

Poncini, Gina 2004. *Discursive Strategies in Multicultural Business Meetings.* Frankfurt: Peter Lang.

Vandermeeren, Sonja 1999. English as a Lingua Franca in Corporate Writing. In Bargiela-Chiappini, Francesca / Nickerson, Catherine (eds) *Writing Business: Genres, Media and Discourses.* London: Longman, 273-291.

Notes on Contributors

GRAHAME T. BILBOW currently holds the post of Dean of Education at the Higher Colleges of Technology in Abu Dhabi, United Arab Emirates. Prior to taking up this position in 2005, Professor Bilbow was Head of the Department of English at the Hong Kong Polytechnic University, Hong Kong's largest university. Professor Bilbow's interests are mainly in the area of intercultural communication and discourse analysis in business contexts. His PhD was a study of spoken discourse between Chinese and English speakers in business meetings at a large airline in Hong Kong. He has also published a number of textbooks in Business English for Longman that are used throughout Hong Kong and China.

CORINE VAN DEN BRANDT is an Associate Professor in the Department of Business Communication and the Center for Language Studies at the Radboud University Nijmegen in the Netherlands. She holds a Ph.D. in Spanish and Applied Linguistics, and she teaches courses in Communicative Skills, Business Spanish and Research into Intercultural Communication. She has published on training foreign language reading strategies and cultural values in international advertising, and her current research interests include the role of cultural background for the effectiveness of persuasive and instructional documents.

PAOLA CATENACCIO holds a PhD in English literature from the Catholic University of Milan with a discourse-based study of seventeenth-century drama, and later an MA in Applied Linguistics from Birkbeck College, London. She holds a research and teaching position at the University of Milan, where she teaches English Linguistics courses for the degree programme in Linguistic and Cultural Mediation. Her research interests span from second language acquisition (the topic of her MA dissertation) to translation and discourse analysis, especially in the context of LSP research. She has presented paper at several international conferences and symposia, and has contributed essays to periodicals and edited volumes. Her most recent contributions focus on the genre of the press release and, more in general, on linguistic aspects of corporate communication. She has also co-authored two volumes on English for Medicine (Milan, Hoepli, 2006).

ORA-ONG CHAKORN is an applied linguist and discourse analyst with a deep interest in business discourse. With a PhD in Applied Linguistics from the University of Warwick in the UK, she has been working as a lecturer in the Graduate School of Language and Communication at the National Institute of Development Administration (NIDA), the only government-owned graduate institution in Bangkok, Thailand. She is responsible for MA courses on English discourse analysis, business communication, and ESP. Her research interests also include genre analysis, contrastive rhetoric and narrative discourse analysis. She supervises and co-supervises, internally and externally, both MA and PhD theses in these fields. Occasionally she is invited as a full-time guest lecturer to teach discourse analysis to graduate students at Chulalongkorn University, Bangkok. She is now conducting a research project on the analysis of the chairman's message in Thai annual reports in time of economic crisis.

DELIA CHIARO holds a chair in English Language and Linguistics at the University of Bologna, Italy. Her main research interests are Humour and Screen Translation which she combines in her audience based, data driven work on the perception of Verbally Expressed Humour when it is translated for television, cinema and the Internet. She is also interested in global communication and especially how companies in different cultures promote their products via the New Economy. Her publications include *The Language of Jokes: Analyzing Verbal Play* (London, Routledge: 1992), a Special Issue (2005) of *Humor, International Journal of Humor Research* (Berlin: De Gruyter) on Humor and Translation and a number of articles in international journals.

ROGIER CRIJNS studied German at the Radboud University Nijmegen in the Netherlands. In his capacity as a lecturer (German) and Socrates coordinator he has given guest lectures at several European universities (Hamburg, Potsdam, Regensburg, Graz, Vienna, Lugano). Since 1994 he has been Head of Business Communications Studies for

German at the Radboud University Nijmegen. He has published on several business communication topics (business email, international advertising, intercultural teambuilding), and he is currently participating in a European research project with the Universities of Turku (FIN), Arhus (DEN), Regensburg and Darmstadt (GER).

NÚRIA DOMÍNGUEZ studied Spanish at the University of Barcelona. She then worked for several years for a number of Spanish corporations. Since 1990 she has taught Spanish in the Department of Business Communication at the Radboud University Nijmegen, the Netherlands. Her courses include Business Spanish, Research into Intercultural Communication and Spanish for Academic Purposes.

BRUCE T. DOWNING is Associate Professor of Linguistics and Director of the Program in Translation and Interpreting at the University of Minnesota. He was co-author of the monograph *Professional Training for Community Interpreters* (1991) and has published numerous articles on linguistics, translation, and interpreting. His current research is concerned mainly with language policy as it affects the provision of interpreting services for minority and immigrant populations and with discourse analysis of mediated bilingual discourse. Dr. Downing is a member of the Standards, Training and Certification Committee of the National Council on Interpreting in Health Care (USA). He also belongs to the American Translation and Interpretation Studies Association (ATISA), and the American Translators Association (ATA), and served (1999-2001) as the ATA representative to the ASTM Subcommittee on Interpreting Standards.

GIULIANA GARZONE is Professor of English Language, Linguistics and Translation at the University of Milan, Italy. In a methodological perspective, she has explored the integration of micro- and macro-linguistic analysis in studying discourse, and in particular specialized discourse ("The Use of Discursive Features Expressing Causal Relations in Annual Company Reports", 2006), and the application of corpus linguistics to Critical Discourse Analysis ("What can corpus linguistics do for Critical Discourse Analysis?", 2004). Specialized discourse in its different domains is her main field of investigation. In particular, she has worked on legal language (*Performatività e linguaggio giuridico*, 1996), on scientific discourse (*Perspectives on ESP and popularization*, 2006) and on business communication, focussing on intercultural aspects ("Annual Company Reports and CEO's Letters: Discoursal Features and Cultural Markedness", 2004; "Letters to shareholders and Chairman's Statements: Textual variability and Generic Integrity", 2005). She has also published extensively and edited several works on translation (*L'italiano delle traduzioni*, 2005, with A. Cardinaletti; *Esperienze del tradurre*, 2005) and interpreting (*Perspectives on Interpreting*, with P. Mead and M. Viezzi; *Interpreting in the 21ˢᵗ Century*, with M. Viezzi, 2002). Her other research interests include the phonology and the syntax of the English language.

MARINEL GERRITSEN holds the Christine Mohrmann chair at the Department of Business Communication Studies at the Radboud University Nijmegen and the Center for Language Studies in the Netherlands. Prior to this she worked for the government and for several multinational organizations in the Netherlands, France, Italy and Germany, and she also held positions at a number of Dutch universities (Amsterdam, Leiden, Utrecht, Nijmegen) and the Royal Netherlands Academy of Arts and Sciences. Marinel Gerritsen's business communication research is primarily focussed on the differences between cultures in communication and the impact that this has on intercultural communication and on the use of English as an international language. She has also published widely on the sociolinguistic in-bedding of language variation and change.

CORNELIA ILIE is Professor of English linguistics at Örebro University, Sweden. She is currently holding a Visiting Professorship at Södertörn University College. Several of her publications include interdisciplinary approaches to topics pertaining to the fields of pragmatics, institutional discourse analysis, argumentation and rhetoric. One of the linguistic fields to which she has contributed extensively is the pragmatic and argumentative study of questions in English (especially non-standard questions like rhetorical questions, echo questions, expository questions, etc.) that occur in three main types of British and American institutional discourses, namely political speeches, courtroom dialogue and talk shows. Her recent publications focus on institutional genre analysis ('Talk shows',

'Parliamentary discourses', in *Encyclopedia of Language and Linguistics*, 2006), as well as on cross-cultural and rhetorical perspectives on language use (her volume *Language, culture, rhetoric: Cultural and rhetorical perspectives on communication*, 2004). In several studies on dialogic discourse she has explored the relation between language and ideology, the interlocutors' rhetorical appeals, fallacies, metadiscursive devices, personal deixis, as well as types of abusive institutional language as cognitive forms of confrontation. Her current research concerns particularly the pragma-rhetorical devices and argumentation strategies that are used in institutional dialogue.

CYNTHIA JANE KELLETT BIDOLI is Associate Professor of Consecutive Interpretation at the Advanced School of Modern Languages, University of Trieste. Her research interests lie in lexicography, history of interpretation and interpretation quality assessment with particular focus on non-verbal aspects of consecutive delivery. Interest in non-verbal communication has led her to research signed language and subsequently to highlight this emerging, little known form of interpretation within the mainstream interpreting community. She has focussed on specific aspects of cultural and linguistic mediation between the English speaking world and the Italian deaf signing community through a multimodal corpus approach, to identify textual recasting and the mechanisms at play during the complex translation process from the oral/aural channel to the visual/gestural one. Electronic analysis of an English-LIS corpus has identified lexical items related to the field of linguistics leading to the compilation (in progress) of a multimodal trilingual terminological electronic glossary for students of sign language. Her current research has now turned to audiovisual translation of films and TV programmes for the deaf.

FRANK VAN MEURS teaches English in the Department of Business Communication Studies and the Center for Language Studies at the Radboud University Nijmegen, the Netherlands. He has published on product recall notices and on the effect of the use of English in Dutch TV commercials and in Dutch job advertisements.

KUMIKO MURATA Kumiko Murata received her M.A. and Ph.D. from the Institute of Education, University of London and is currently professor of English and applied linguistics at the School of Education and the Graduate School of Education, Waseda University, Japan. Her research interests include conversation analysis, discourse analysis, cross-cultural communication, language teaching and pragmatics. She has published *A Cross-Cultural Approach to the Analysis of Conversation and Its Implications for Language Pedagogy* (Liber Press, Tokyo 1994), and her articles and book reviews have appeared in international journals such as *The International Journal of Applied Linguistics, The Journal of Asia TEFL, The Journal of Pragmatics, Pragmatics, Language and Society,* and *World Englishes.*

ULRIKE NEDERSTIGT studied English and German at the Free University Berlin, the University of Manchester and the Albert-Ludwigs University Freiburg. In 1997, she was awarded a PhD-stipend from the Max-Planck Society. In 2003, she received her doctoral degree in General Linguistics from the Humboldt University Berlin. She recently joined the Department of Business Communication at the Radboud University Nijmegen as an Associate Professor. She works on structural differences between different languages and the consequences for these differences in text construction and communication across languages. She has also worked on child language acquisition and focus particles.

CATHERINE NICKERSON is Professor of Business Communication at the Alliance Business School in Bangalore. She has been teaching and researching business communication for many years, and her current research interests are focused on the use of English as an international business language as it is used in settings such as global advertising, corporate web-site communication, and the BPO industry. She has authored and co-authored many international scholarly publications and her latest book volume – *Business Discourse* – was published by Palgrave-MacMillan in 2006 (co-authored with Francesca Bargiela-Chiappini and Brigitte Planken). She is an Associate Editor for the *Journal of Business Communication* (Sage) and she is on the Editorial Boards for the *English for Specific Purposes Journal* (Elsevier) and for *Hermes – Journal of Language and Communication Studies* (Aarhus School of Business, Denmark).

GINA PONCINI is an Associate Professor at the University of Milan, where she teaches English Business Communication in the Faculty of Political Science. She also teaches a seminar in Business Writing in the Master's program in Corporate Communication at the University of Lugano. Her Ph.D. in Applied English Linguistics is from the University of Birmingham (UK). Her publications include the book *Discursive Strategies in Multicultural Business Meetings* (Peter Lang 2004), winner of the Association for Business Communication Award for Distinguished Publication on Business Communication. Her articles have appeared in volumes and journals, including the *International Review of Applied Linguistics, Journal of Intercultural Studies, English for Specific Purposes* and *Business Communication Quarterly*. Her research interests concern business discourse, meetings, intercultural communication, financial communication and tourism communication. Gina Poncini is currently Vice President Europe of the Association for Business Communication and a member of the editorial boards of *Business Communication Quarterly* and *Hermes – Journal of Language and Communication Studies*.

CARMEN VALERO-GARCÉS, Ph.D. is a Senior Lecturer at the University of Alcalá, Madrid (Spain), and the Director of the Post Graduate and Undergraduate Program on Public Service Interpreting and Translation, offered in five language pairs (Spanish-Arabic; Spanish-Rumanian, Spanish-French, Spanish-English, Spanish-Russian) since 2000. She is also the coordinator of *The International Conference on Translation and Interpreting* held at Alcalá since 1995 and the editor of the Proceedings as well as the author of some books and articles dealing with interpreting and translating in public services, cross-cultural communication, interpreting and translating, SLA and Contrastive Linguistics.

MARIA CRISTINA PAGANONI is a lecturer in English at the Faculty of Political Science, State University of Milan, Italy. She holds a Ph.D. in English from the University of Northumbria, Newcastle, U.K. Her publications include *Lettere dal Sudafrica. La saggistica di Nadine Gordimer* (FrancoAngeli, 1997), *Counterdiscourses of Globalisation: "Another World is Possible"* (Lubrina, 2004), besides essays on Dickens and Victorian literature, on contemporary British fiction and on postcolonial writers, such as Zadie Smith and Arundhati Roy. She has edited the Italian translation of Paul Scott's India-set novel *Staying on* (*Gente in ombra*, Lubrina, 2001) within the European project "Culture 2000", and translated two novels by the British author Anita Brookner, *Nostalgia* (Edizioni dell'Arco, 2000) and *Una strana estate* (Lubrina, 2002). She is now investigating the issues of globalisation and multiculturalism and the construction of these discourses in the Western media.

STEPHANIE ZILLES POHLE holds an M.A. degree in English Linguistics, History and Educational Science. She studied at the University of Bonn/Germany, and at Trinity College, Dublin/Ireland. Currently, she is a PhD candidate in Applied English Linguistics at the University of Bonn. Her thesis, an empirical analysis of Irish English business negotiations, focuses on micropragmatic and macropragmatic aspects of offers and related commissive speech acts. Her main research interests include pragmatics, discourse analysis, business and intercultural communication as well as research technology. She has presented at numerous conferences Europe-wide, for instance at the conventions of the Association for Business Communication. Stefanie Pohle was a re-search assistant in the English and History Departments of the University of Bonn, has gained work experience in the training, consulting and archiving sector, and currently works in the area of information and records management in an international sports organisation.

DANIELA WAWRA teaches English Language and Culture at the University of Passau. She studied English and Economics at the Universities of Passau and Eastern Illinois, USA. She wrote her dissertation on *Männer und Frauen im Job Interview: Eine evolutions-psychologische Studie zu ihrem Sprachgebrauch im Englischen* (2004, Münster: LIT) [Men and women in the job interview: An evolutionary study of their language use in English]. Her main research interests are linguistic gender studies, discourse analysis, business and intercultural communication as well as media communication. Other major publi-cations are: "Language and Peacock Tails: The Evolution of Language by Sexual Selection" (2006) and "The Male and the Female Self in Job Interviews: On Personal, Impersonal and Dominant Language Use" (2005).

Linguistic Insights

Studies in Language and Communication

This series aims to promote specialist language studies in the fields of linguistic theory and applied linguistics, by publishing volumes that focus on specific aspects of language use in one or several languages and provide valuable insights into language and communication research. A cross-disciplinary approach is favoured and most European languages are accepted.

The series includes two types of books:

- **Monographs** – featuring in-depth studies on special aspects of language theory, language analysis or language teaching.
- **Collected papers** – assembling papers from workshops, conferences or symposia.

Vol. 1   Maurizio Gotti & Marina Dossena (eds)
           Modality in Specialized Texts. Selected Papers of the
           1st CERLIS Conference.
           421 pages. 2001. ISBN 3-906767-10-8. US-ISBN 0-8204-5340-4

Vol. 2   Giuseppina Cortese & Philip Riley (eds)
           Domain-specific English. Textual Practices across
           Communities and Classrooms.
           420 pages. 2002. ISBN 3-906768-98-8. US-ISBN 0-8204-5884-8

Vol. 3   Maurizio Gotti, Dorothee Heller & Marina Dossena (eds)
           Conflict and Negotiation in Specialized Texts. Selected Papers of
           the 2nd CERLIS Conference.
           470 pages. 2002. ISBN 3-906769-12-7. US-ISBN 0-8204-5887-2

Editorial address:

Prof. Maurizio Gotti   Università di Bergamo, Facoltà di Lingue e Letterature Straniere,
                        Via Salvecchio 19, 24129 Bergamo, Italy
                        Fax: 0039 035 2052789, E-Mail: m.gotti@unibg.it

Juan Carlos Palmer-Silveira / Miguel F. Ruiz-Garrido /
Inmaculada Fortanet-Gómez (Eds)

Intercultural and International Business Communication

Theory, Research, and Teaching

Bern, Berlin, Bruxelles, Frankfurt am Main, New York, Oxford, Wien, 2006. 343 pp.
Linguistic Insights. Studies in Language and Communication. Vol. 38
Edited by Maurizio Gotti
ISBN 978-3-03910-954-8 / US-ISBN 978-0-8204-8356-6 pb.
sFr. 82.– / €* 56.60 / €** 58.20 / € 52.90 / £ 37.– / US-$ 62.95

* includes VAT – valid for Germany   ** includes VAT – valid for Austria

This volume originates from the editors' interest in one of the most relevant fields
of research these days: Intercultural and International Business Communication.
The needs of the business world to communicate effectively at an international
level in order to overcome language differences have proved to be a fascinating
topic for many scholars. International business discourse is culturally-situated and
therefore context-dependent, and all three – discourse, culture and context – play
a key role in the communication process. The present contributions analyse this
topic under the perspective of theory, research and teaching. Different scholars have
offered their views on the subject, presenting contributions on different areas related to business communication all over the world.

Contents: Juan C. Palmer-Silveira/Miguel F. Ruiz-Garrido/Inmaculada Fortanet-
Gómez: Introduction: Facing the Future of Intercultural and International Busi-
ness Communication (IIBC) – Leena Louhiala-Salminen/Mirjaliisa Charles: English
as the Lingua Franca of International Business Communication: Whose English?
What English? – Bertha Du-Babcock/Richard D. Babcock: Developing Linguistic
and Cultural Competency in International Business Communication – Aud
Solbjørg Skulstad: Genre Analysis of Corporate Communication – Belinda
Crawford Camiciottoli: Corporate Earnings Calls: a Hybrid Genre? – Frank van
Meurs/Hubert Korzilius/Adriënne den Hollander: The Persuasive Effect of the Use
of English in External Business Communication on Non-Native Speakers of
English: an Experimental Case Study of the Impact of the Use of English on a Dutch
Job Site – Yunxia Zhu: Cross-Cultural Genre Study: a Dual Perspective – Hilkka
Yli-Jokipii: Translating Professional Discourse: a Genre-Based View on Corporate
ESP – Jakob Lauring: The Exclusive Group - Expatriates Working against Corporate
Goals – Britt-Louise Gunnarsson: Swedish Companies and their Multilingual Practice
– Vijay K. Bhatia/Jane Lung: Corporate Identity and Generic Integrity in Business
Discourse – Julio C. Giménez: International Business Communication: Helping
Advanced Learners of English Cope with the Demands – Gina Poncini: Evaluation
in Written and Spoken Business Discourse: Integrating Research into Teaching.

PETER LANG
Bern · Berlin · Bruxelles · Frankfurt am Main · New York · Oxford · Wien